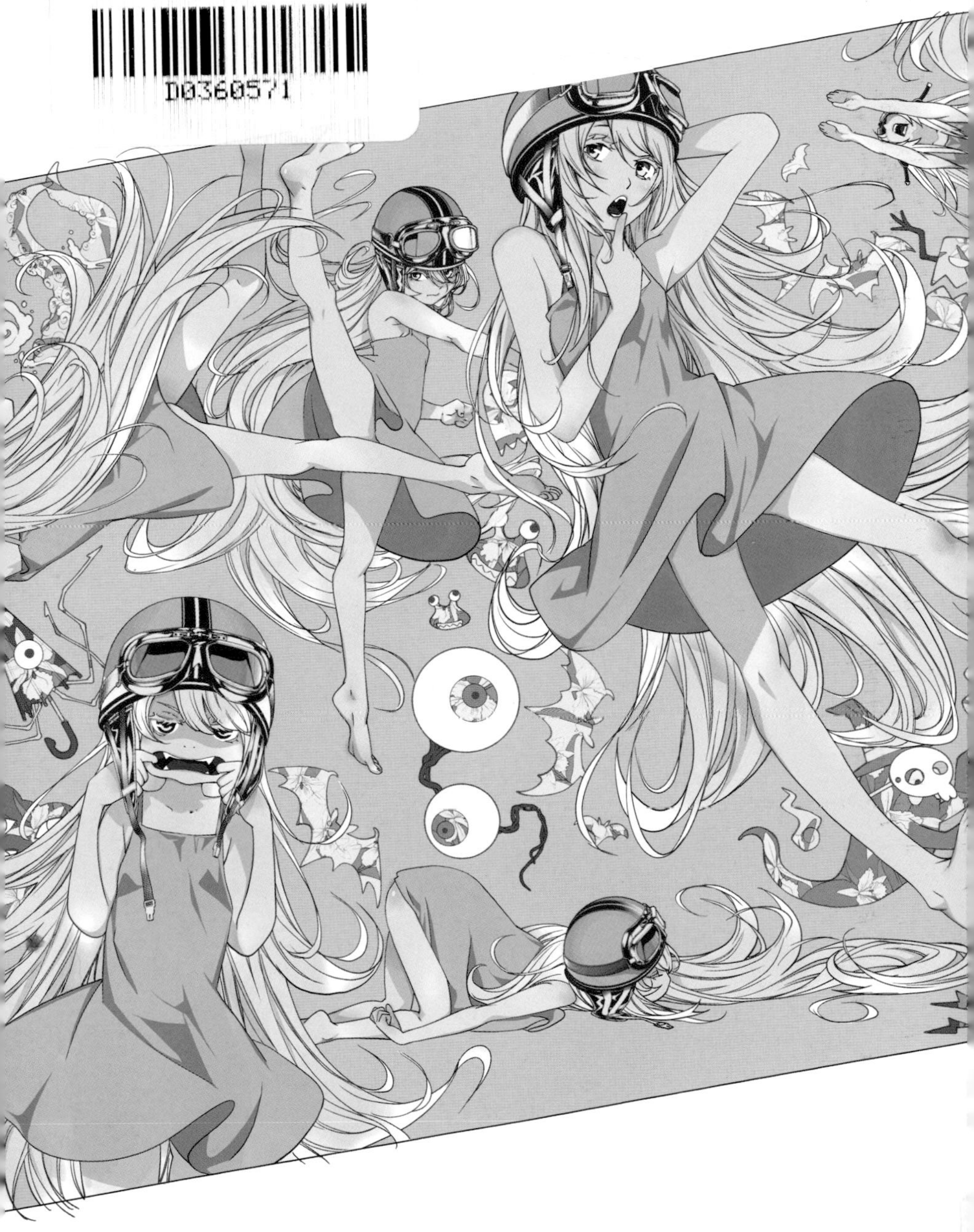

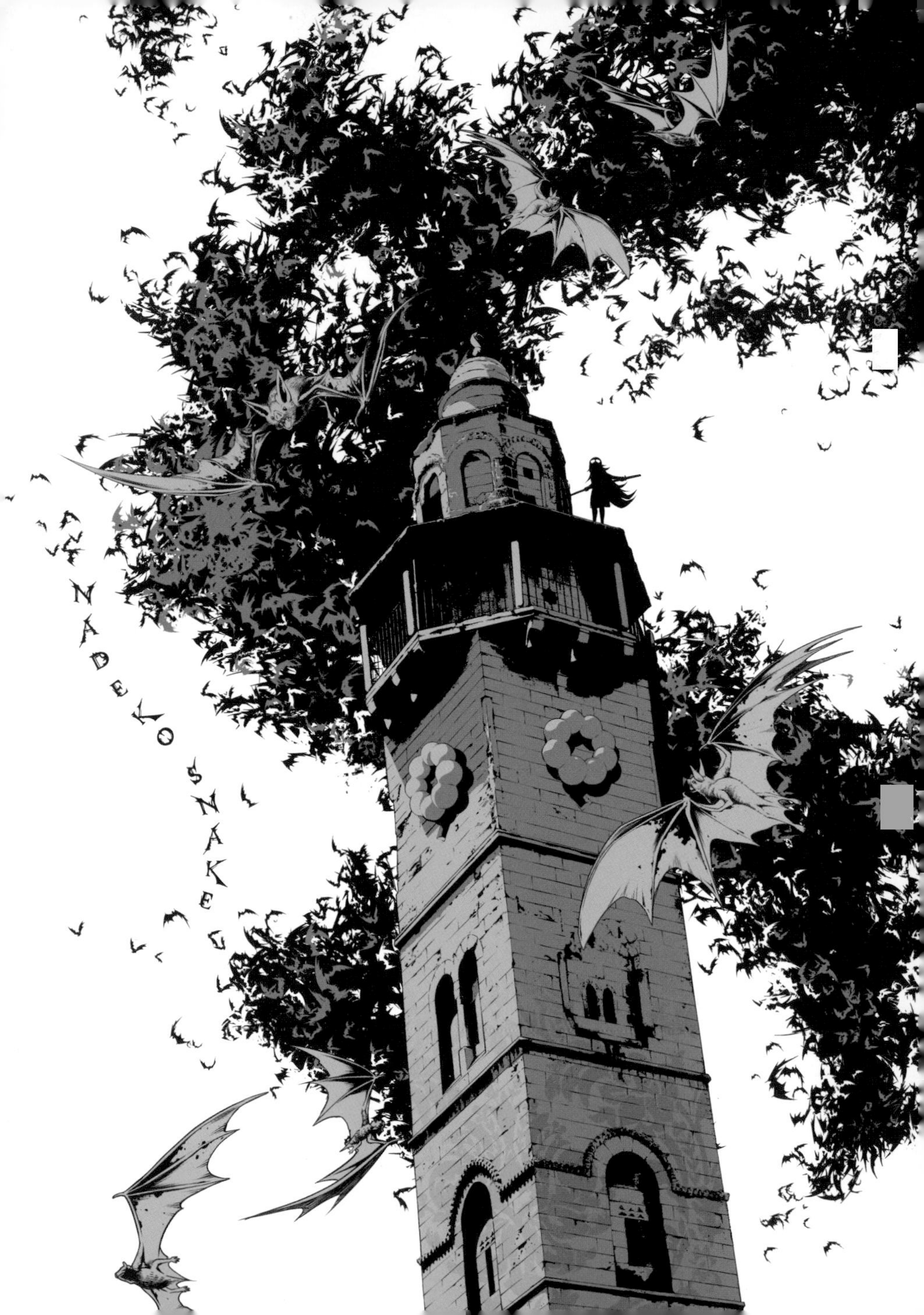
NADEKO SNAKE

BAKEMONOGATARI

OH!GREAT

ORIGINAL STORY:

NISIOISIN

7

ORIGINAL CHARACTER
DESIGN: VOFAN

MAIN CHARACTERS

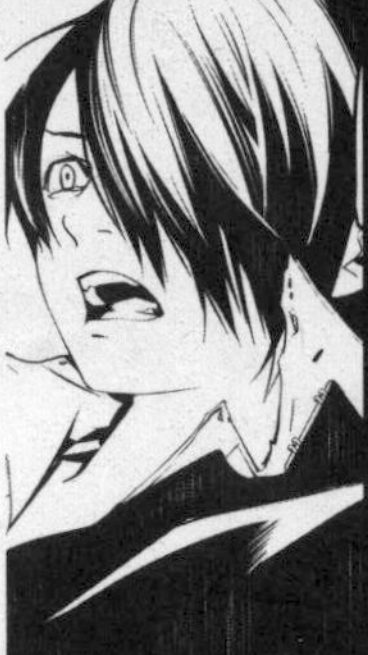

Koyomi Araragi

A boy who was attacked by a vampire. After that attack, he was saved by Mèmè and is sometimes asked to perform tasks to pay off the large debt he owes as a result.

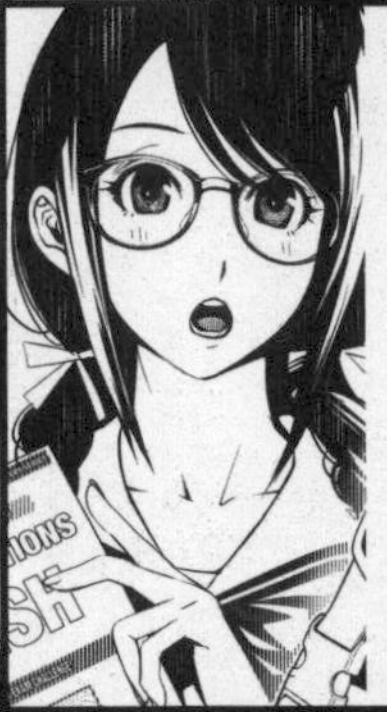

Tsubasa Hanekawa

Koyomi's classmate, who was once bewitched by a "cat." She denies it, but she's a class president among class presidents who knows everything.

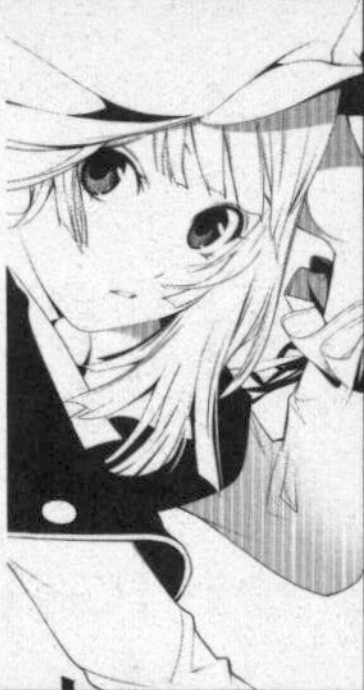

Nadeko Sengoku

Classmates with Tsukihi, Koyomi's youngest sister. Koyomi and Suruga happen to cross paths with her as they head through the mountains to a shrine.

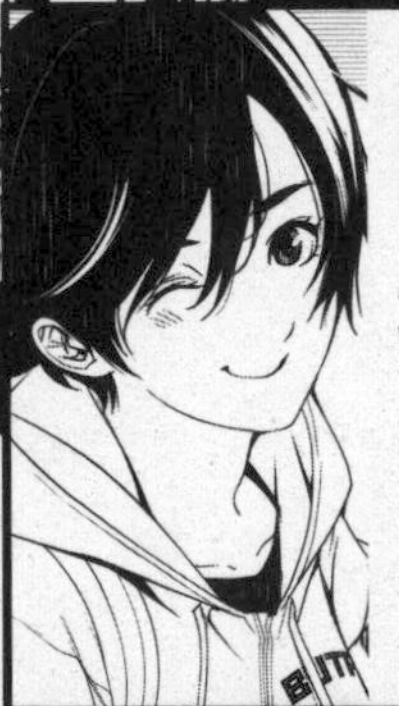

Suruga Kanbaru

A girl who made a wish to a "monkey." Though the aberration ended up remaining in her left arm, Koyomi and Hitagi were able to work to make her wish come half-true.

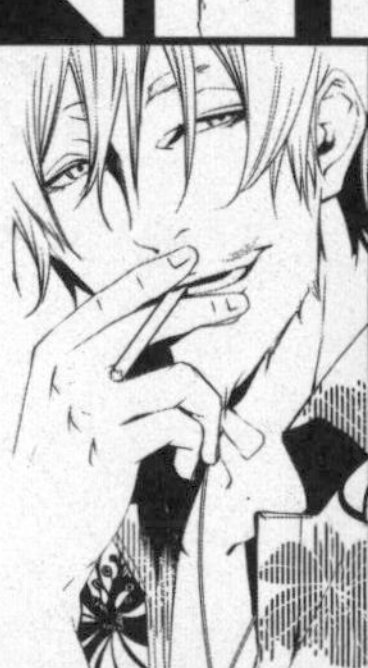

Mèmè Oshino

An expert on aberrations who Koyomi relies on whenever he has a problem. He makes the ruins of a former cram school his home.

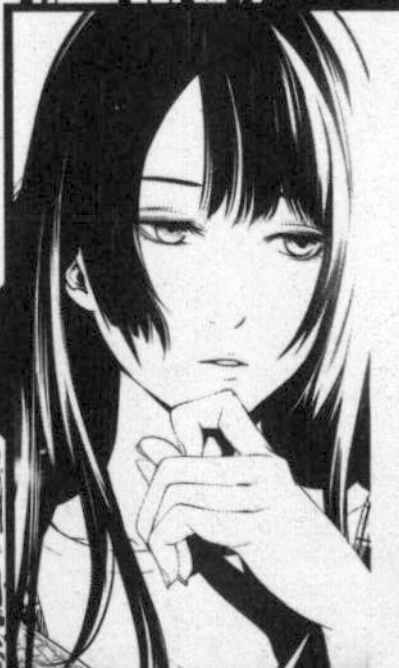

Hitagi Senjogahara

A girl whose weight was once stolen by a "crab." Suruga has been her junior ever since middle school, and the two have now reconciled.

THE STORY SO FAR

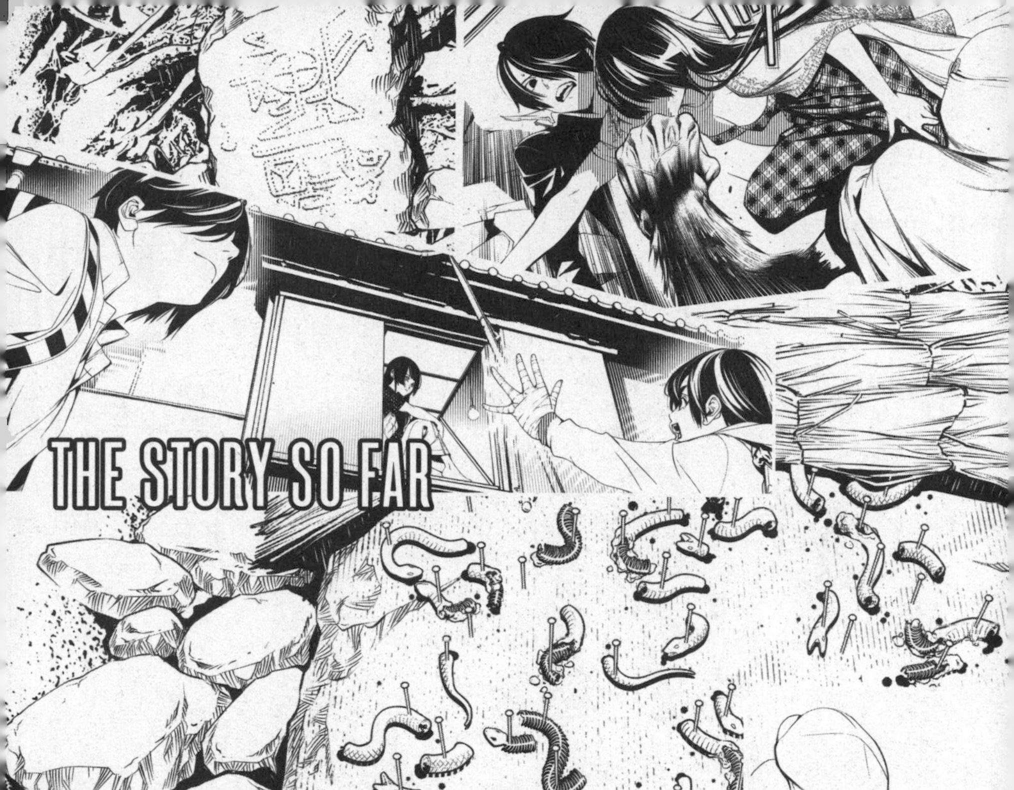

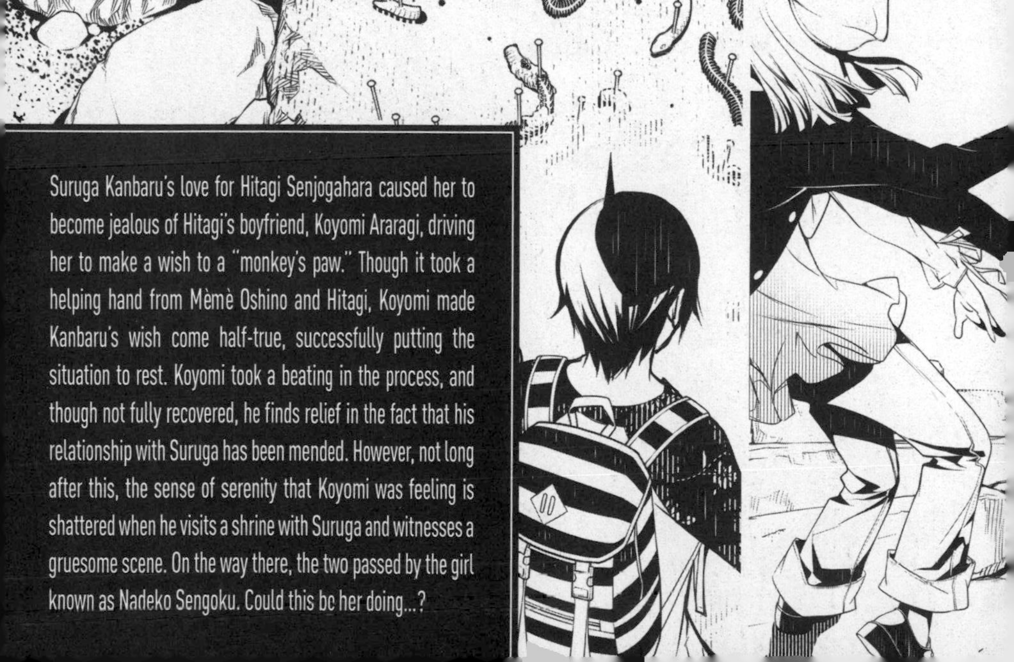

Suruga Kanbaru's love for Hitagi Senjogahara caused her to become jealous of Hitagi's boyfriend, Koyomi Araragi, driving her to make a wish to a "monkey's paw." Though it took a helping hand from Mèmè Oshino and Hitagi, Koyomi made Kanbaru's wish come half-true, successfully putting the situation to rest. Koyomi took a beating in the process, and though not fully recovered, he finds relief in the fact that his relationship with Suruga has been mended. However, not long after this, the sense of serenity that Koyomi was feeling is shattered when he visits a shrine with Suruga and witnesses a gruesome scene. On the way there, the two passed by the girl known as Nadeko Sengoku. Could this be her doing...?

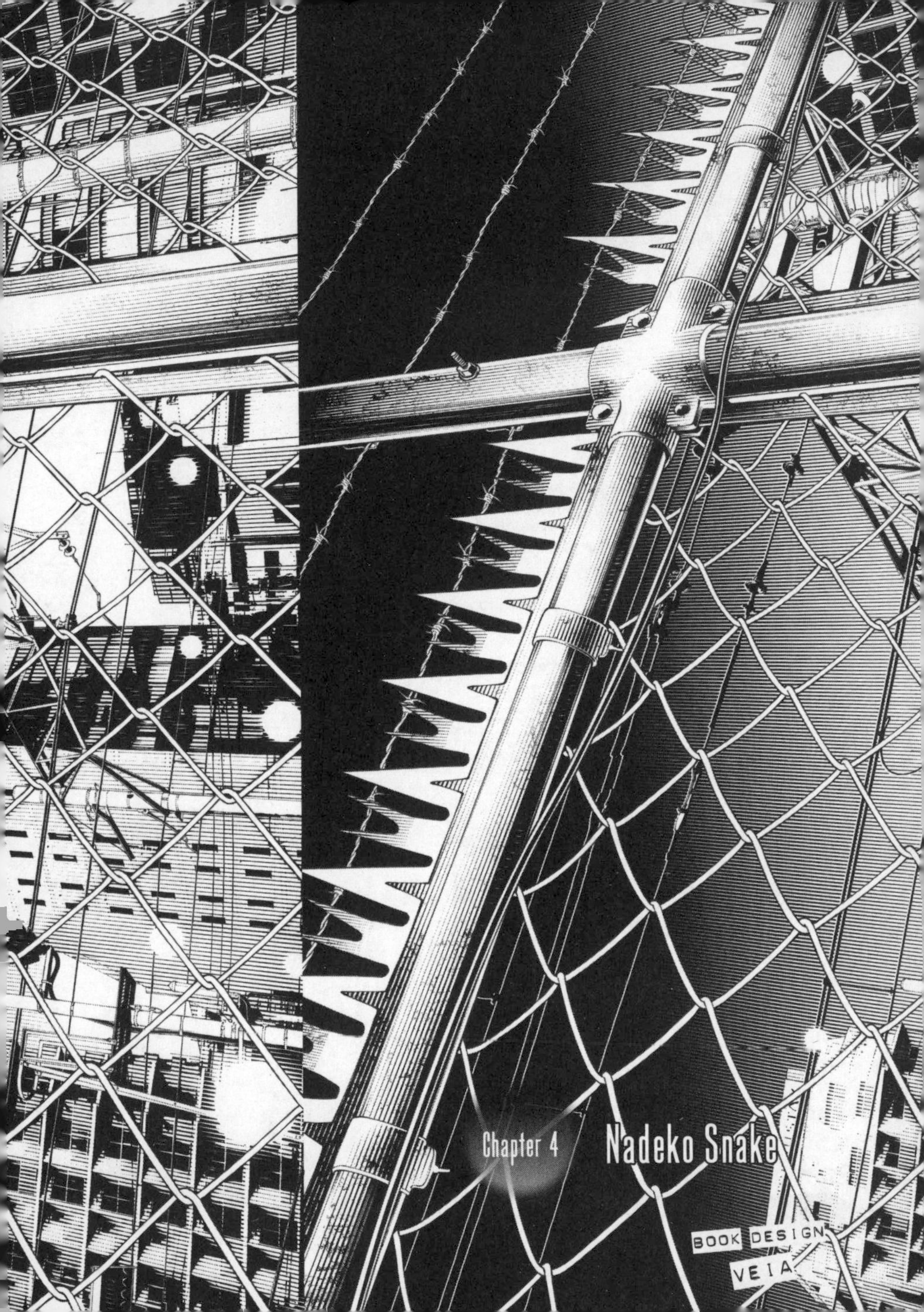
Chapter 4 Nadeko Snake
BOOK DESIGN
VEIA

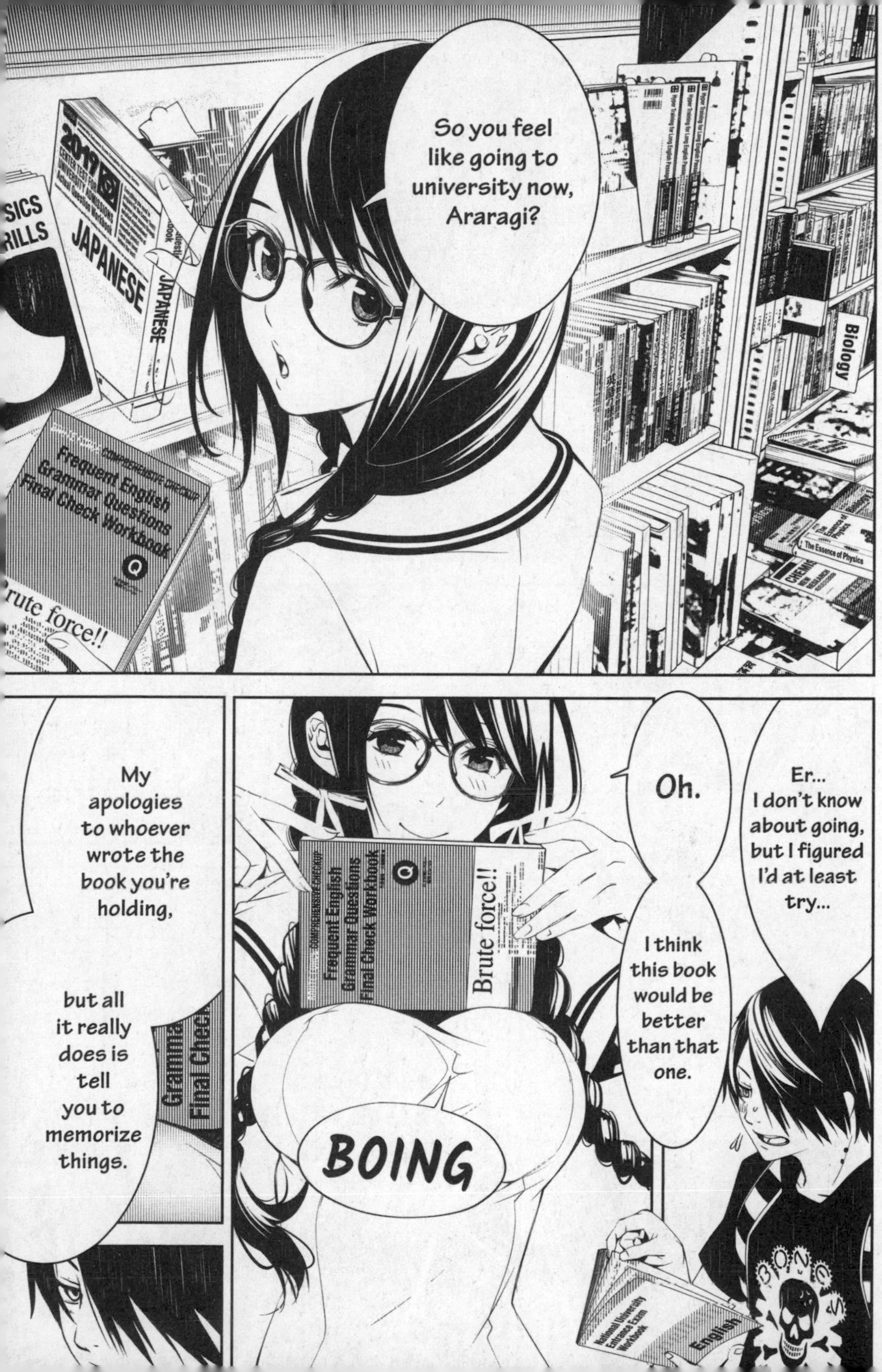

So you feel like going to university now, Araragi?
2019 CENTER TEST FOR UNIVERSITY ADMISSIONS Actual Question Workbook
JAPANESE
JAPANESE
SICS
RILLS
COMPREHENSIVE CHECKUP
Frequent English Grammar Questions Final Check Workbook
Brute force!!
Biology
The Essence of Physics
Er... I don't know about going, but I figured I'd at least try...
Oh.
I think this book would be better than that one.
COMPREHENSIVE CHECKUP
Frequent English Grammar Questions Final Check Workbook
Brute force!!
BOING
My apologies to whoever wrote the book you're holding,
but all it really does is tell you to memorize things.
Gramma
Final Check
National University Entrance Exam Workbook
English

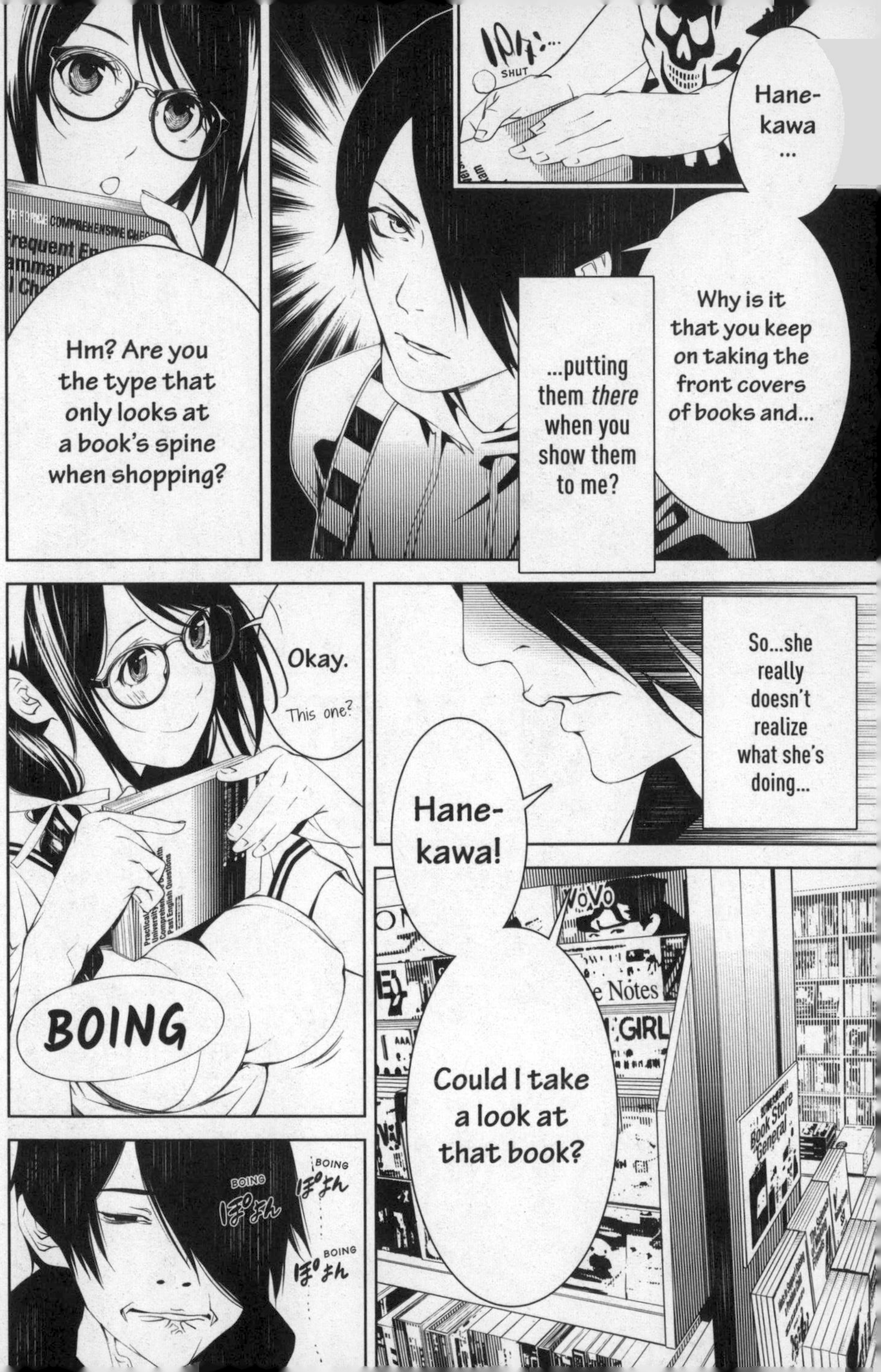
SHUT
Hane-kawa...
Why is it that you keep on taking the front covers of books and...
...putting them *there* when you show them to me?
Hm? Are you the type that only looks at a book's spine when shopping?
So...she really doesn't realize what she's doing...
Hane-kawa!
Okay.
This one?
BOING
Could I take a look at that book?
BOING
ぽよん
BOING
ぽよん
BOING
ぽよん

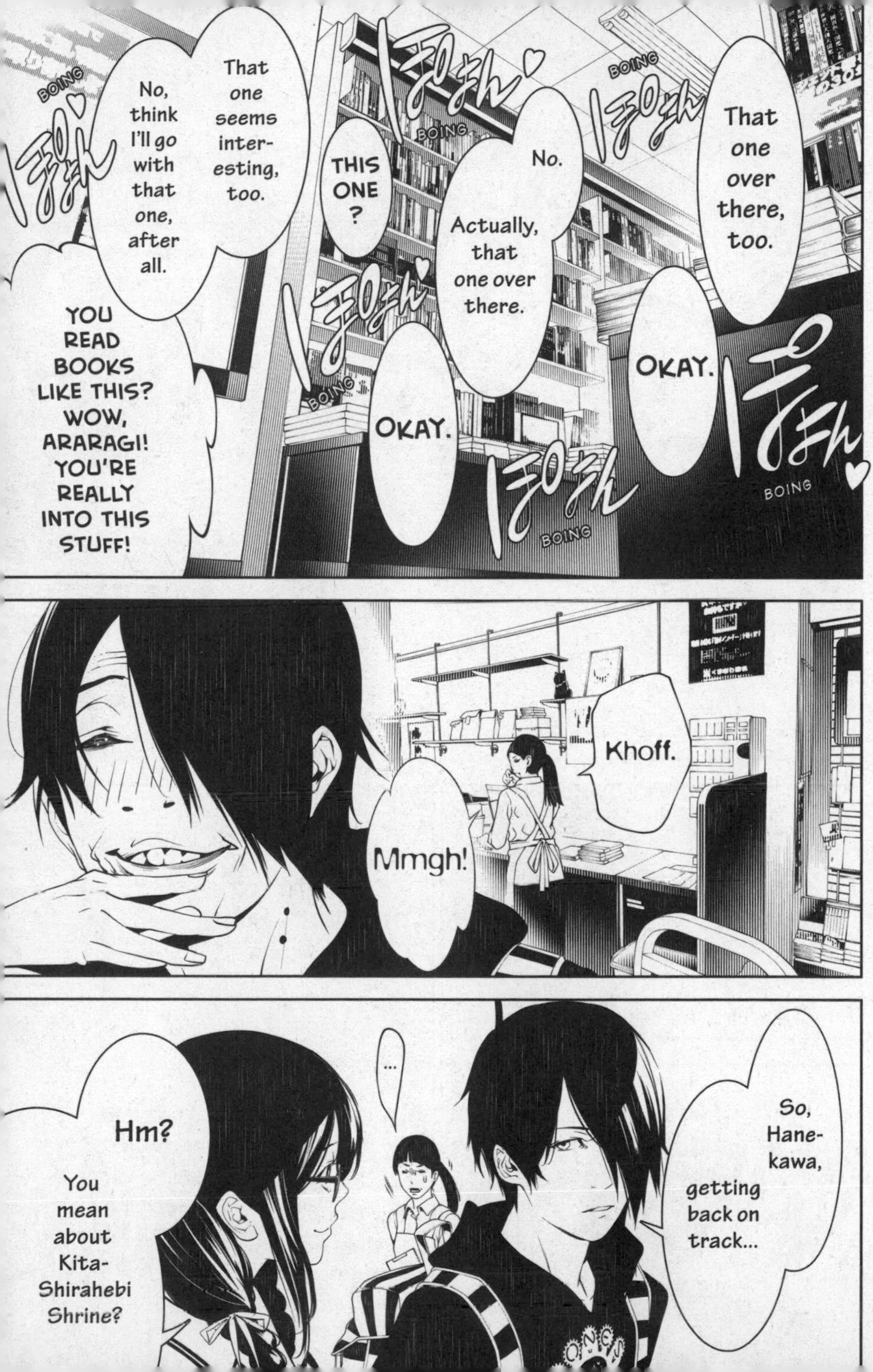
That one over there, too.
BOING
OKAY.
BOING
No.
Actually, that one over there.
BOING
OKAY.
BOING
THIS ONE ?
BOING
That one seems interesting, too.
No, think I'll go with that one, after all.
BOING
YOU READ BOOKS LIKE THIS? WOW, ARARAGI! YOU'RE REALLY INTO THIS STUFF!
Khoff.
Mmgh!
So, Hanekawa, getting back on track...
...
Hm?
You mean about Kita-Shirahebi Shrine?

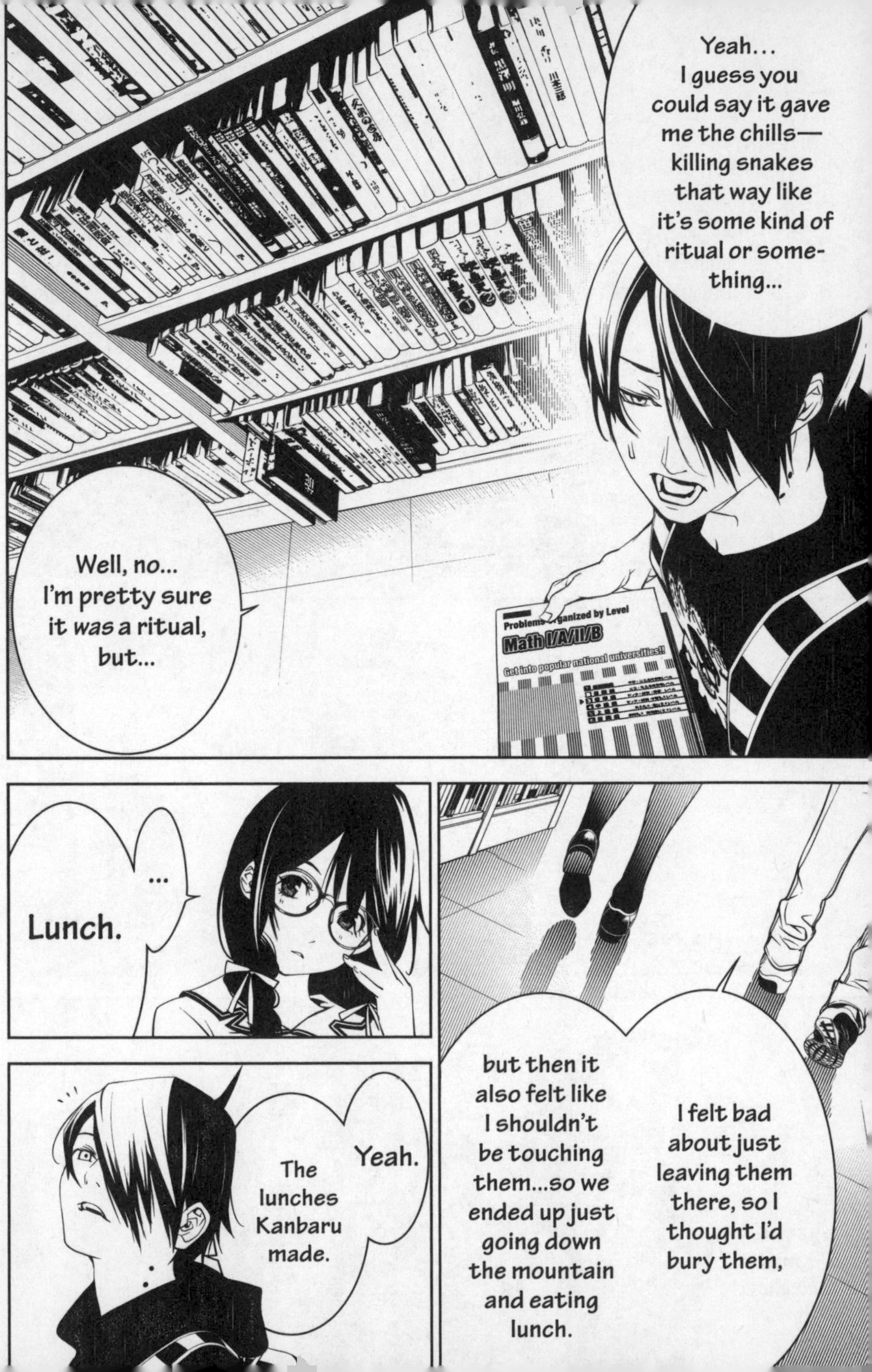
Yeah… I guess you could say it gave me the chills— killing snakes that way like it's some kind of ritual or something…
Well, no… I'm pretty sure it *was* a ritual, but…
Math I/A/II/B
Get into popular national universities!!
I felt bad about just leaving them there, so I thought I'd bury them,
but then it also felt like I shouldn't be touching them…so we ended up just going down the mountain and eating lunch.
…
Lunch.
Yeah.
The lunches Kanbaru made.

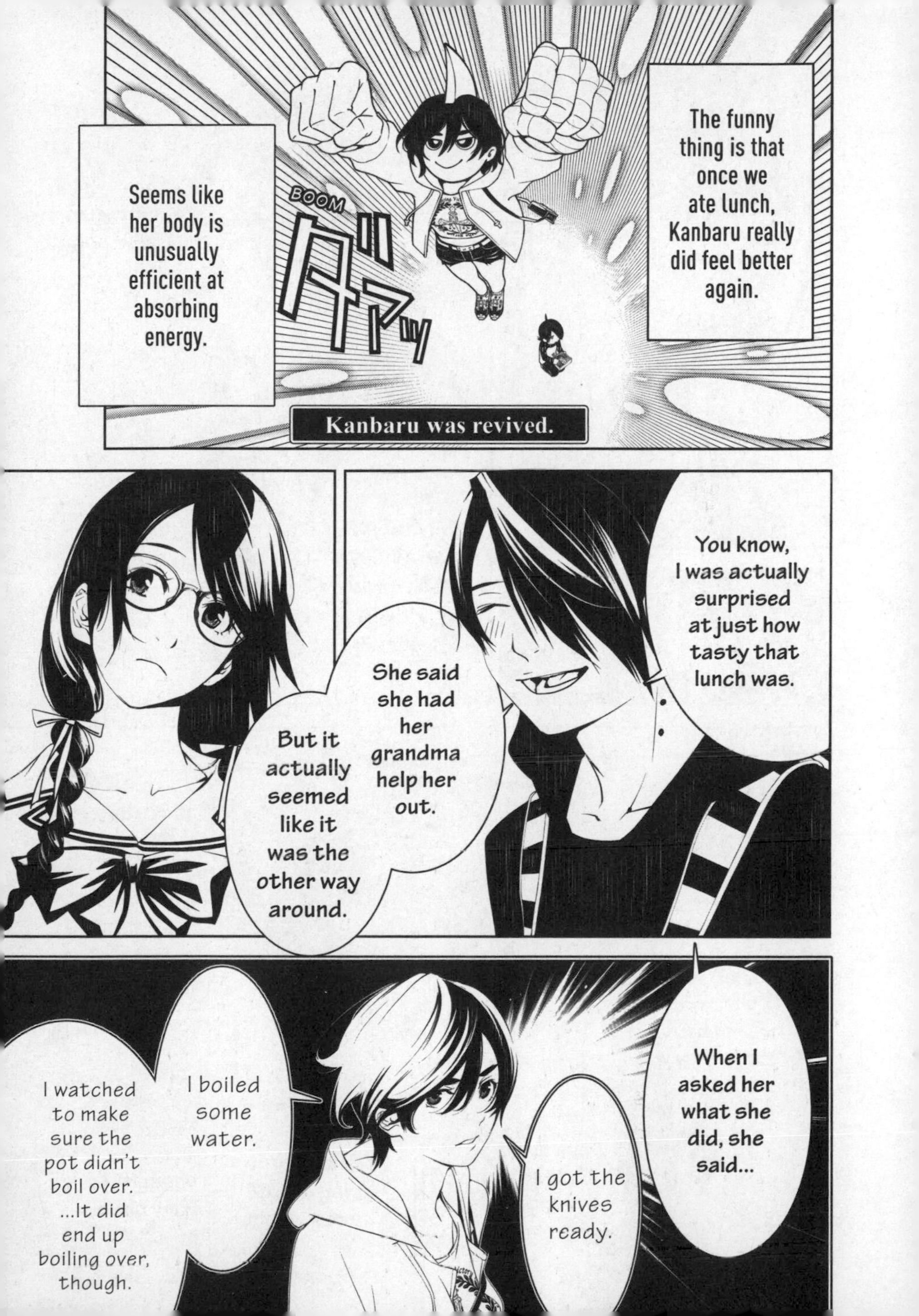
The funny thing is that once we ate lunch, Kanbaru really did feel better again.
BOOM
ダァッ
Seems like her body is unusually efficient at absorbing energy.
Kanbaru was revived.
You know, I was actually surprised at just how tasty that lunch was.
She said she had her grandma help her out.
But it actually seemed like it was the other way around.
When I asked her what she did, she said...
I got the knives ready.
I boiled some water.
I watched to make sure the pot didn't boil over. ...It did end up boiling over, though.

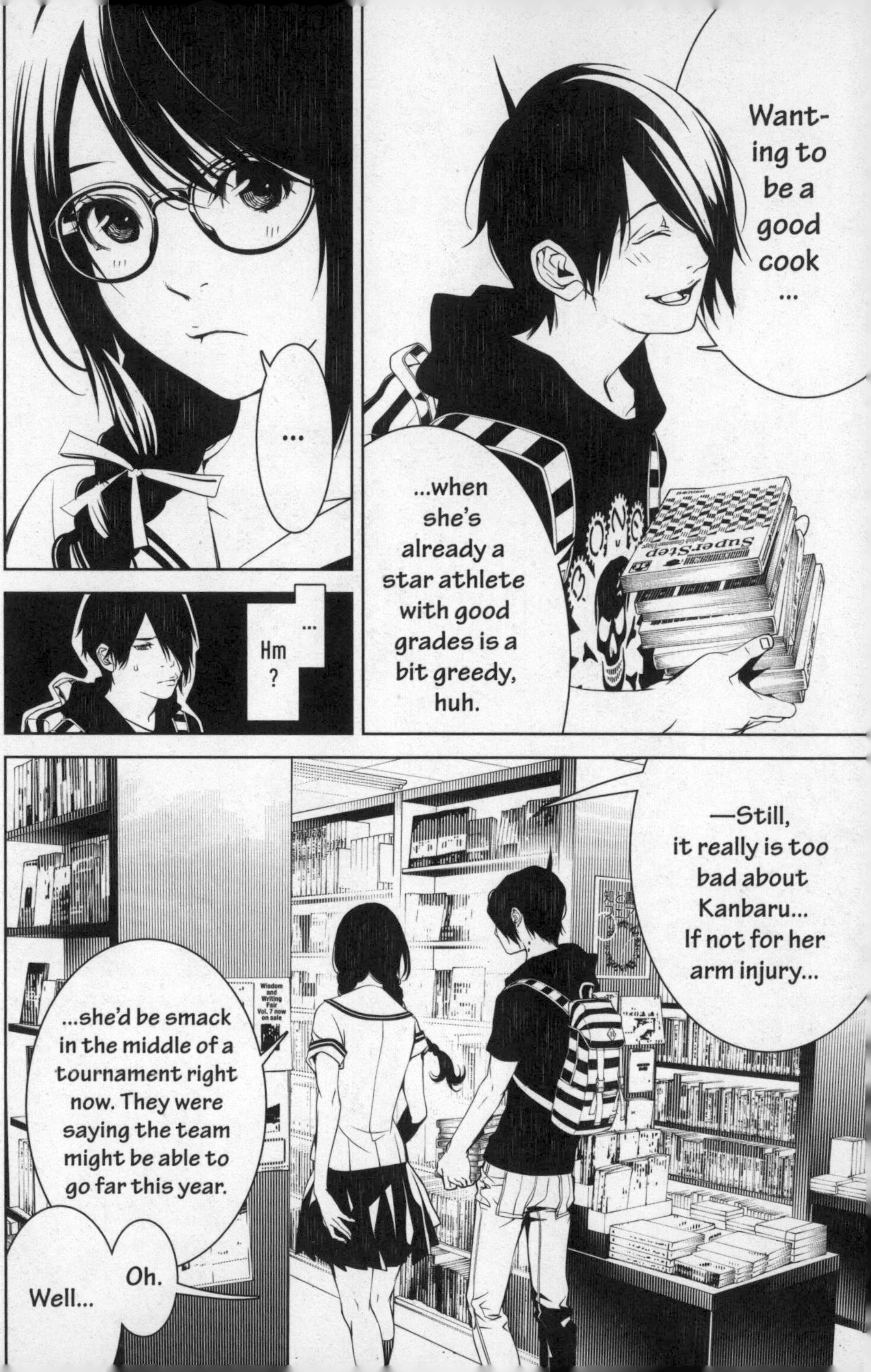
Wanting to be a good cook...
...when she's already a star athlete with good grades is a bit greedy, huh.
...
... Hm?
—Still, it really is too bad about Kanbaru... If not for her arm injury...
Wisdom and Writing Fair Vol. 7 now on sale
...she'd be smack in the middle of a tournament right now. They were saying the team might be able to go far this year.
Oh.
Well...

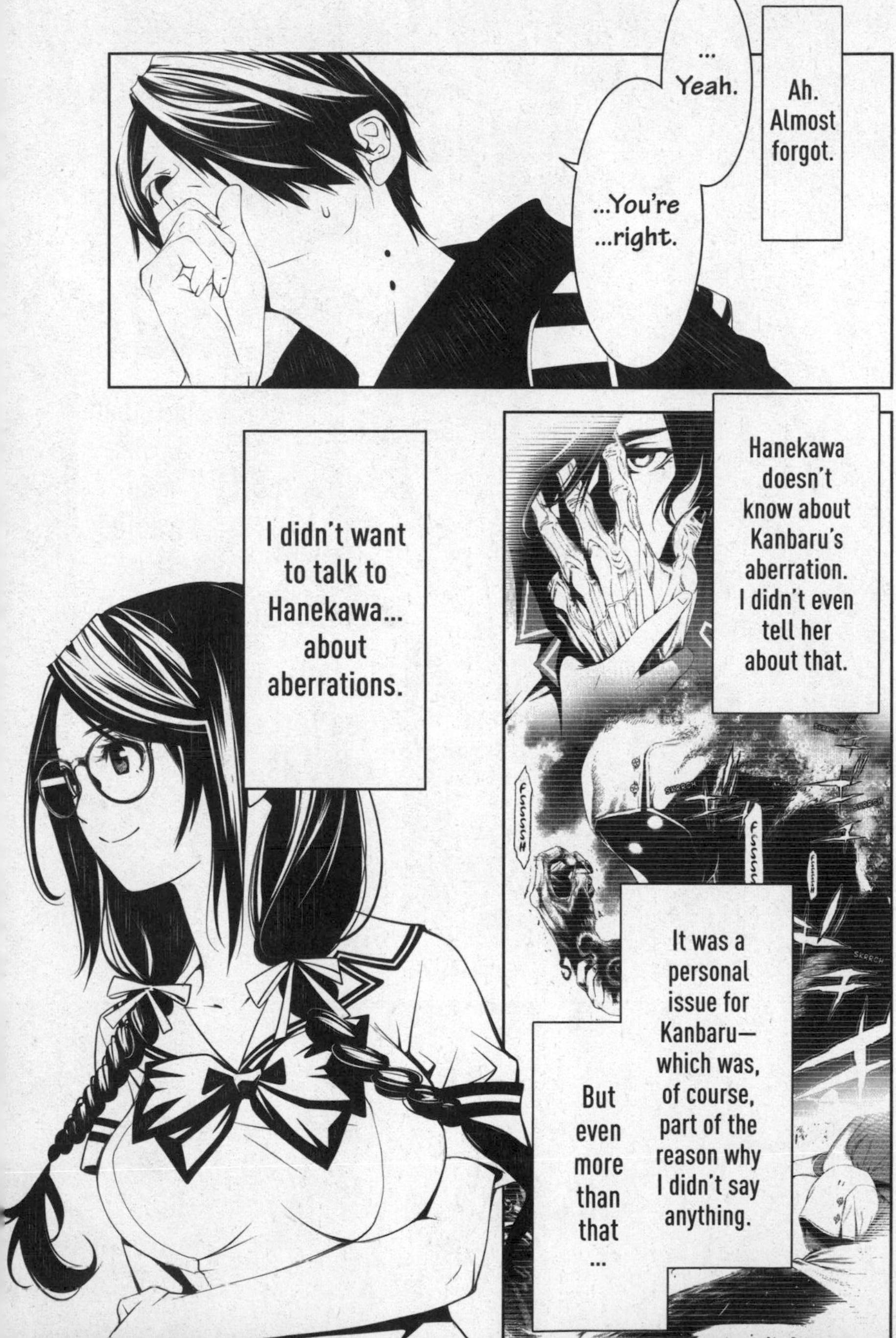

Ah. Almost forgot.
... Yeah.
...You're ...right.
Hanekawa doesn't know about Kanbaru's aberration. I didn't even tell her about that.
SKRRCH
SKRRCH
FSSSSH
It was a personal issue for Kanbaru—which was, of course, part of the reason why I didn't say anything.
SKRRCH
But even more than that ...
I didn't want to talk to Hanekawa... about aberrations.

More than anyone else, I wanted Hanekawa...

...to be as far away as possible from aberrations.

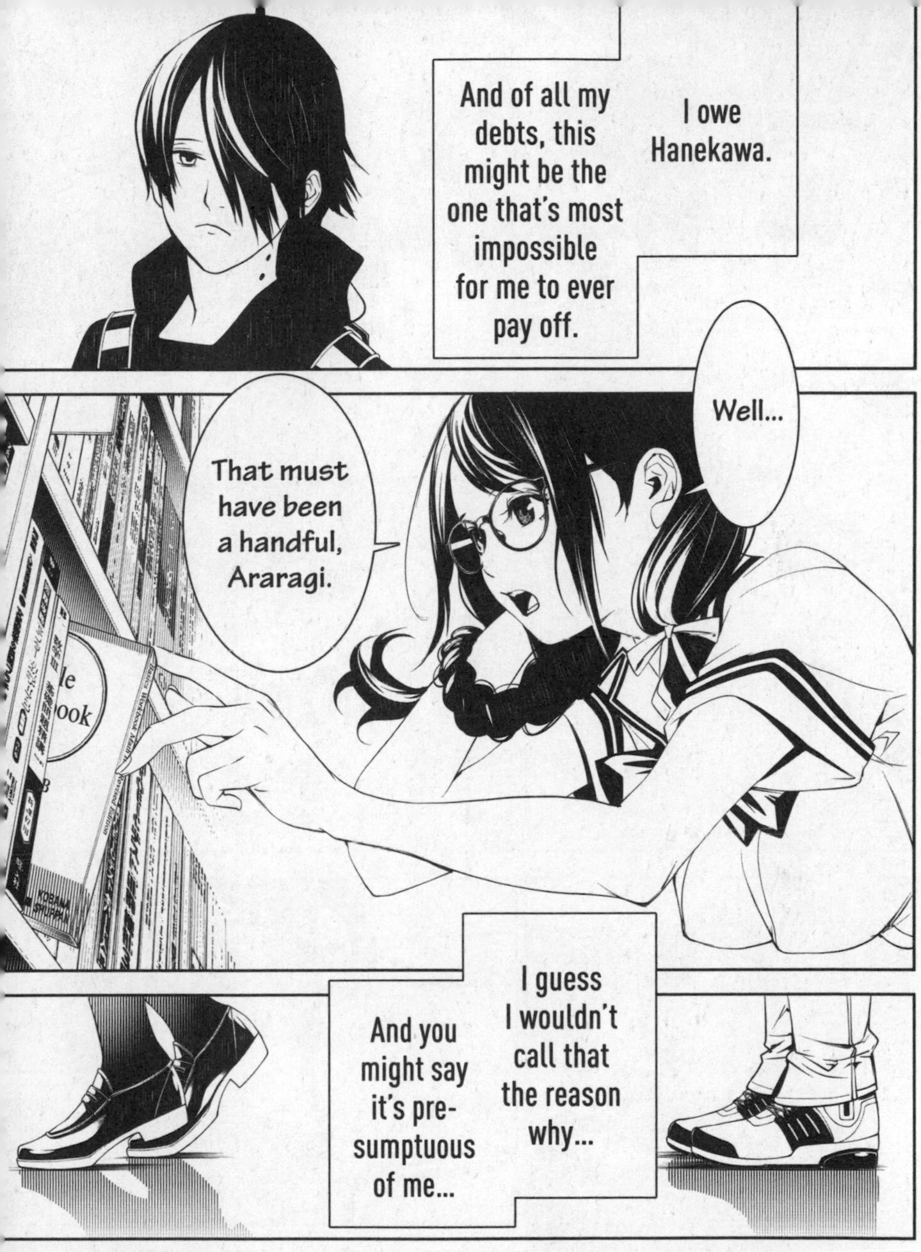
I owe Hanekawa.
And of all my debts, this might be the one that's most impossible for me to ever pay off.
Well...
That must have been a handful, Araragi.
I guess I wouldn't call that the reason why...
And you might say it's pre-sumptuous of me...

But I want to protect Hanekawa.
And I want to be even closer to her as I do.

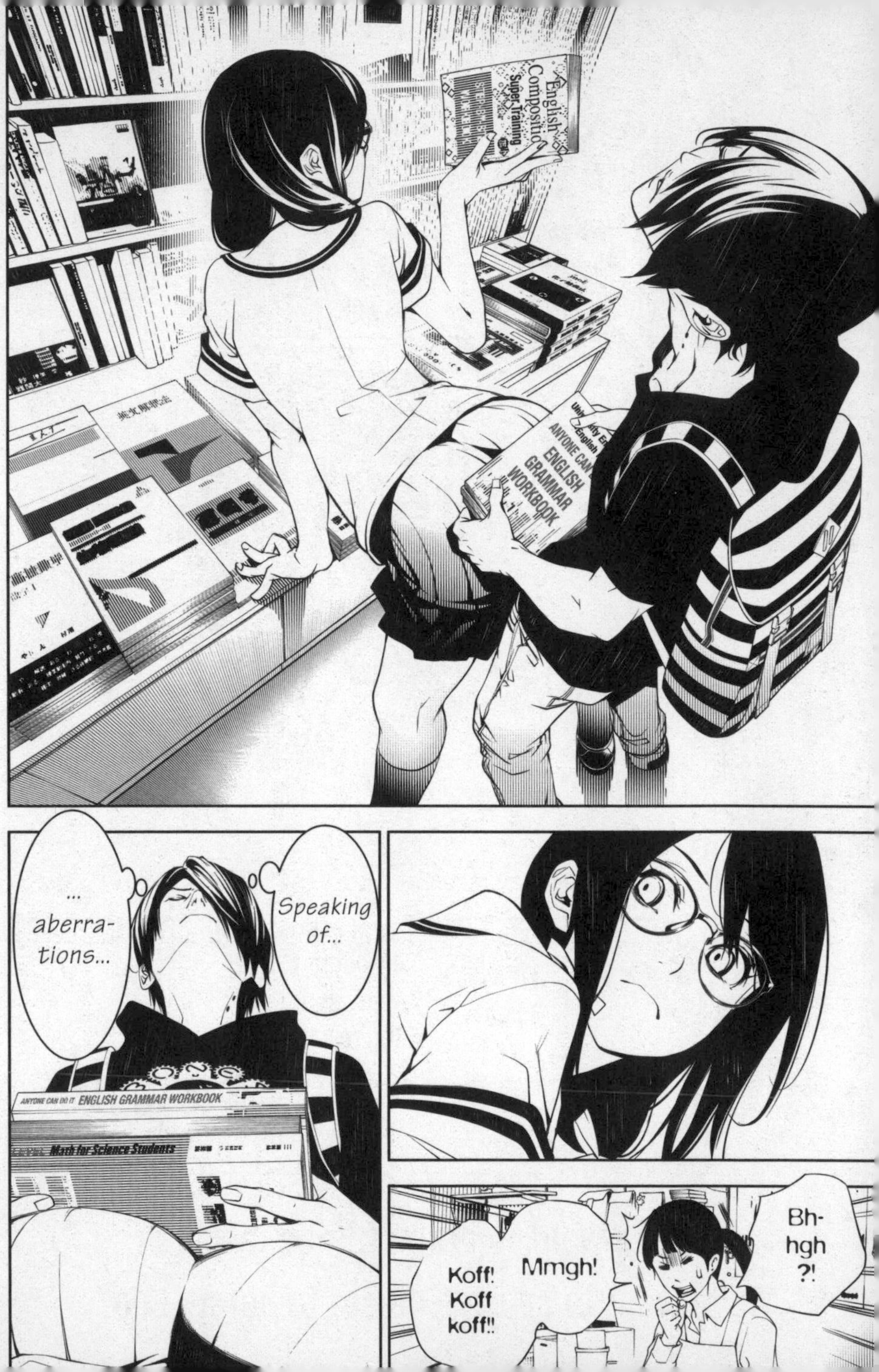
Super Training
ANYONE CAN
ENGLISH
GRAMMAR
WORKBOOK
Speaking of...
... aberra-tions...
ANYONE CAN DO IT ENGLISH GRAMMAR WORKBOOK
Math for Science Students
Bh-hgh?!
Mmgh!
Koff! Koff koff!!

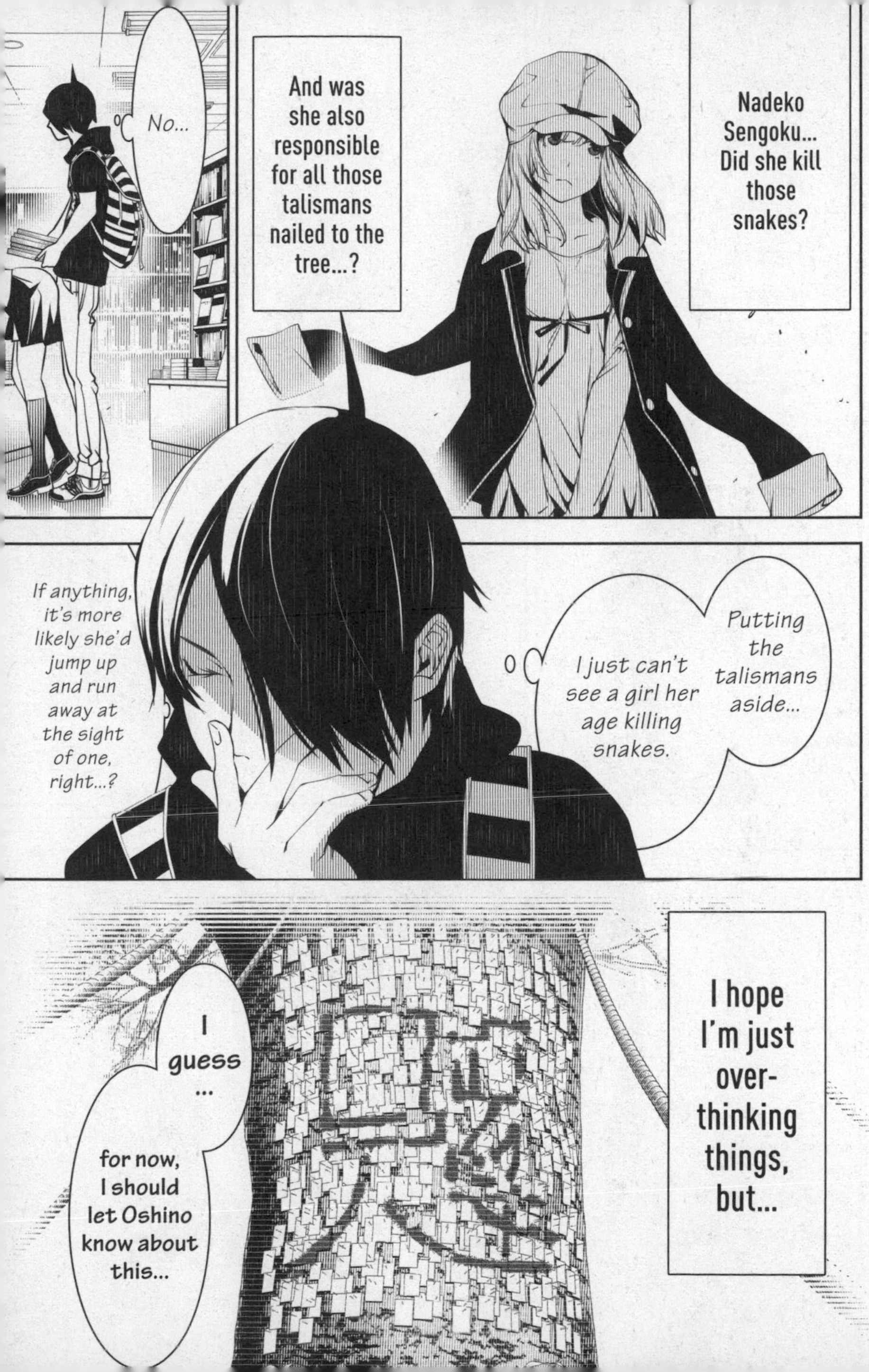
Nadeko Sengoku... Did she kill those snakes?
And was she also responsible for all those talismans nailed to the tree...?
No...
Putting the talismans aside...
I just can't see a girl her age killing snakes.
If anything, it's more likely she'd jump up and run away at the sight of one, right...?
I hope I'm just over-thinking things, but...
I guess...
for now, I should let Oshino know about this...

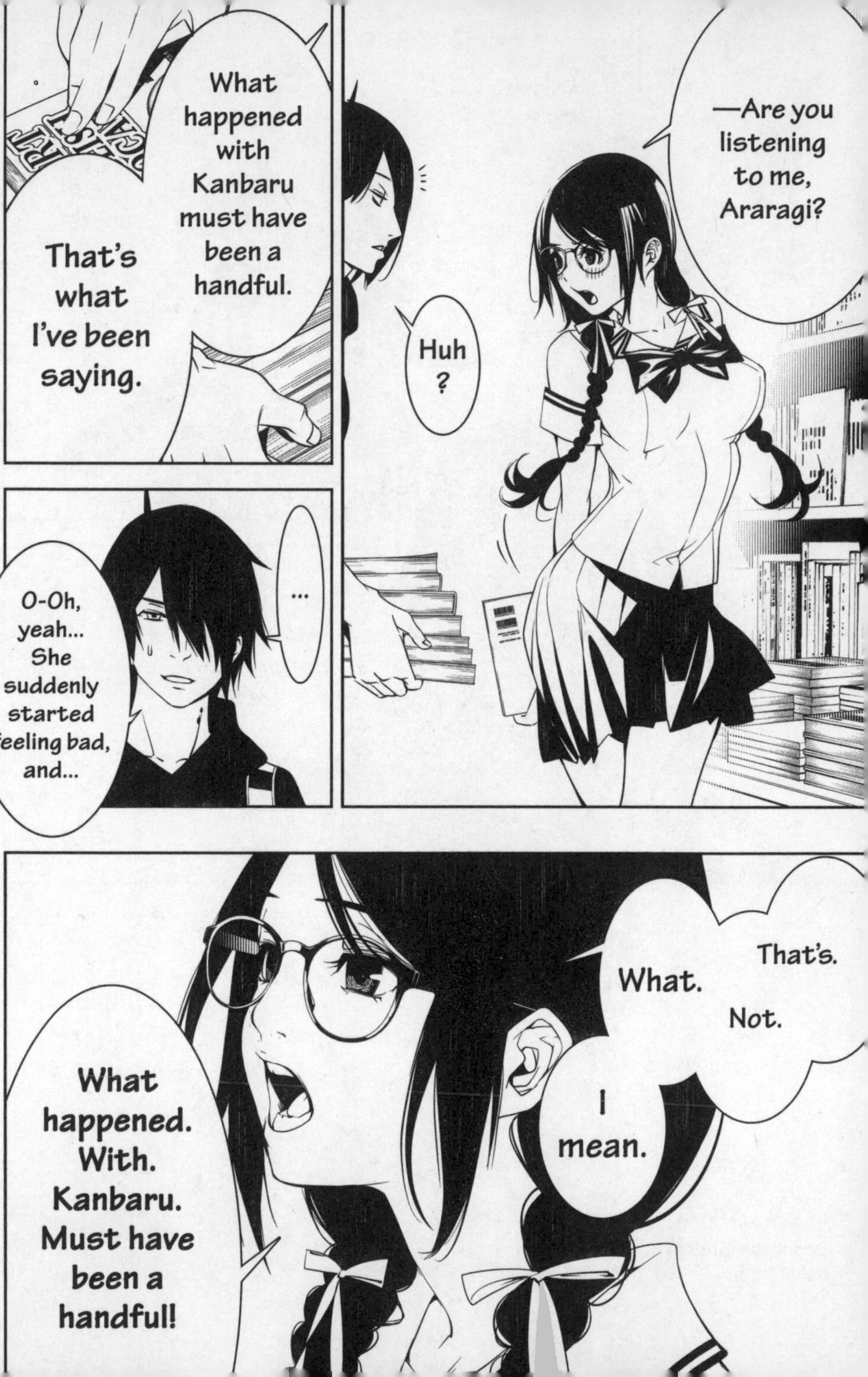
—Are you listening to me, Araragi?
Huh?
What happened with Kanbaru must have been a handful.
That's what I've been saying.
...
O-Oh, yeah... She suddenly started feeling bad, and...
That's. Not. What. I mean.
What happened. With. Kanbaru. Must have been a handful!

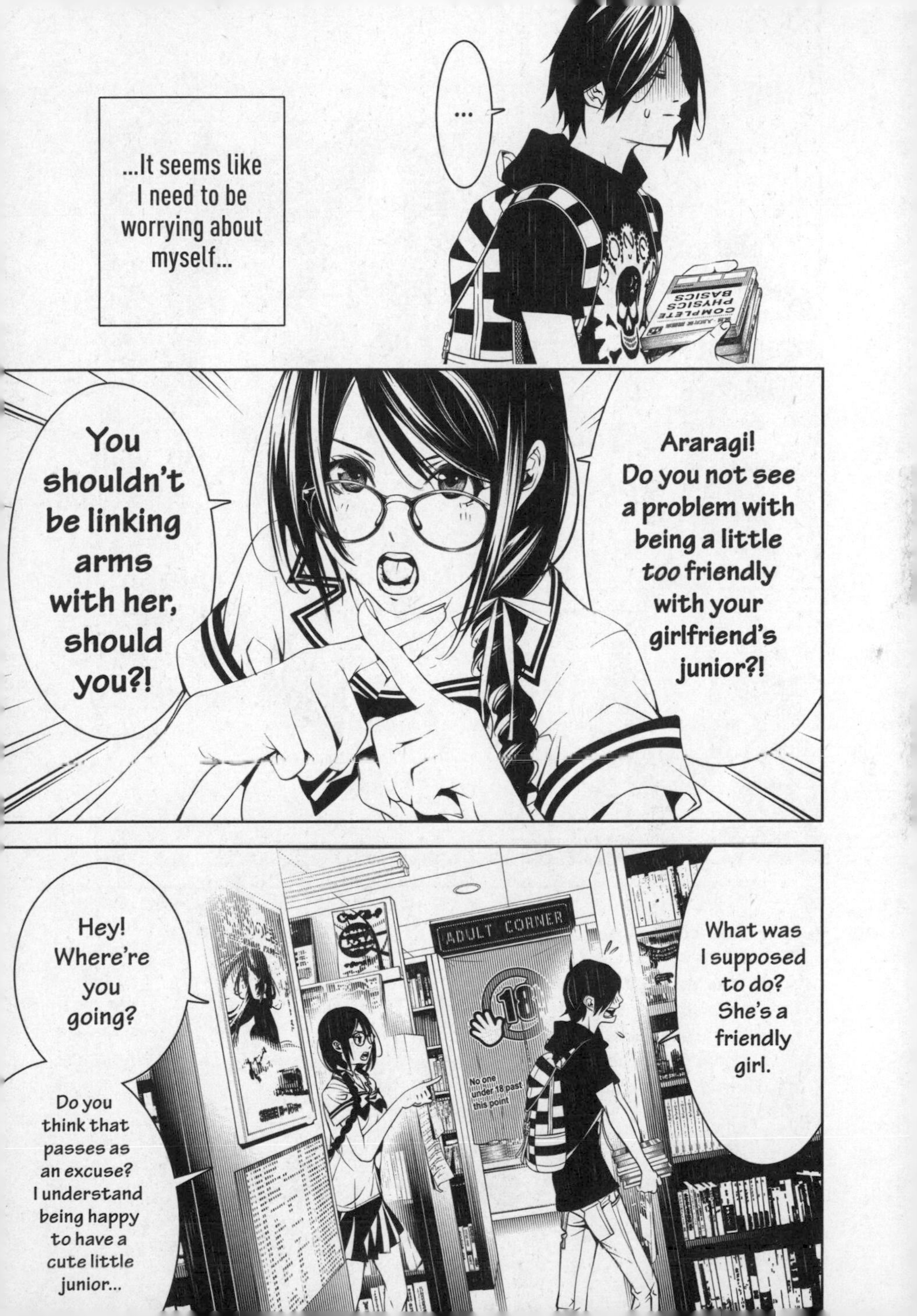
...
...It seems like I need to be worrying about myself...
COMPLETE PHYSICS BASICS
Araragi! Do you not see a problem with being a little *too* friendly with your girlfriend's junior?!
You shouldn't be linking arms with her, should you?!
What was I supposed to do? She's a friendly girl.
ADULT CORNER
18
No one under 18 past this point
Hey! Where're you going?
Do you think that passes as an excuse? I understand being happy to have a cute little junior...

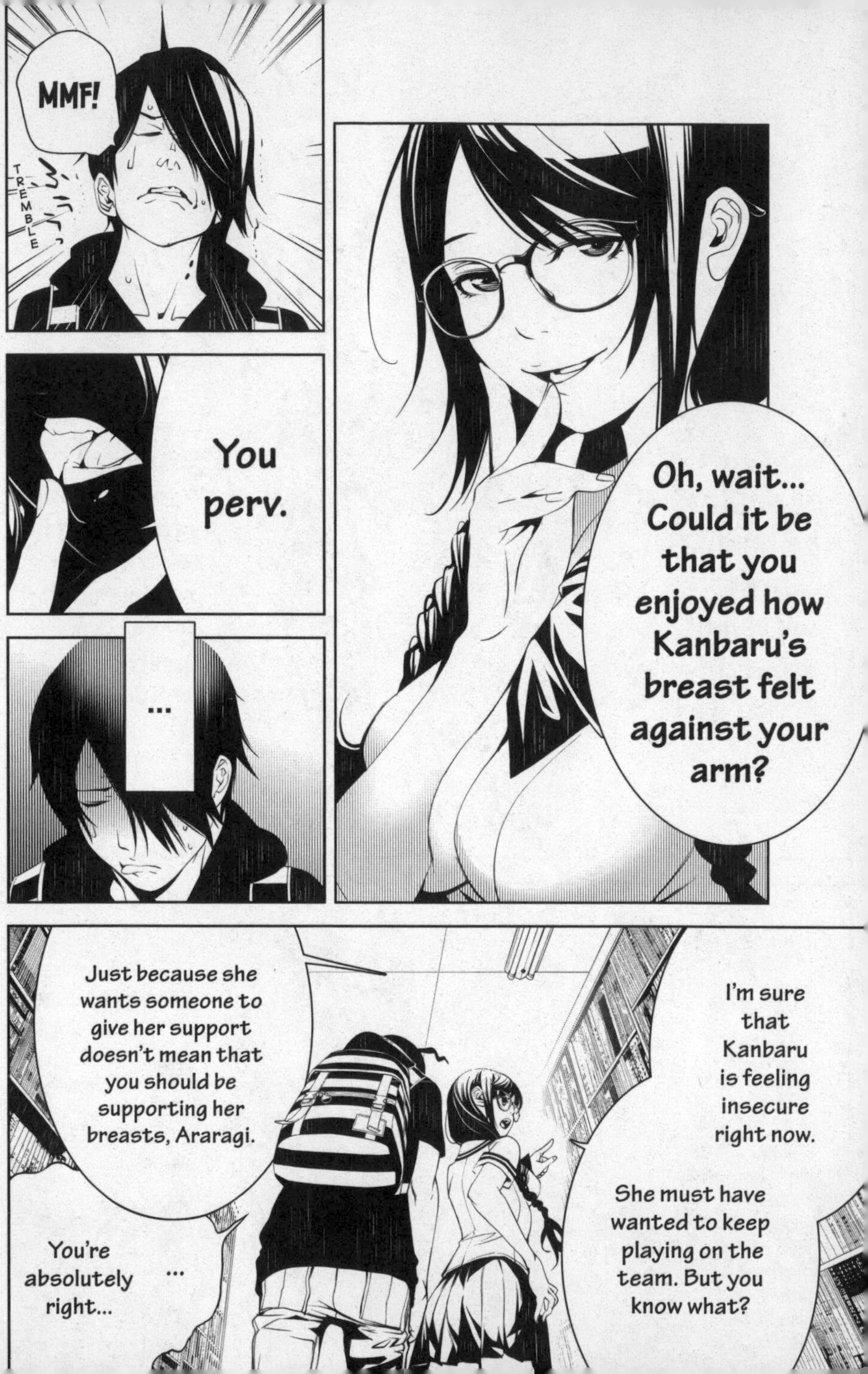
Oh, wait... Could it be that you enjoyed how Kanbaru's breast felt against your arm?
MMF!
TREMBLE
You perv.
...
I'm sure that Kanbaru is feeling insecure right now.
She must have wanted to keep playing on the team. But you know what?
Just because she wants someone to give her support doesn't mean that you should be supporting her breasts, Araragi.
...
You're absolutely right...

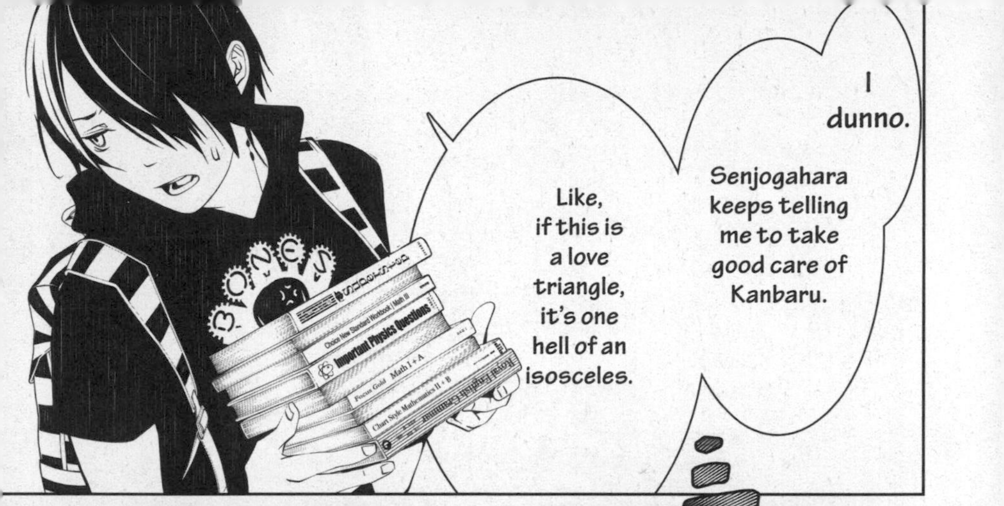

I dunno.
Senjogahara keeps telling me to take good care of Kanbaru.
Like, if this is a love triangle, it's one hell of an isosceles.
BONES
Choice New Standard Workbook | Math III
Important Physics Questions
Focus Gold Math I + A
Chart Style Mathematics III + B
Royal English Grammar

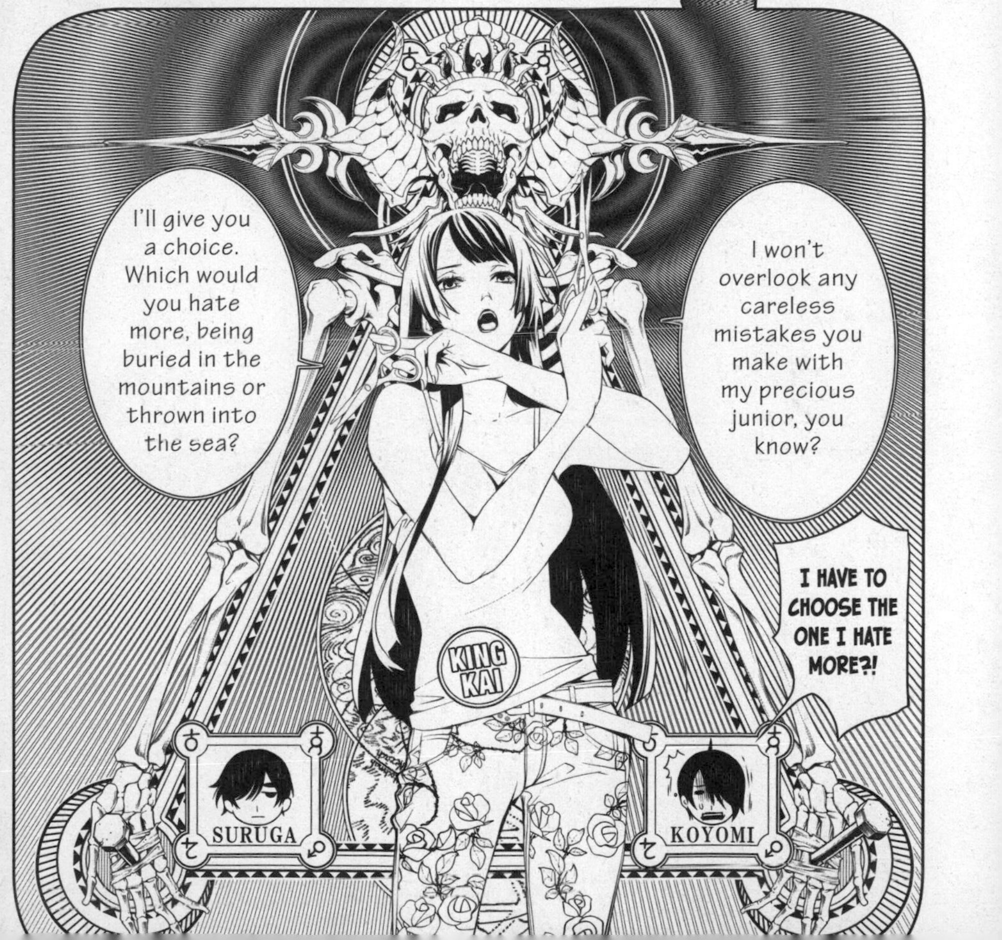

I won't overlook any careless mistakes you make with my precious junior, you know?
I'll give you a choice. Which would you hate more, being buried in the mountains or thrown into the sea?
I HAVE TO CHOOSE THE ONE I HATE MORE?!
KING KAI
KOYOMI
SURUGA

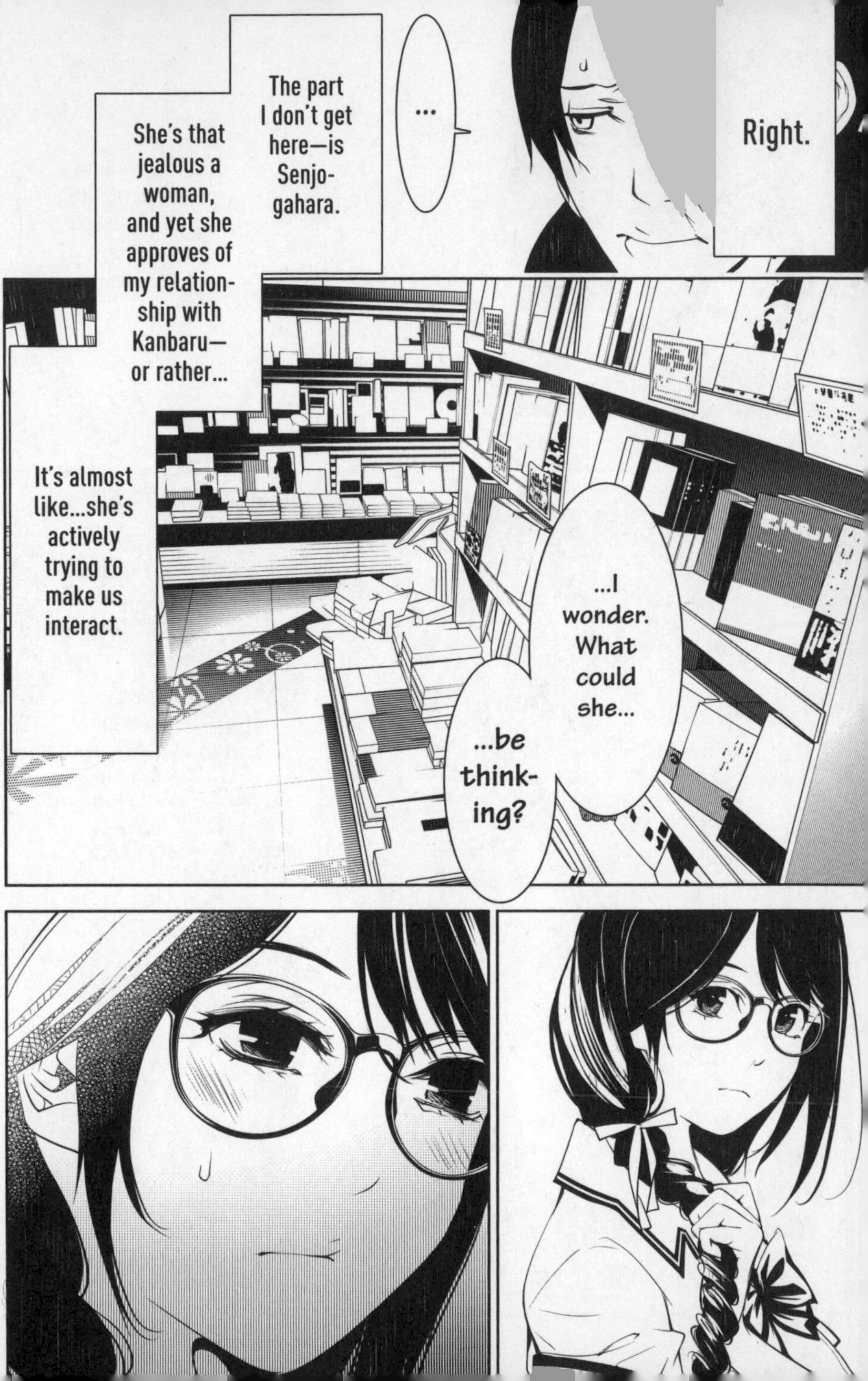
Right.
...
The part I don't get here—is Senjo-gahara.
She's that jealous a woman, and yet she approves of my relationship with Kanbaru—or rather...
It's almost like...she's actively trying to make us interact.
...I wonder. What could she...
...be thinking?

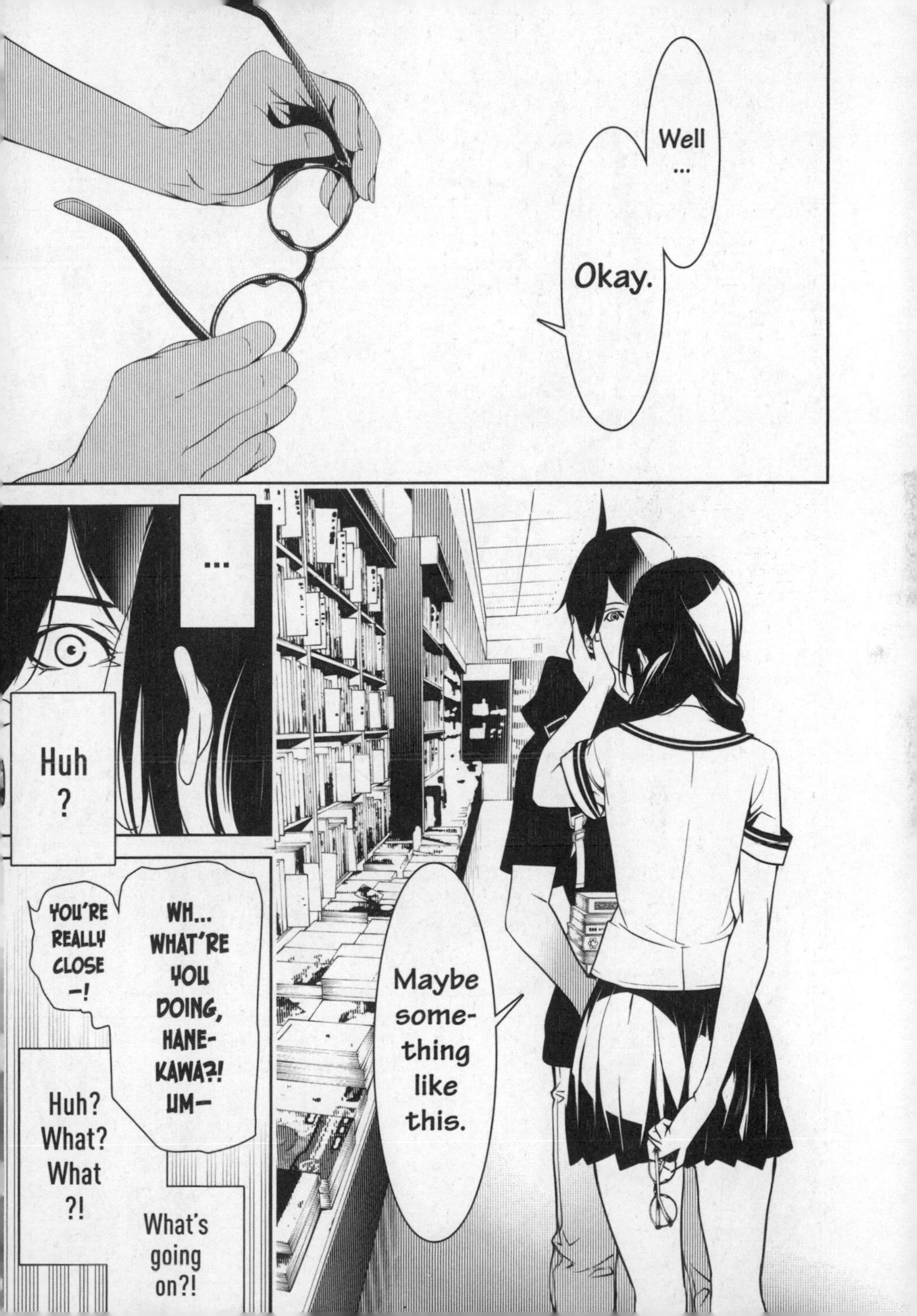
Well ...
Okay.
Maybe some-thing like this.
...
Huh ?
WH... WHAT'RE YOU DOING, HANE-KAWA?! UM—
YOU'RE REALLY CLOSE —!
Huh? What? What ?!
What's going on?!

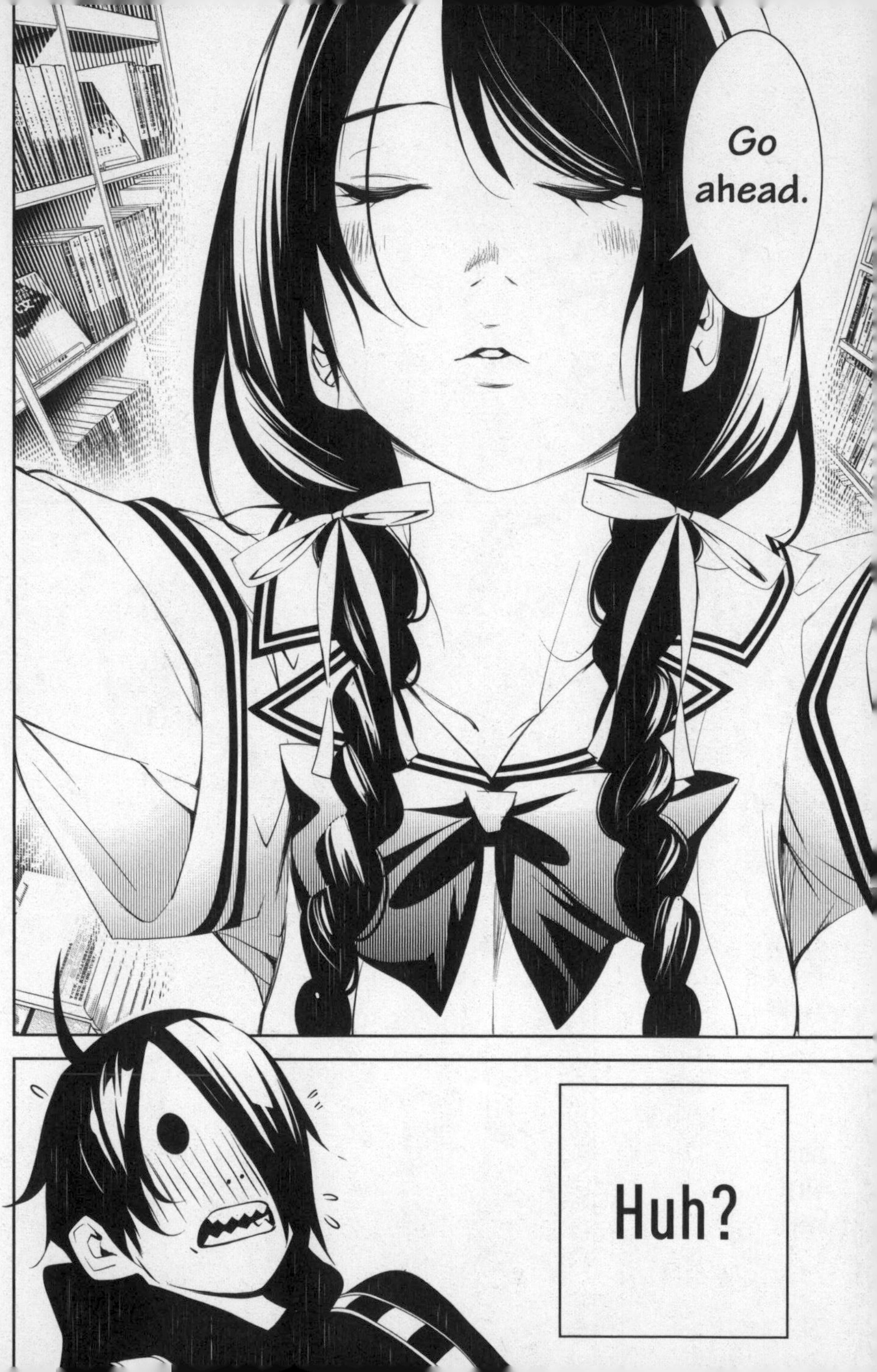
Go ahead.
Huh?

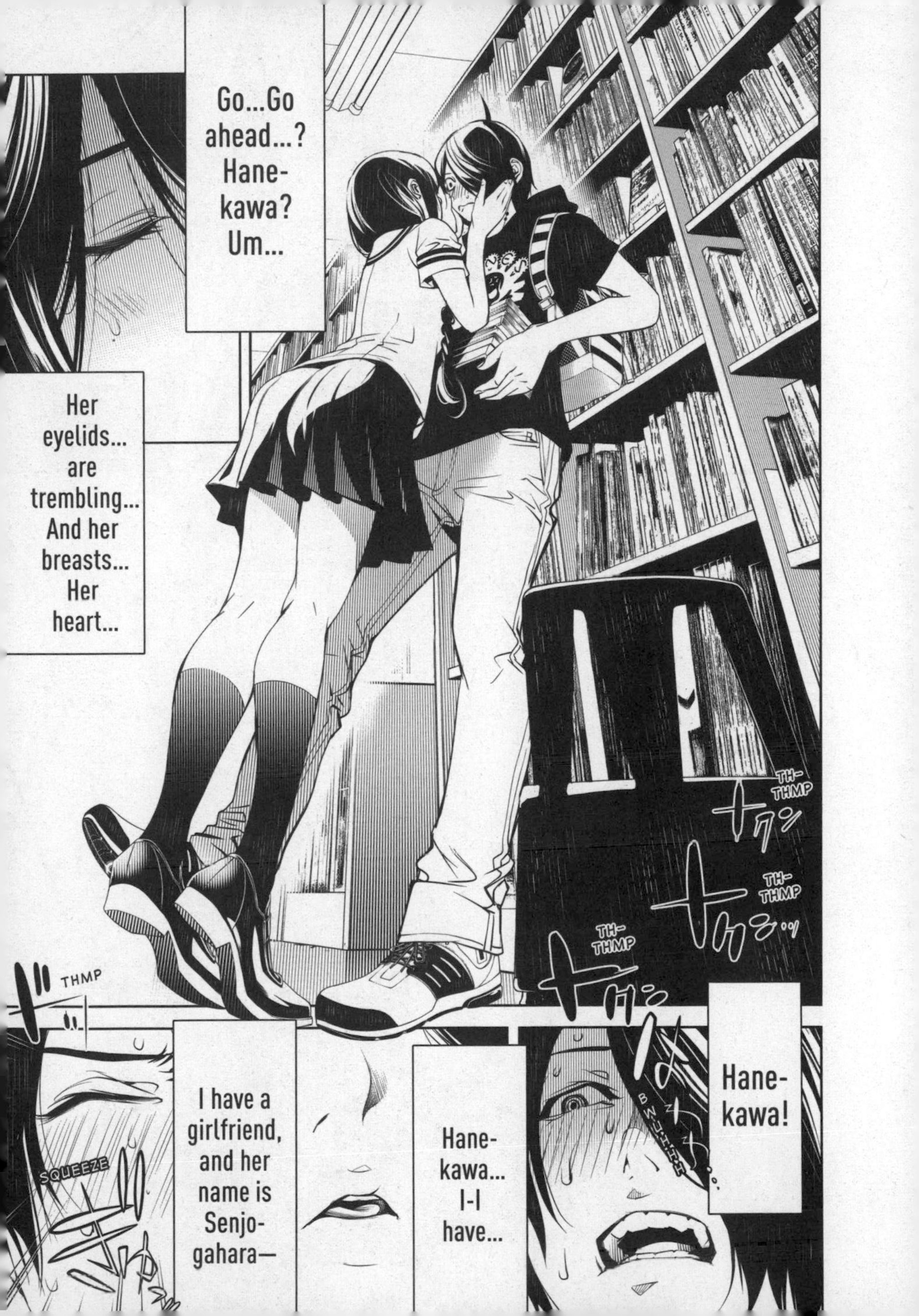
Go...Go ahead...? Hane-kawa? Um...
TH-THMP
TH-THMP
TH-THMP
Her eyelids... are trembling... And her breasts... Her heart...
THMP
Hane-kawa!
BWUHHHH
Hane-kawa... I-I have...
I have a girlfriend, and her name is Senjo-gahara—
SQUEEZE

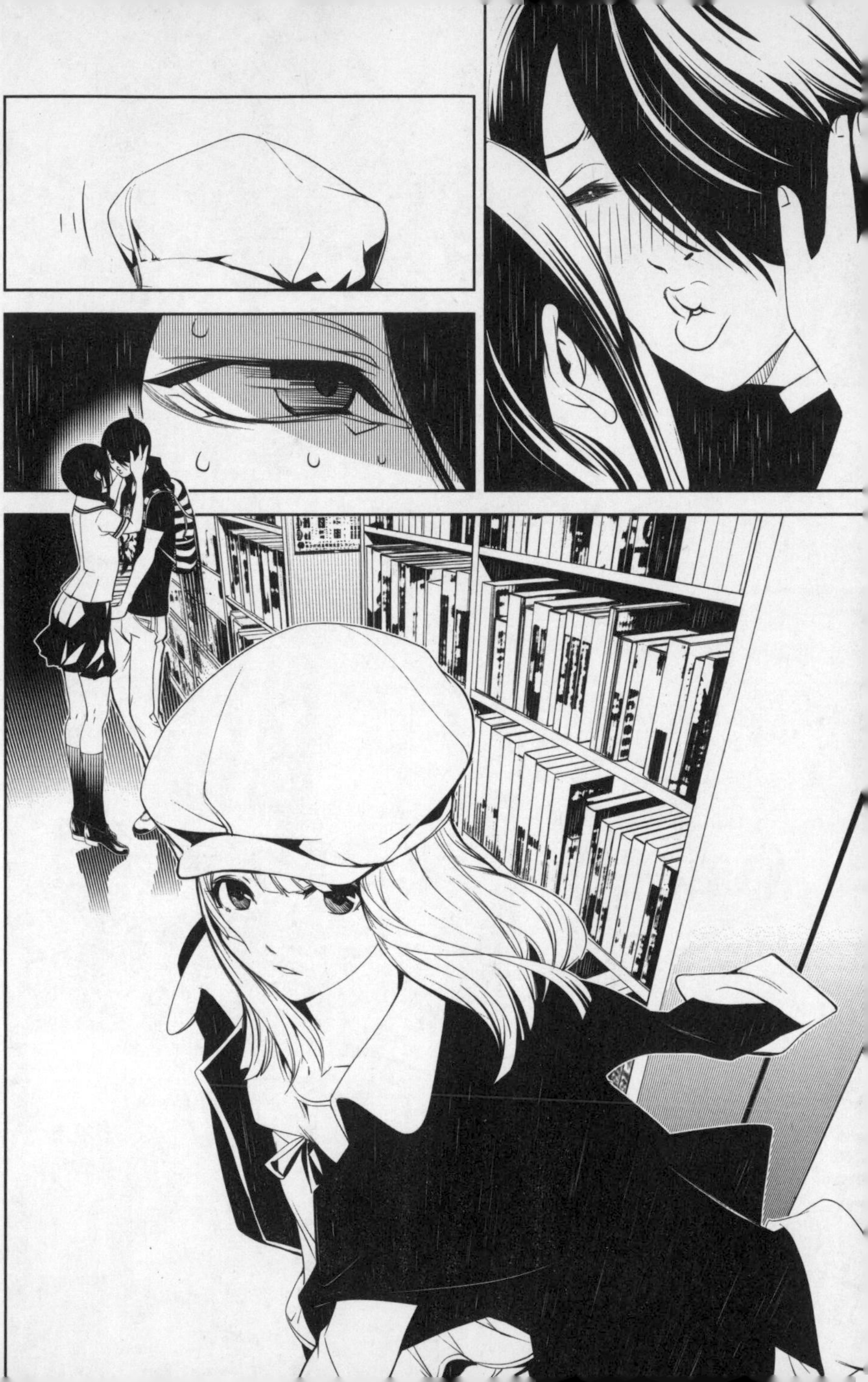

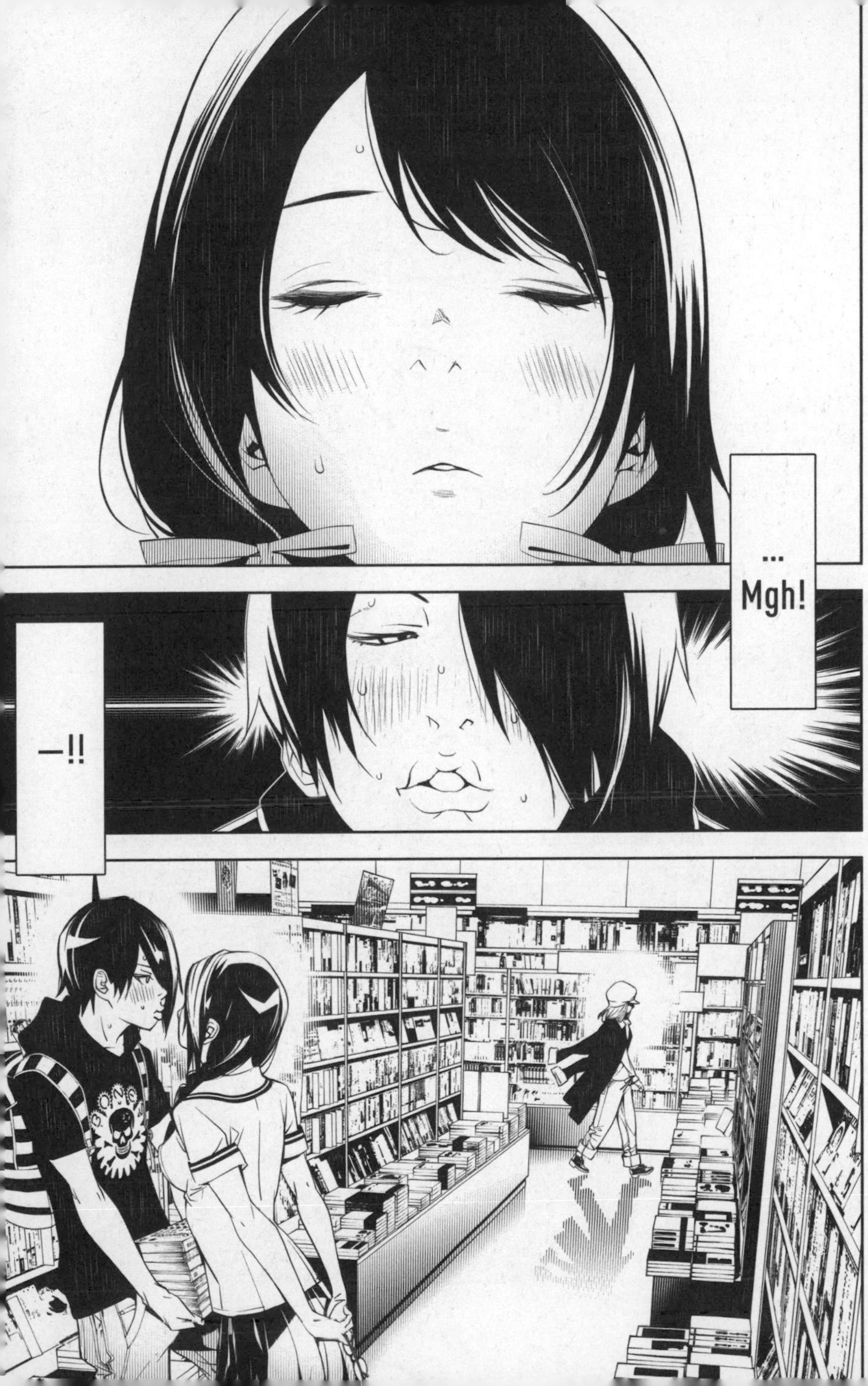

... Mgh!
—!!

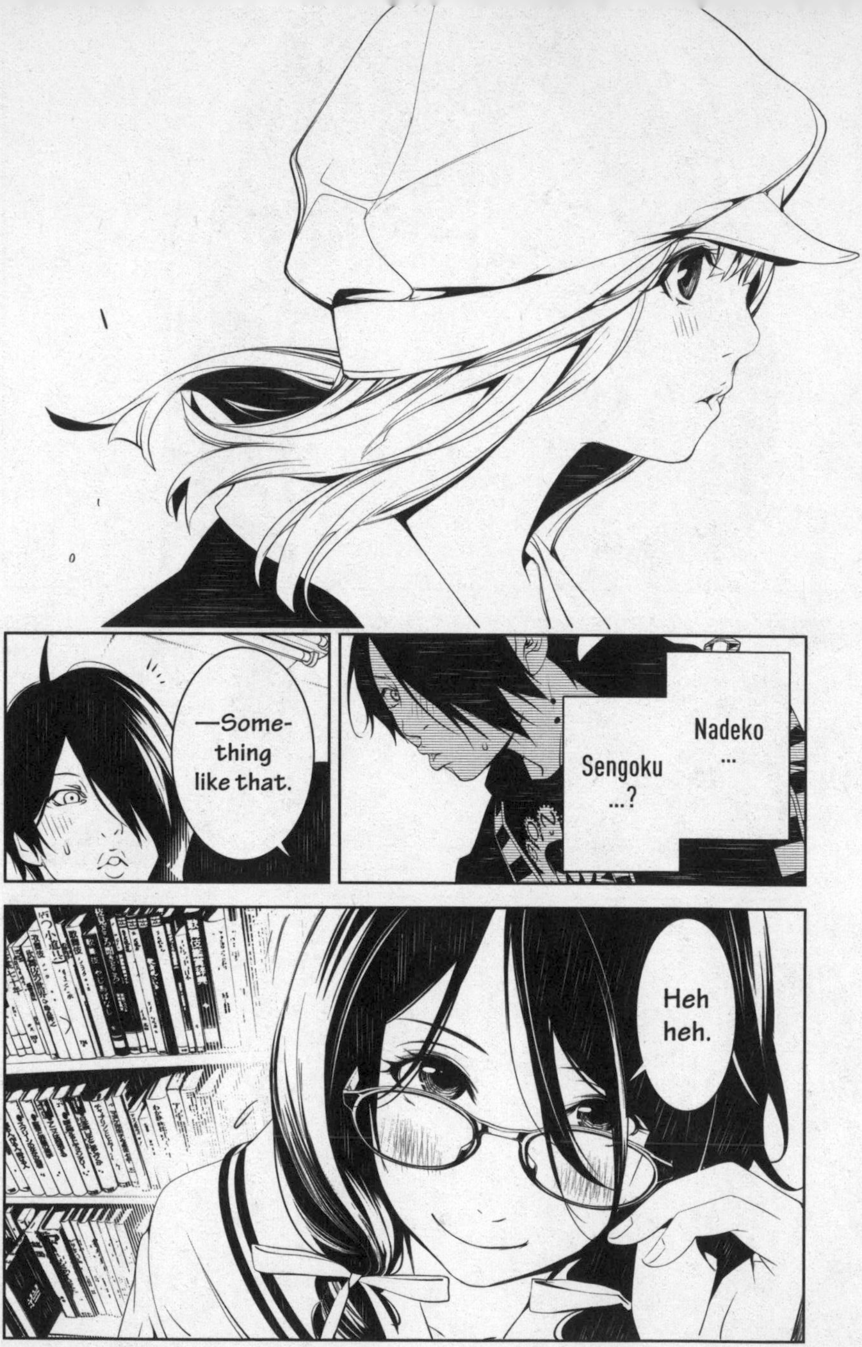
Nadeko ...
Sengoku ...?
—Something like that.
Heh heh.

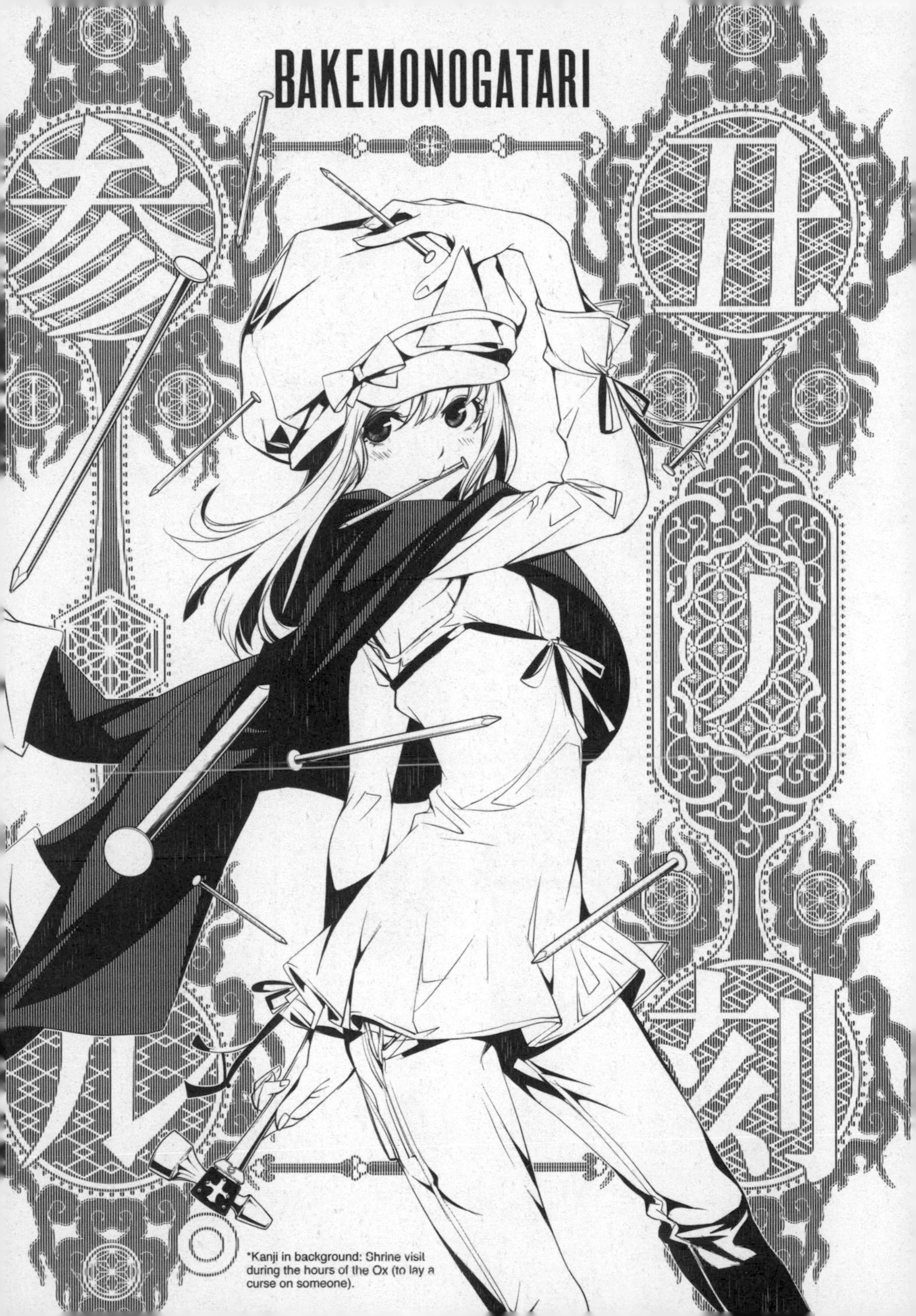
BAKEMONOGATARI

*Kanji in background: Shrine visit during the hours of the Ox (to lay a curse on someone).

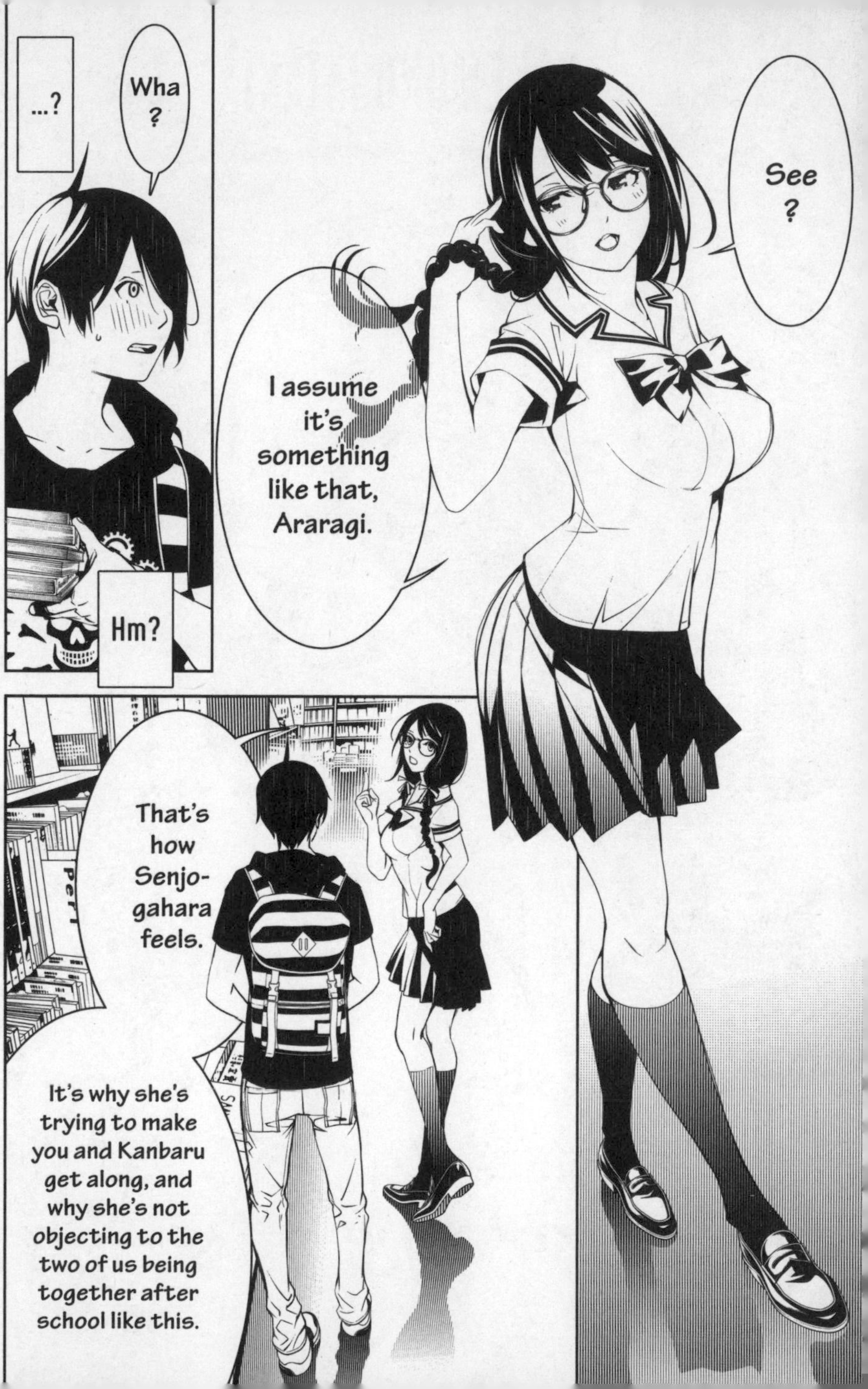
See?
I assume it's something like that, Araragi.
Wha?
...?
Hm?
That's how Senjo-gahara feels.
It's why she's trying to make you and Kanbaru get along, and why she's not objecting to the two of us being together after school like this.

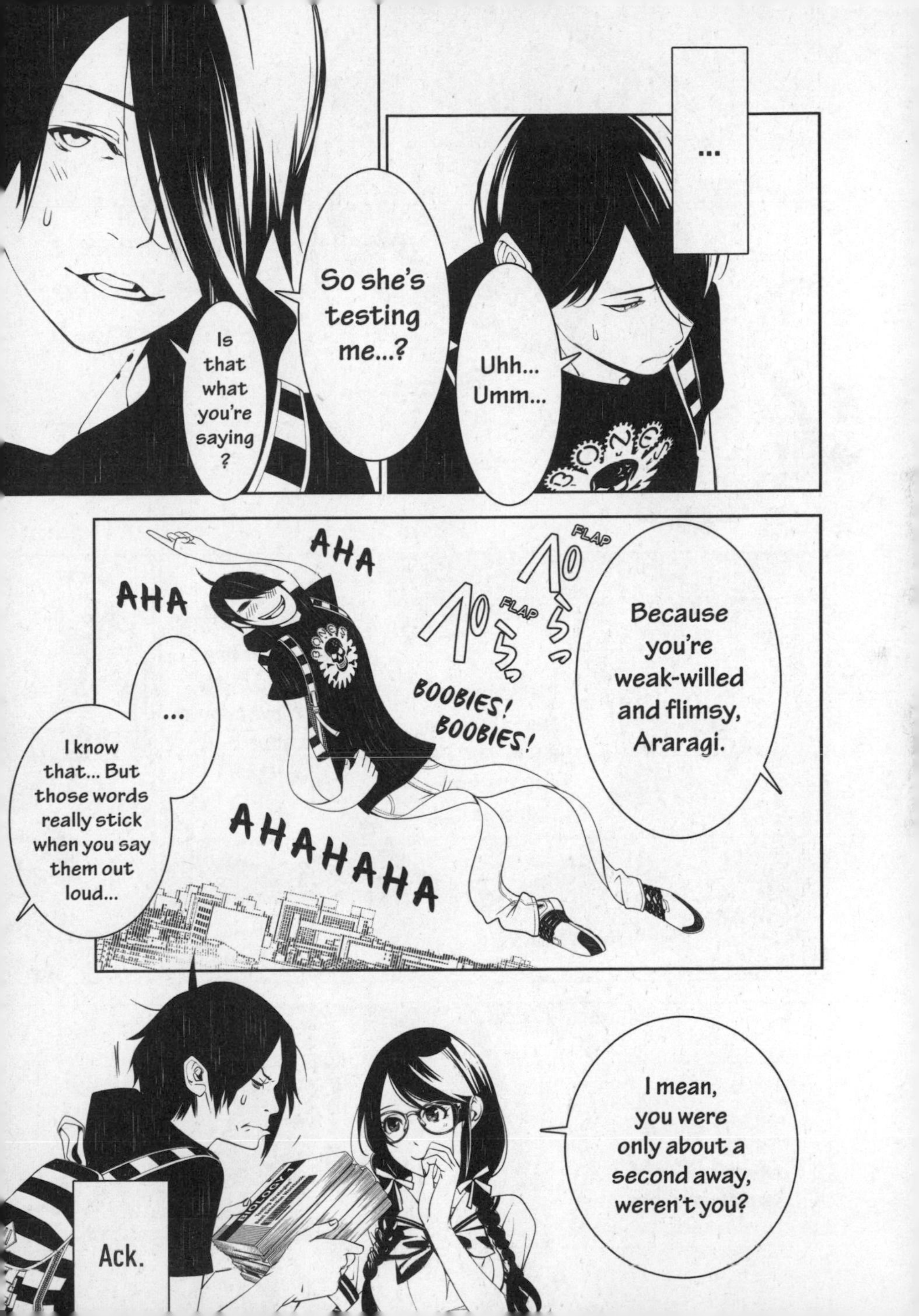
...
Uhh... Umm...
So she's testing me...?
Is that what you're saying?
Because you're weak-willed and flimsy, Araragi.
FLAP
FLAP
AHA
AHA
BOOBIES! BOOBIES!
AHAHAHA
...
I know that... But those words really stick when you say them out loud...
I mean, you were only about a second away, weren't you?
Ack.

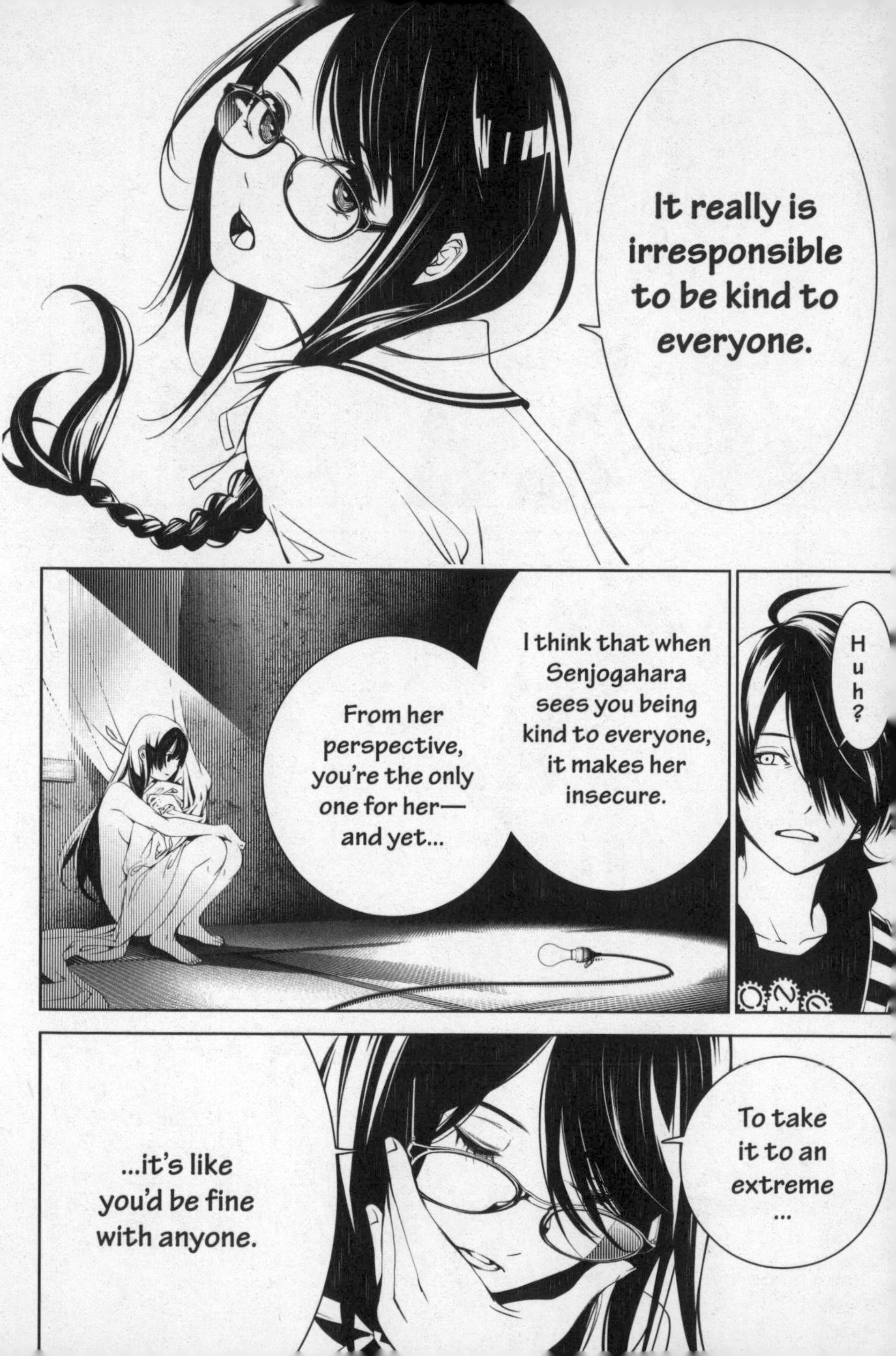
It really is irresponsible to be kind to everyone.
Huh?
I think that when Senjogahara sees you being kind to everyone, it makes her insecure.
From her perspective, you're the only one for her— and yet...
To take it to an extreme ...
...it's like you'd be fine with anyone.

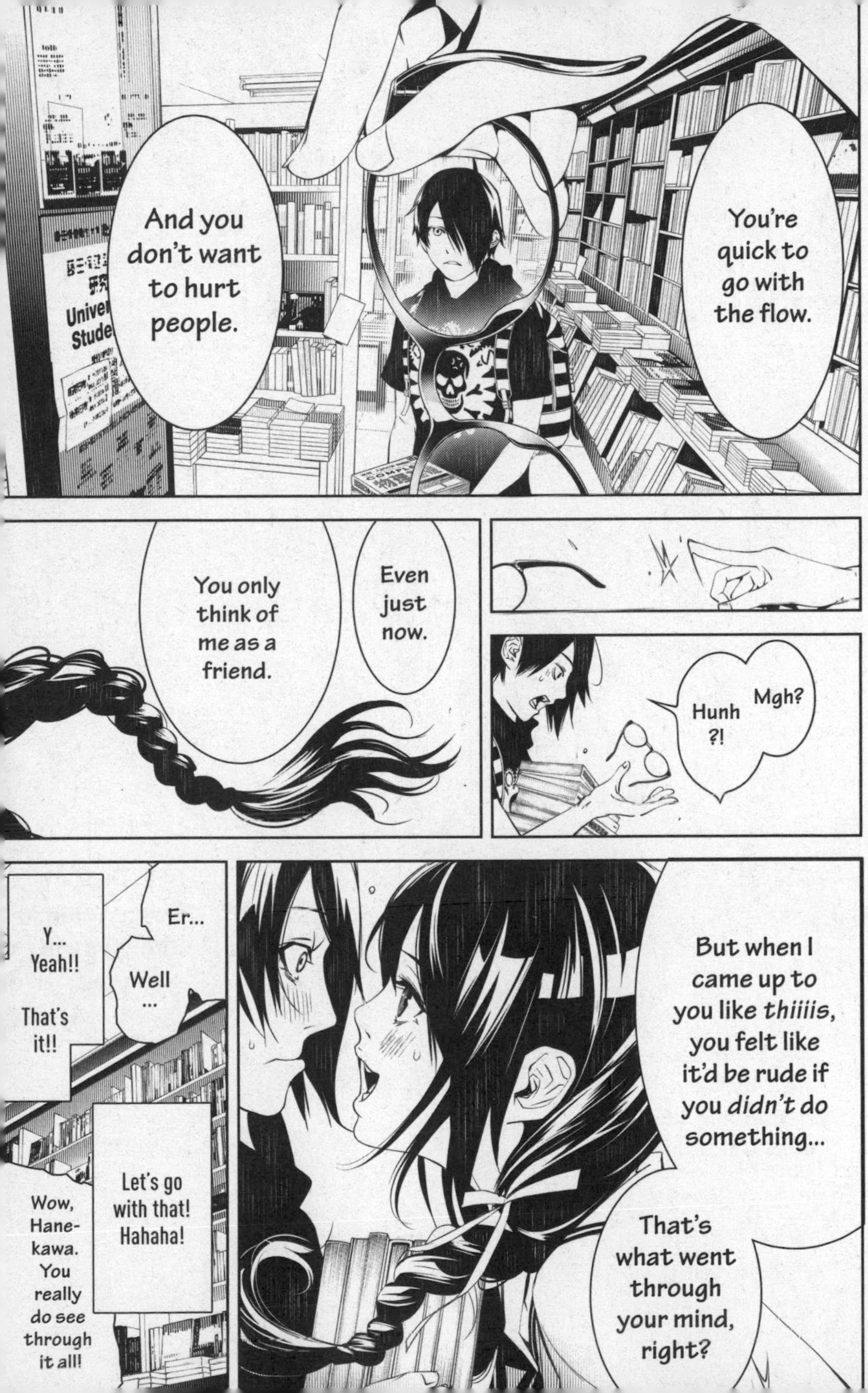
You're quick to go with the flow.
And you don't want to hurt people.
Mgh?
Hunh ?!
Even just now.
You only think of me as a friend.
But when I came up to you like *thiiiis*, you felt like it'd be rude if you *didn't* do something...
That's what went through your mind, right?
Er...
Well ...
Y... Yeah!!
That's it!!
Let's go with that! Hahaha!
Wow, Hane-kawa. You really do see through it all!

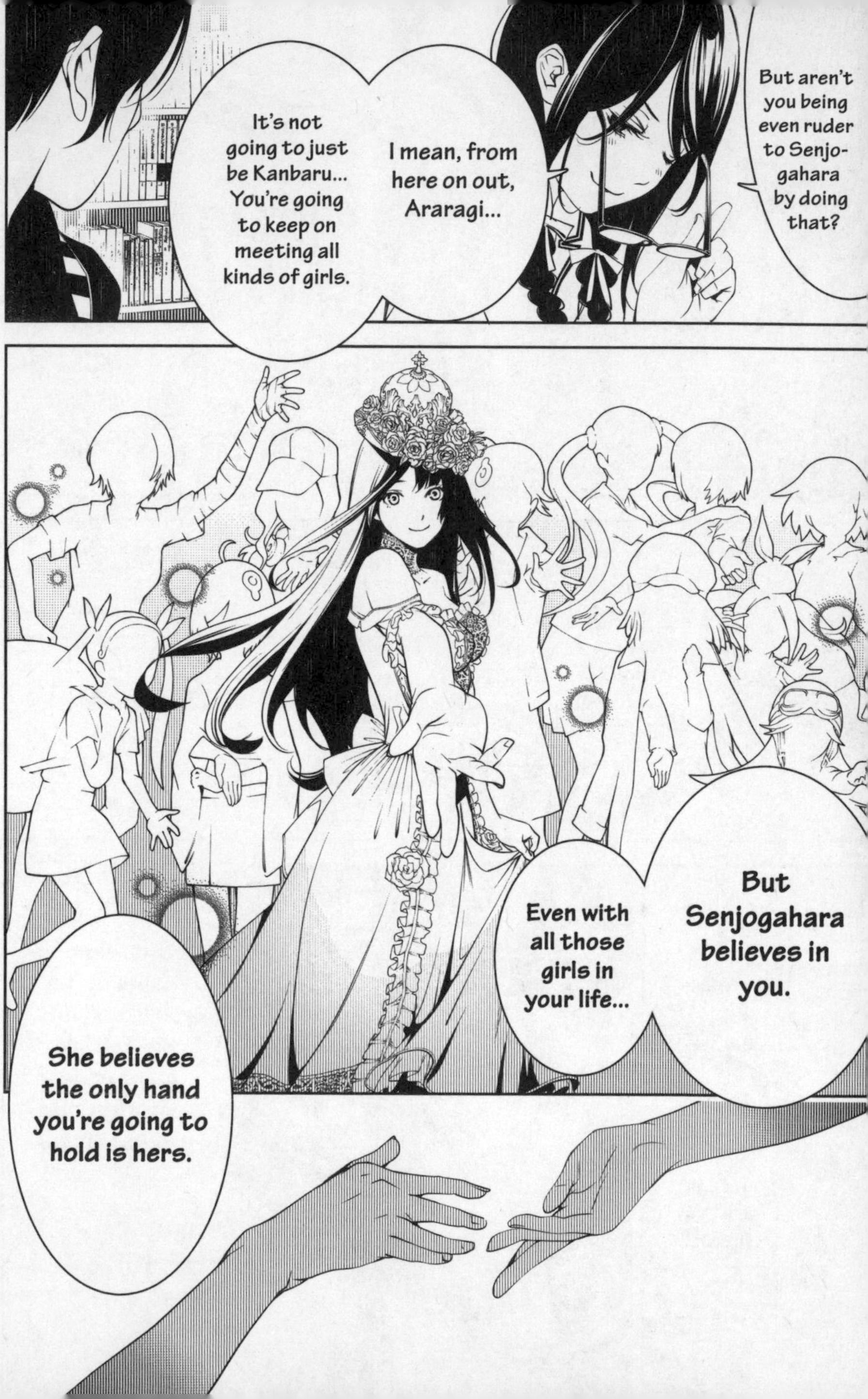
But aren't you being even ruder to Senjogahara by doing that?
I mean, from here on out, Araragi...
It's not going to just be Kanbaru... You're going to keep on meeting all kinds of girls.
But Senjogahara believes in you.
Even with all those girls in your life...
She believes the only hand you're going to hold is hers.

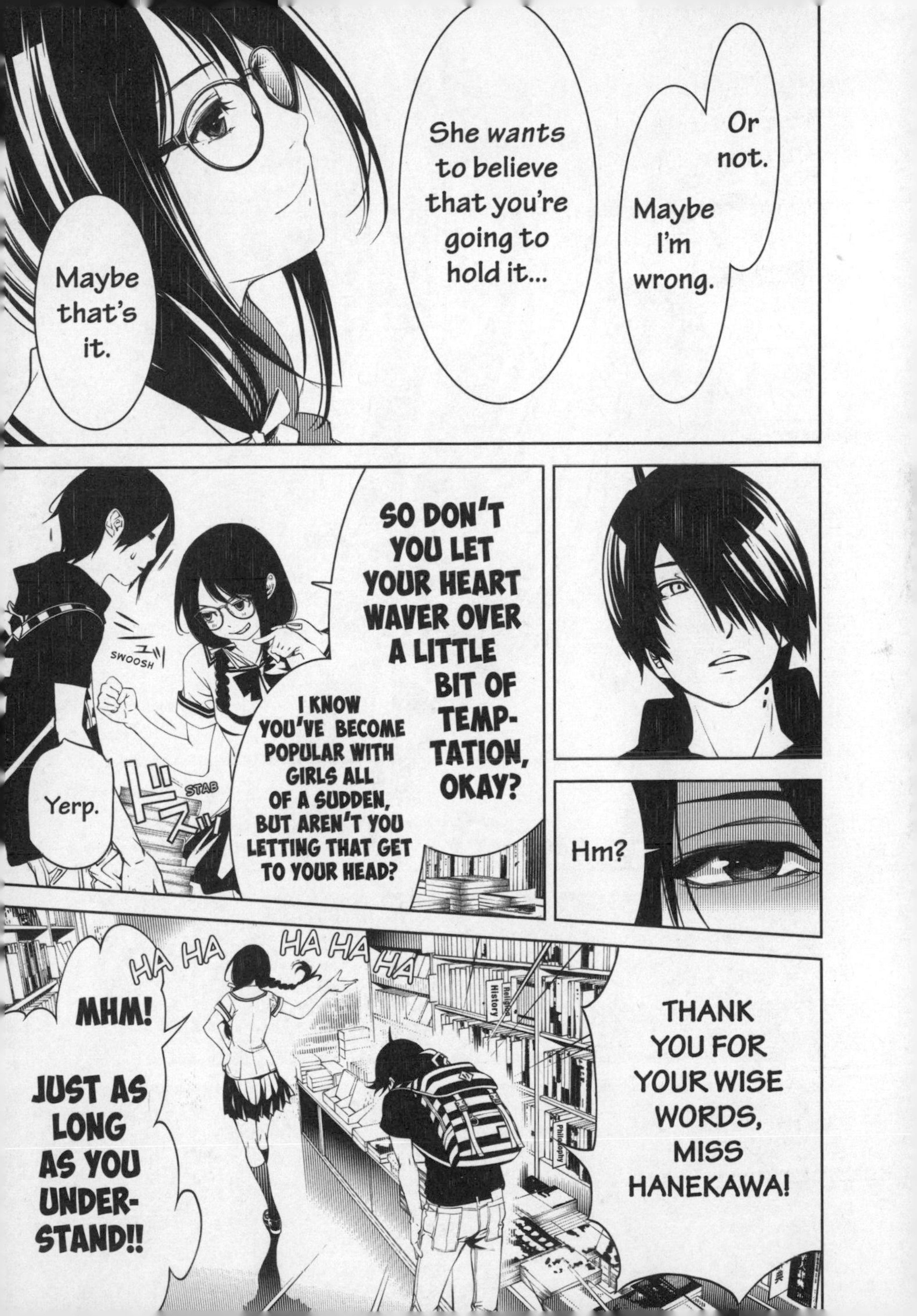
Or not.
Maybe I'm wrong.
She wants to believe that you're going to hold it...
Maybe that's it.
Hm?
SO DON'T YOU LET YOUR HEART WAVER OVER A LITTLE BIT OF TEMPTATION, OKAY?
I KNOW YOU'VE BECOME POPULAR WITH GIRLS ALL OF A SUDDEN, BUT AREN'T YOU LETTING THAT GET TO YOUR HEAD?
SWOOSH
STAB
Yerp.
THANK YOU FOR YOUR WISE WORDS, MISS HANEKAWA!
Religion
History
Philosophy
HA HA HA HA HA
MHM!
JUST AS LONG AS YOU UNDER-STAND!!

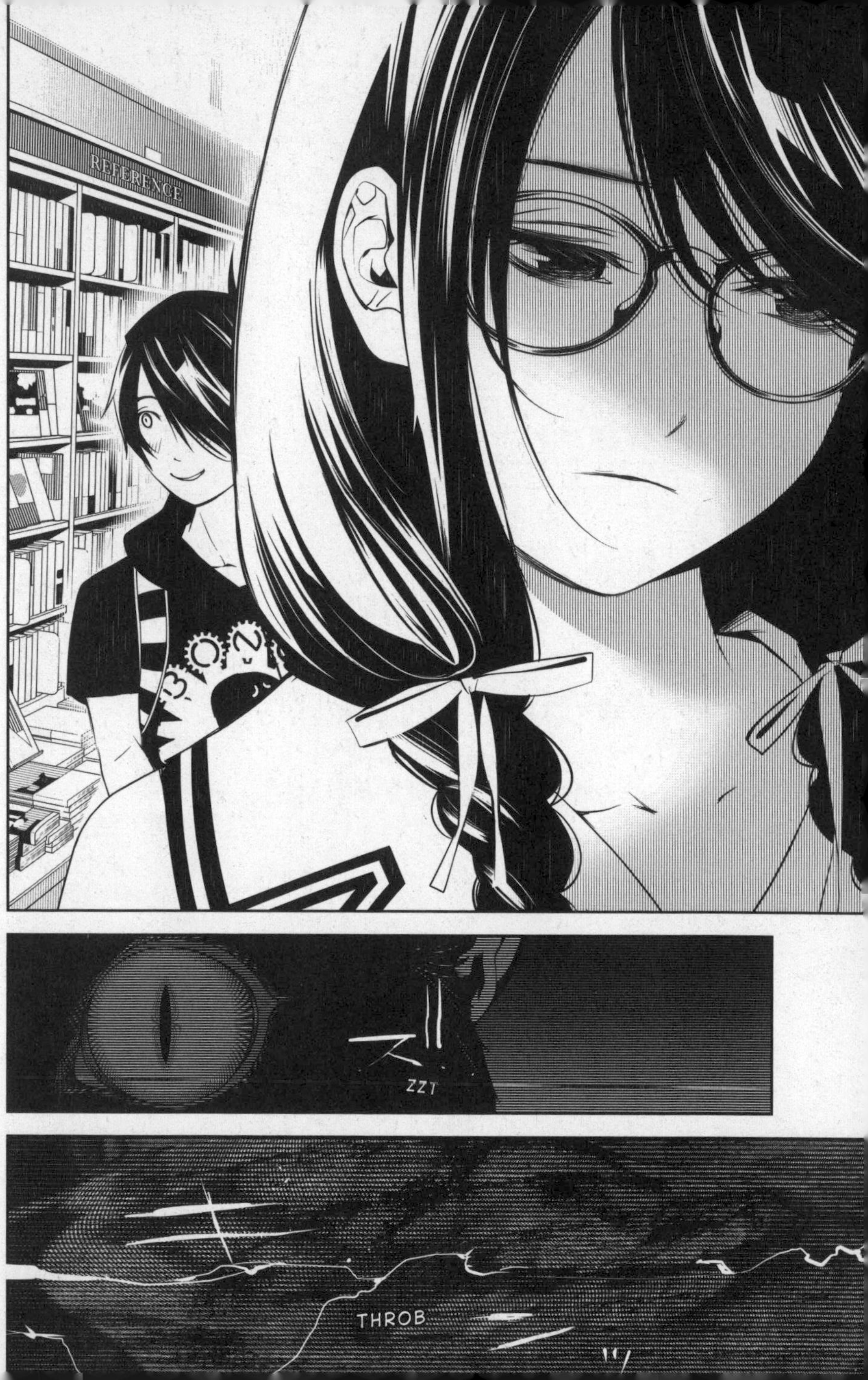
REFERENCE
ZZT
THROB

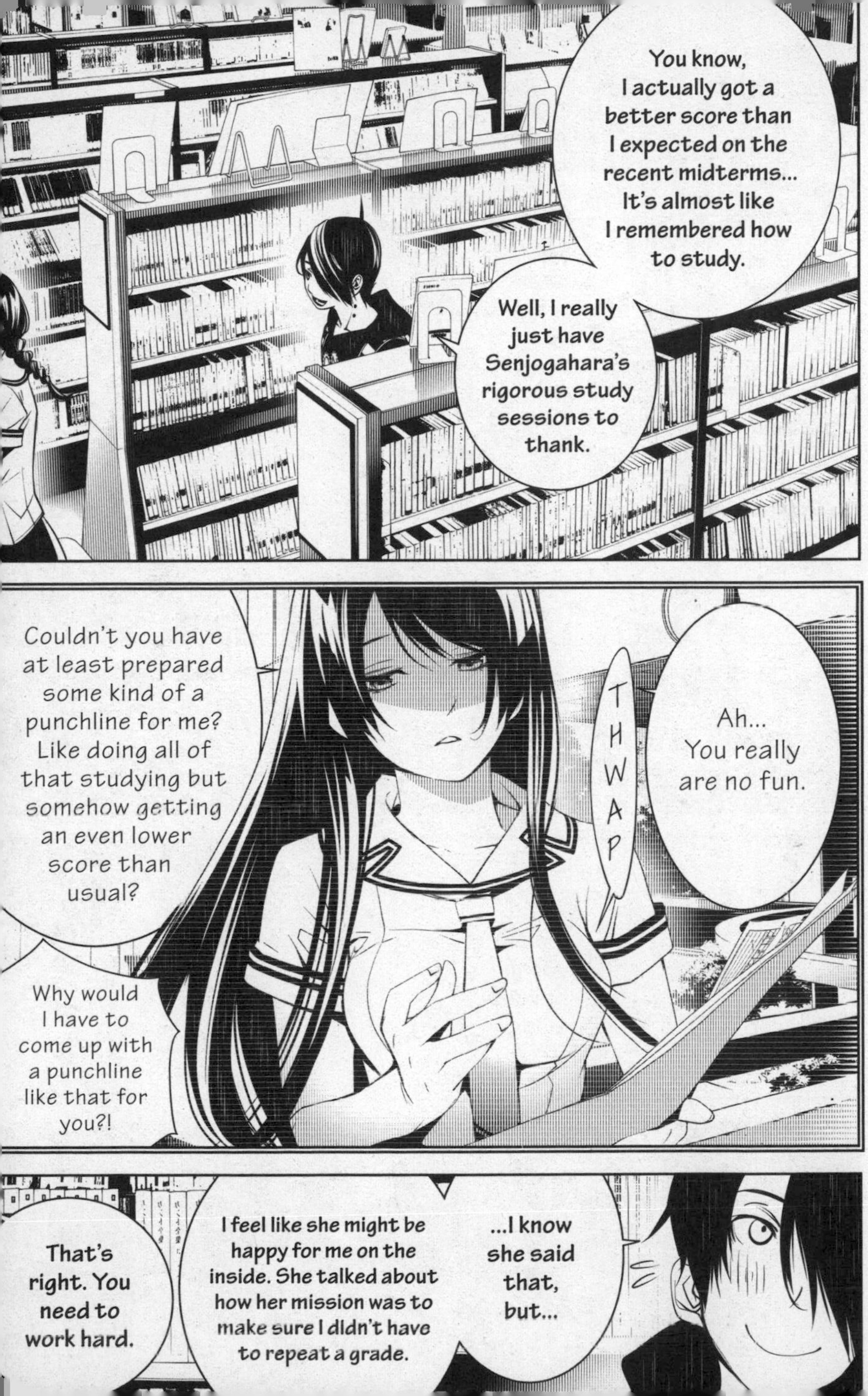
You know, I actually got a better score than I expected on the recent midterms... It's almost like I remembered how to study.
Well, I really just have Senjogahara's rigorous study sessions to thank.
Ah... You really are no fun.
THWAP
Couldn't you have at least prepared some kind of a punchline for me? Like doing all of that studying but somehow getting an even lower score than usual?
Why would I have to come up with a punchline like that for you?!
...I know she said that, but...
I feel like she might be happy for me on the inside. She talked about how her mission was to make sure I didn't have to repeat a grade.
That's right. You need to work hard.

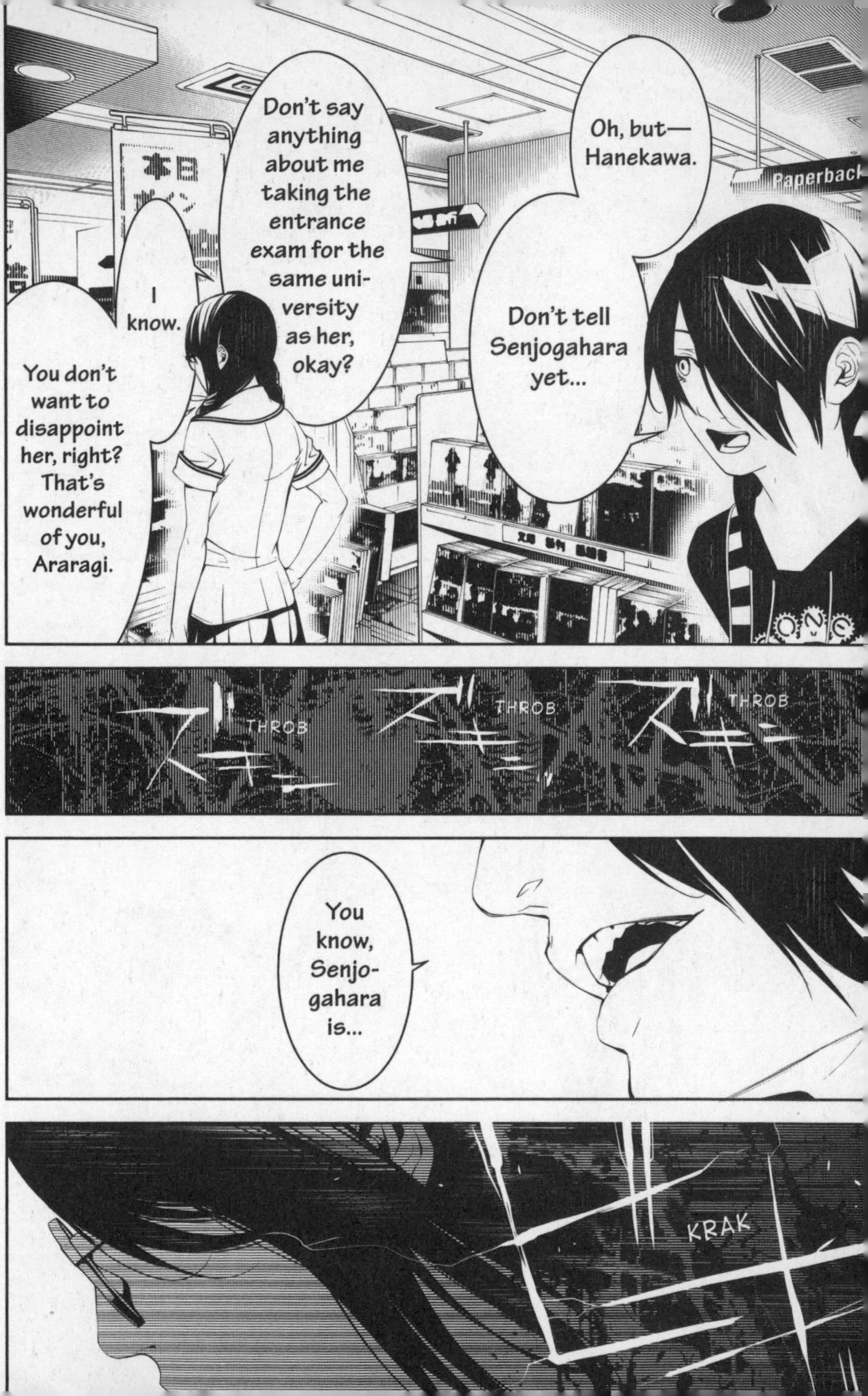
Paperback
Oh, but— Hanekawa.
Don't tell Senjogahara yet...
Don't say anything about me taking the entrance exam for the same university as her, okay?
I know.
You don't want to disappoint her, right? That's wonderful of you, Araragi.
THROB
THROB
THROB
You know, Senjogahara is...
KRAK

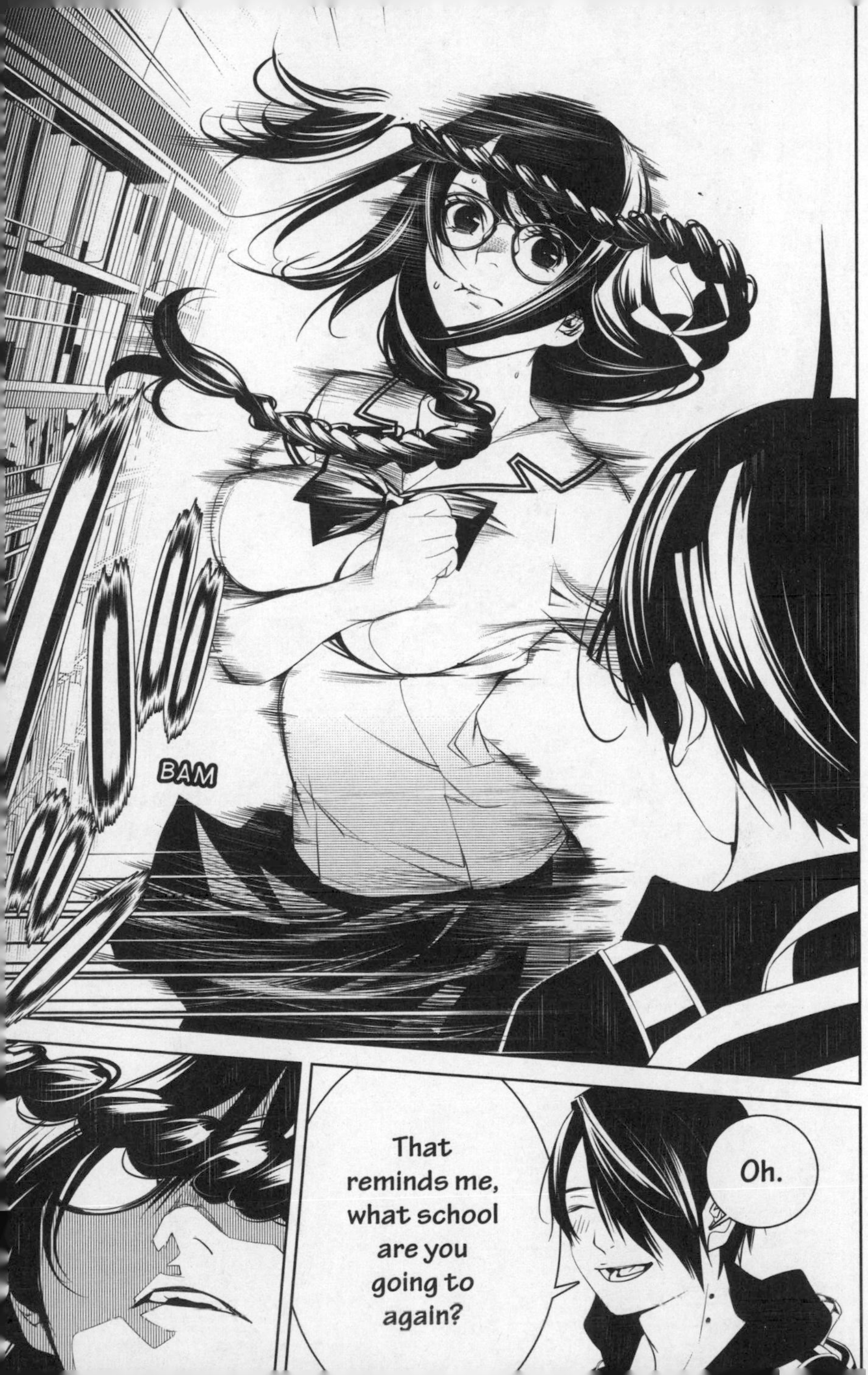
BAM
Oh.
That reminds me, what school are you going to again?

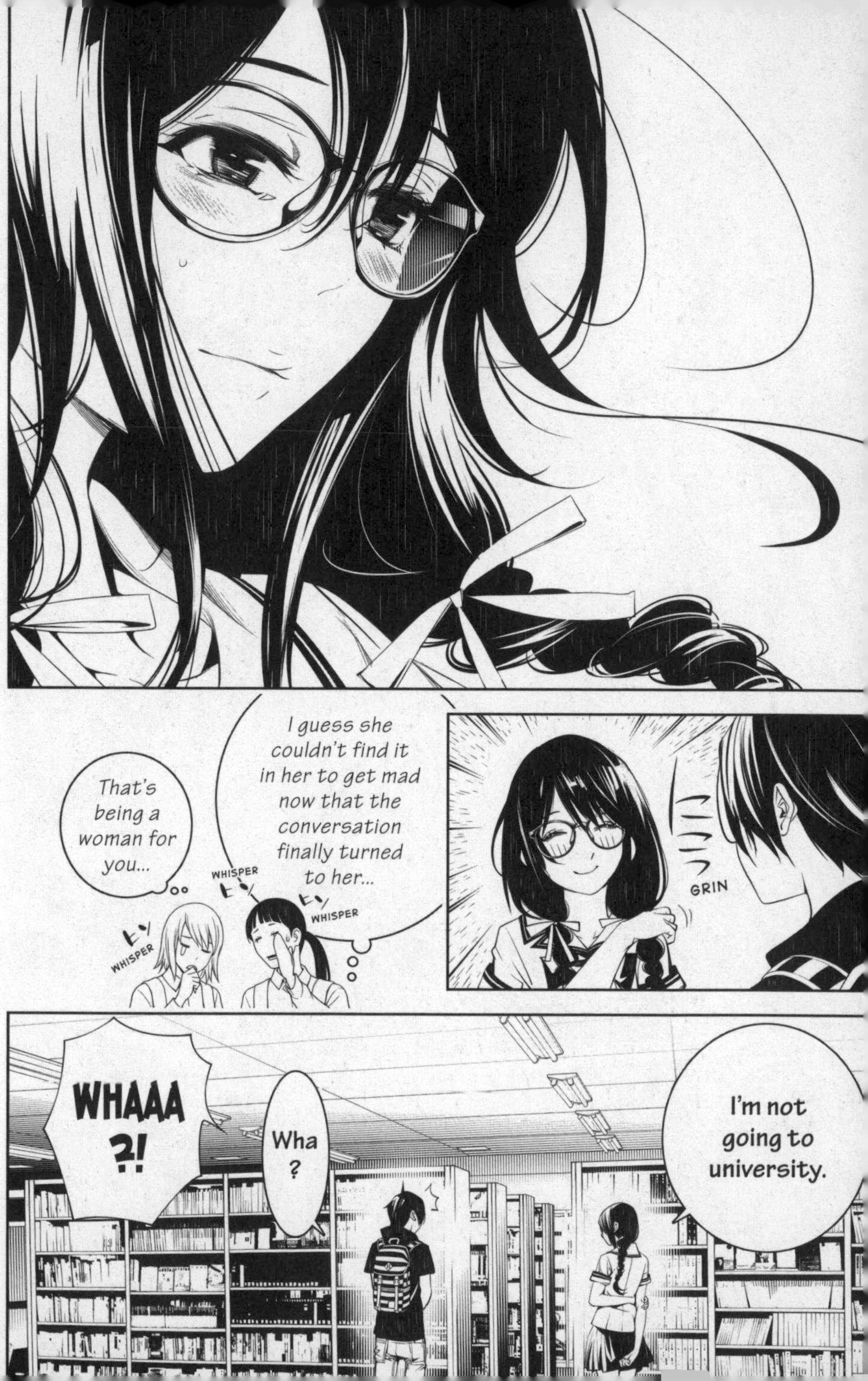
GRIN
I guess she couldn't find it in her to get mad now that the conversation finally turned to her...
WHISPER ヒソ
ヒソ WHISPER
That's being a woman for you...
ヒソ WHISPER
I'm not going to university.
Wha?
WHAAA?!

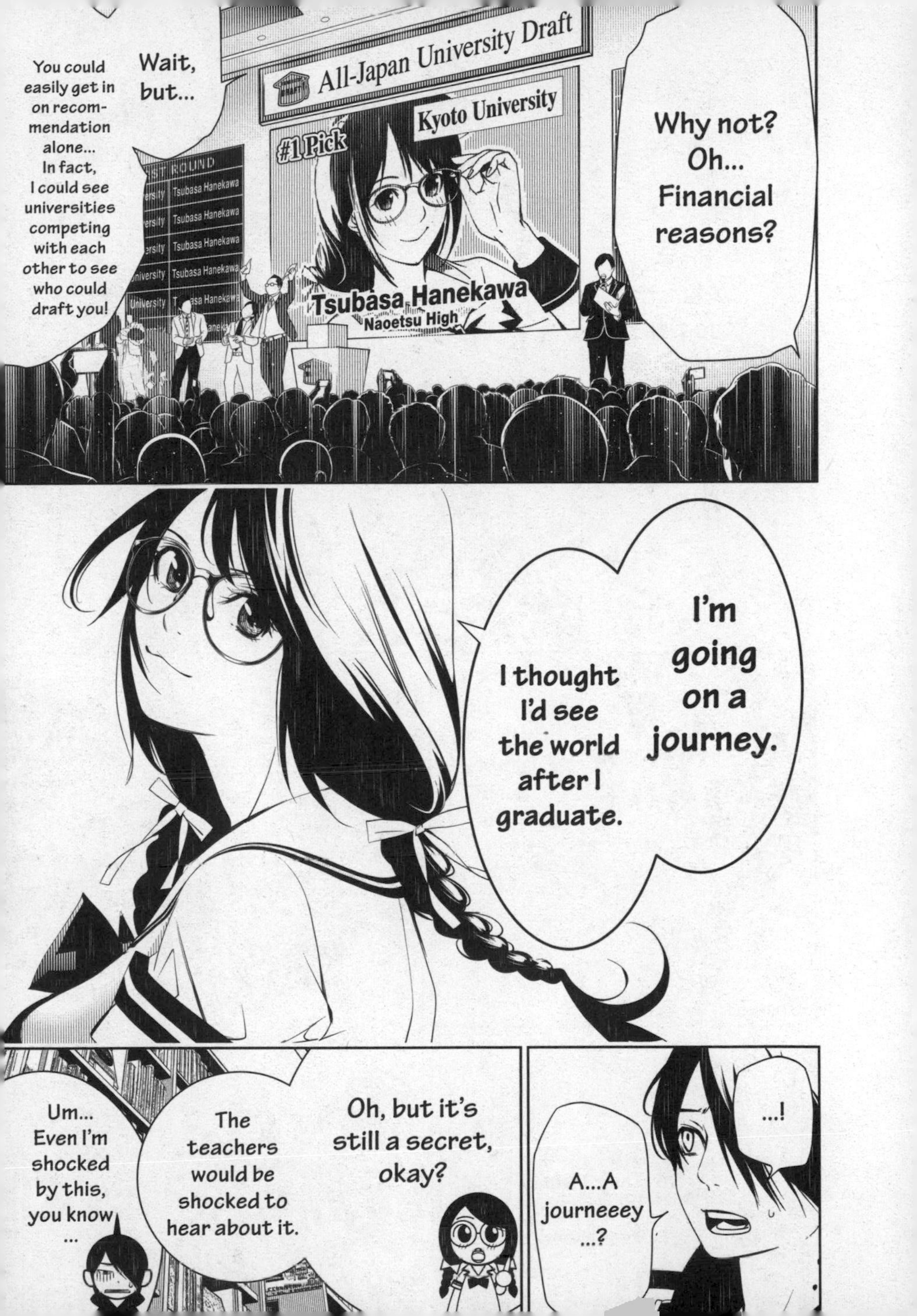
Why not? Oh... Financial reasons?
Wait, but...
You could easily get in on recommendation alone... In fact, I could see universities competing with each other to see who could draft you!
All-Japan University Draft
Kyoto University
#1 Pick
Tsubasa Hanekawa
Naoetsu High
I'm going on a journey.
I thought I'd see the world after I graduate.
...!
A...A journeeey ...?
Oh, but it's still a secret, okay?
The teachers would be shocked to hear about it.
Um... Even I'm shocked by this, you know...

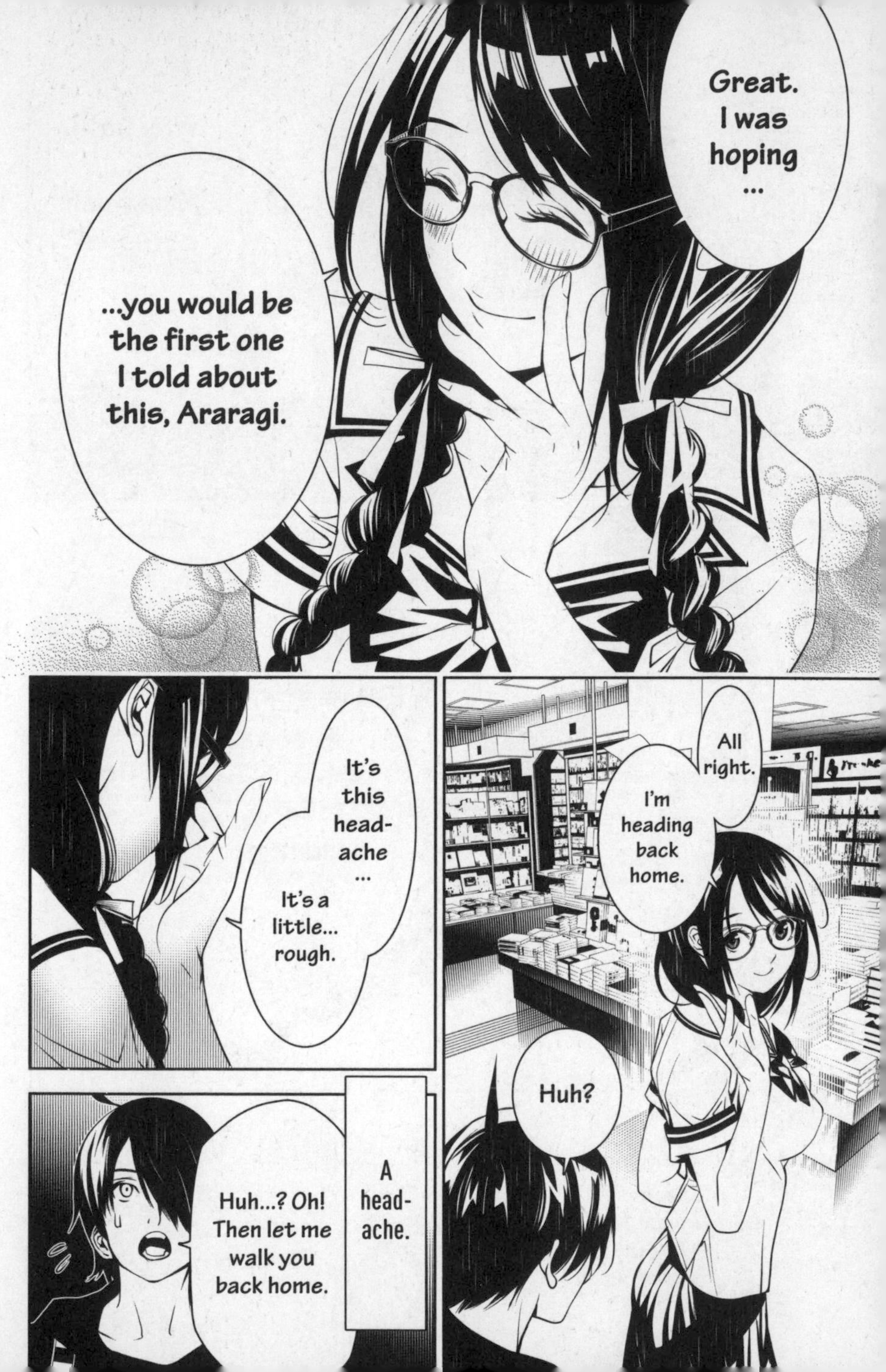
Great. I was hoping...
...you would be the first one I told about this, Araragi.
All right.
I'm heading back home.
Huh?
It's this headache...
It's a little... rough.
A headache.
Huh...? Oh! Then let me walk you back home.

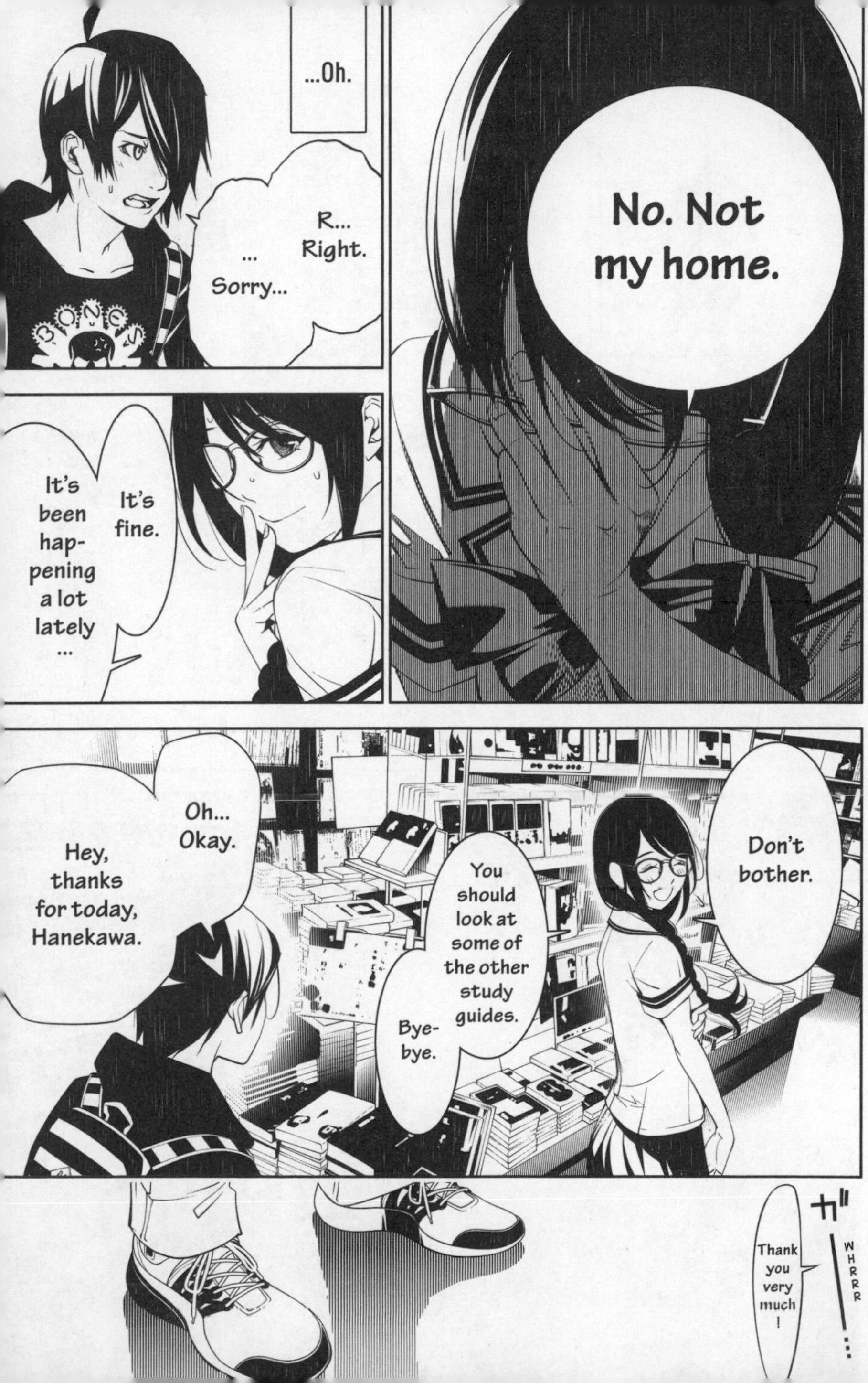
No. Not my home.
...Oh.
R... Right.
... Sorry...
It's fine.
It's been hap-pening a lot lately ...
Don't bother.
You should look at some of the other study guides.
Bye-bye.
Oh... Okay.
Hey, thanks for today, Hanekawa.
ガ
WHRRR
Thank you very much!

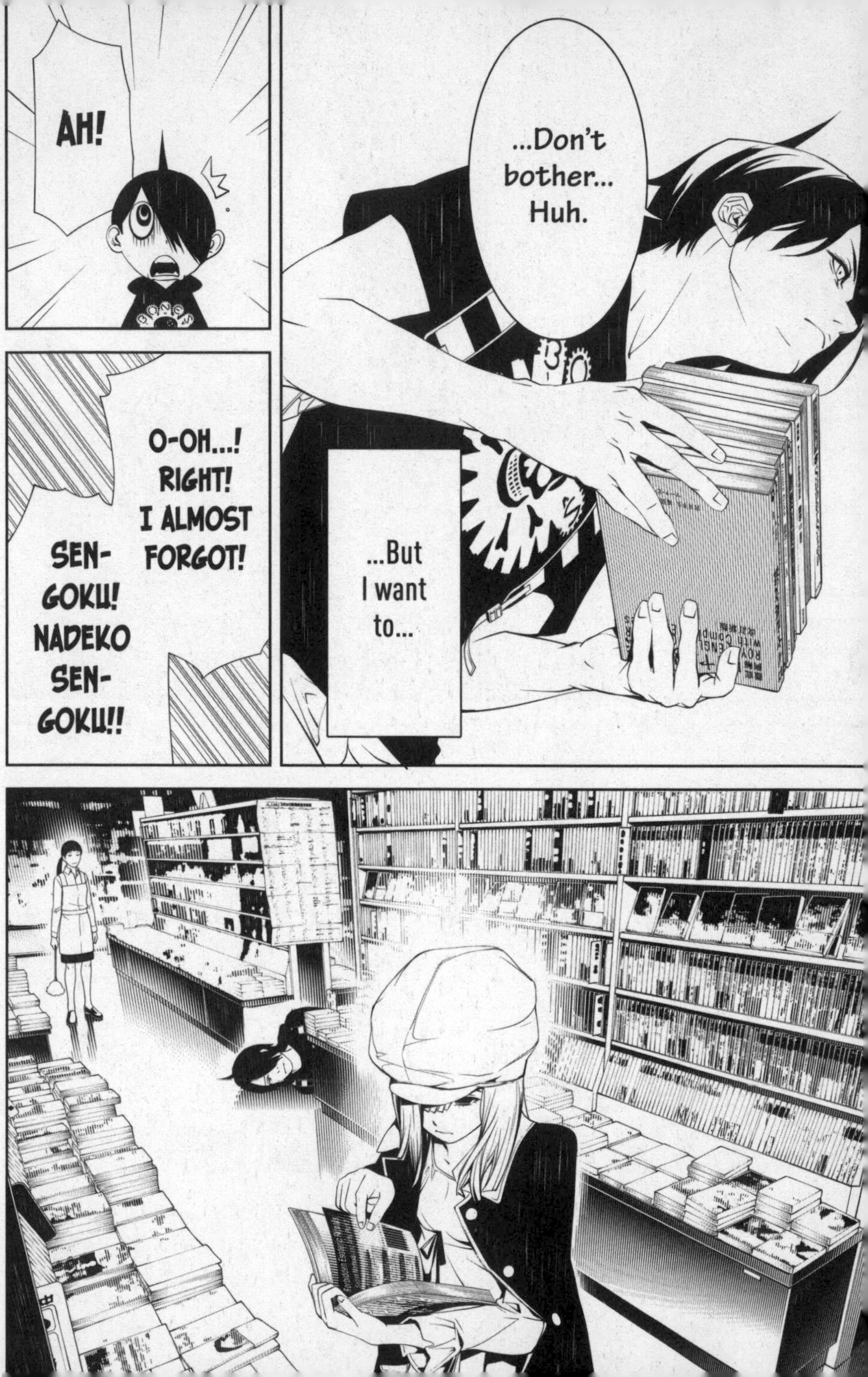
...Don't bother... Huh.
...But I want to...
AH!
O-OH...! RIGHT! I ALMOST FORGOT!
SEN-GOKU! NADEKO SEN-GOKU!!

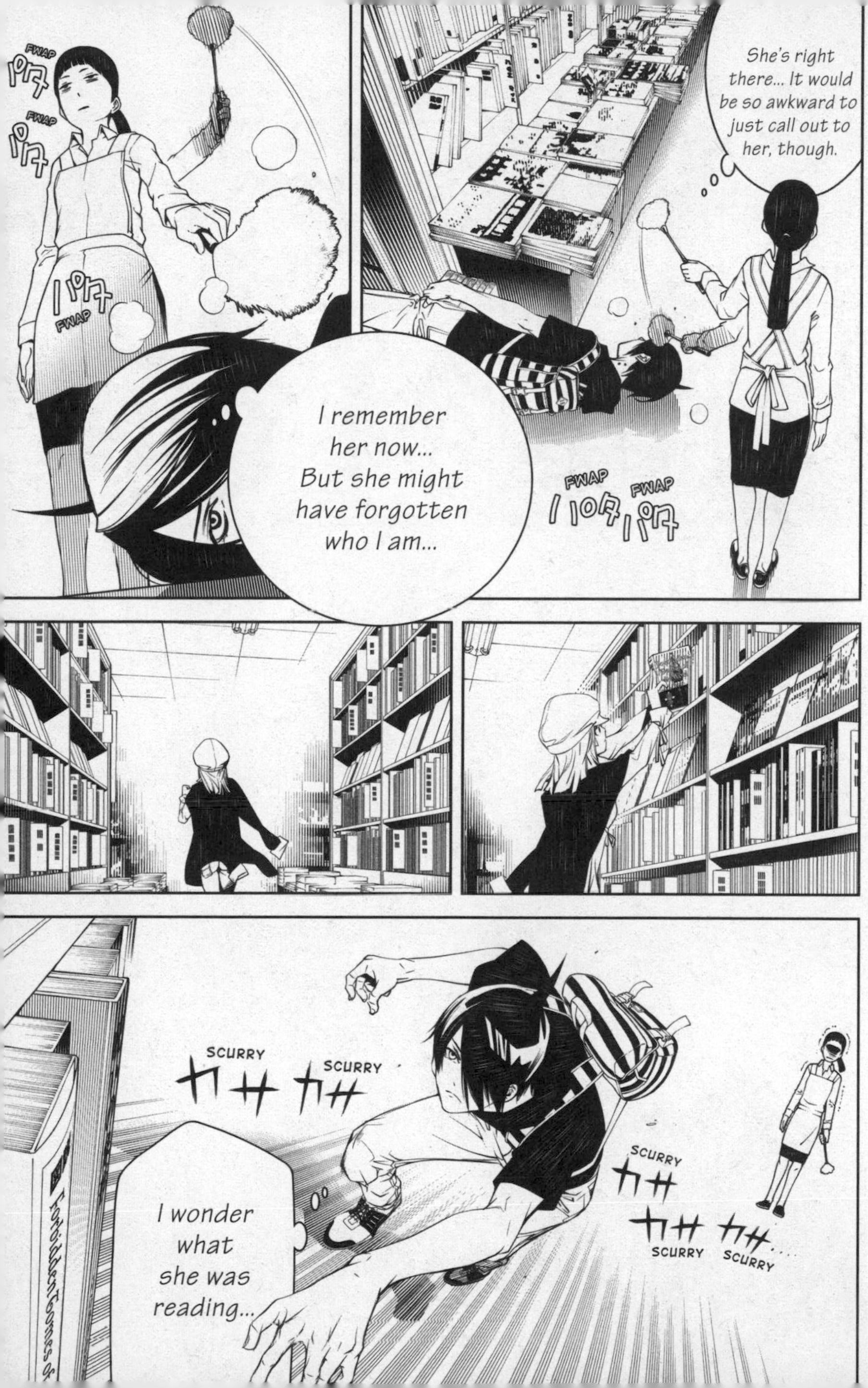
She's right there... It would be so awkward to just call out to her, though.
FWAP FWAP
FWAP
FWAP
FWAP
I remember her now... But she might have forgotten who I am...
SCURRY
SCURRY SCURRY
SCURRY
SCURRY
I wonder what she was reading...

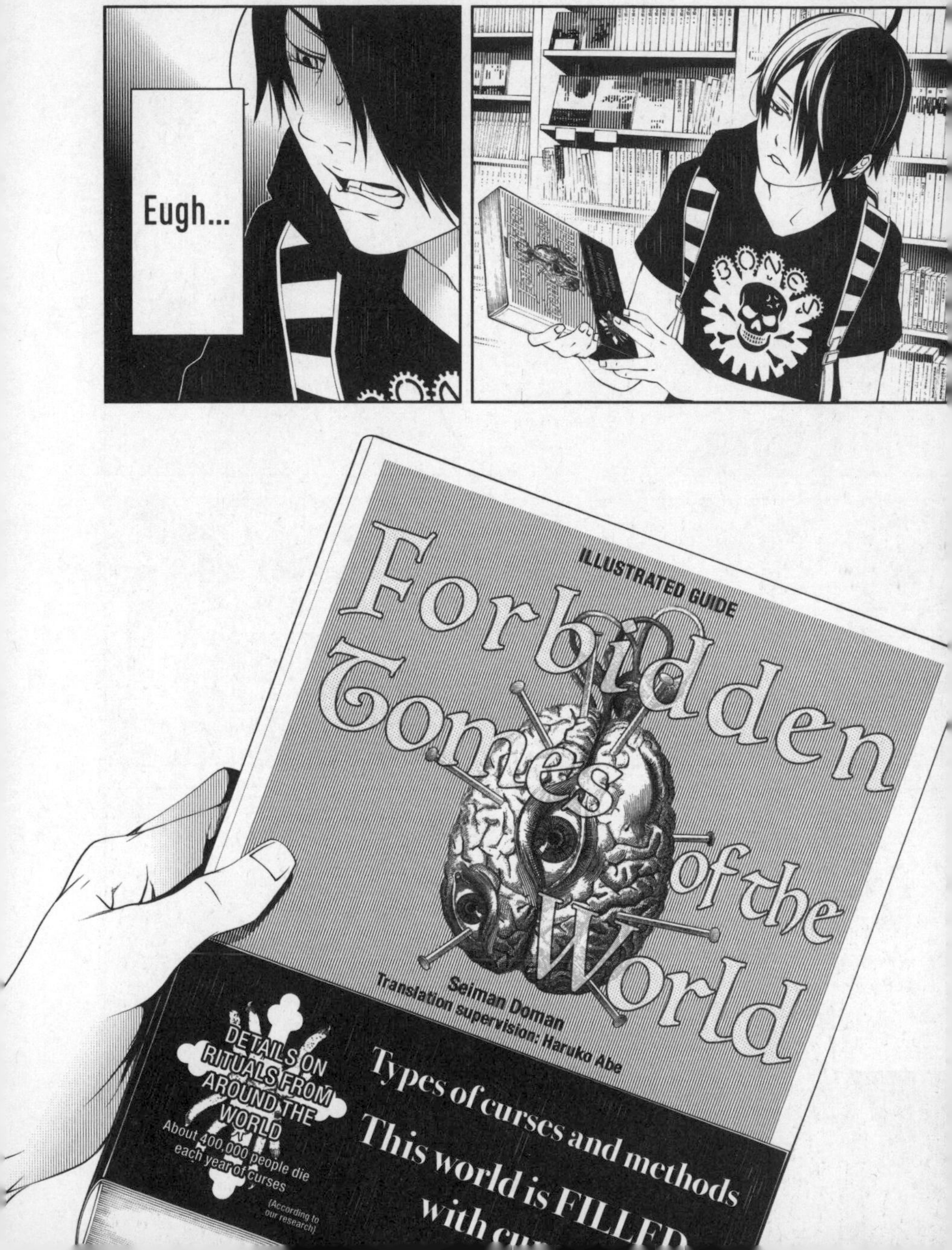

Eugh...
ILLUSTRATED GUIDE
Forbidden Tomes of the World
Seiman Doman
Translation supervision: Haruko Abe
DETAILS ON RITUALS FROM AROUND THE WORLD
About 400,000 people die each year of curses
(According to our research)
Types of curses and methods
This world is FILLED
with

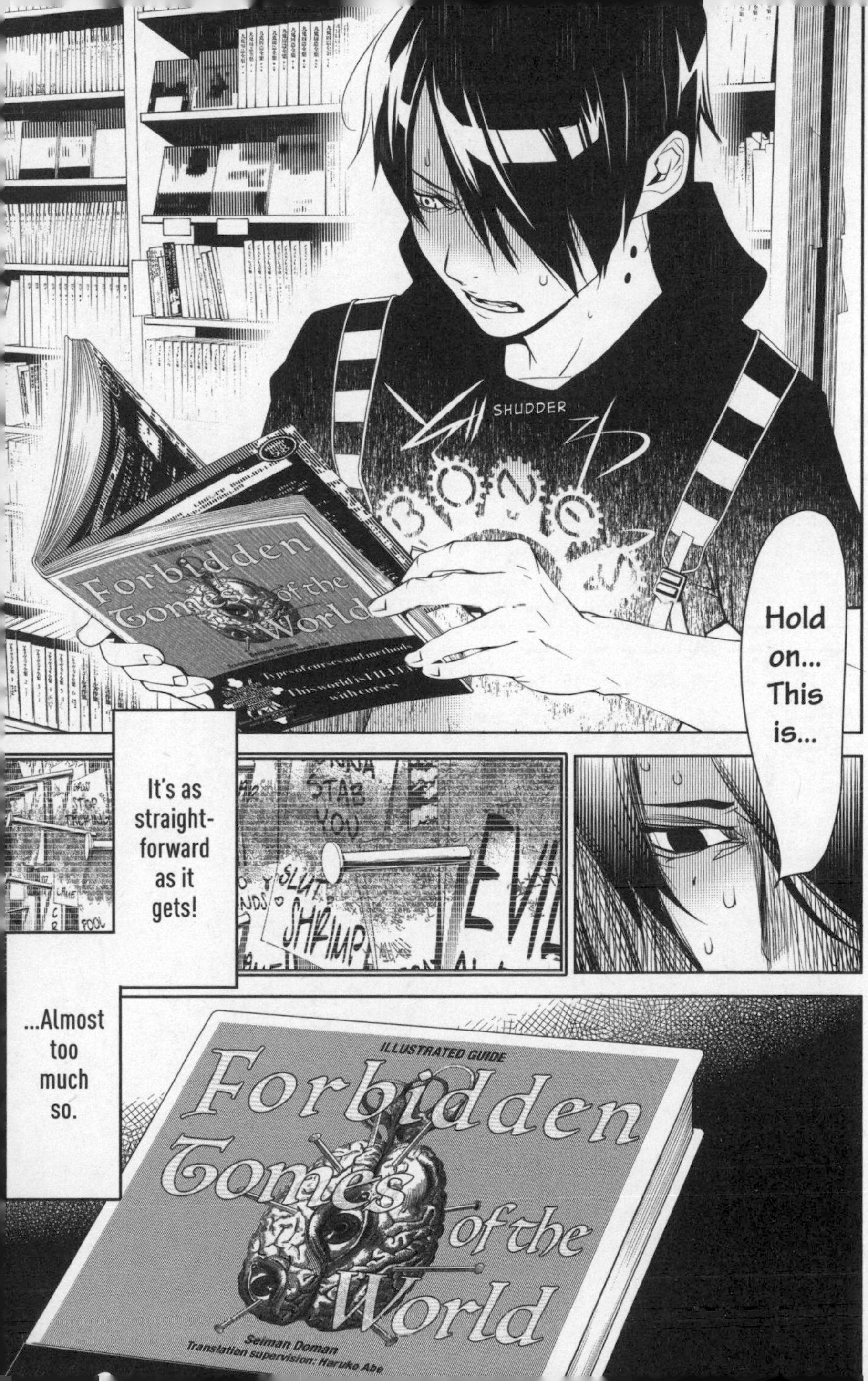
SHUDDER
ILLUSTRATED GUIDE
Forbidden Tomes of the World
Types of curses and methods
Hold on... This is...
STAB YOU
SLUT
SHRIMP
EVIL
FOOL
It's as straight-forward as it gets!
...Almost too much so.
ILLUSTRATED GUIDE
Forbidden Tomes of the World
Seiman Doman
Translation supervision: Haruko Abe

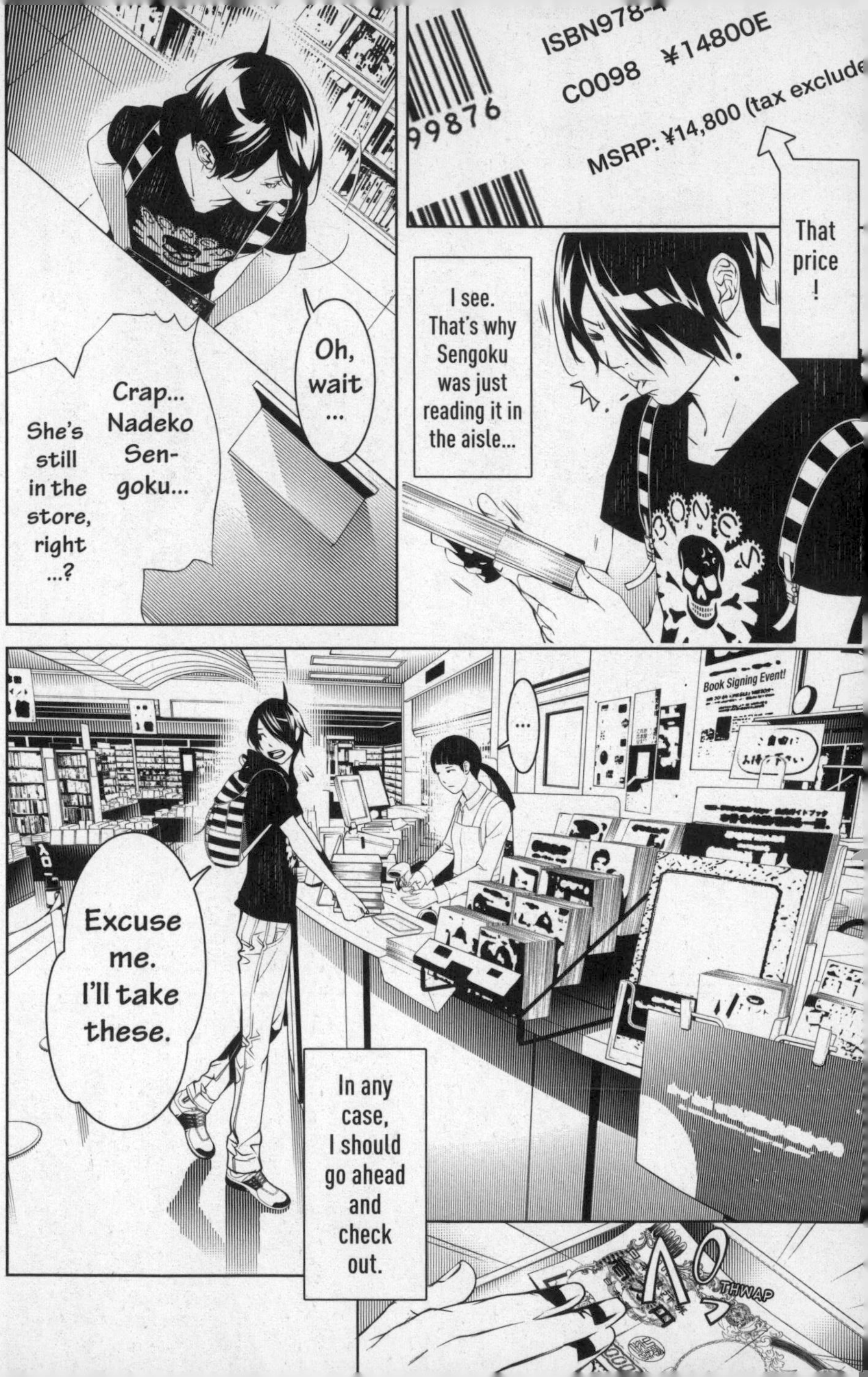
ISBN978-4
C0098 ¥14800E
99876
MSRP: ¥14,800 (tax exclude
That price!
I see. That's why Sengoku was just reading it in the aisle...
Oh, wait...
Crap... Nadeko Sengoku...
She's still in the store, right...?
...
Book Signing Event!
Excuse me. I'll take these.
In any case, I should go ahead and check out.
THWAP

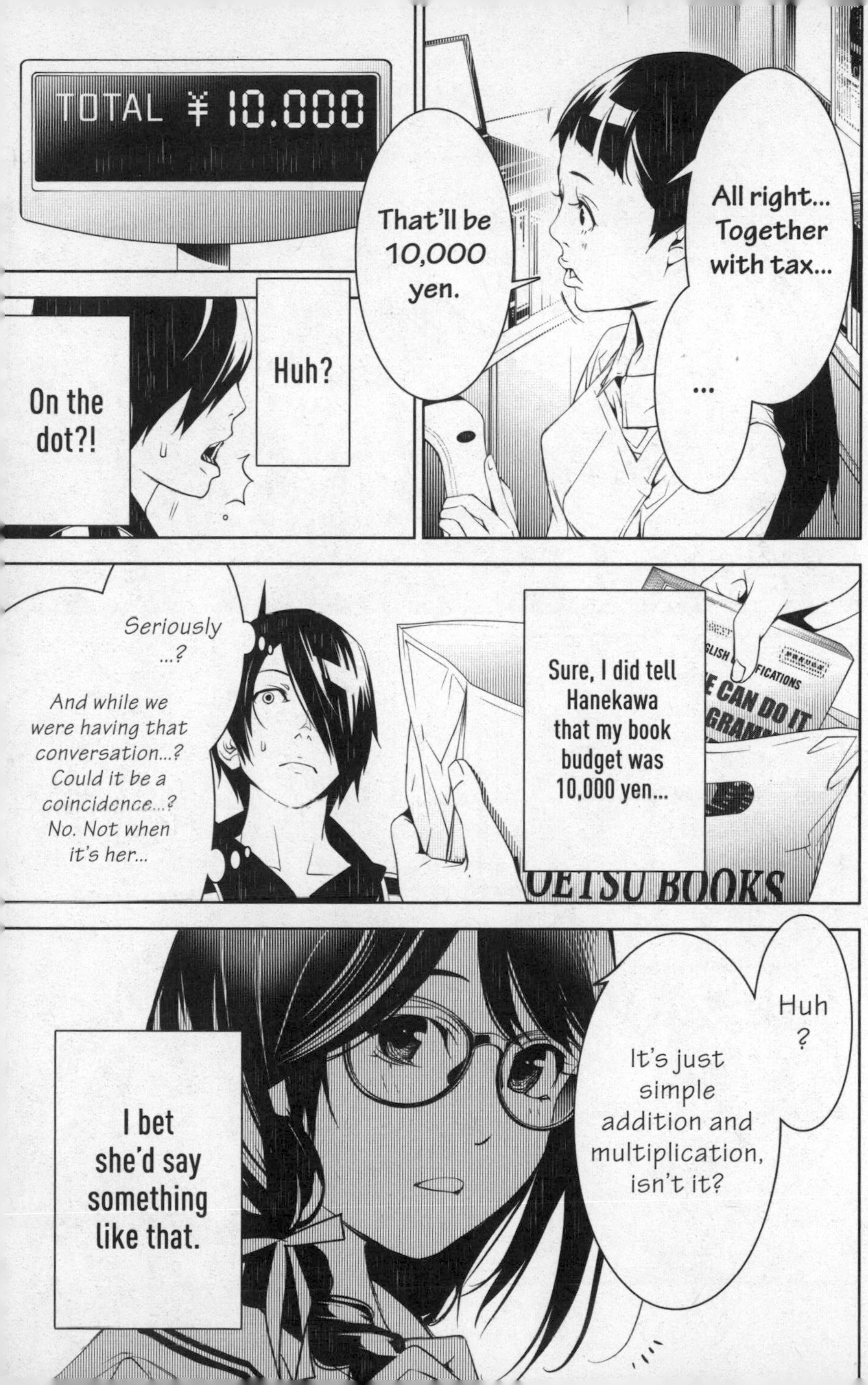
All right... Together with tax...
That'll be 10,000 yen.
...
TOTAL ¥10.000
Huh?
On the dot?!
Sure, I did tell Hanekawa that my book budget was 10,000 yen...
Seriously ...?
And while we were having that conversation...? Could it be a coincidence...? No. Not when it's her...
ENGLISH
FICATIONS
CAN DO IT
GRAM
OETSU BOOKS
Huh ?
It's just simple addition and multiplication, isn't it?
I bet she'd say something like that.

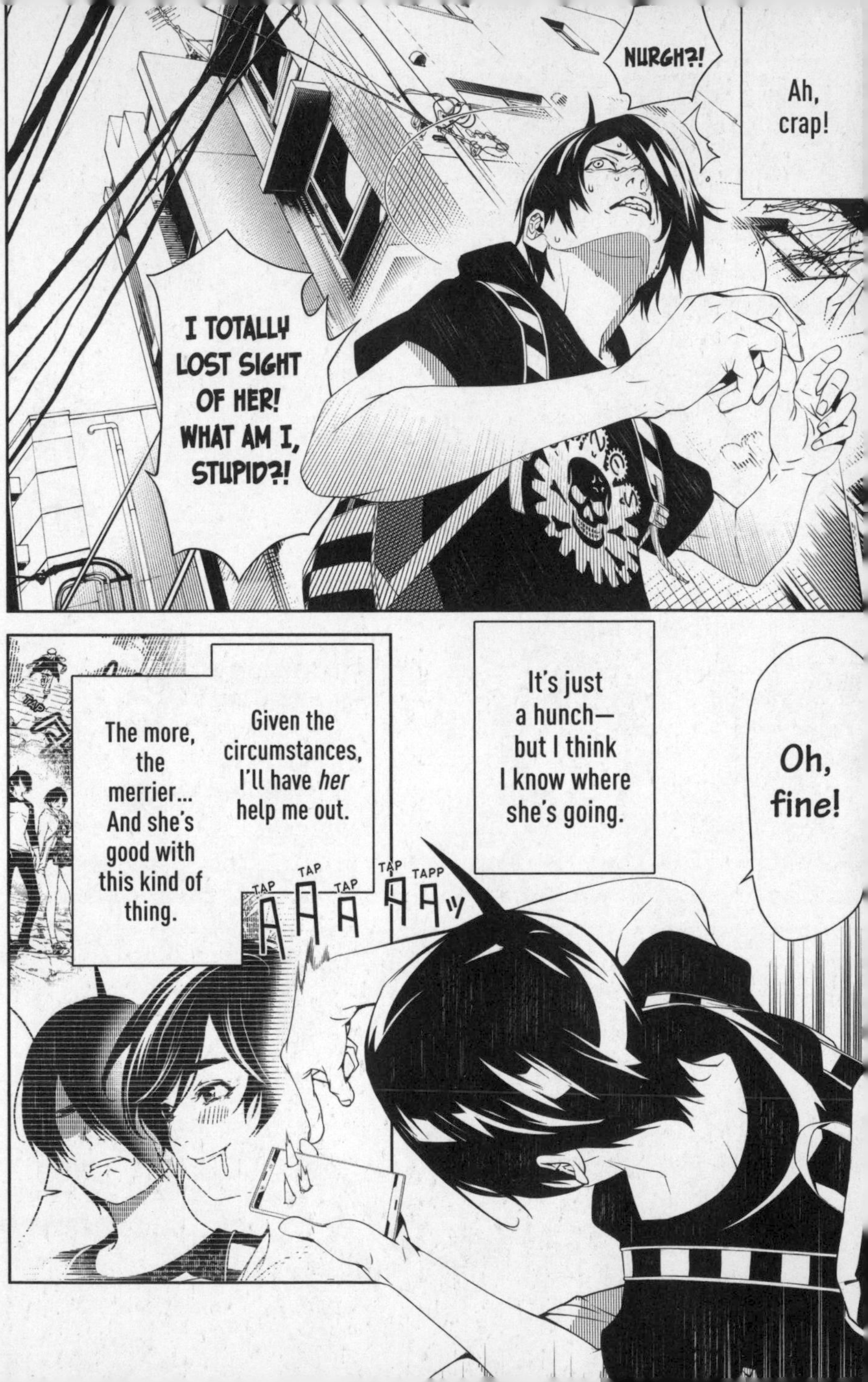
Ah, crap!
NURGH?!
I TOTALLY LOST SIGHT OF HER! WHAT AM I, STUPID?!
Oh, fine!
It's just a hunch— but I think I know where she's going.
Given the circumstances, I'll have *her* help me out.
TAP TAP TAP TAP TAPP
The more, the merrier... And she's good with this kind of thing.
TAP

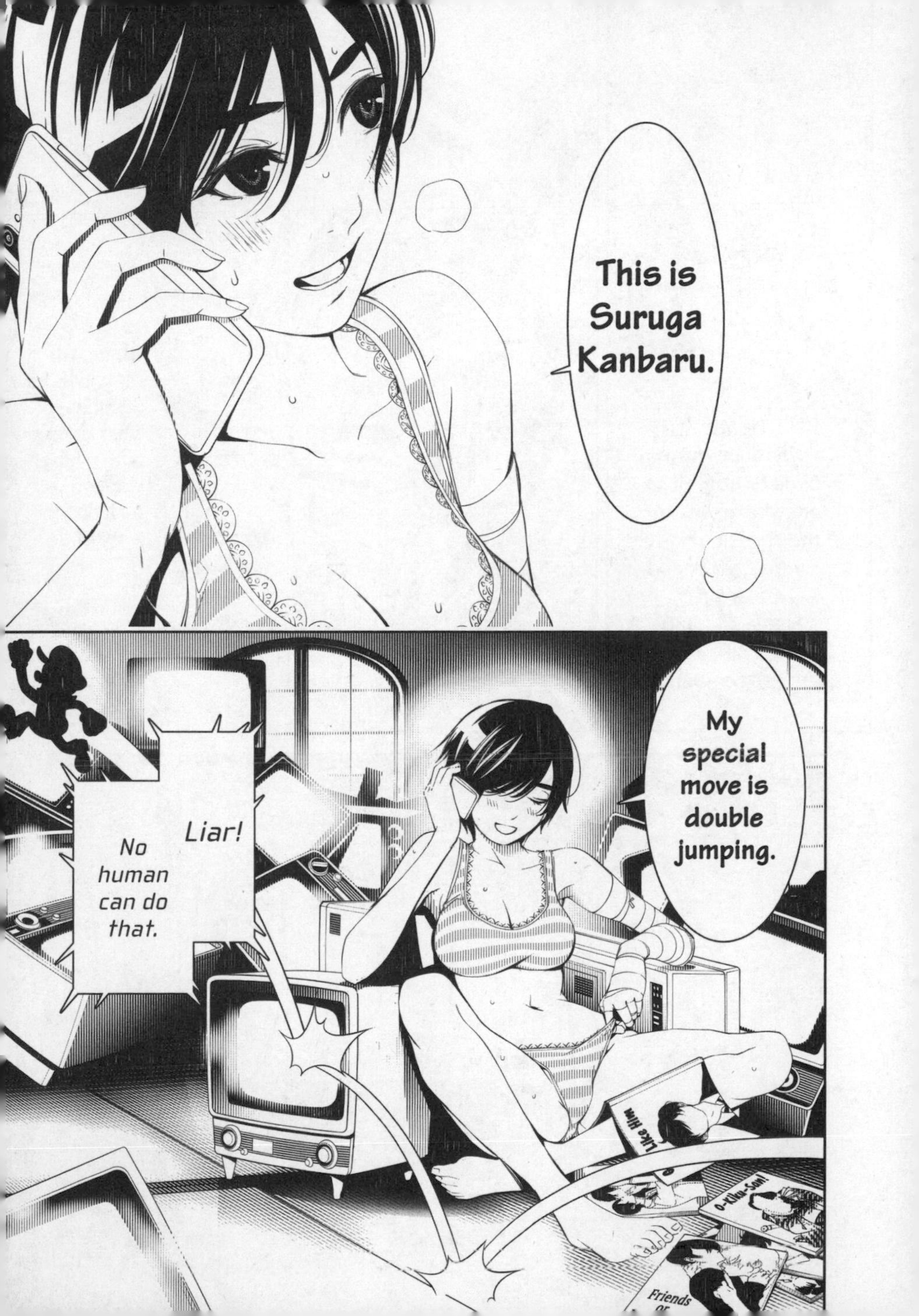
This is Suruga Kanbaru.
My special move is double jumping.
Liar!
No human can do that.
Like Him
O-Kiku-San!

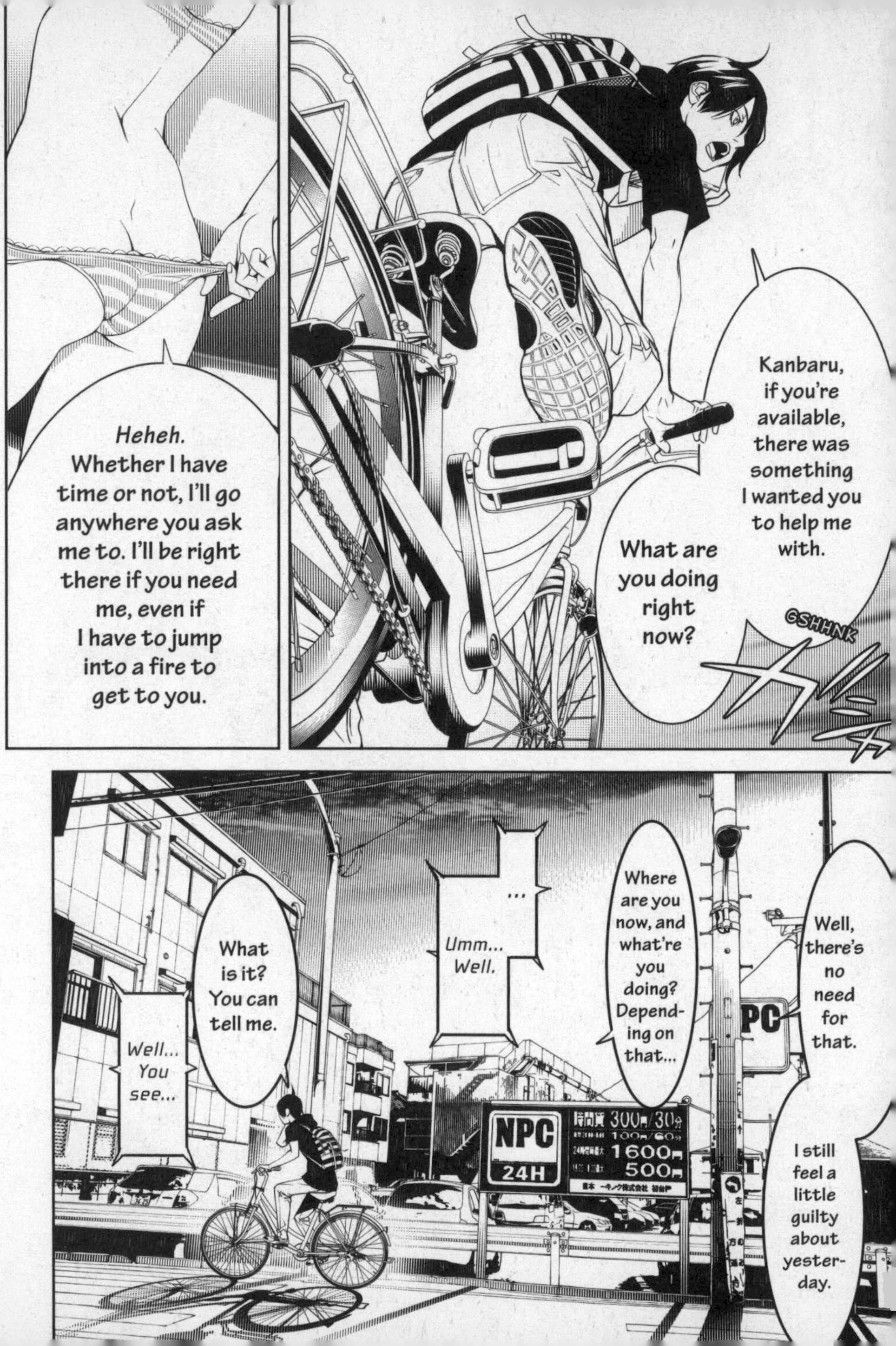
Kanbaru, if you're available, there was something I wanted you to help me with.
What are you doing right now?
GSHHNK
Heheh. Whether I have time or not, I'll go anywhere you ask me to. I'll be right there if you need me, even if I have to jump into a fire to get to you.
Well, there's no need for that.
I still feel a little guilty about yesterday.
Where are you now, and what're you doing? Depending on that...
...
Umm... Well.
What is it? You can tell me.
Well... You see...
NPC
NPC
24H
300円/30分
100円/60分
1600円
500円

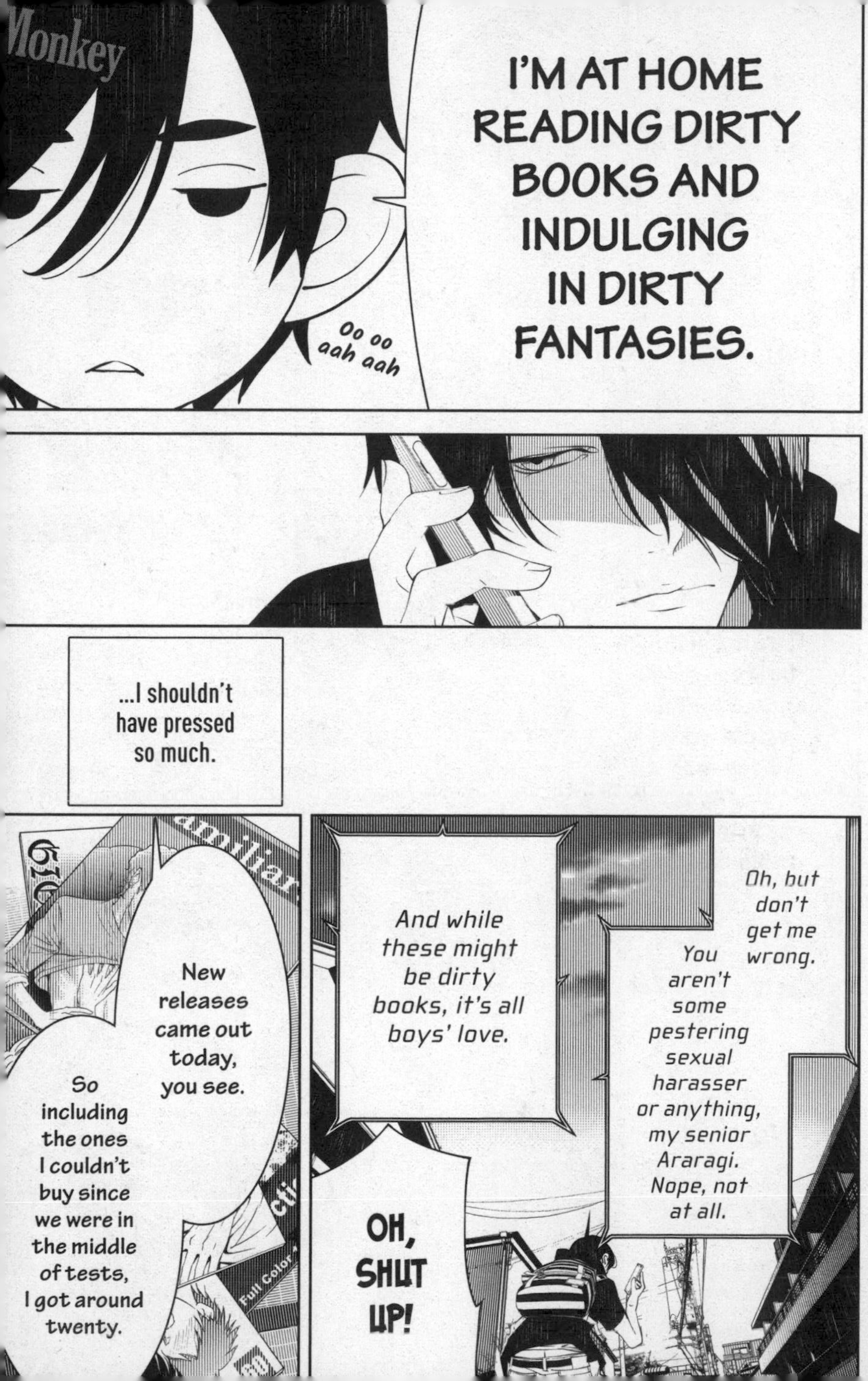
I'M AT HOME READING DIRTY BOOKS AND INDULGING IN DIRTY FANTASIES.
Oo oo aah aah
Monkey
...I shouldn't have pressed so much.
Oh, but don't get me wrong.
You aren't some pestering sexual harasser or anything, my senior Araragi. Nope, not at all.
And while these might be dirty books, it's all boys' love.
OH, SHUT UP!
New releases came out today, you see.
So including the ones I couldn't buy since we were in the middle of tests, I got around twenty.

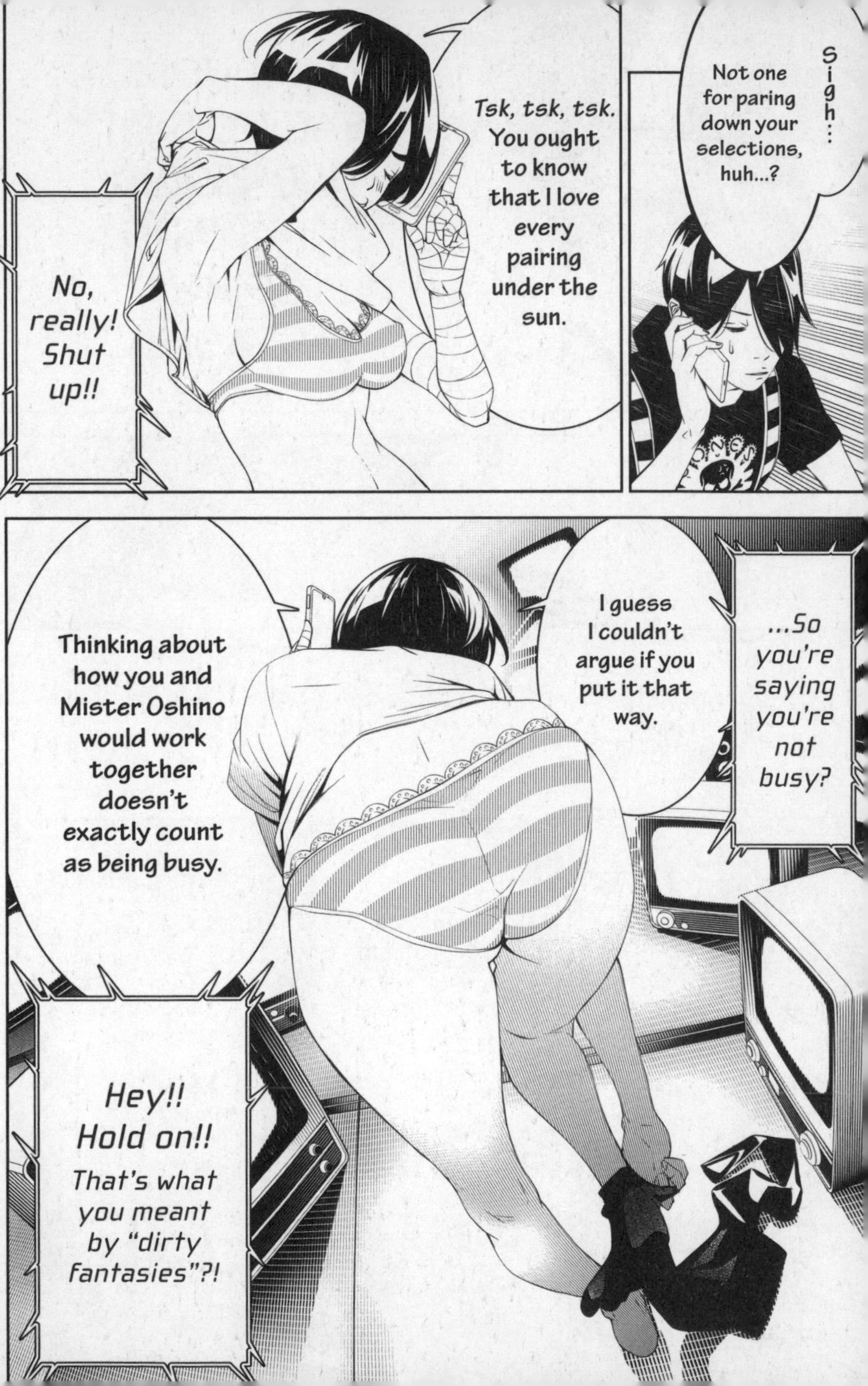
Sigh…
Not one for paring down your selections, huh...?
Tsk, tsk, tsk. You ought to know that I love every pairing under the sun.
No, really! Shut up!!
...So you're saying you're not busy?
I guess I couldn't argue if you put it that way.
Thinking about how you and Mister Oshino would work together doesn't exactly count as being busy.
Hey!! Hold on!! That's what you meant by "dirty fantasies"?!

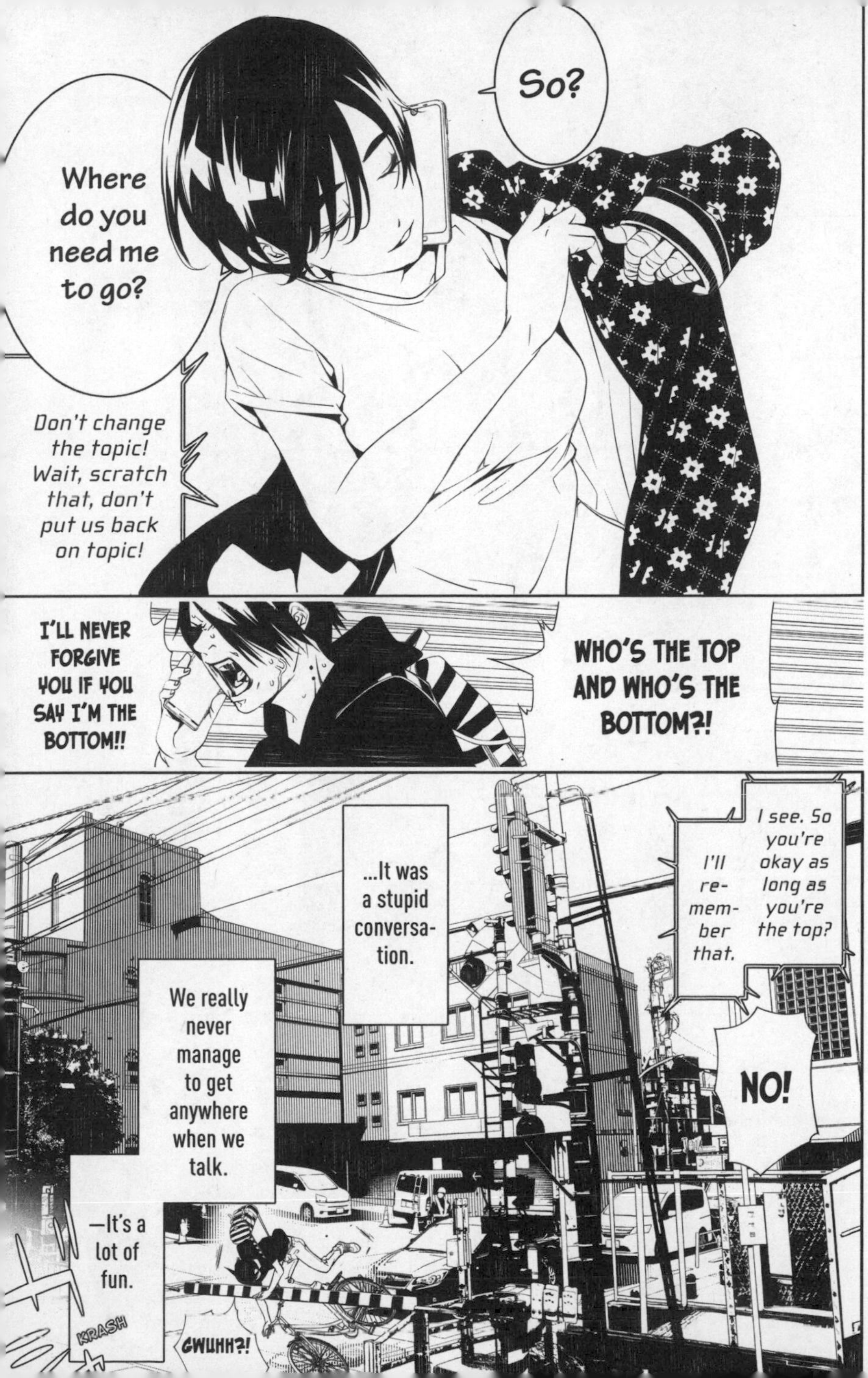
So?
Where do you need me to go?
Don't change the topic! Wait, scratch that, don't put us back on topic!
WHO'S THE TOP AND WHO'S THE BOTTOM?!
I'LL NEVER FORGIVE YOU IF YOU SAY I'M THE BOTTOM!!
I see. So you're okay as long as you're the top?
I'll re-mem-ber that.
NO!
...It was a stupid conversa-tion.
We really never manage to get anywhere when we talk.
—It's a lot of fun.
GWUHH?!
KRASH

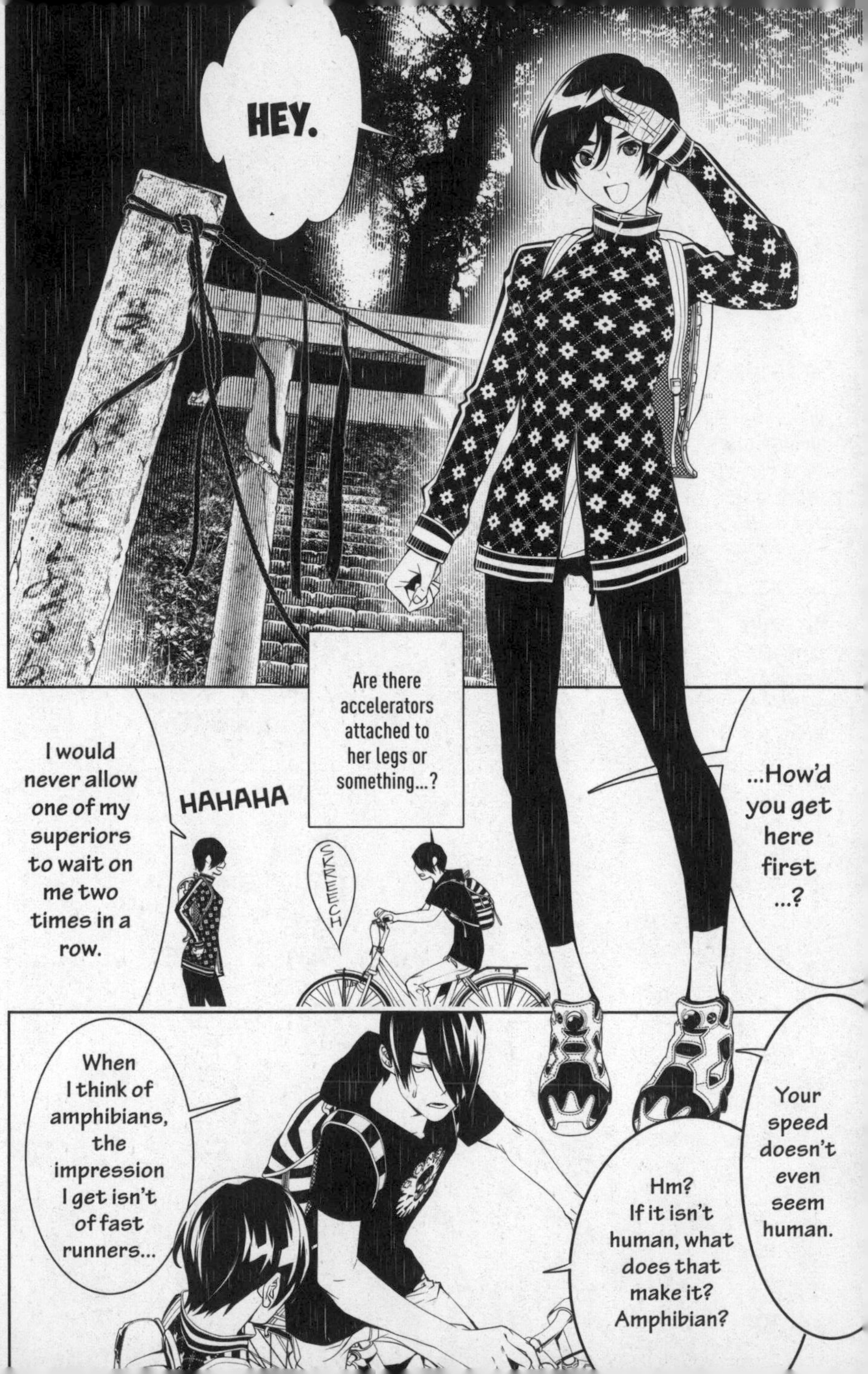
HEY.
...How'd you get here first ...?
Are there accelerators attached to her legs or something...?
SKREECH
HAHAHA
I would never allow one of my superiors to wait on me two times in a row.
Your speed doesn't even seem human.
Hm? If it isn't human, what does that make it? Amphibian?
When I think of amphibians, the impression I get isn't of fast runners...

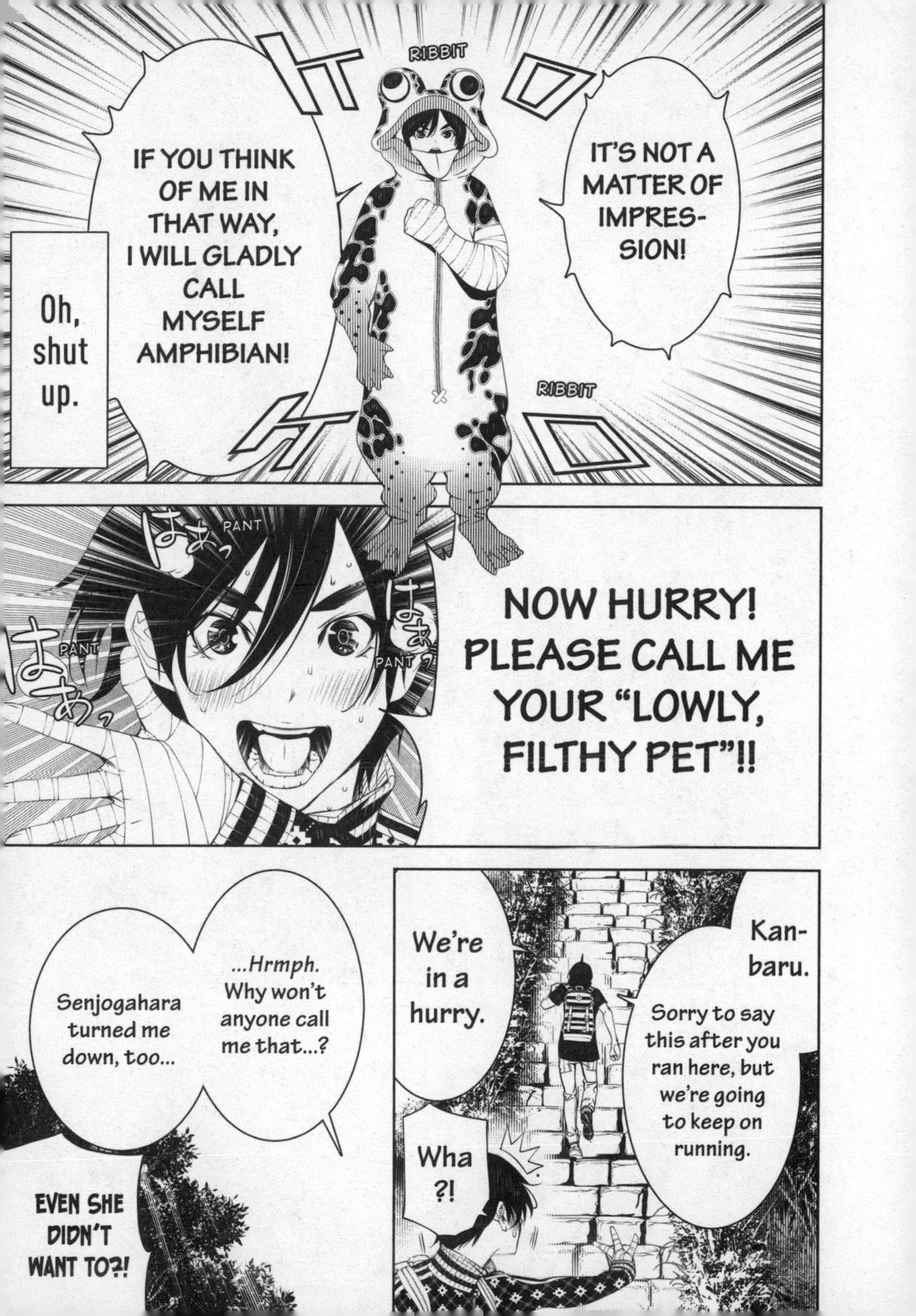
IT'S NOT A MATTER OF IMPRES-SION!
RIBBIT
IF YOU THINK OF ME IN THAT WAY, I WILL GLADLY CALL MYSELF AMPHIBIAN!
RIBBIT
Oh, shut up.
NOW HURRY! PLEASE CALL ME YOUR "LOWLY, FILTHY PET"!!
PANT
PANT
PANT
Kan-baru.
Sorry to say this after you ran here, but we're going to keep on running.
We're in a hurry.
Wha ?!
...Hrmph. Why won't anyone call me that...?
Senjogahara turned me down, too...
EVEN SHE DIDN'T WANT TO?!

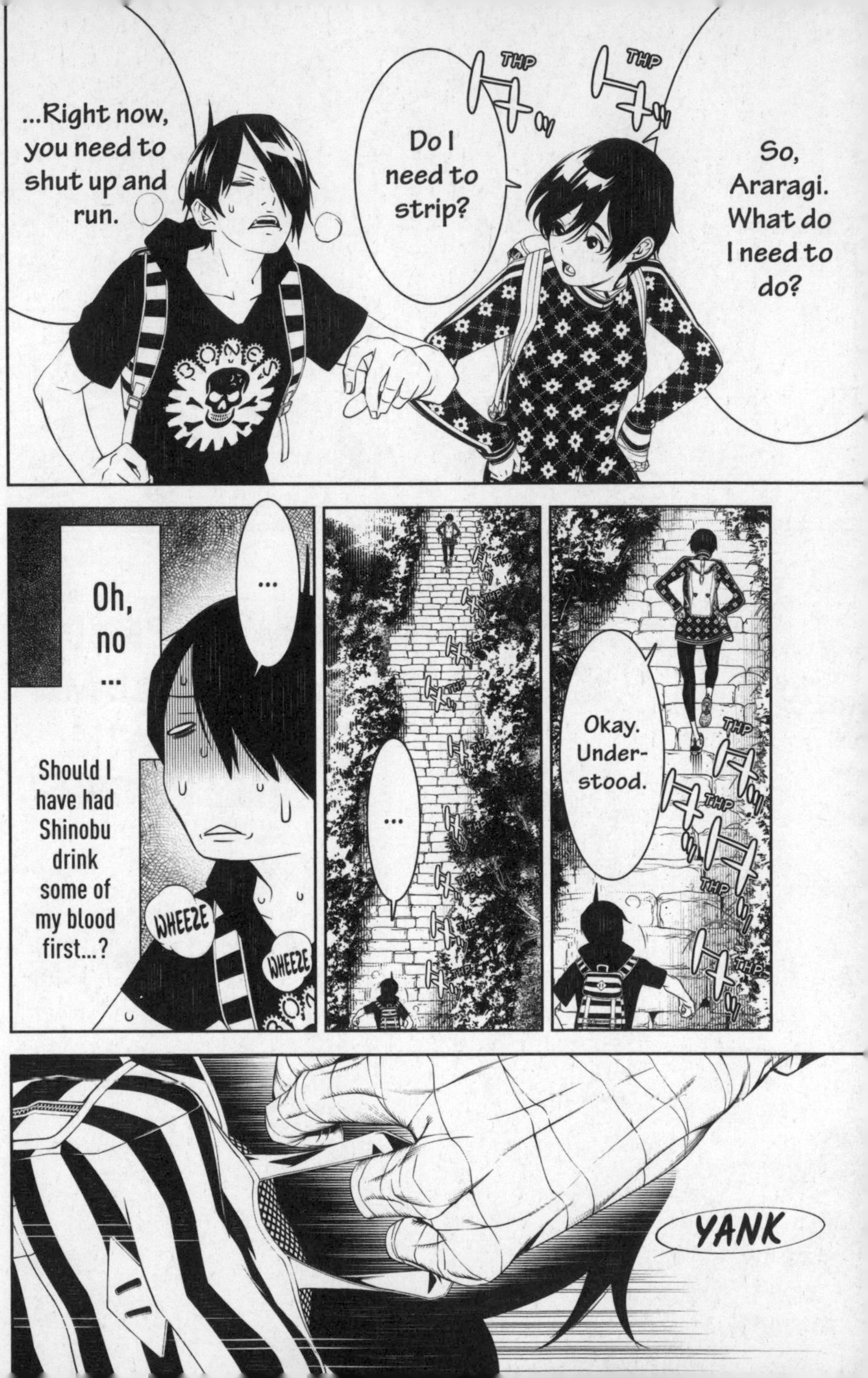
So, Araragi. What do I need to do?
THP
THP
Do I need to strip?
...Right now, you need to shut up and run.
Okay. Understood.
THP
THP
THP
THP
...
...
THP
THP
THP
THP
THP
THP
THP
THP
...
Oh, no ...
Should I have had Shinobu drink some of my blood first...?
WHEEZE
WHEEZE
YANK

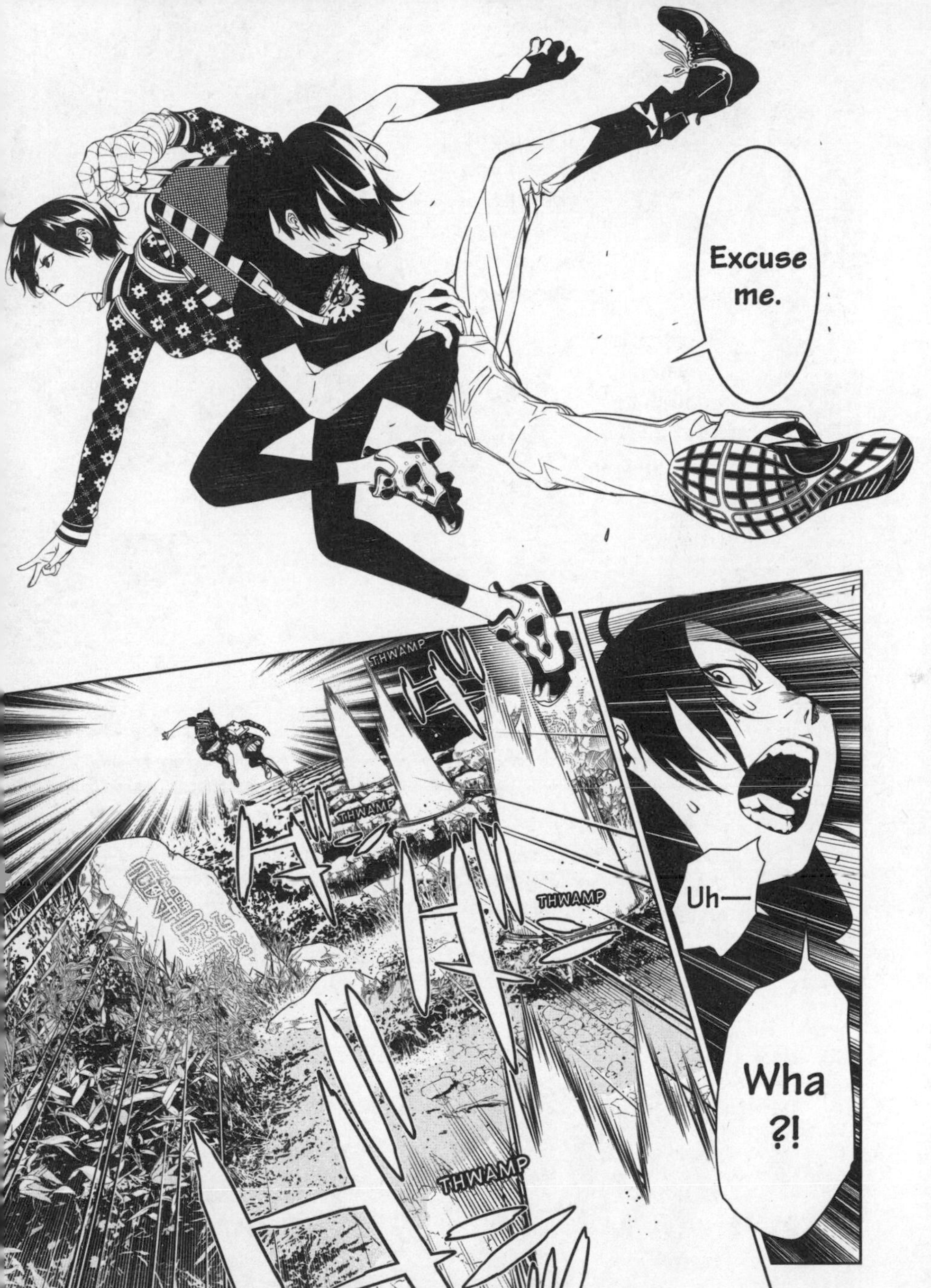
Excuse me.
Uh—
Wha ?!
THWAMP
THWAMP
THWAMP
THWAMP

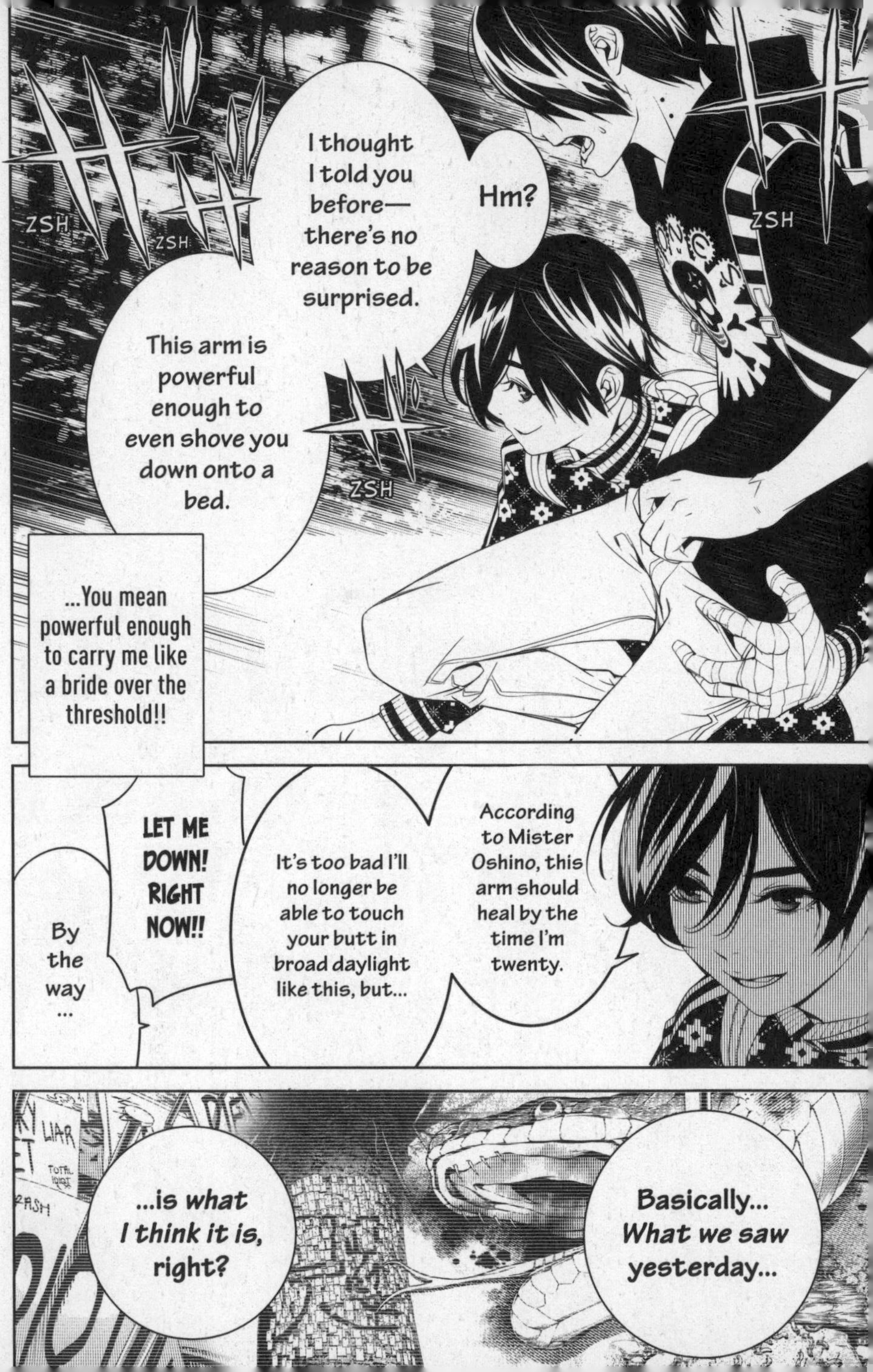
ZSH
Hm?
I thought I told you before—there's no reason to be surprised.
ZSH
ZSH
This arm is powerful enough to even shove you down onto a bed.
ZSH
...You mean powerful enough to carry me like a bride over the threshold!!
According to Mister Oshino, this arm should heal by the time I'm twenty.
It's too bad I'll no longer be able to touch your butt in broad daylight like this, but...
LET ME DOWN! RIGHT NOW!!
By the way...
Basically... *What we saw yesterday...*
...is *what I think it is,* right?
LIAR

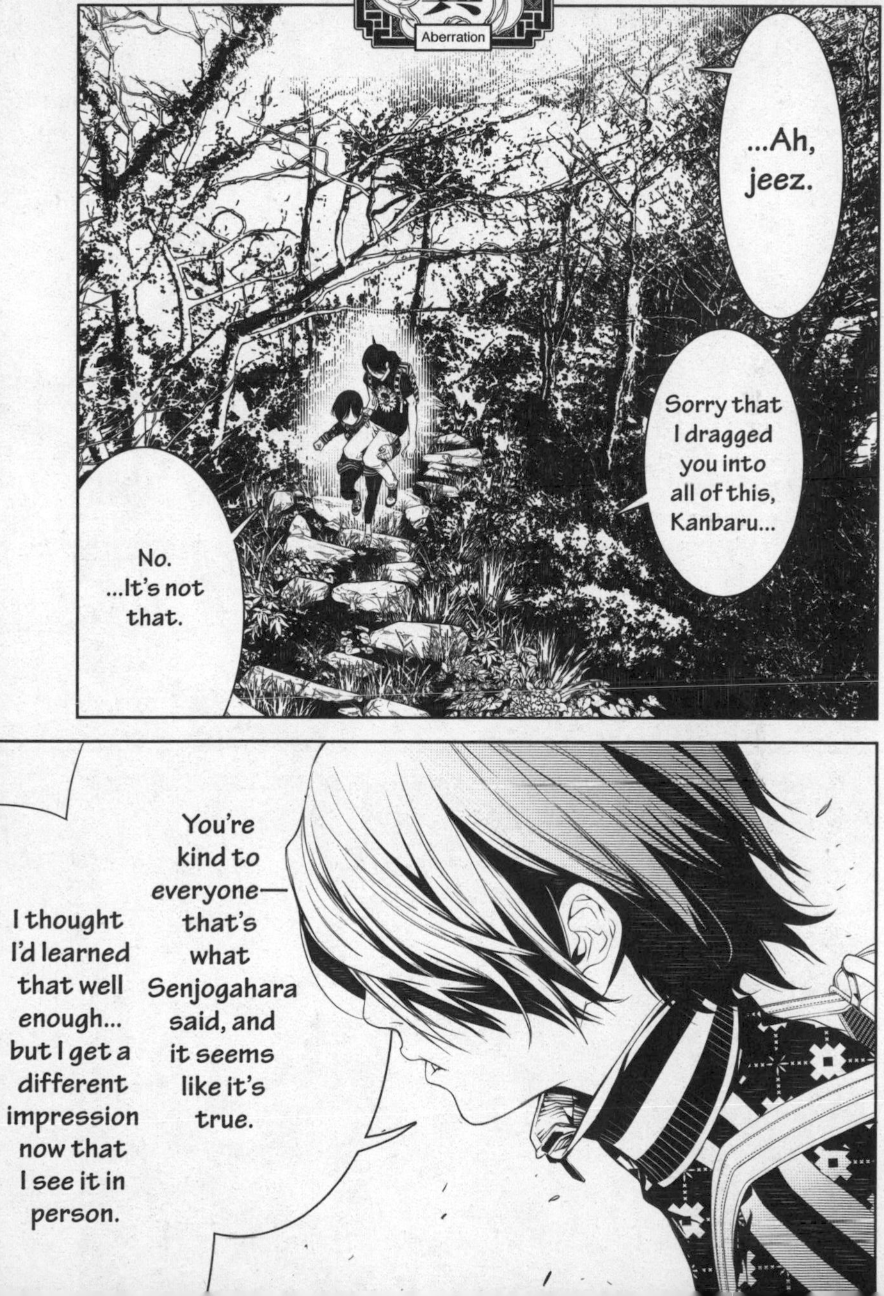
...Ah, jeez.
Sorry that I dragged you into all of this, Kanbaru...
No. ...It's not that.
You're kind to everyone—that's what Senjogahara said, and it seems like it's true.
I thought I'd learned that well enough... but I get a different impression now that I see it in person.

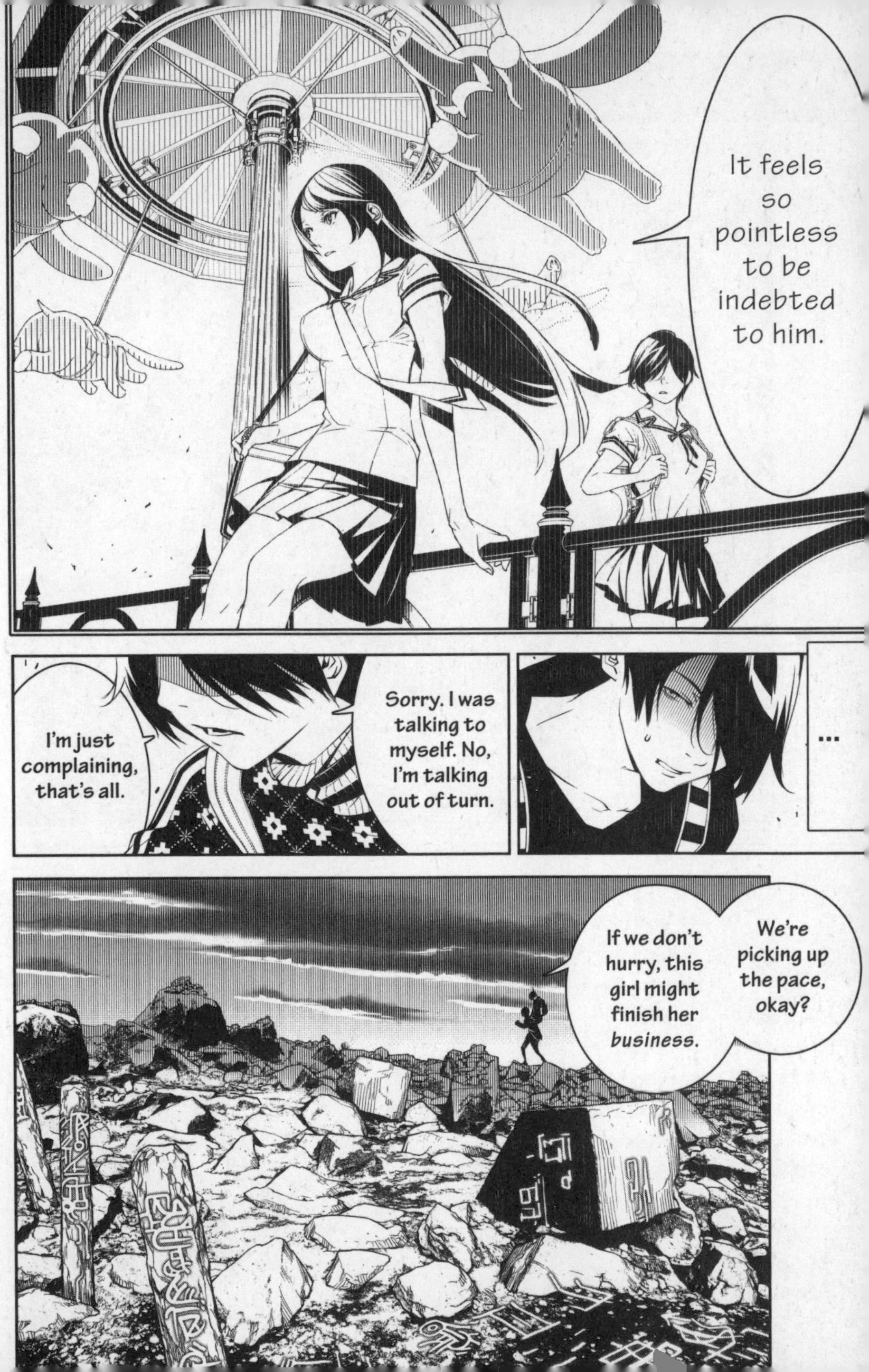
It feels so pointless to be indebted to him.
...
Sorry. I was talking to myself. No, I'm talking out of turn.
I'm just complaining, that's all.
We're picking up the pace, okay?
If we don't hurry, this girl might finish her *business*.

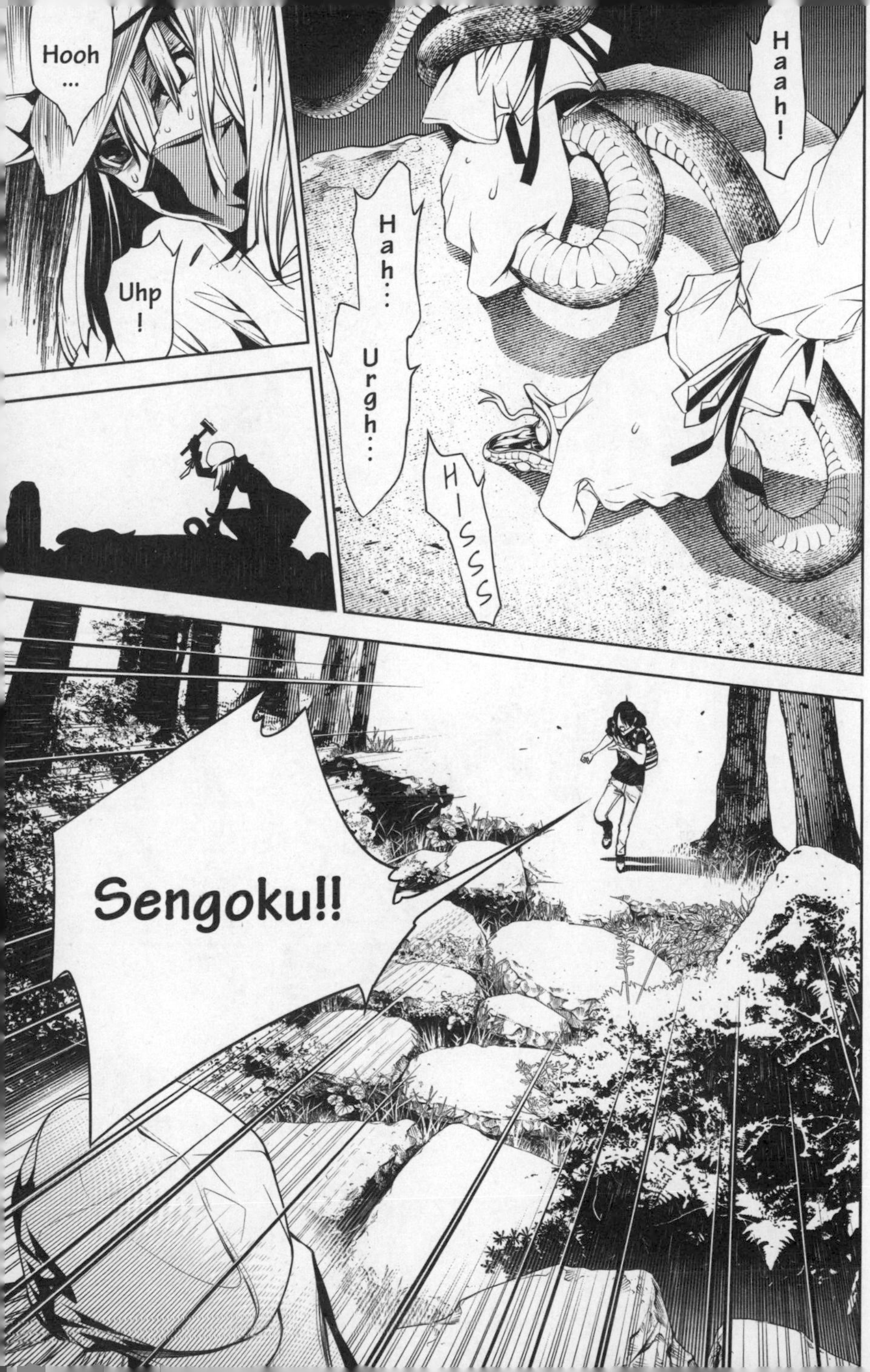

Haaah!
Hah… Urgh…
HISSS
Hooh …
Uhp !
Sengoku!!

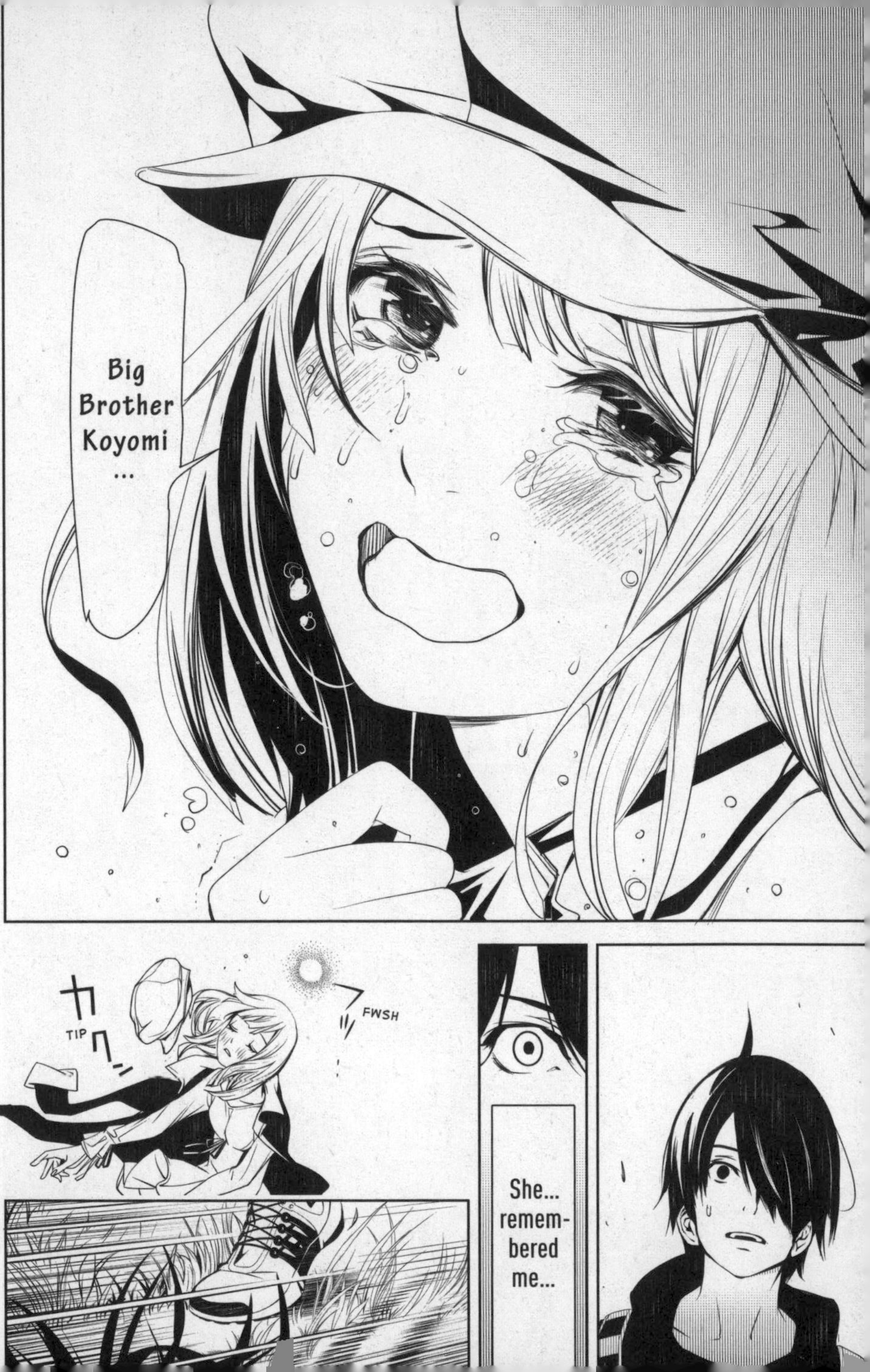
Big Brother Koyomi ...
She... remembered me...
FWSH
TIP

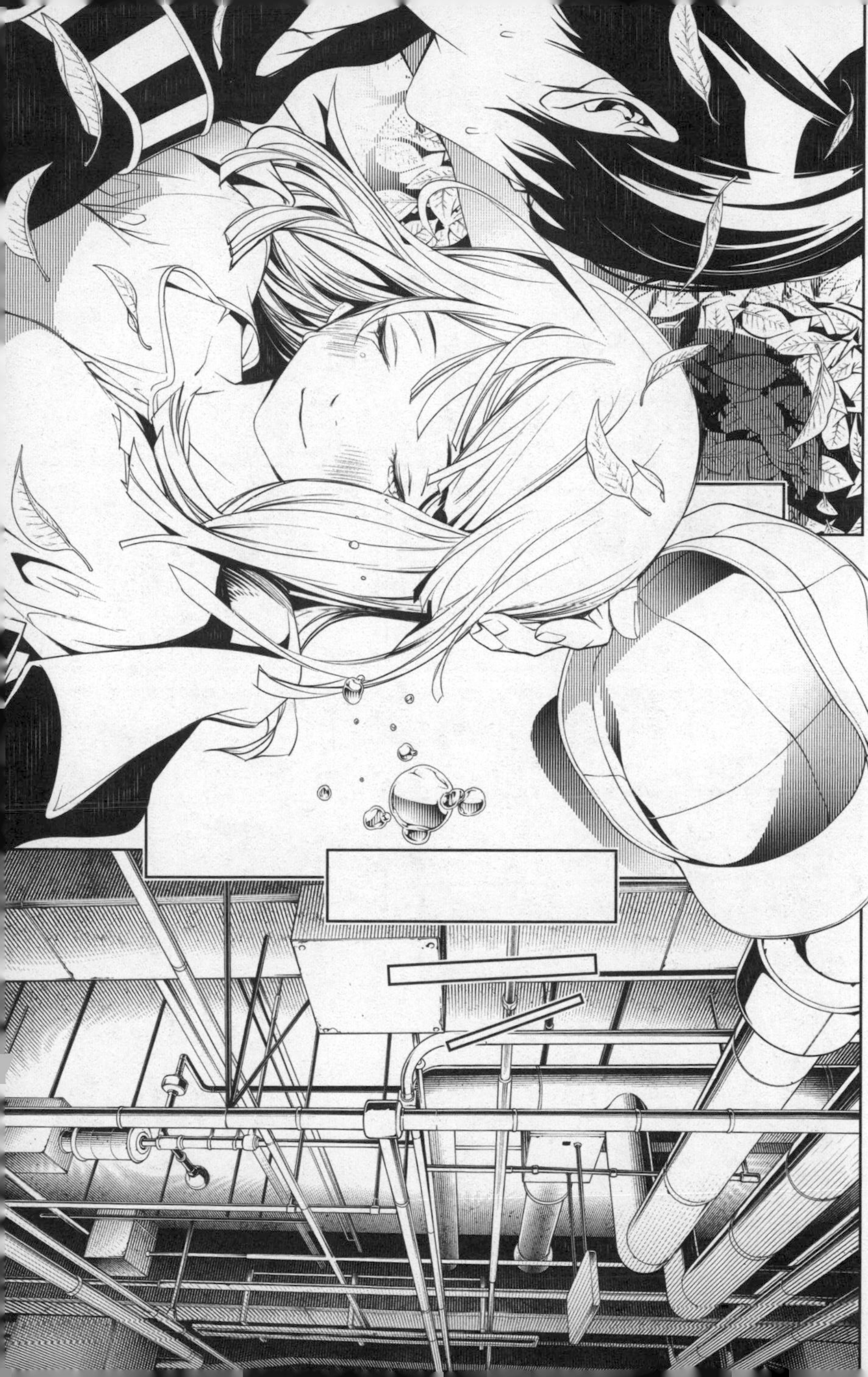

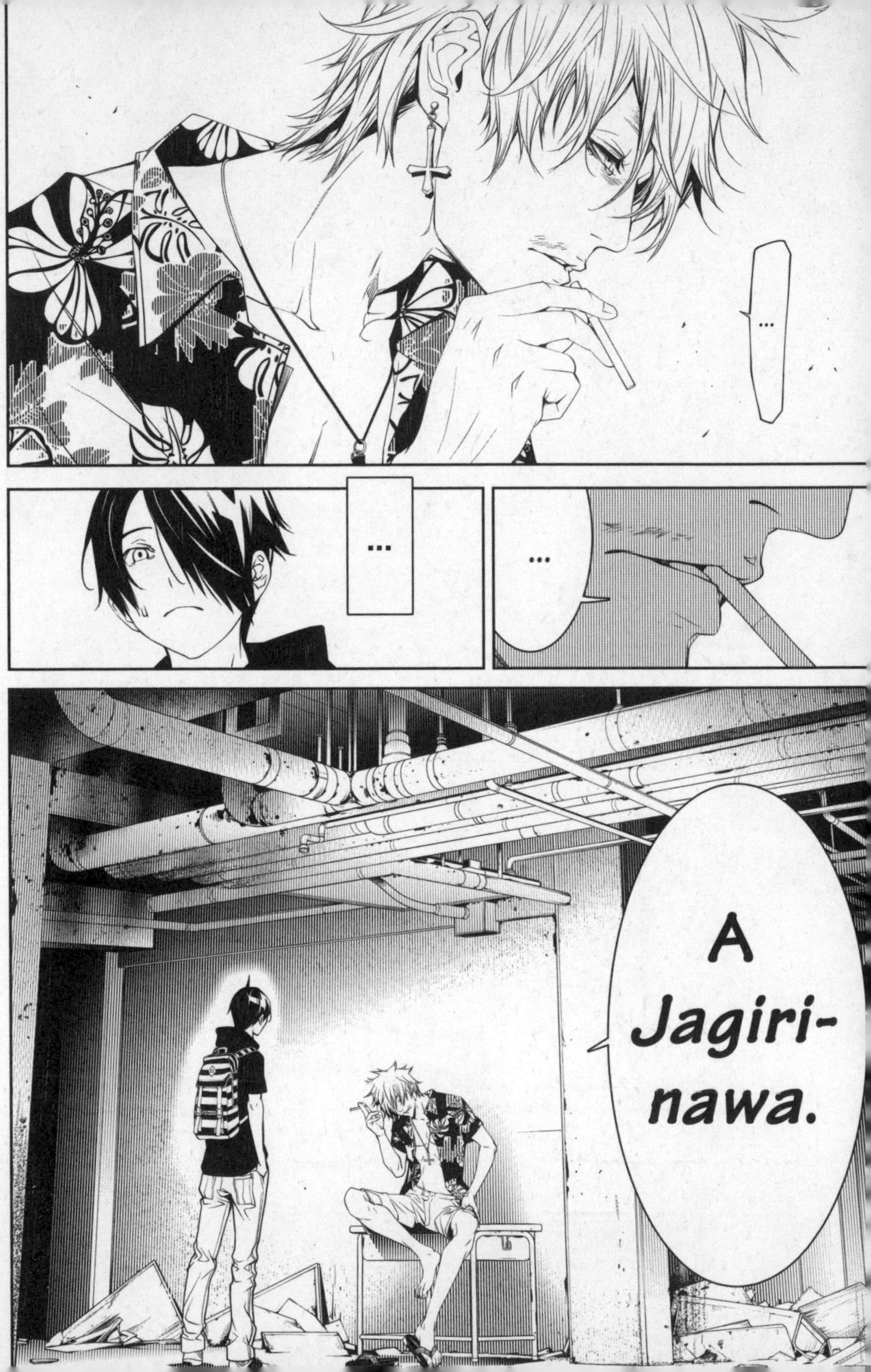
...
...
...
A Jagiri-nawa.

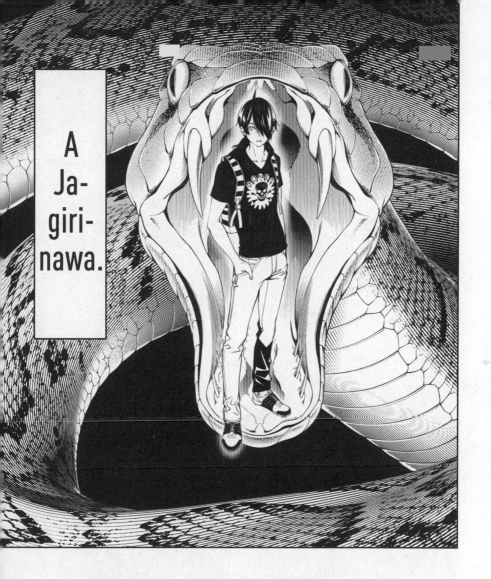

A
Ja-
giri-
nawa.

Snake: The general term for reptiles in Class Reptilia, Order Squamata, Suborder Serpentes. Noted for their long, thin, cylindrical bodies covered in scales. They have hundreds of vertebrae and are able to squirm about freely.

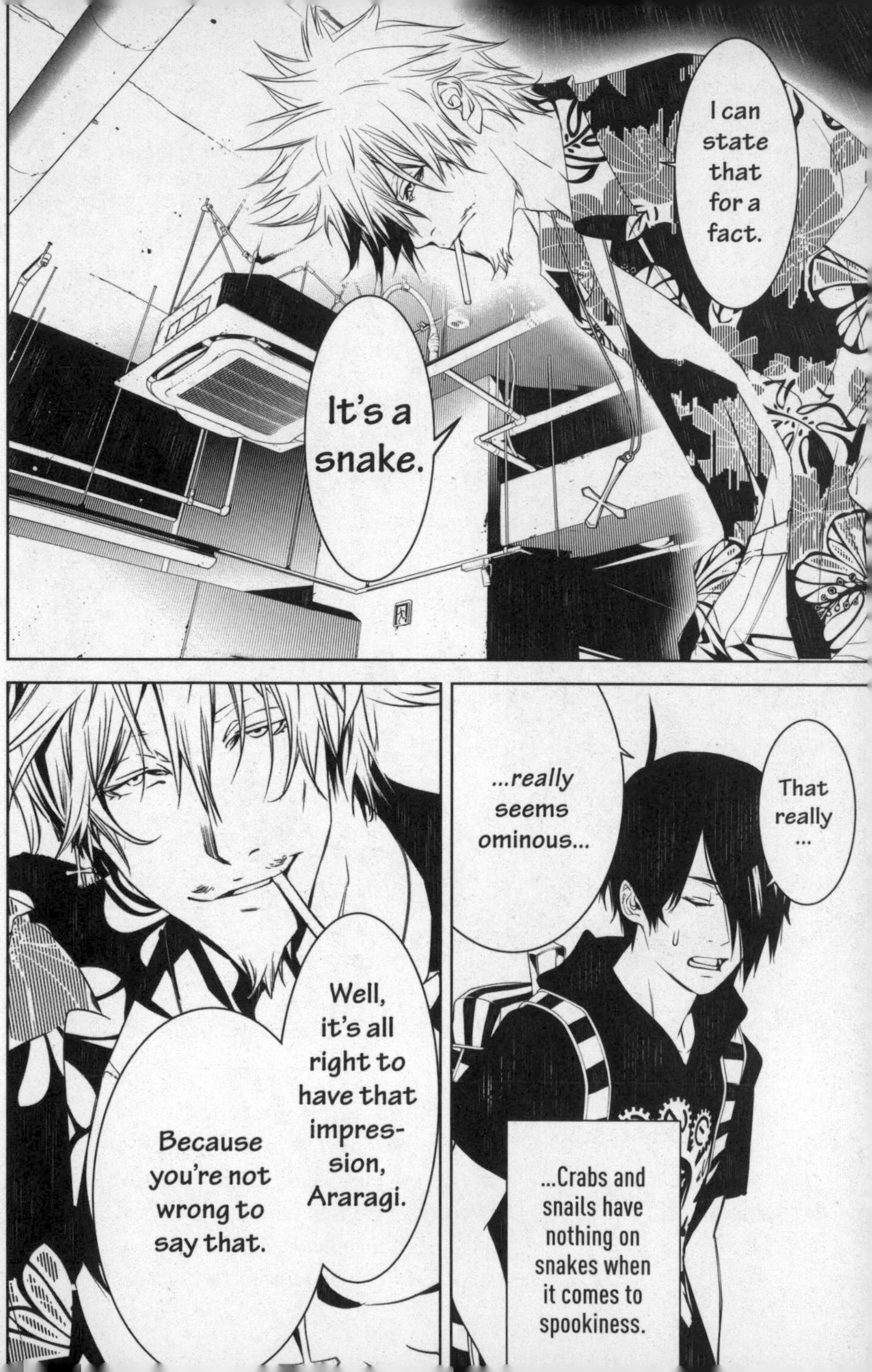
I can state that for a fact.
It's a snake.
That really...
...really seems ominous...
...Crabs and snails have nothing on snakes when it comes to spookiness.
Well, it's all right to have that impression, Araragi.
Because you're not wrong to say that.

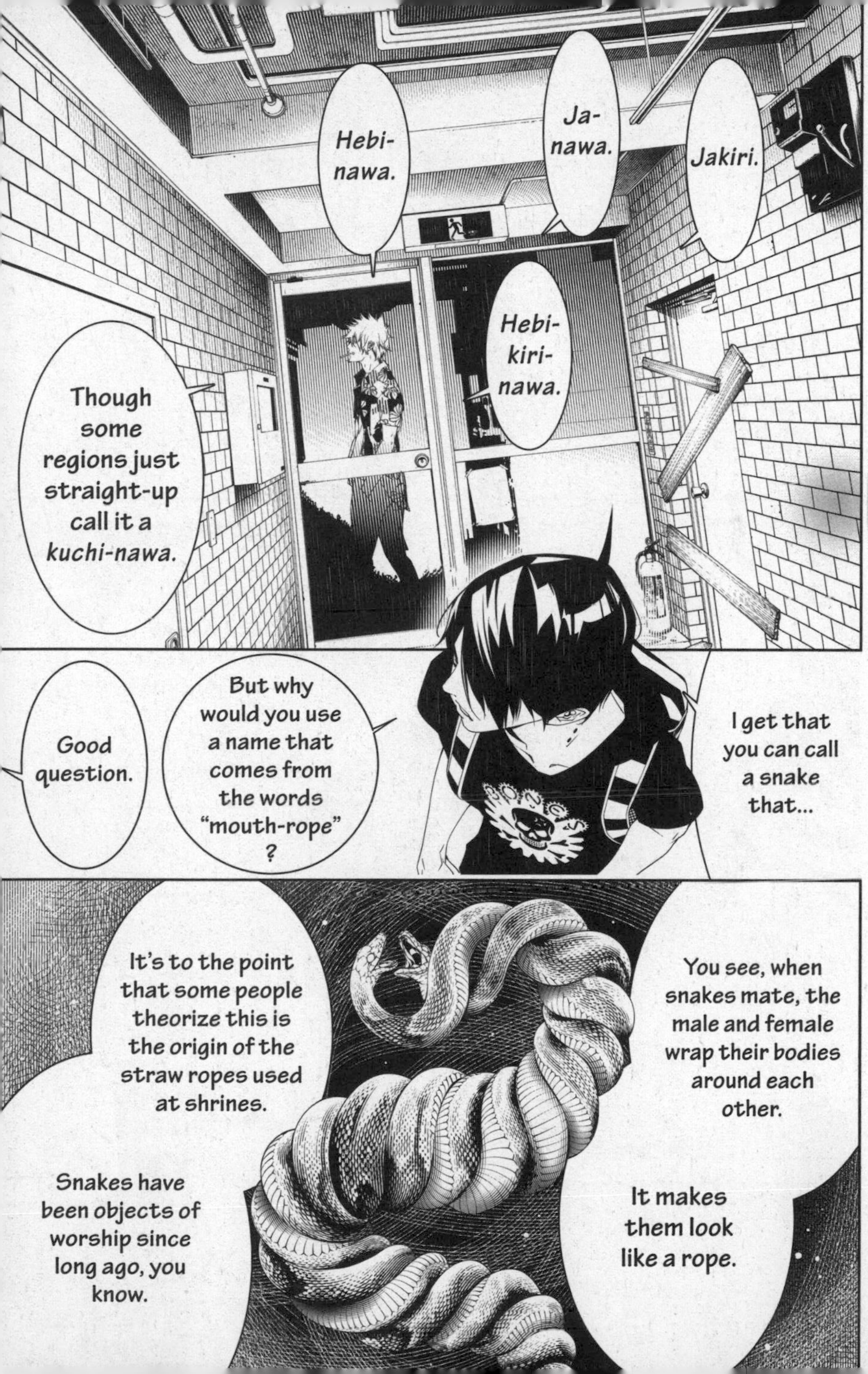
Jakiri.
Ja- nawa.
Hebi- nawa.
Hebi- kiri- nawa.
Though some regions just straight-up call it a *kuchi-nawa*.
I get that you can call a snake that...
But why would you use a name that comes from the words "mouth-rope"?
Good question.
You see, when snakes mate, the male and female wrap their bodies around each other.
It makes them look like a rope.
It's to the point that some people theorize this is the origin of the straw ropes used at shrines.
Snakes have been objects of worship since long ago, you know.

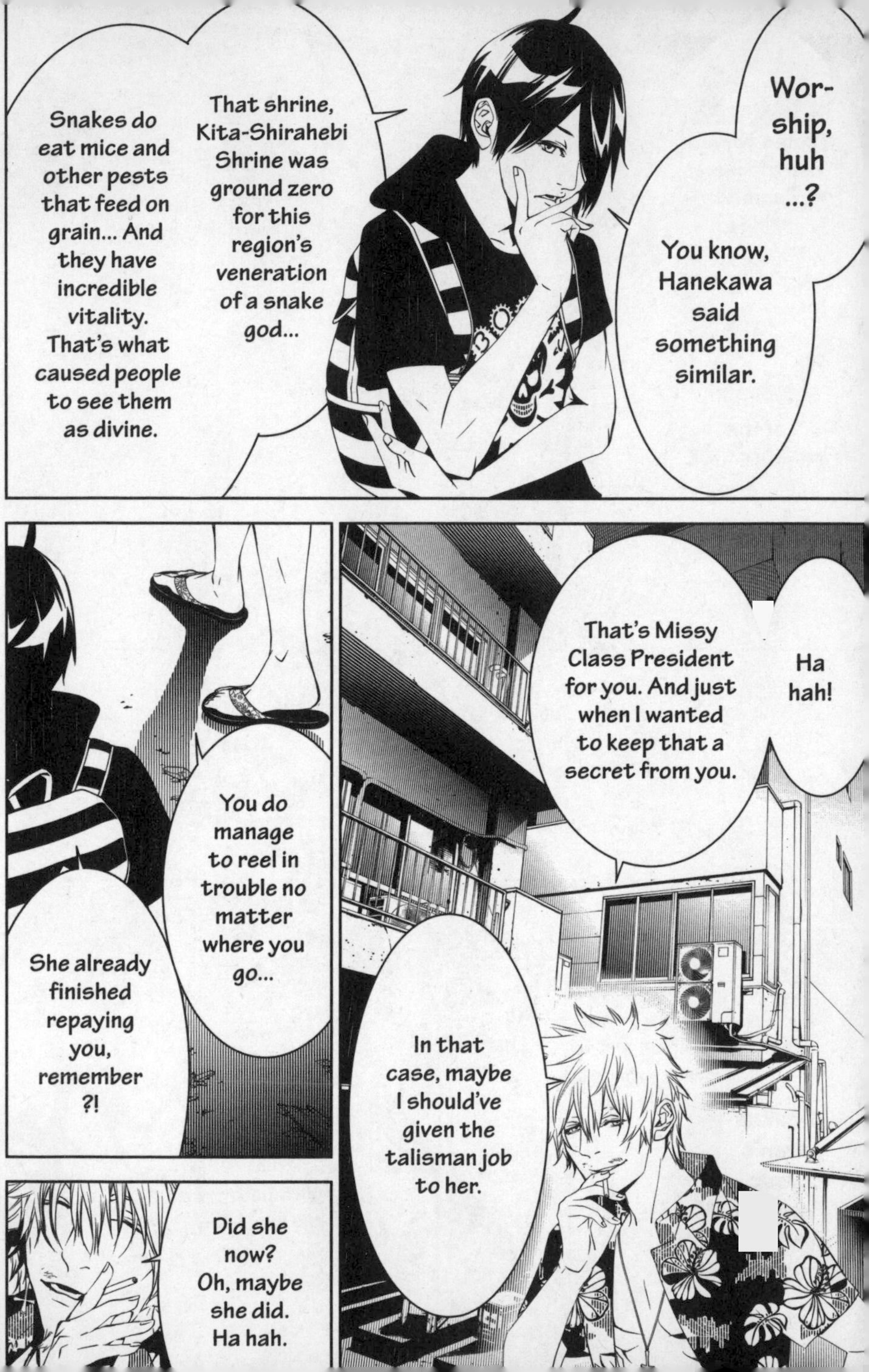
Worship, huh ...?
You know, Hanekawa said something similar.
That shrine, Kita-Shirahebi Shrine was ground zero for this region's veneration of a snake god...
Snakes do eat mice and other pests that feed on grain... And they have incredible vitality. That's what caused people to see them as divine.
Ha hah!
That's Missy Class President for you. And just when I wanted to keep that a secret from you.
In that case, maybe I should've given the talisman job to her.
You do manage to reel in trouble no matter where you go...
She already finished repaying you, remember ?!
Did she now? Oh, maybe she did. Ha hah.

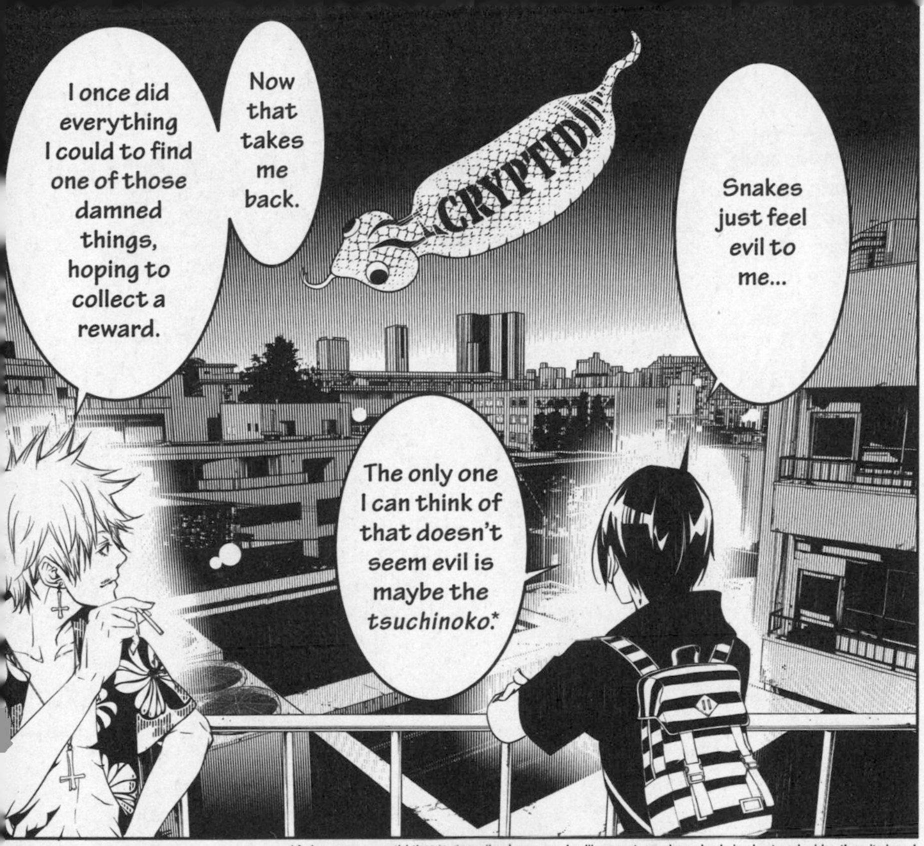
Snakes just feel evil to me...
The only one I can think of that doesn't seem evil is maybe the tsuchinoko.*
CRYPTID!!
Now that takes me back.
I once did everything I could to find one of those damned things, hoping to collect a reward.

*A Japanese cryptid that is described as a snake-like creature whose body is short and wider than its head.

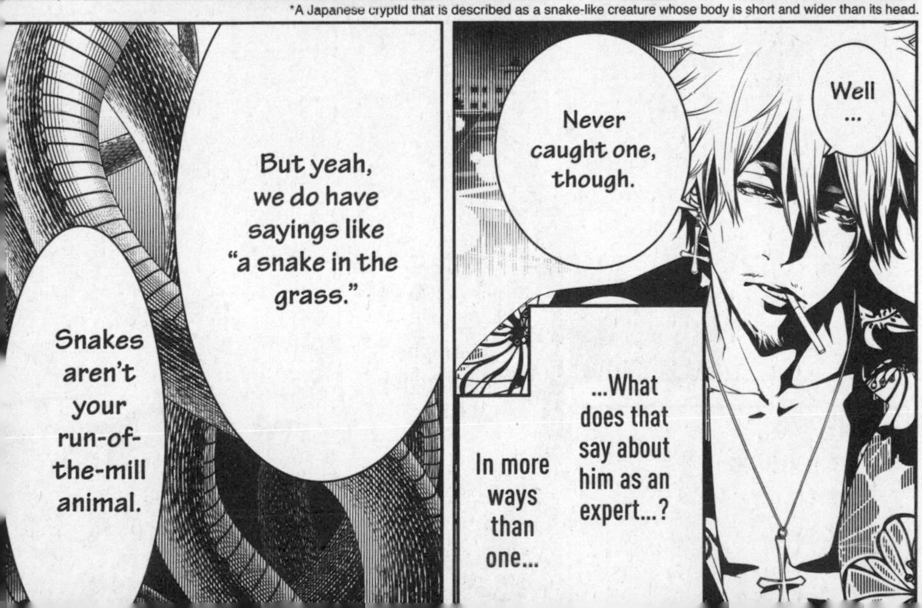
Well...
Never caught one, though.
...What does that say about him as an expert...?
In more ways than one...
But yeah, we do have sayings like "a snake in the grass."
Snakes aren't your run-of-the-mill animal.

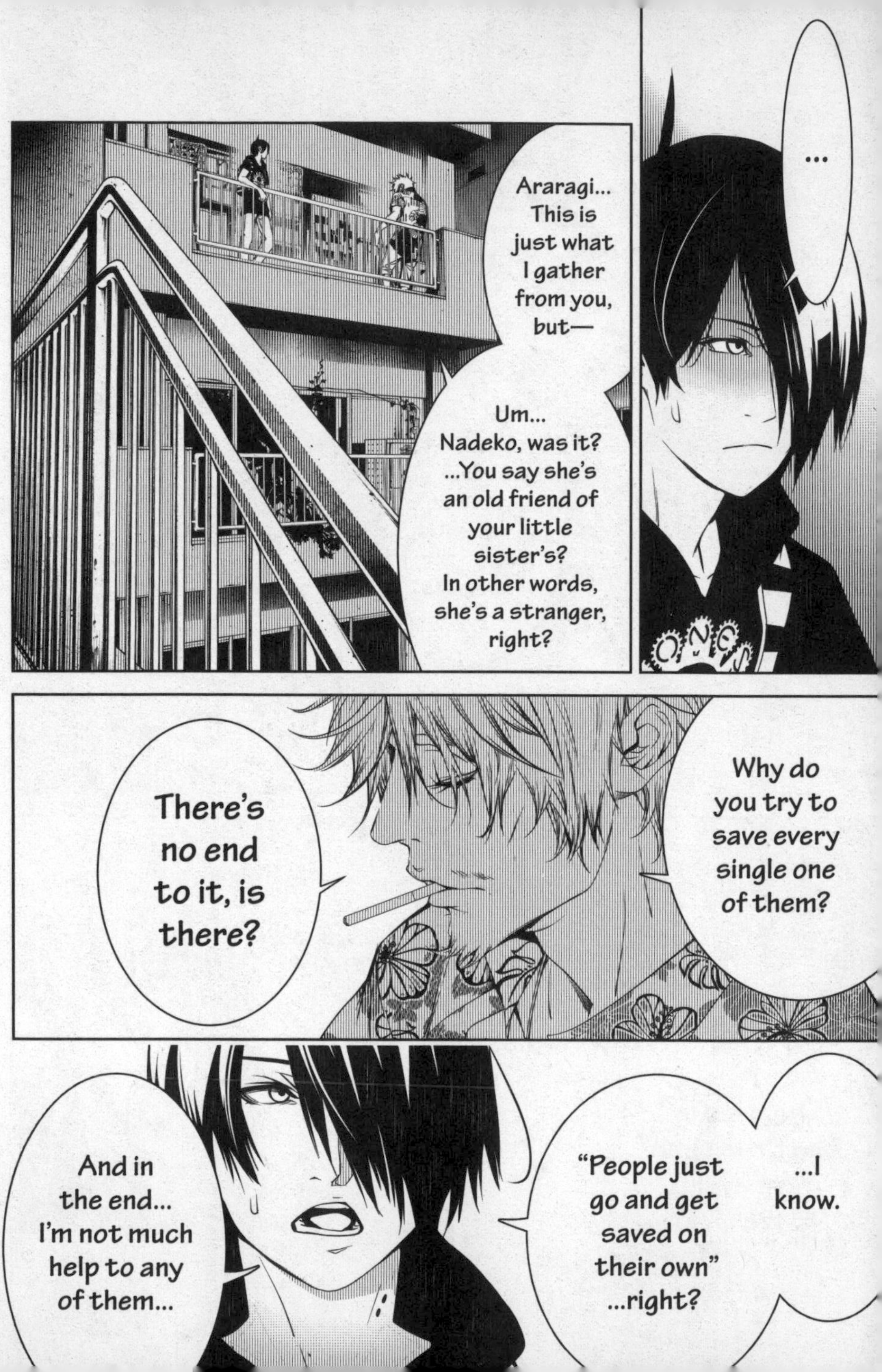
...
Araragi... This is just what I gather from you, but—
Um... Nadeko, was it? ...You say she's an old friend of your little sister's? In other words, she's a stranger, right?
Why do you try to save every single one of them?
There's no end to it, is there?
...I know.
"People just go and get saved on their own" ...right?
And in the end... I'm not much help to any of them...

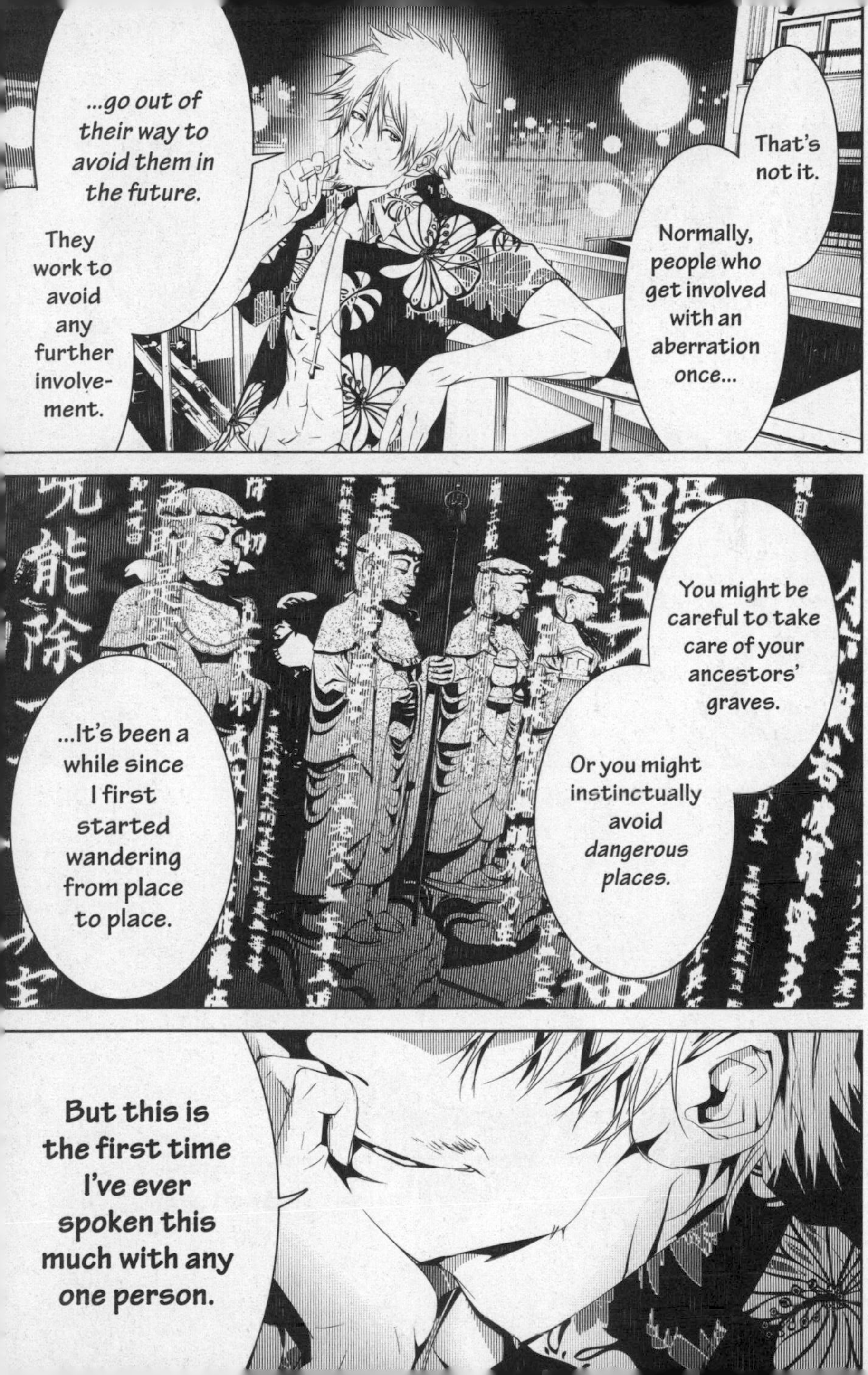
That's not it.
Normally, people who get involved with an aberration once...
...go out of their way to avoid them in the future.
They work to avoid any further involvement.
You might be careful to take care of your ancestors' graves.
Or you might instinctually avoid dangerous places.
...It's been a while since I first started wandering from place to place.
But this is the first time I've ever spoken this much with any one person.

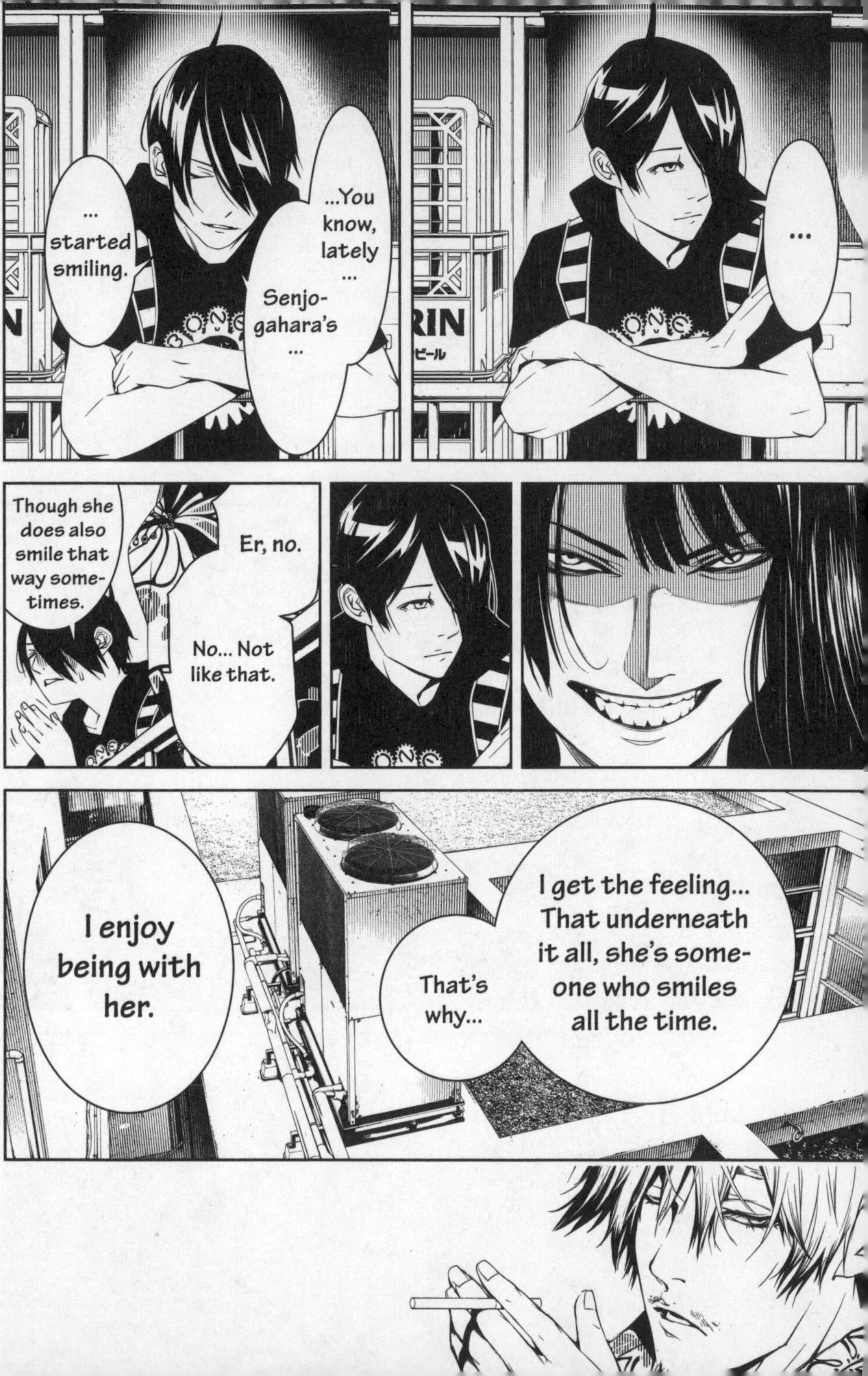
...
...You know, lately ... Senjo-gahara's ...
... started smiling.
Er, no.
No... Not like that.
Though she does also smile that way some-times.
I get the feeling... That underneath it all, she's some-one who smiles all the time.
That's why...
I enjoy being with her.
RIN
ビール

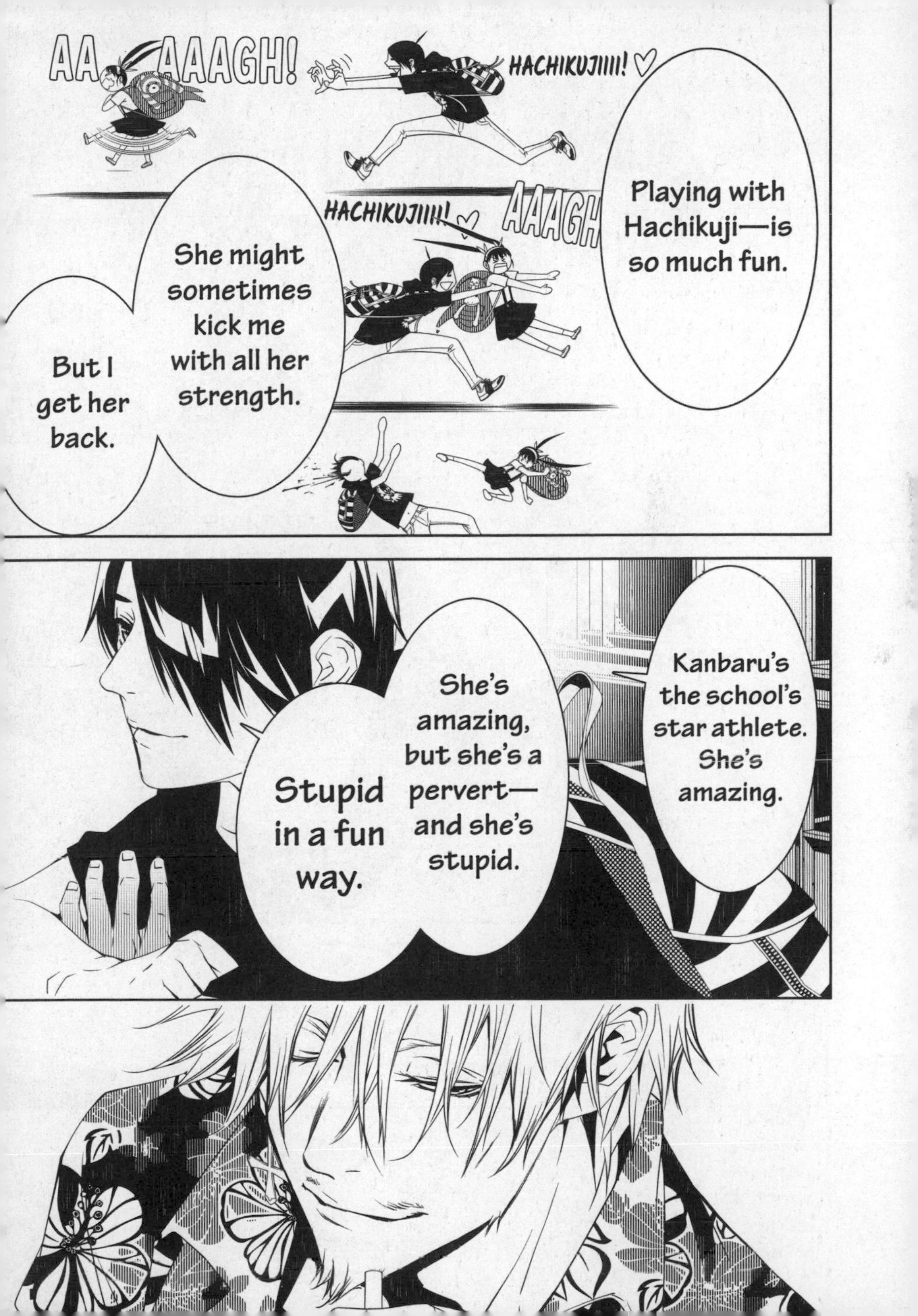
HACHIKUJIIIII! ♡
AA AAAGH!
Playing with Hachikuji—is so much fun.
AAAGH
HACHIKUJIIIII! ♡
She might sometimes kick me with all her strength.
But I get her back.
Kanbaru's the school's star athlete. She's amazing.
She's amazing, but she's a pervert—and she's stupid.
Stupid in a fun way.

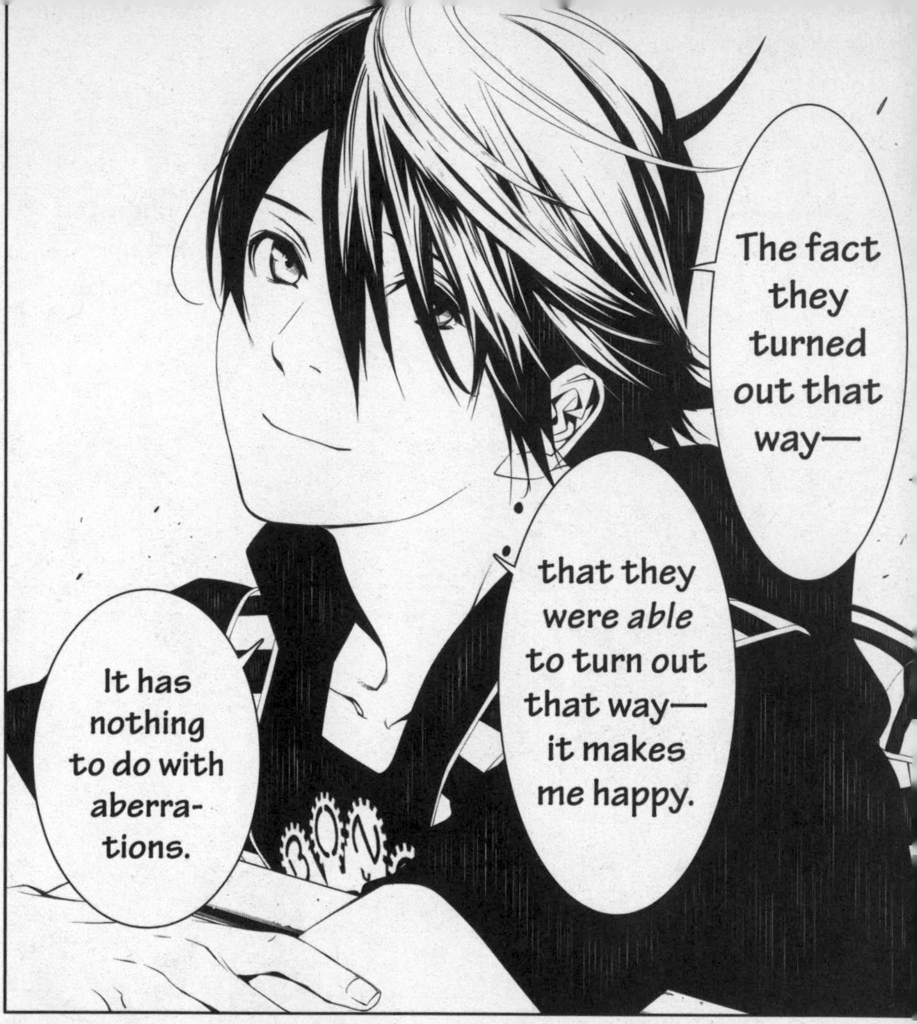
The fact they turned out that way—
that they were *able* to turn out that way— it makes me happy.
It has nothing to do with aberrations.

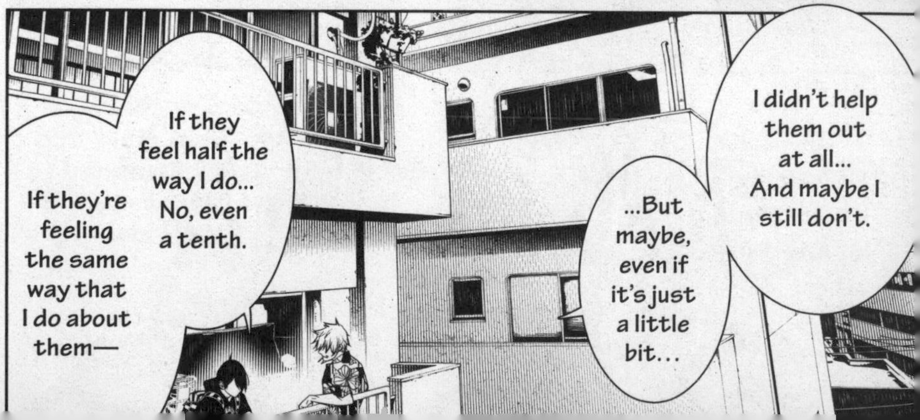
I didn't help them out at all... And maybe I still don't.
...But maybe, even if it's just a little bit...
If they feel half the way I do... No, even a tenth.
If they're feeling the same way that I do about them—

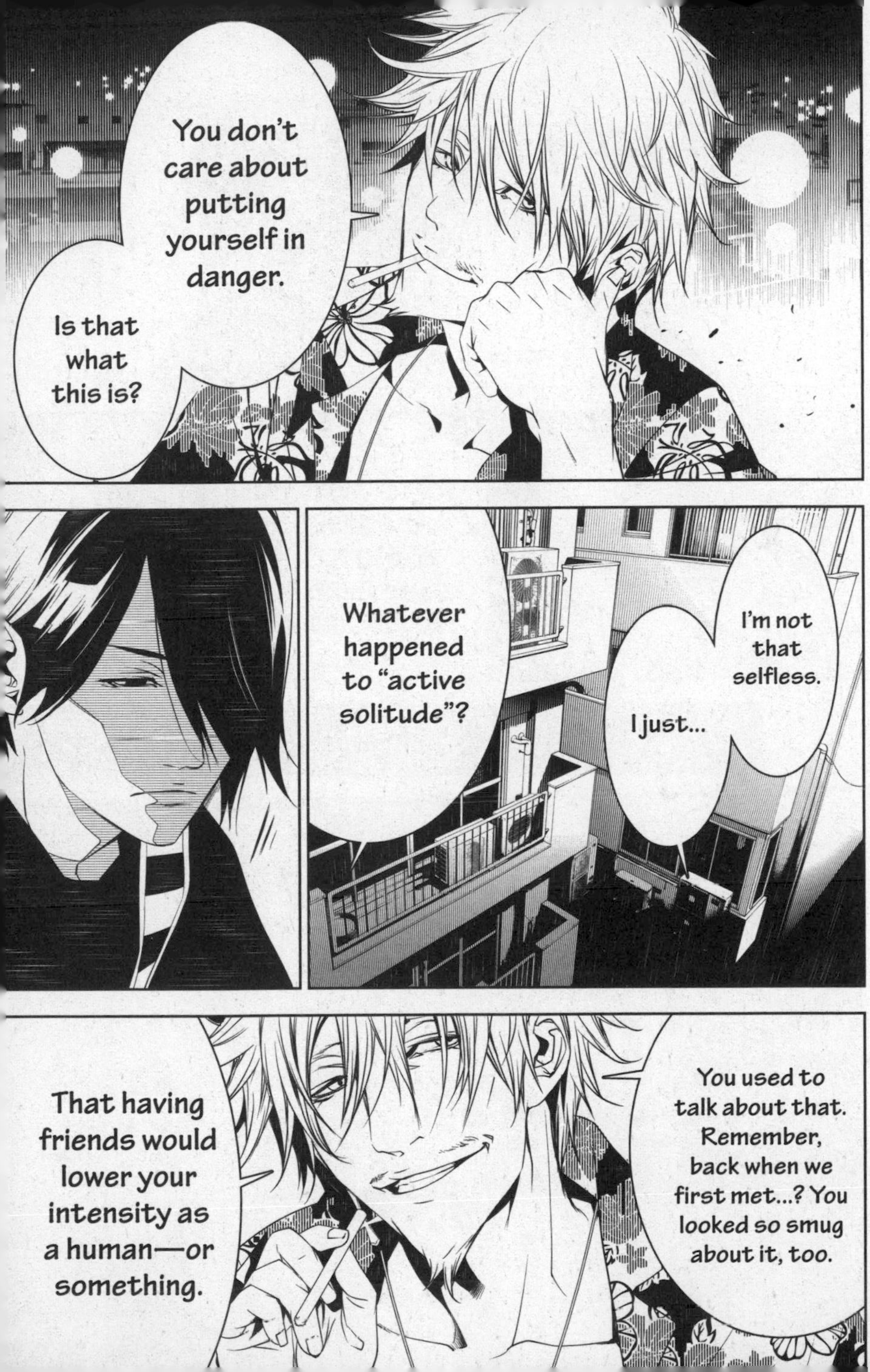
You don't care about putting yourself in danger.
Is that what this is?
I'm not that selfless.
I just...
Whatever happened to "active solitude"?
You used to talk about that. Remember, back when we first met...? You looked so smug about it, too.
That having friends would lower your intensity as a human—or something.

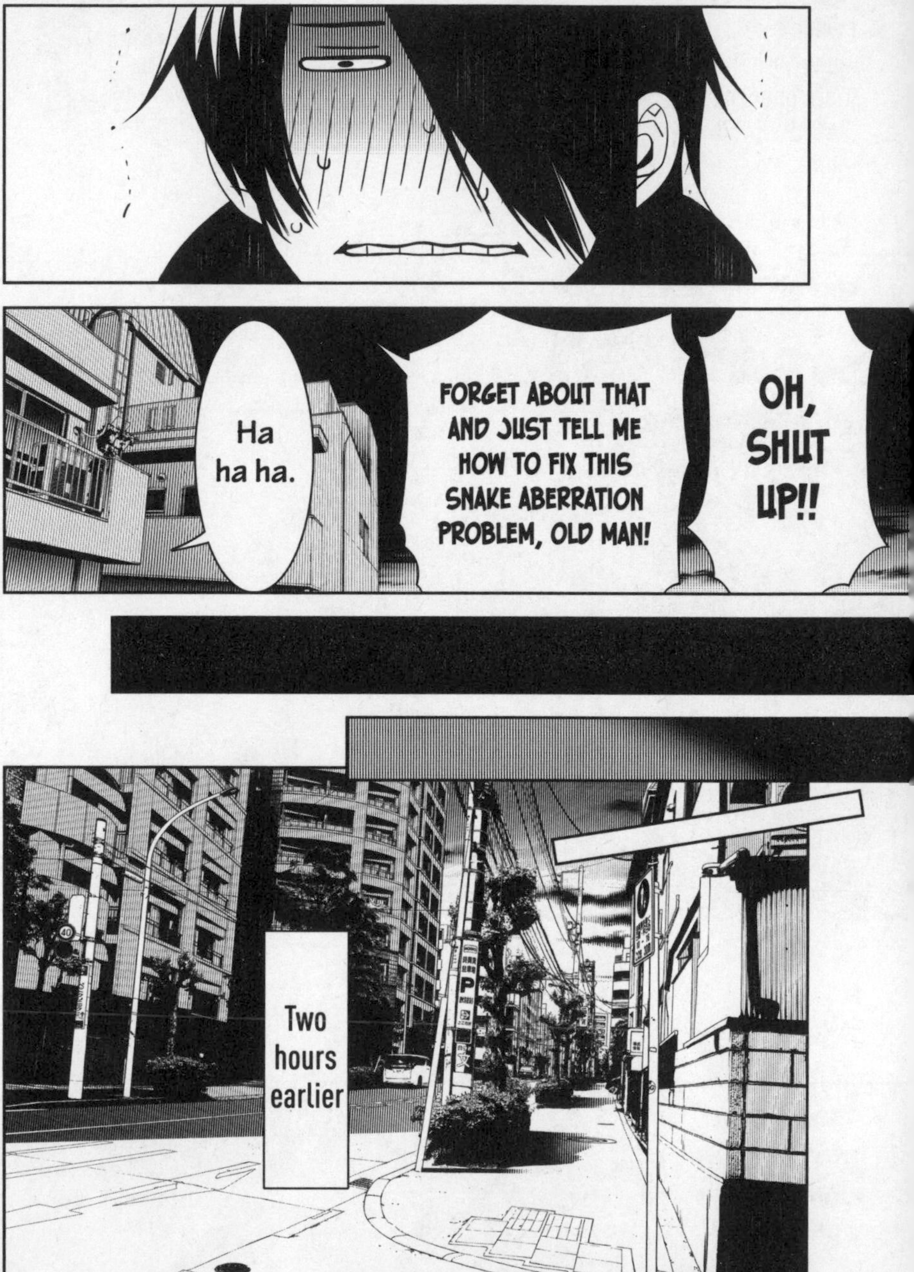
OH, SHUT UP!!
FORGET ABOUT THAT AND JUST TELL ME HOW TO FIX THIS SNAKE ABERRATION PROBLEM, OLD MAN!
Ha ha ha.
Two hours earlier

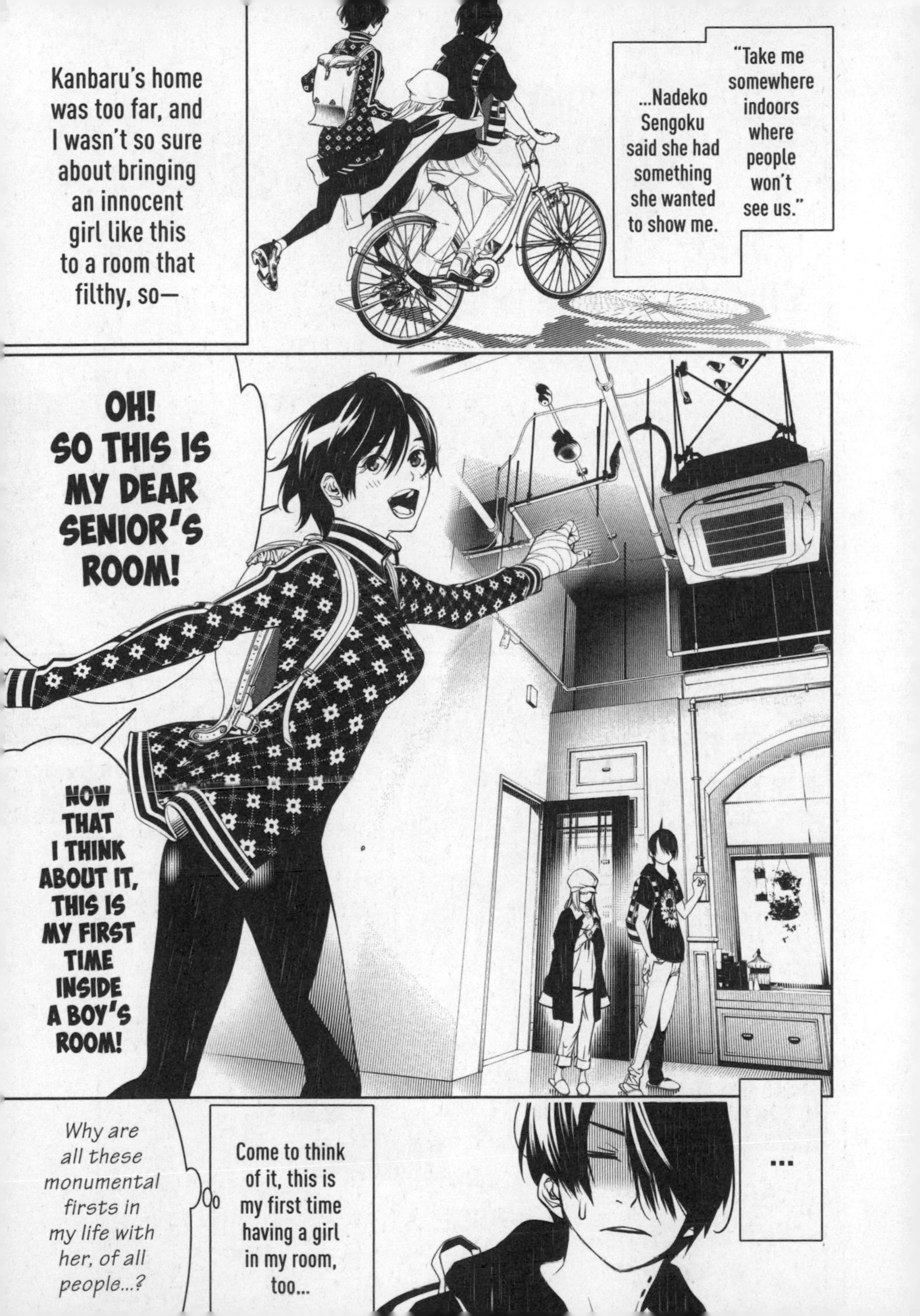
"Take me somewhere indoors where people won't see us."
...Nadeko Sengoku said she had something she wanted to show me.
Kanbaru's home was too far, and I wasn't so sure about bringing an innocent girl like this to a room that filthy, so—
OH! SO THIS IS MY DEAR SENIOR'S ROOM!
NOW THAT I THINK ABOUT IT, THIS IS MY FIRST TIME INSIDE A BOY'S ROOM!
...
Come to think of it, this is my first time having a girl in my room, too...
Why are all these monumental firsts in my life with her, of all people...?

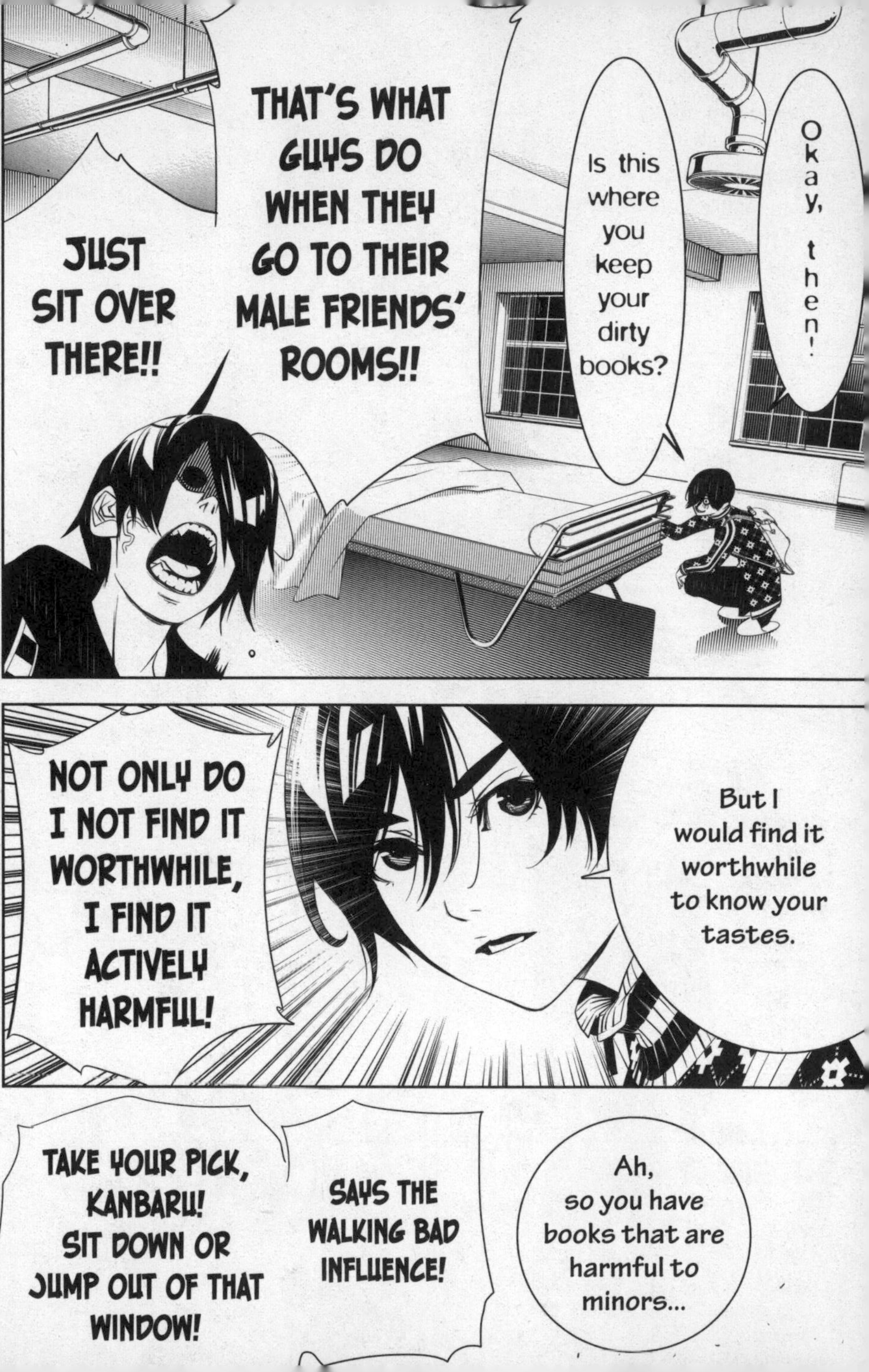
Okay, then!
Is this where you keep your dirty books?
THAT'S WHAT GUYS DO WHEN THEY GO TO THEIR MALE FRIENDS' ROOMS!!
JUST SIT OVER THERE!!
But I would find it worthwhile to know your tastes.
NOT ONLY DO I NOT FIND IT WORTHWHILE, I FIND IT ACTIVELY HARMFUL!
Ah, so you have books that are harmful to minors...
SAYS THE WALKING BAD INFLUENCE!
TAKE YOUR PICK, KANBARU! SIT DOWN OR JUMP OUT OF THAT WINDOW!

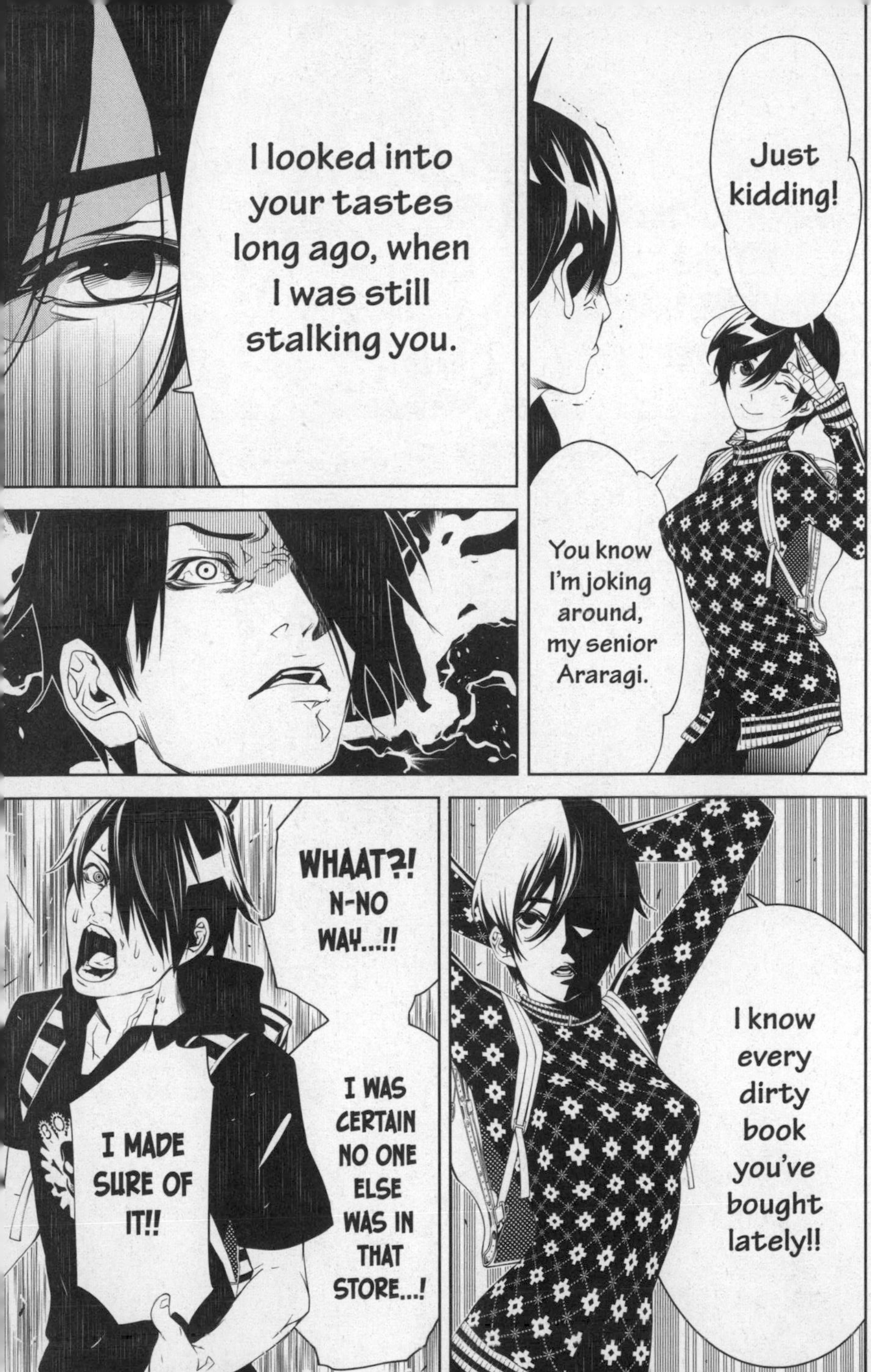
Just kidding!
You know I'm joking around, my senior Araragi.
I looked into your tastes long ago, when I was still stalking you.
I know every dirty book you've bought lately!!
WHAAT?! N-NO WAY...!!
I WAS CERTAIN NO ONE ELSE WAS IN THAT STORE...!
I MADE SURE OF IT!!

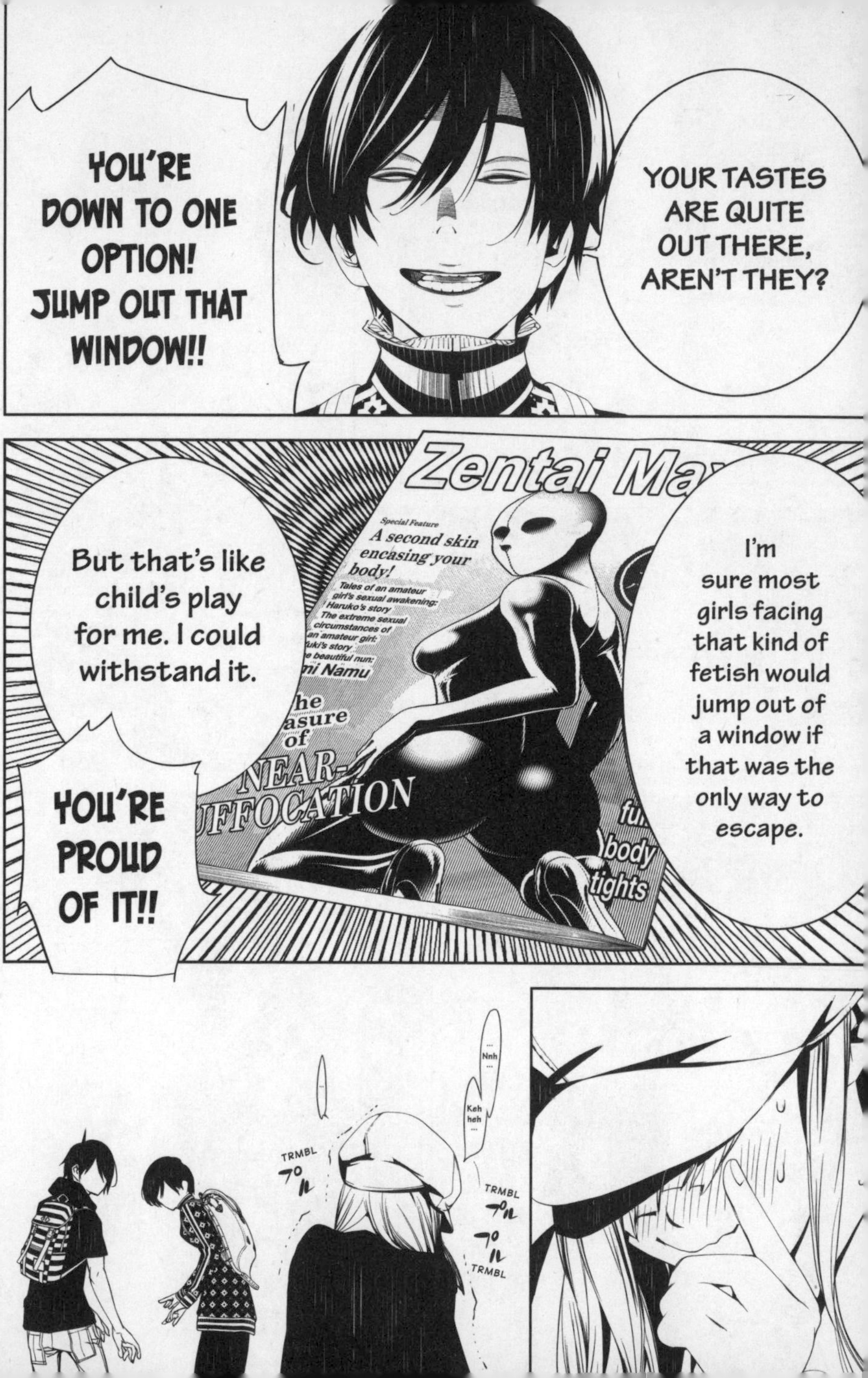
YOUR TASTES ARE QUITE OUT THERE, AREN'T THEY?
YOU'RE DOWN TO ONE OPTION! JUMP OUT THAT WINDOW!!
I'm sure most girls facing that kind of fetish would jump out of a window if that was the only way to escape.
Zentai Ma
Special Feature
A second skin encasing your body!
Tales of an amateur girl's sexual awakening: Haruko's story
The extreme sexual circumstances of an amateur girl: Yuki's story
NEAR-
UFFOCATION
body tights
But that's like child's play for me. I could withstand it.
YOU'RE PROUD OF IT!!
...Nnh...
Keh heh...
...!
TRMBL
TRMBL
TRMBL

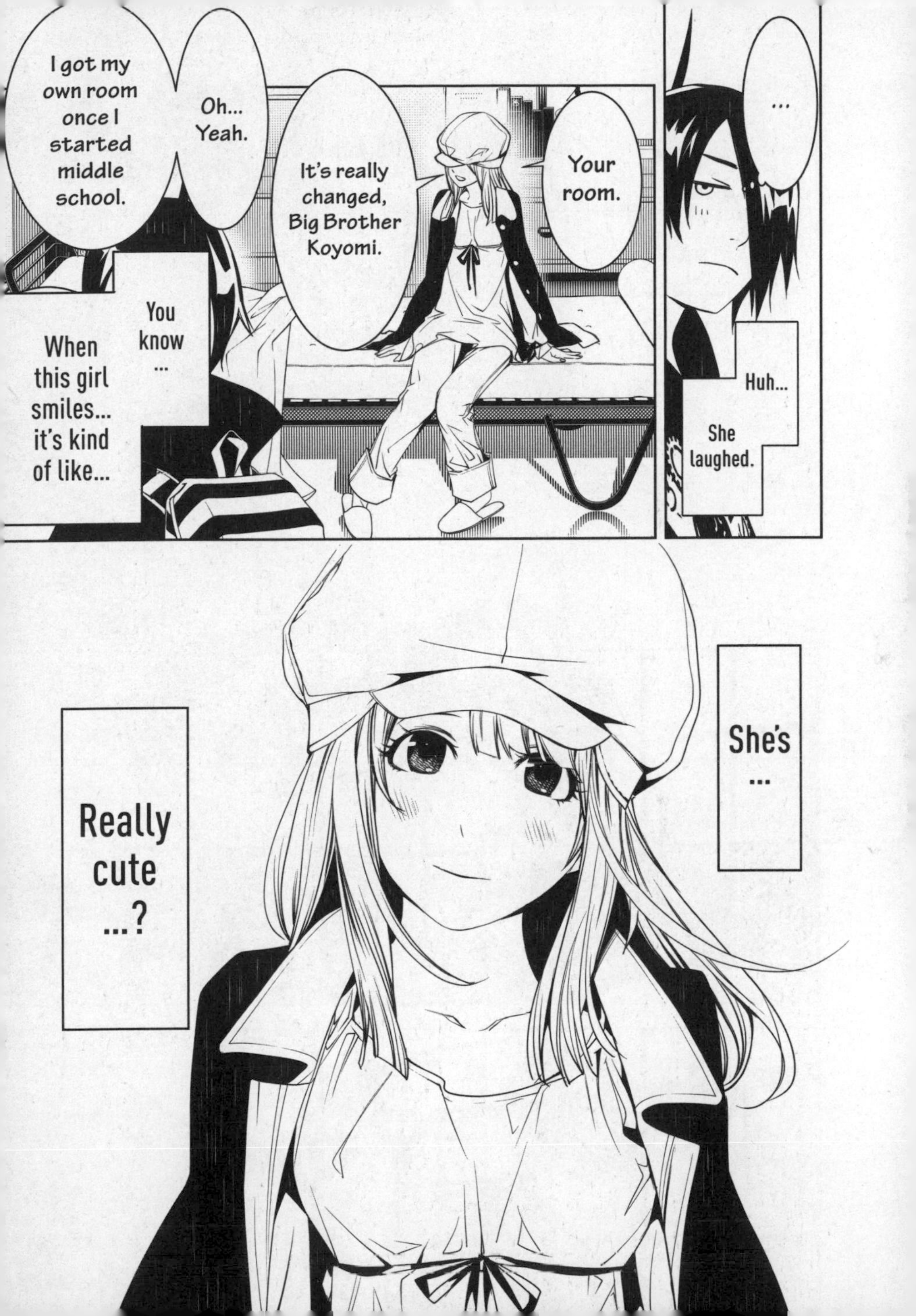
...
Huh...
She laughed.
Your room.
It's really changed, Big Brother Koyomi.
Oh... Yeah.
I got my own room once I started middle school.
You know ...
When this girl smiles... it's kind of like...
She's ...
Really cute ...?

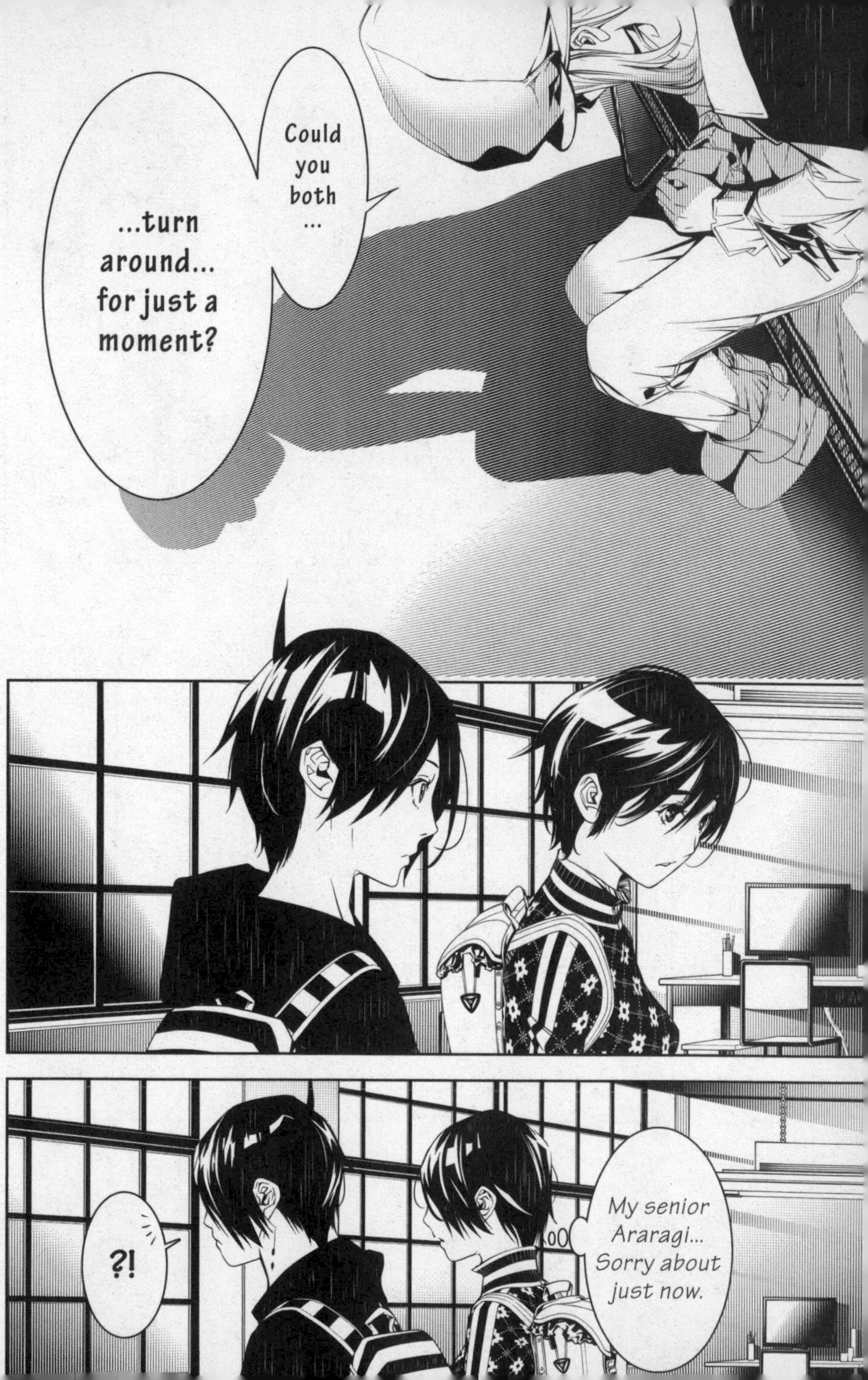
Could you both ...
...turn around... for just a moment?
My senior Araragi... Sorry about just now.
?!

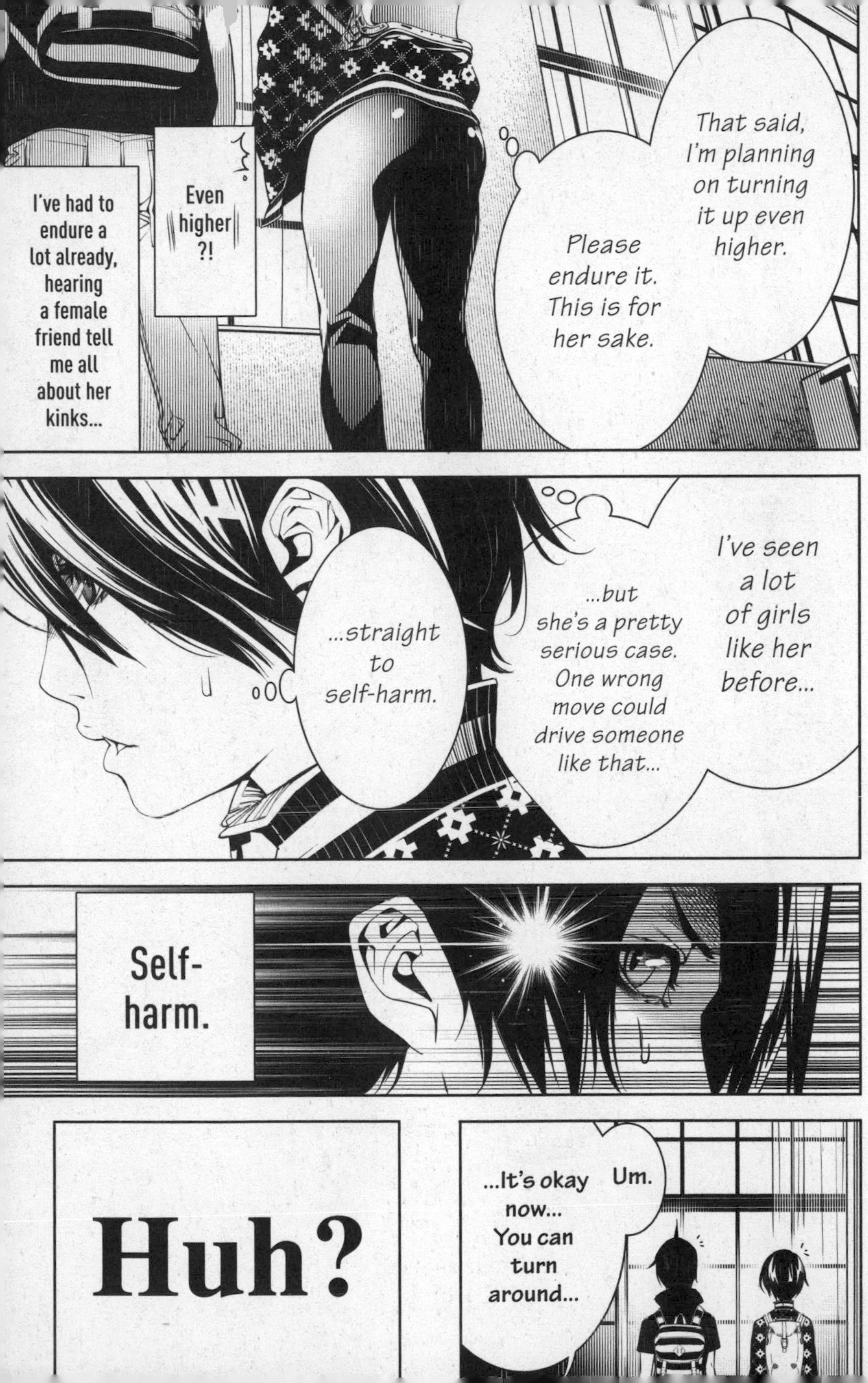
That said, I'm planning on turning it up even higher.
Please endure it. This is for her sake.
Even higher?!
I've had to endure a lot already, hearing a female friend tell me all about her kinks...
I've seen a lot of girls like her before...
...but she's a pretty serious case. One wrong move could drive someone like that...
...straight to self-harm.
Self-harm.
Um.
...It's okay now... You can turn around...
Huh?

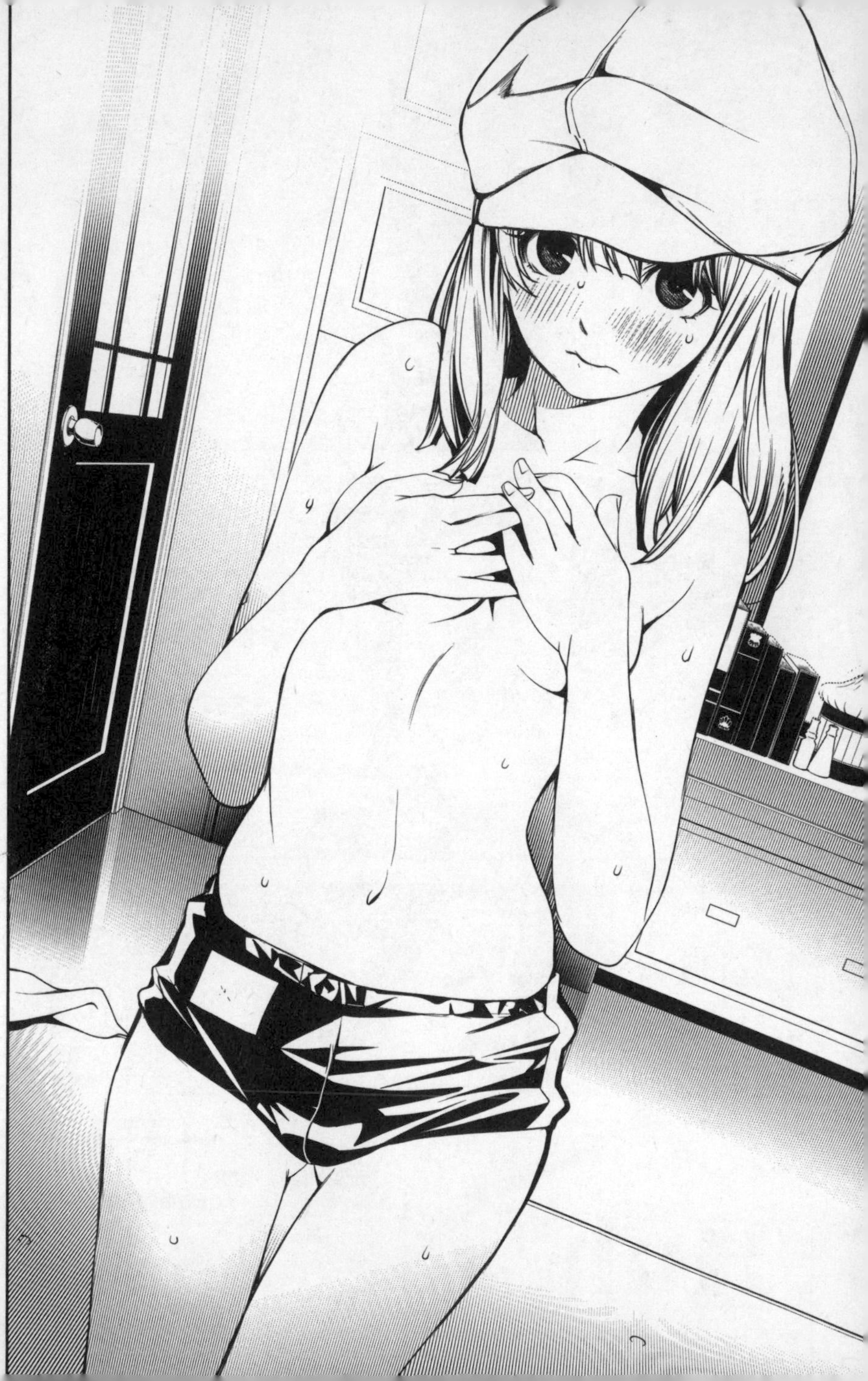

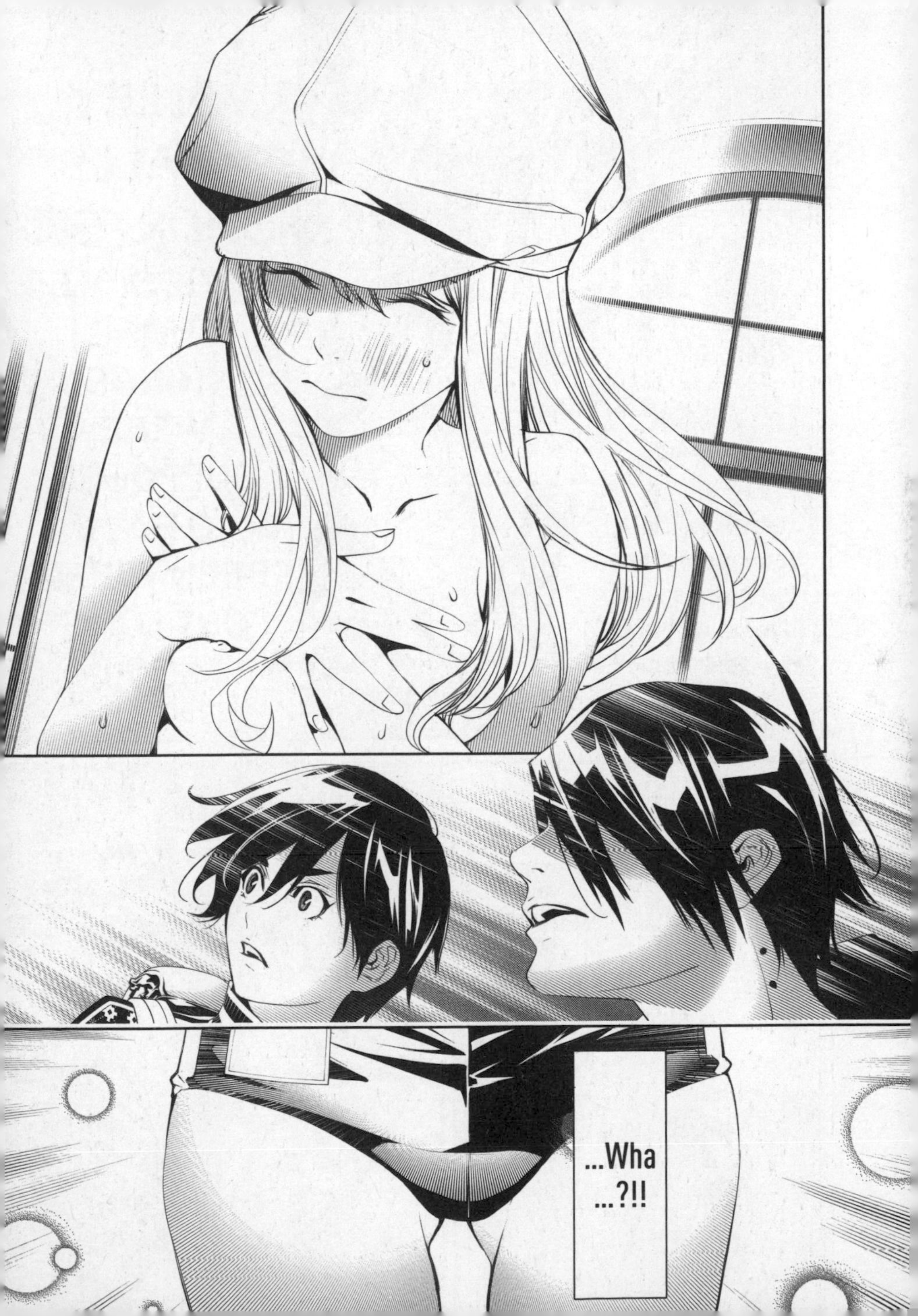
...Wha
...?!!

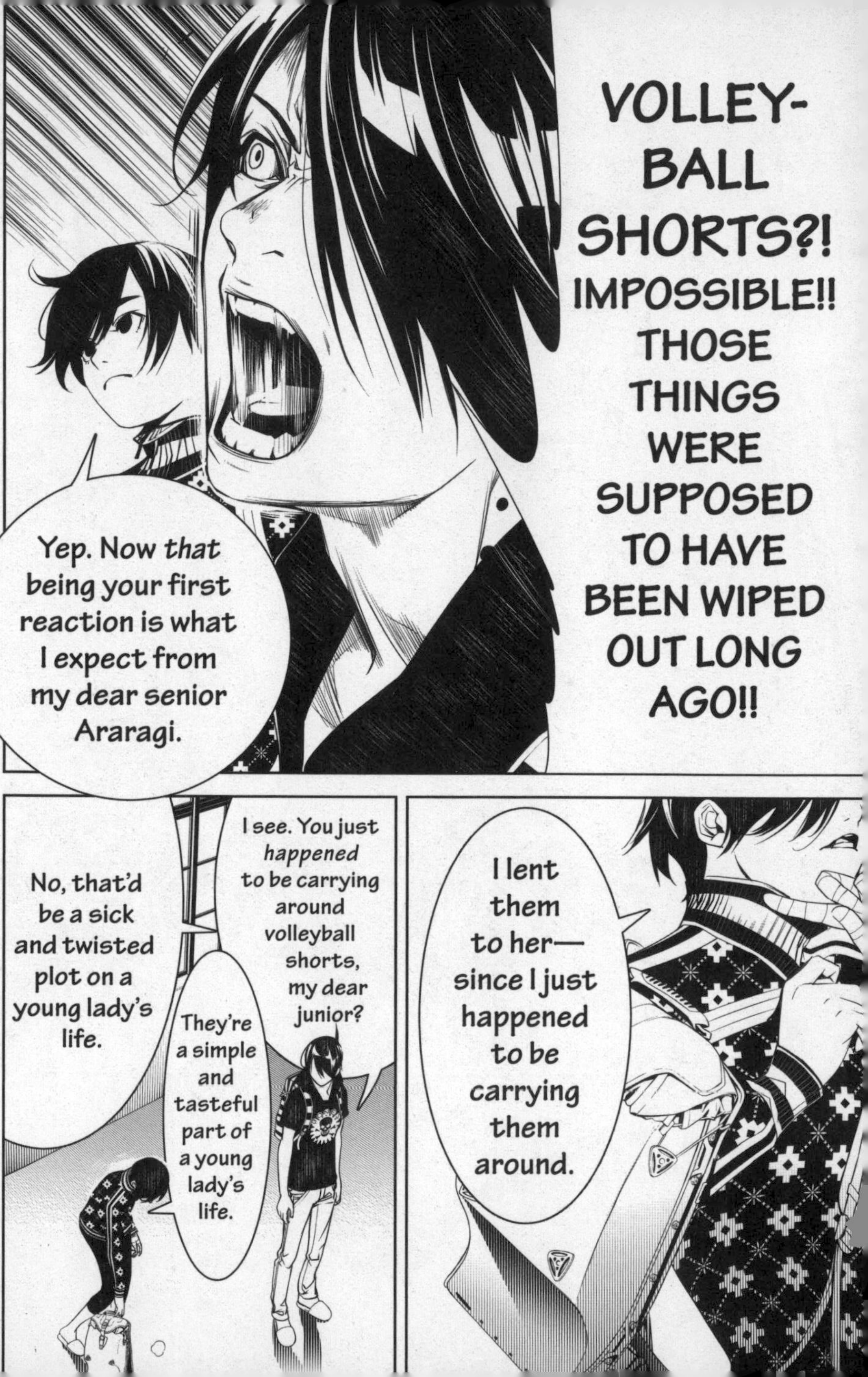
VOLLEY-BALL SHORTS?! IMPOSSIBLE!! THOSE THINGS WERE SUPPOSED TO HAVE BEEN WIPED OUT LONG AGO!!
Yep. Now *that* being your first reaction is what I expect from my dear senior Araragi.
I lent them to her—since I just happened to be carrying them around.
I see. You just *happened* to be carrying around volleyball shorts, my dear junior?
No, that'd be a sick and twisted plot on a young lady's life.
They're a simple and tasteful part of a young lady's life.

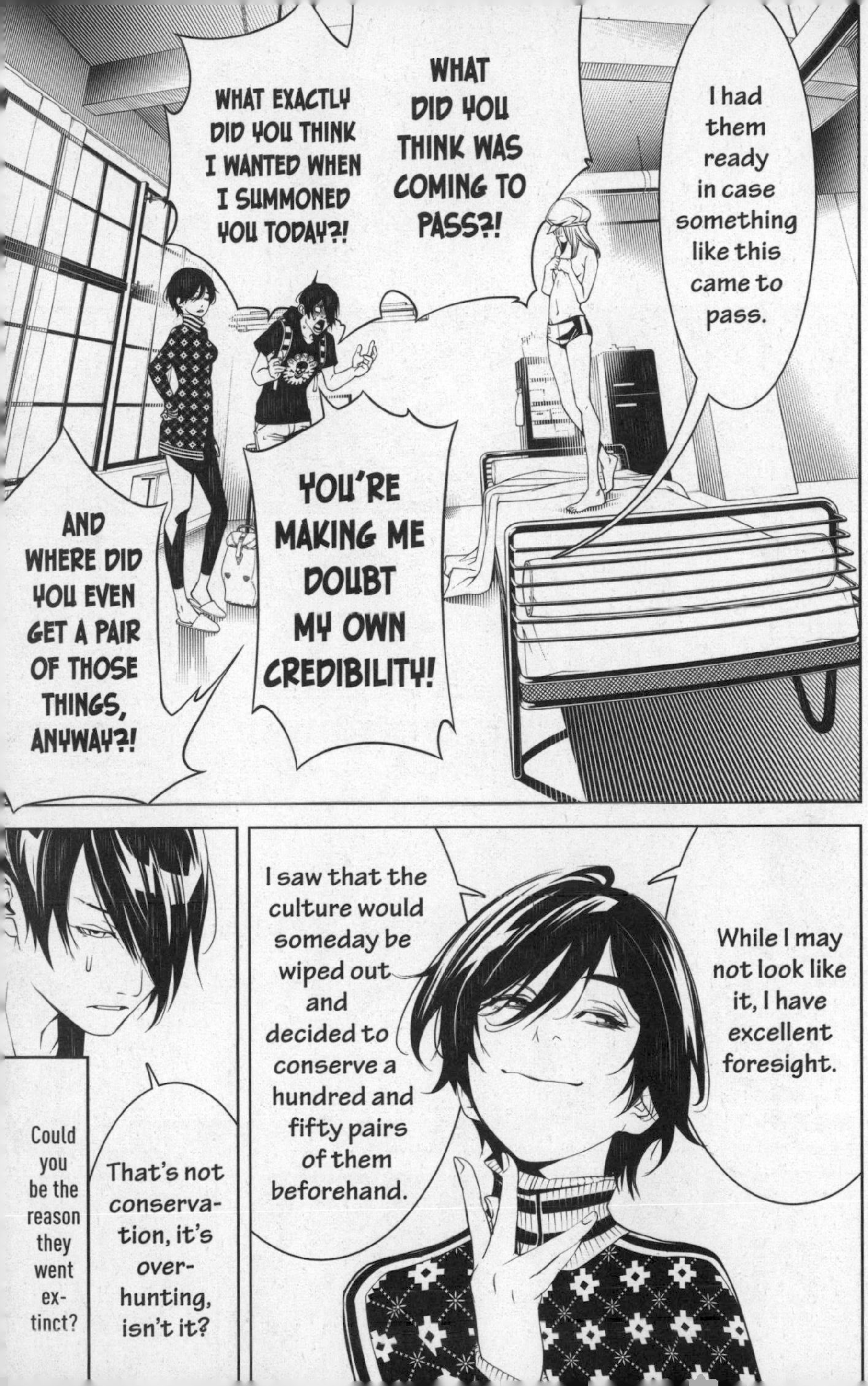
I had them ready in case something like this came to pass.
WHAT DID YOU THINK WAS COMING TO PASS?!
WHAT EXACTLY DID YOU THINK I WANTED WHEN I SUMMONED YOU TODAY?!
YOU'RE MAKING ME DOUBT MY OWN CREDIBILITY!
AND WHERE DID YOU EVEN GET A PAIR OF THOSE THINGS, ANYWAY?!
While I may not look like it, I have excellent foresight.
I saw that the culture would someday be wiped out and decided to conserve a hundred and fifty pairs of them beforehand.
That's not conserva-tion, it's over-hunting, isn't it?
Could you be the reason they went ex-tinct?

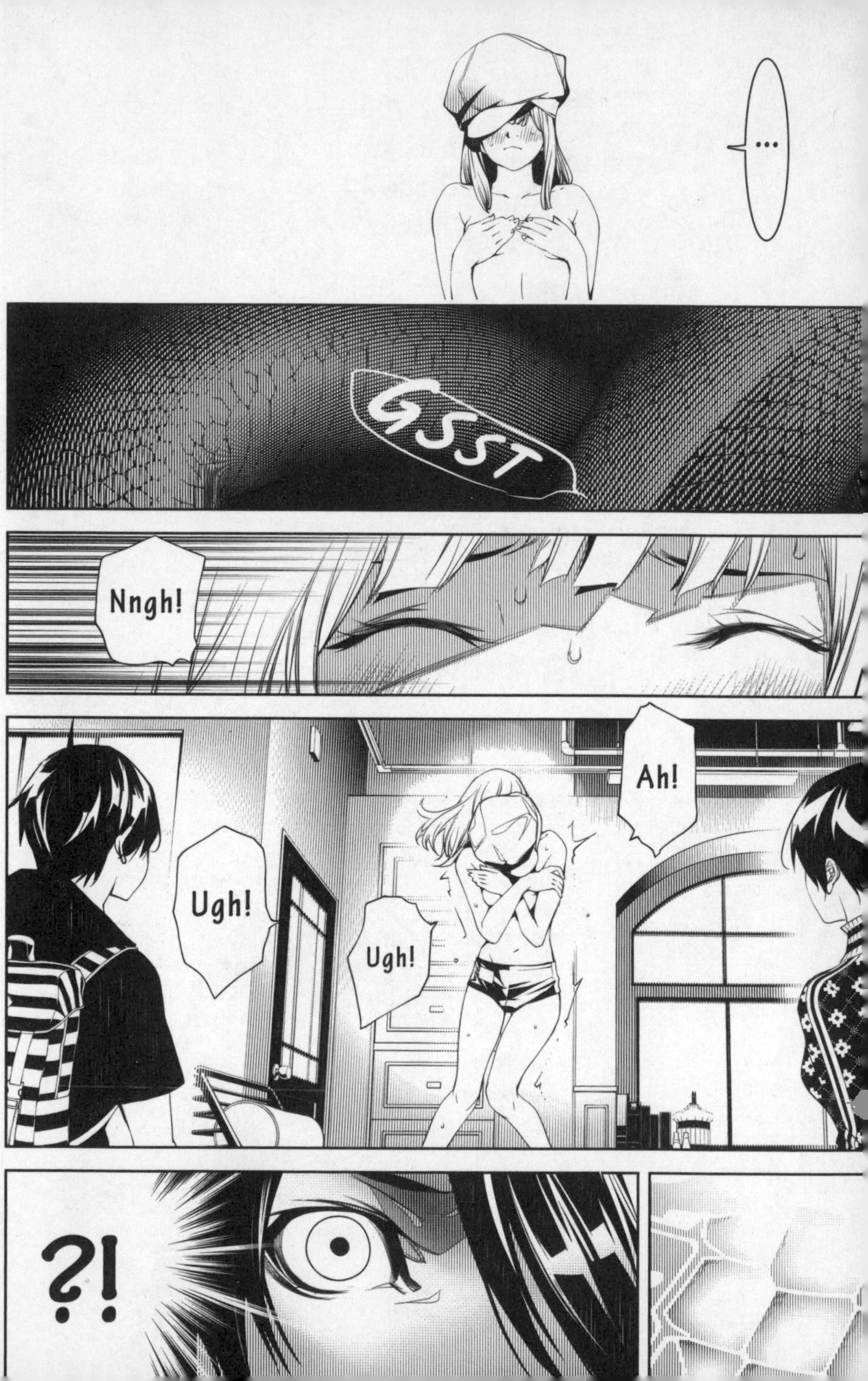
...
GSST
Nngh!
Ah!
Ugh!
Ugh!
?!

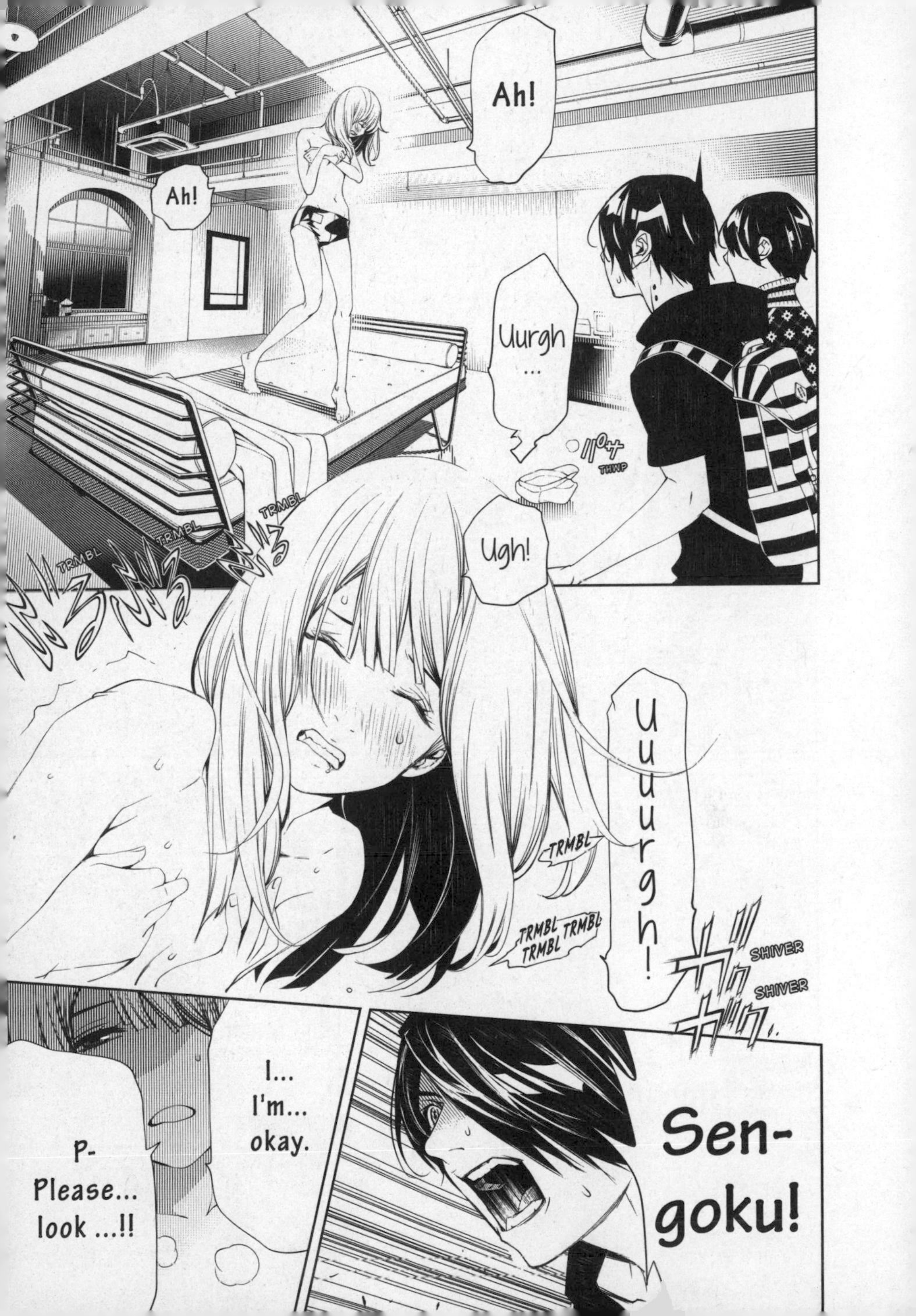
Ah!
Ah!
Uurgh ...
THWP
TRMBL
TRMBL
TRMBL
Ugh!
Uuurgh!
SHIVER
SHIVER
TRMBL
TRMBL TRMBL TRMBL
Sen-goku!
I... I'm... okay.
P- Please... look ...!!

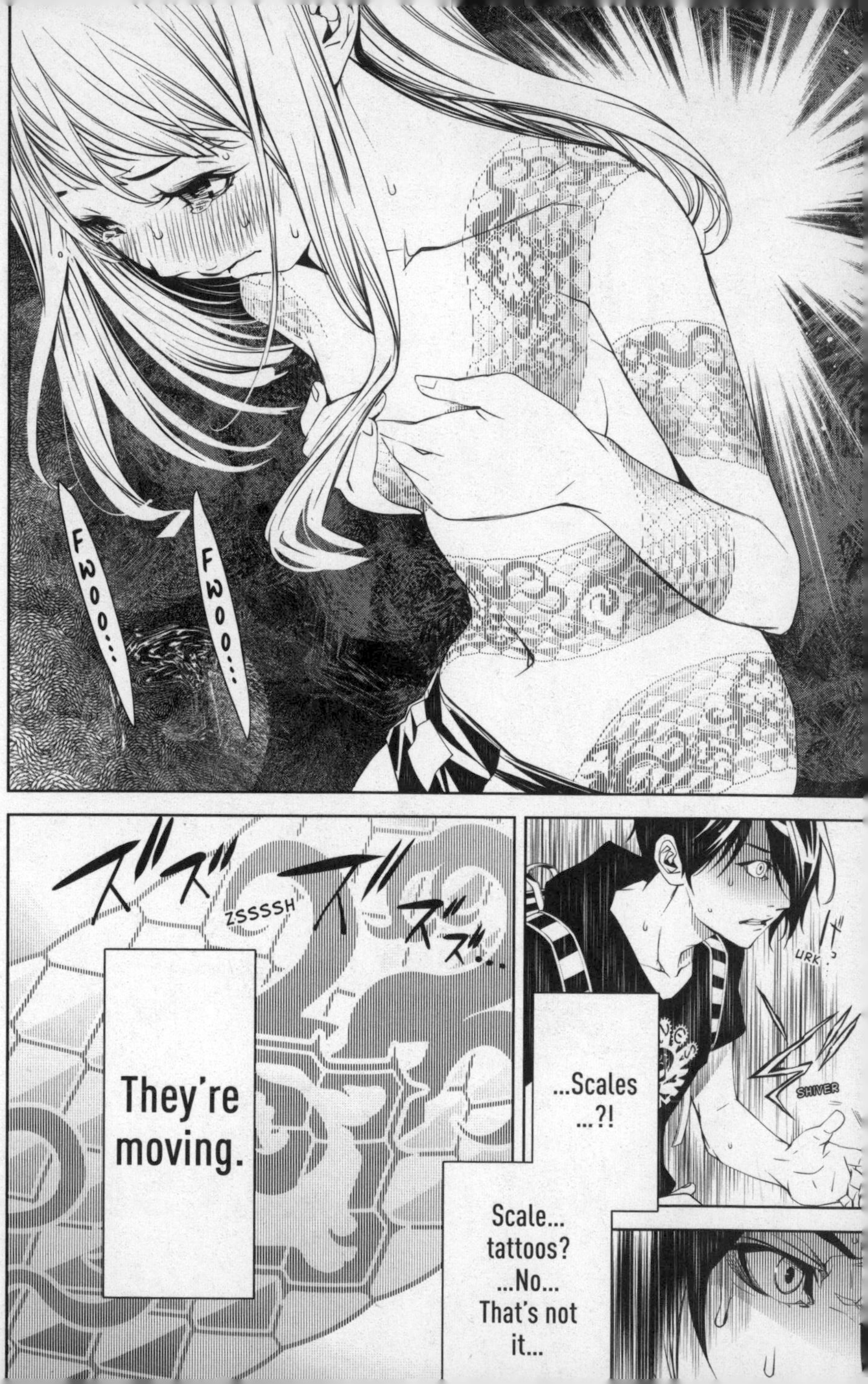
FWOOO...
FWOOO...
URK
SHIVER
...Scales ...?!
Scale... tattoos? ...No... That's not it...
ZSSSSH
They're moving.

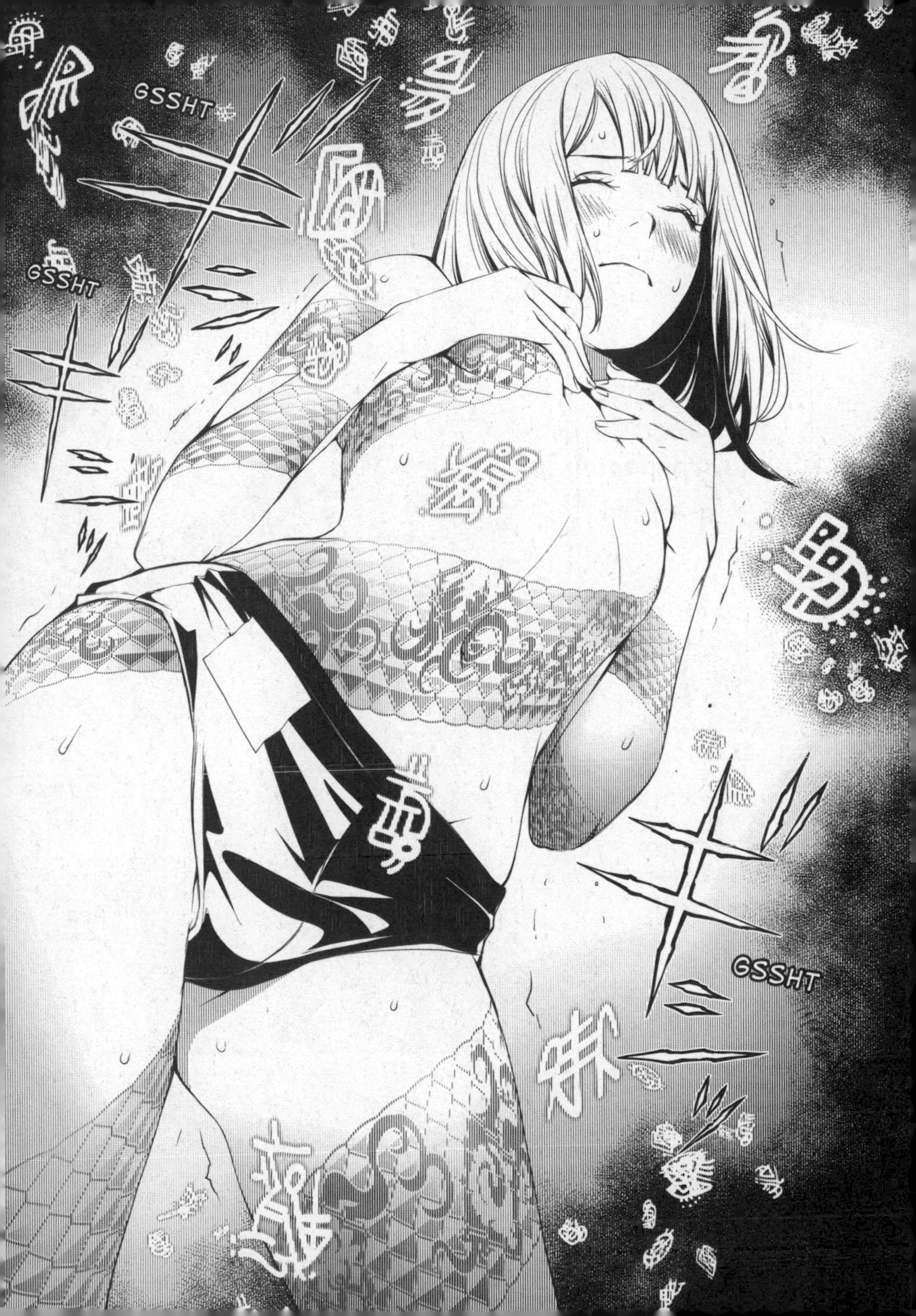
GSSHT
GSSHT
GSSHT

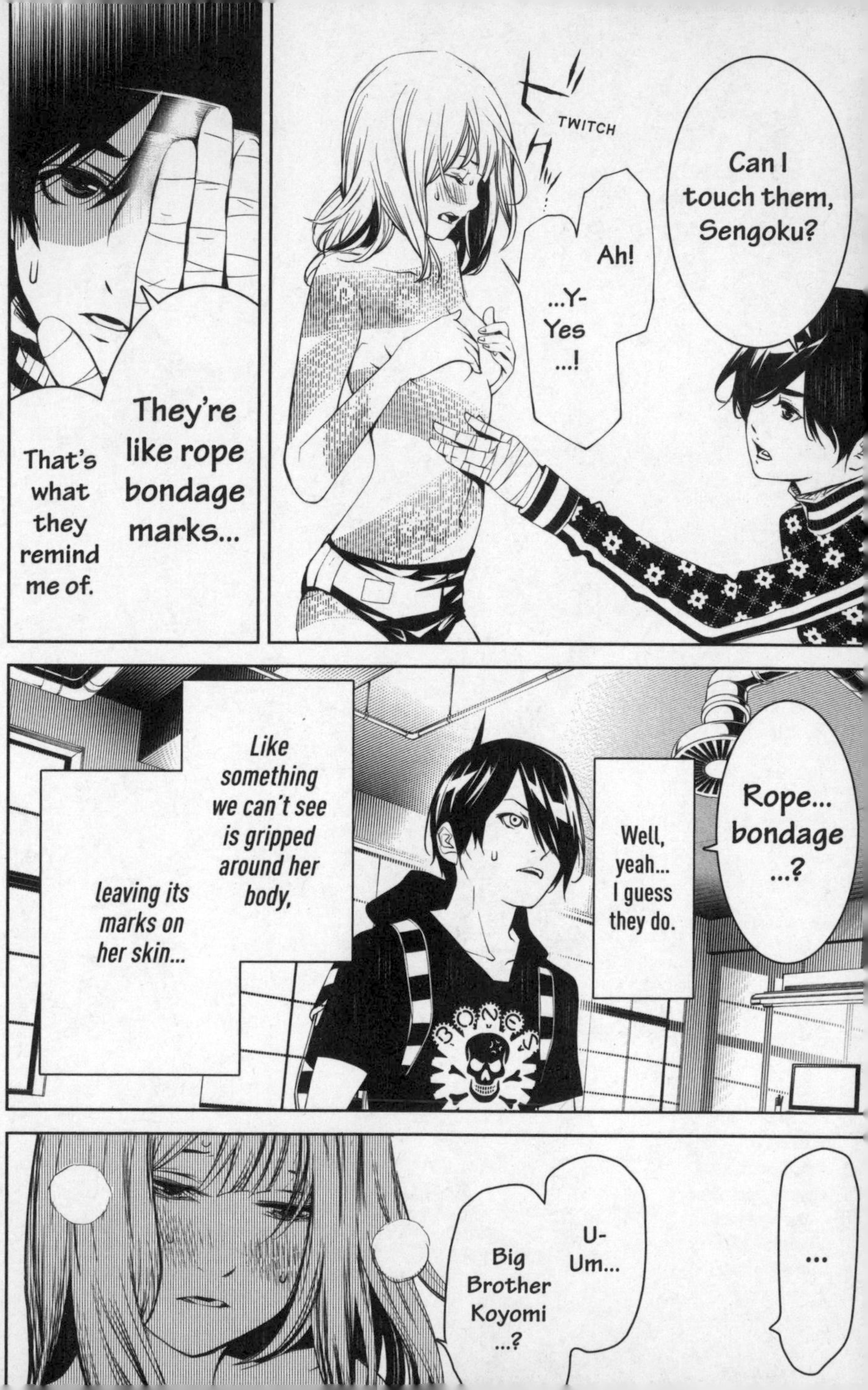
Can I touch them, Sengoku?
TWITCH
Ah!
...Y- Yes ...!
They're like rope bondage marks...
That's what they remind me of.
Rope... bondage ...?
Well, yeah... I guess they do.
Like something we can't see is gripped around her body,
leaving its marks on her skin...
...
U- Um...
Big Brother Koyomi ...?

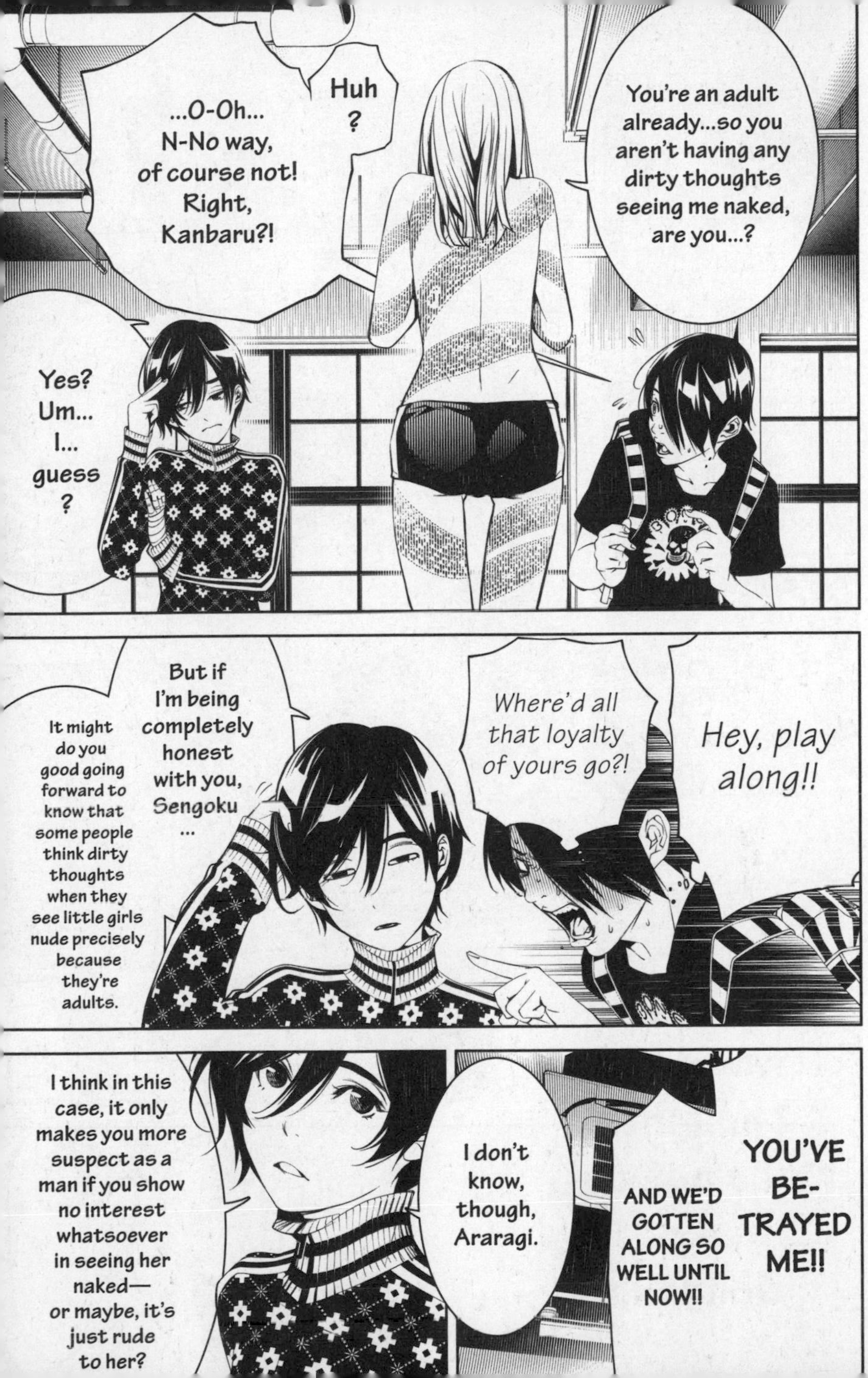
You're an adult already...so you aren't having any dirty thoughts seeing me naked, are you...?
Huh?
...O-Oh... N-No way, of course not! Right, Kanbaru?!
Yes? Um... I... guess?
Hey, play along!!
Where'd all that loyalty of yours go?!
But if I'm being completely honest with you, Sengoku...
It might do you good going forward to know that some people think dirty thoughts when they see little girls nude precisely because they're adults.
YOU'VE BE-TRAYED ME!!
AND WE'D GOTTEN ALONG SO WELL UNTIL NOW!!
I don't know, though, Araragi.
I think in this case, it only makes you more suspect as a man if you show no interest whatsoever in seeing her naked—or maybe, it's just rude to her?

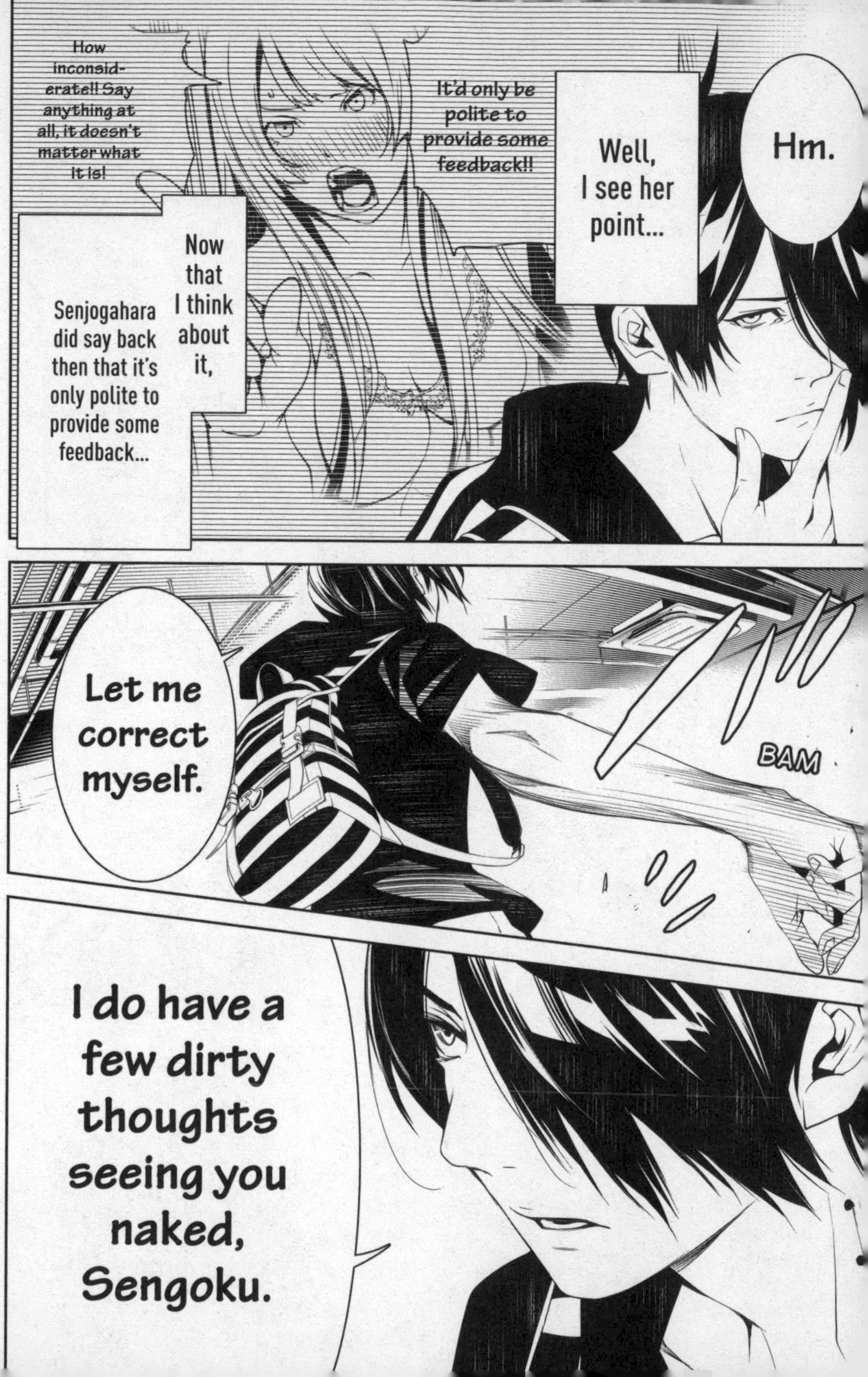
Hm.
Well, I see her point...
It'd only be polite to provide some feedback!!
How inconsiderate!! Say anything at all, it doesn't matter what it is!
Now that I think about it,
Senjogahara did say back then that it's only polite to provide some feedback...
BAM
Let me correct myself.
I do have a few dirty thoughts seeing you naked, Sengoku.

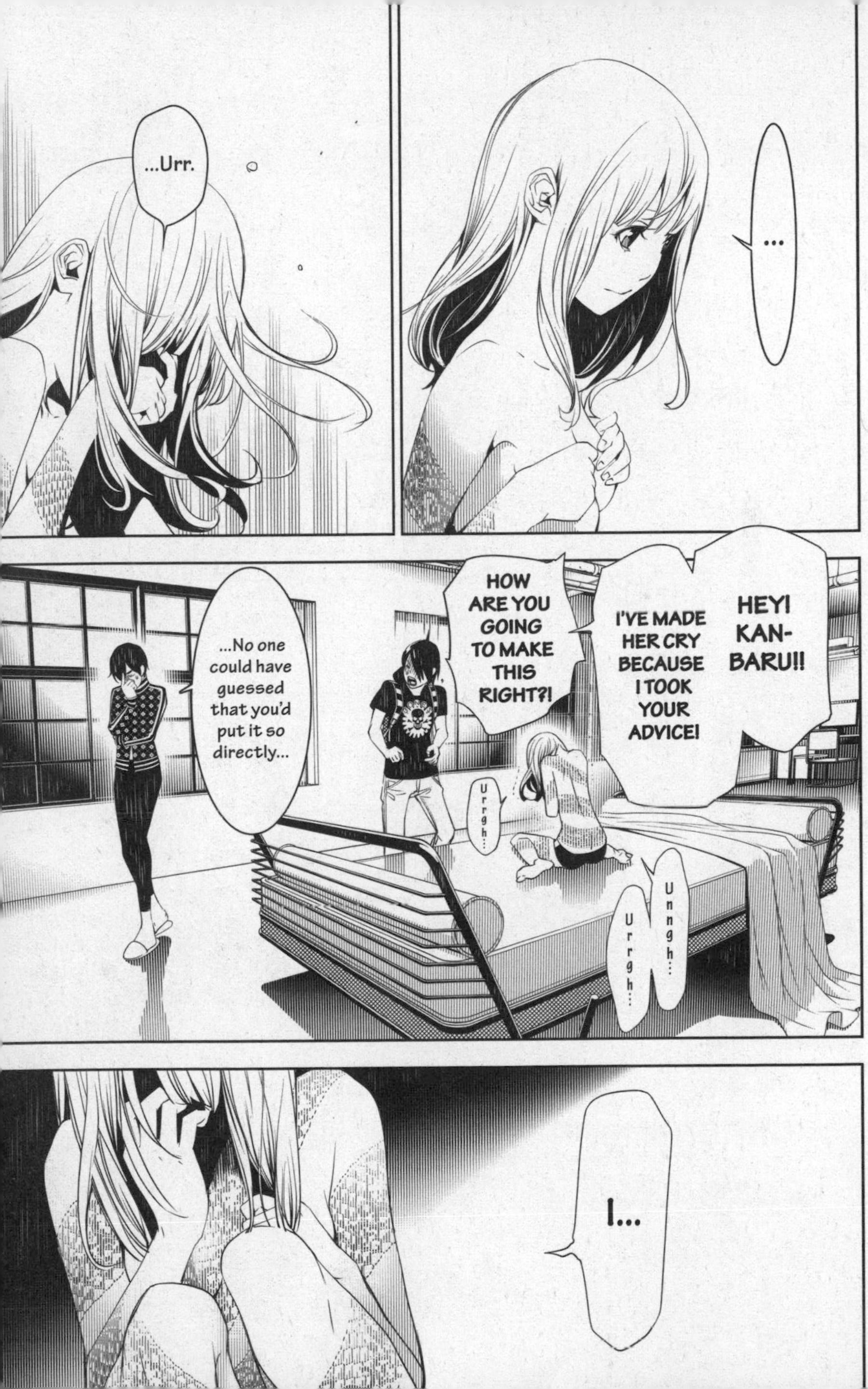
...
...Urr.
HEY! KAN-BARU!!
I'VE MADE HER CRY BECAUSE I TOOK YOUR ADVICE!
HOW ARE YOU GOING TO MAKE THIS RIGHT?!
Unngh...
Urrgh...
Urrgh...
...No one could have guessed that you'd put it so directly...
I...

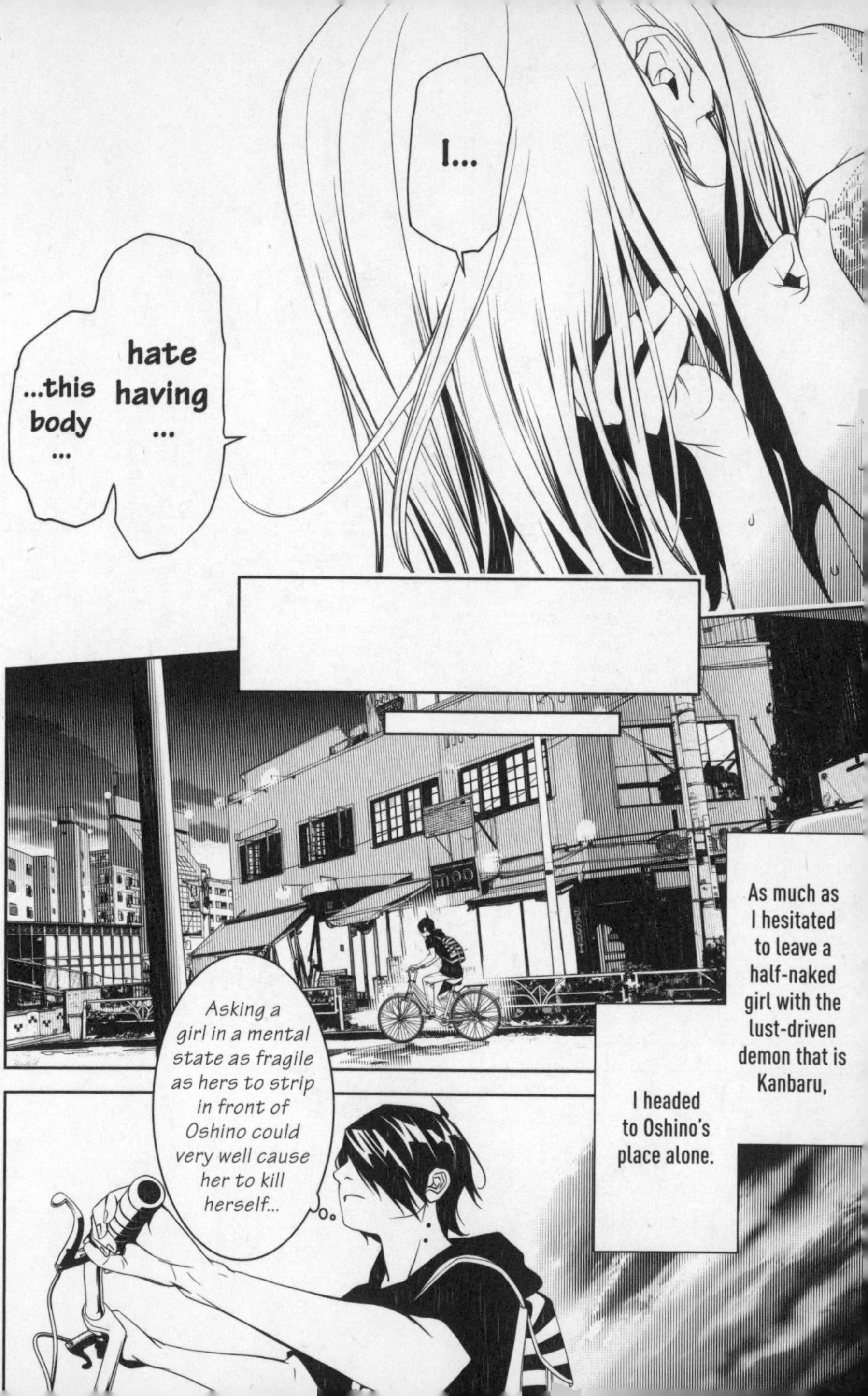
I...
hate having ...
...this body ...
As much as I hesitated to leave a half-naked girl with the lust-driven demon that is Kanbaru,
I headed to Oshino's place alone.
Asking a girl in a mental state as fragile as hers to strip in front of Oshino could very well cause her to kill herself...

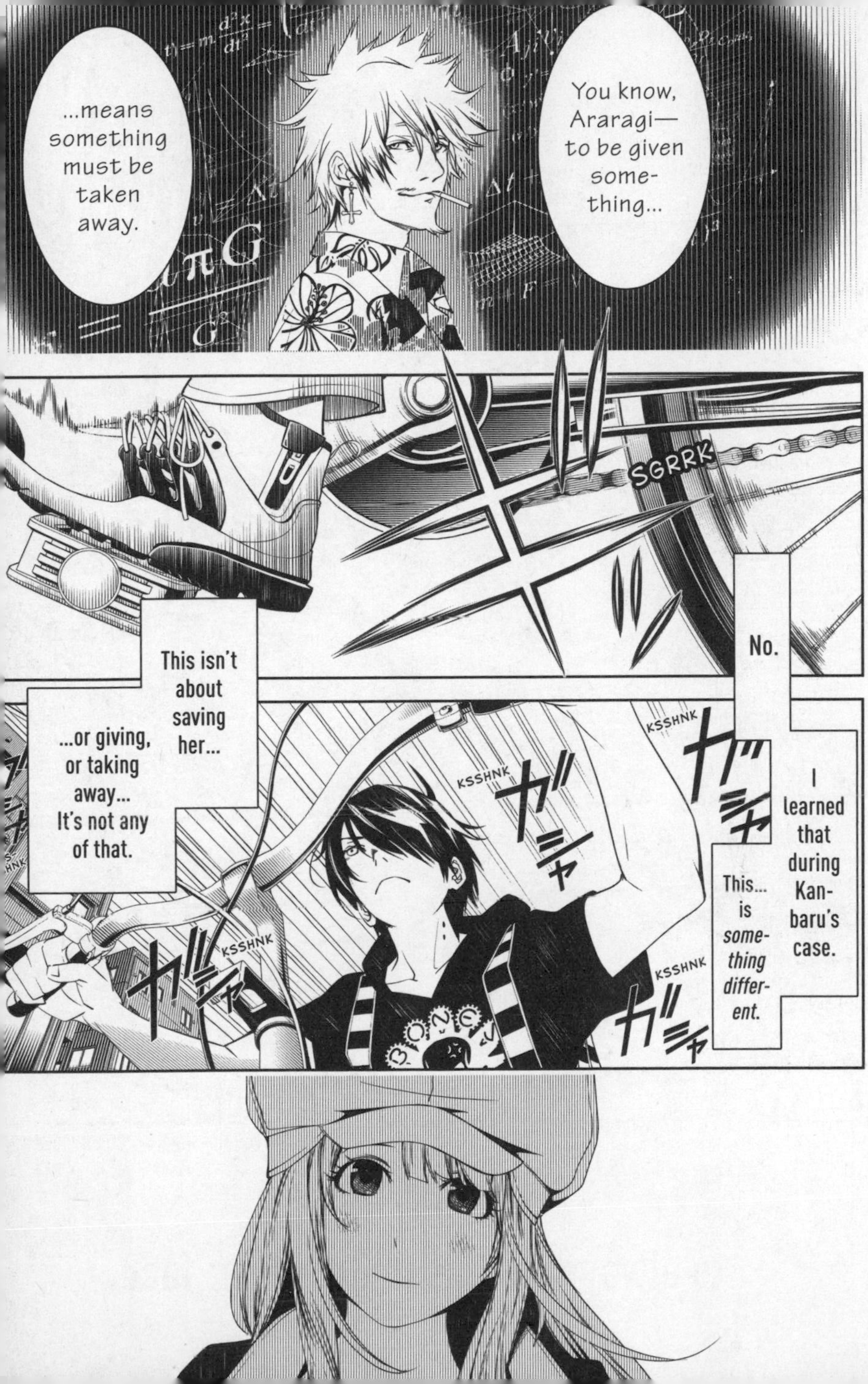
You know, Araragi—to be given some-thing...
...means something must be taken away.
SGRRK
No.
I learned that during Kan-baru's case.
KSSHNK
This... is *some-thing differ-ent.*
KSSHNK
KSSHNK
KSSHNK
This isn't about saving her...
...or giving, or taking away... It's not any of that.

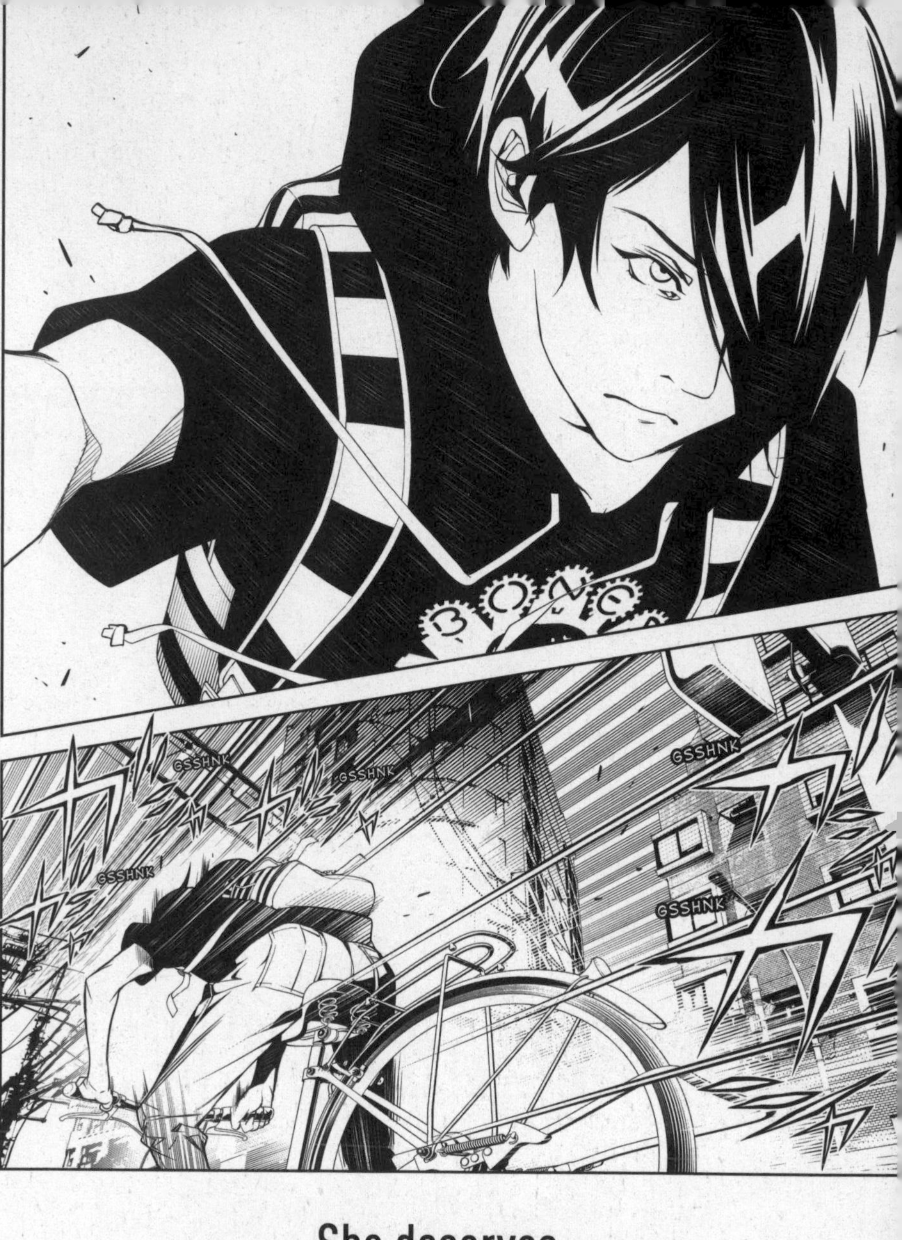
BONE
GSSHNK
GSSHNK
GSSHNK
GSSHNK

She deserves...

...to always wear a smile on her face.

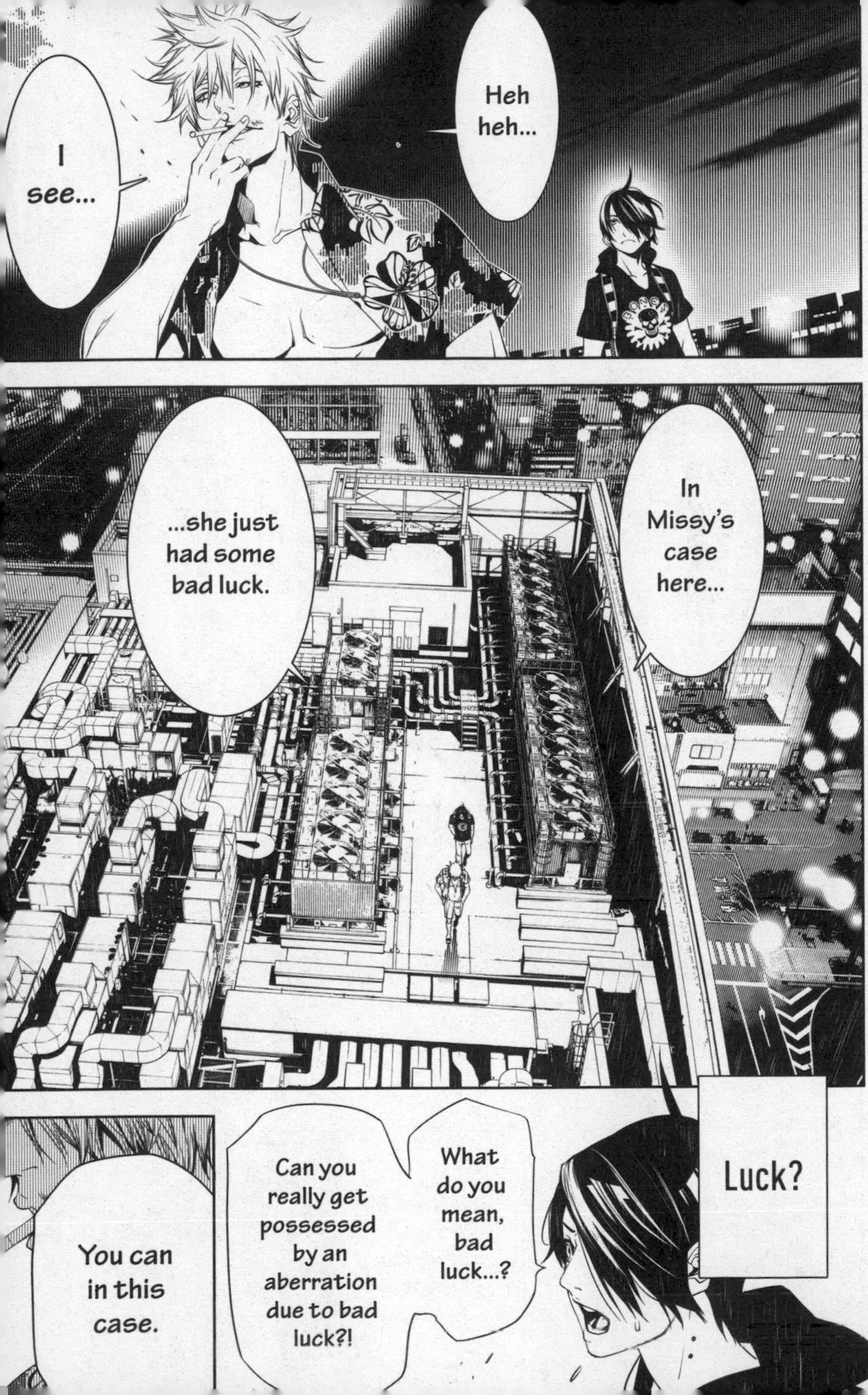
Heh heh...
I see...
In Missy's case here...
...she just had some bad luck.
Luck?
What do you mean, bad luck...?
Can you really get possessed by an aberration due to bad luck?!
You can in this case.

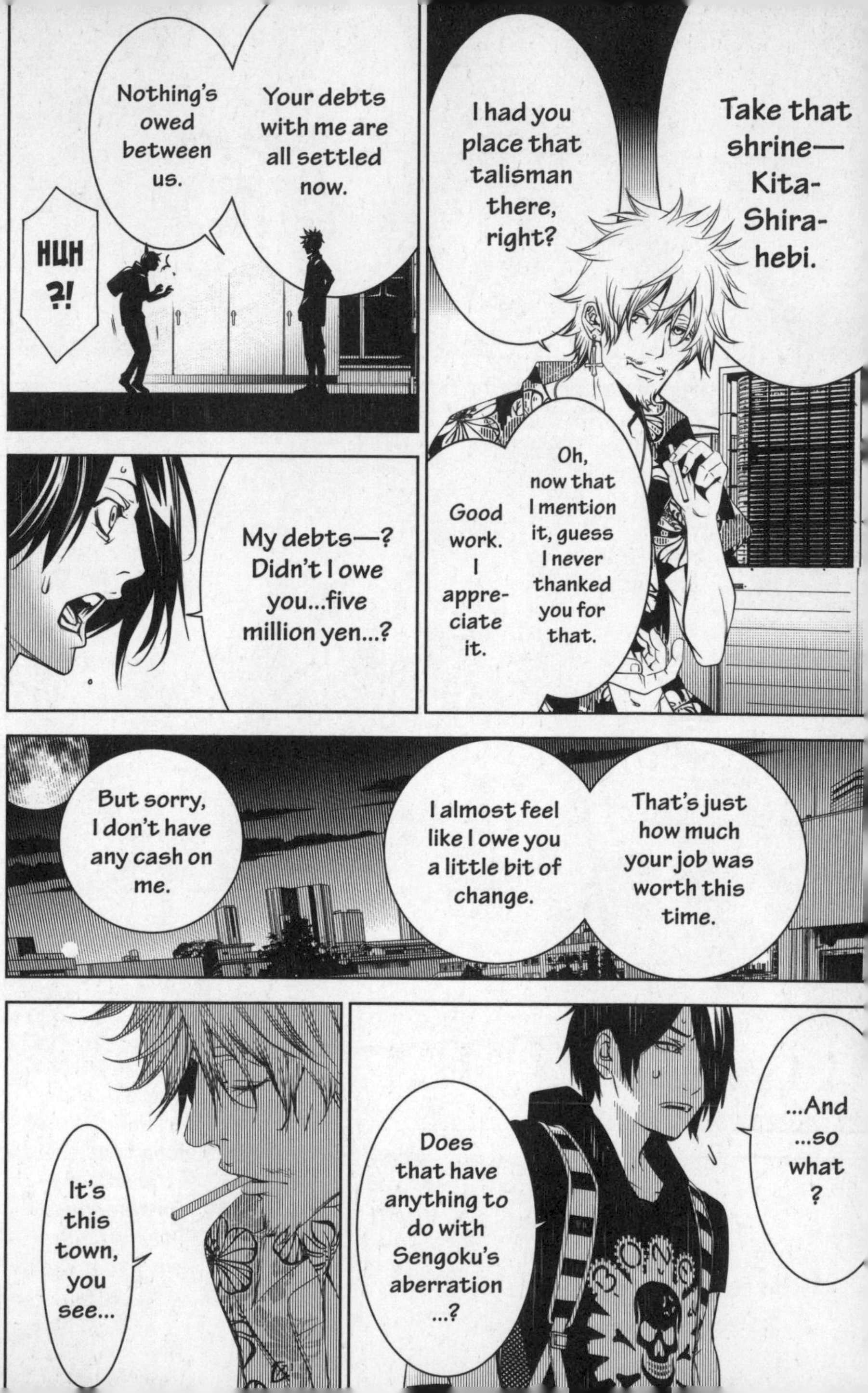
Take that shrine—Kita-Shira-hebi.
I had you place that talisman there, right?
Oh, now that I mention it, guess I never thanked you for that.
Good work. I appreciate it.
Your debts with me are all settled now.
Nothing's owed between us.
HUH ?!
My debts—? Didn't I owe you...five million yen...?
That's just how much your job was worth this time.
I almost feel like I owe you a little bit of change.
But sorry, I don't have any cash on me.
...And ...so what?
Does that have anything to do with Sengoku's aberration ...?
It's this town, you see...

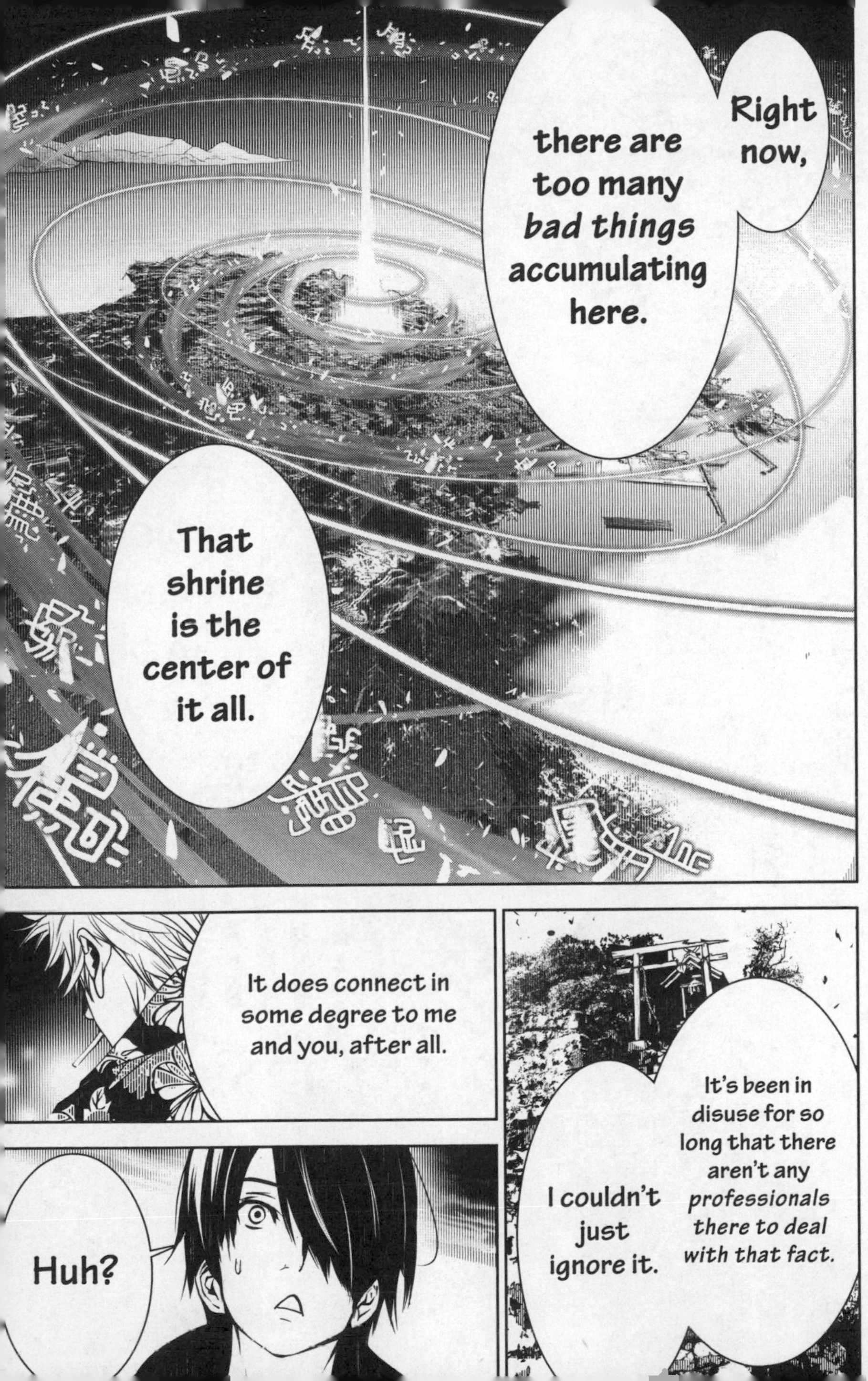
Right now, there are too many *bad things* accumulating here.
That shrine is the center of it all.
It's been in disuse for so long that there aren't any *professionals there to deal with that fact.*
I couldn't just ignore it.
It does connect in some degree to me and you, after all.
Huh?

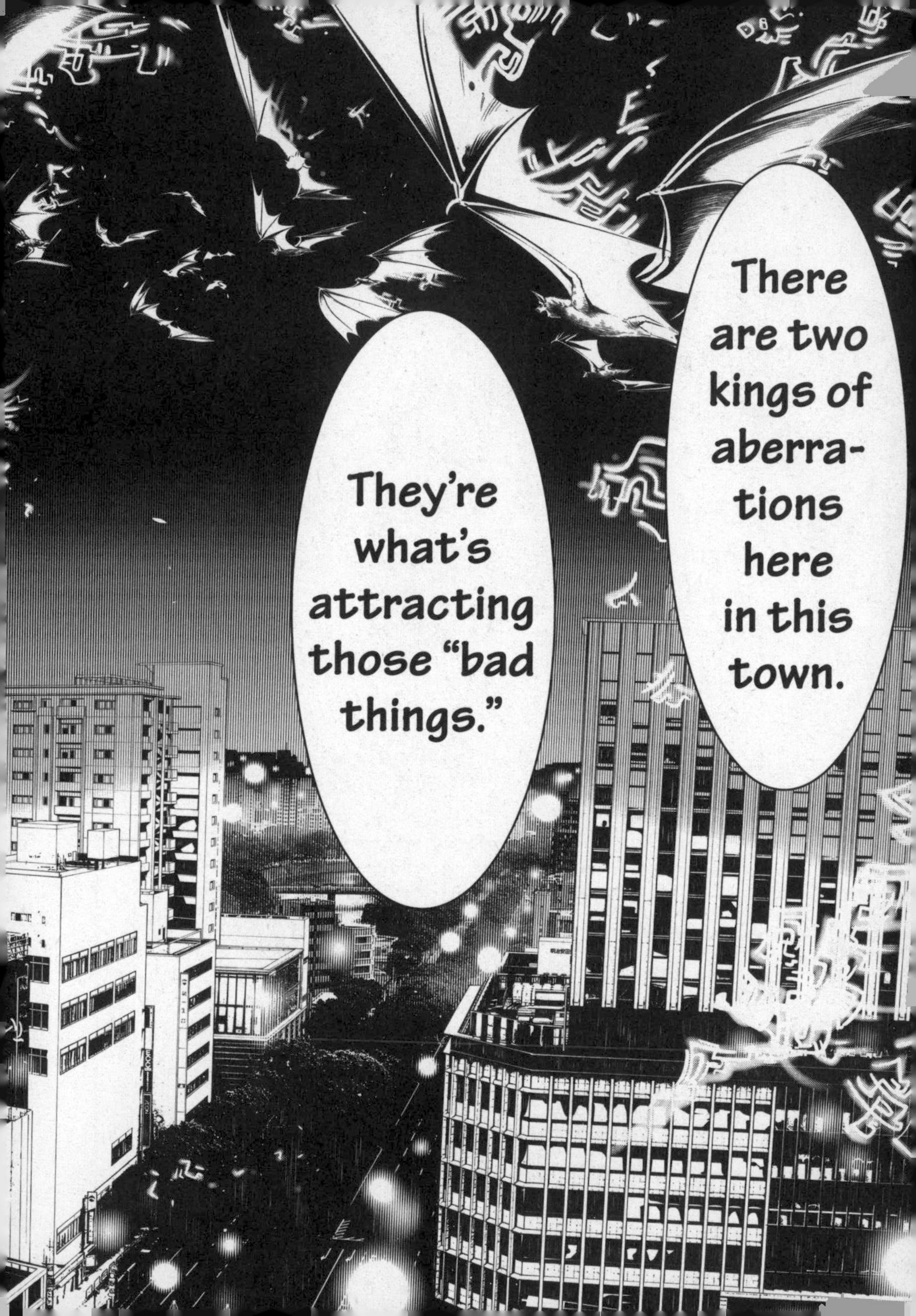
There are two kings of aberra-tions here in this town.
They're what's attracting those "bad things."

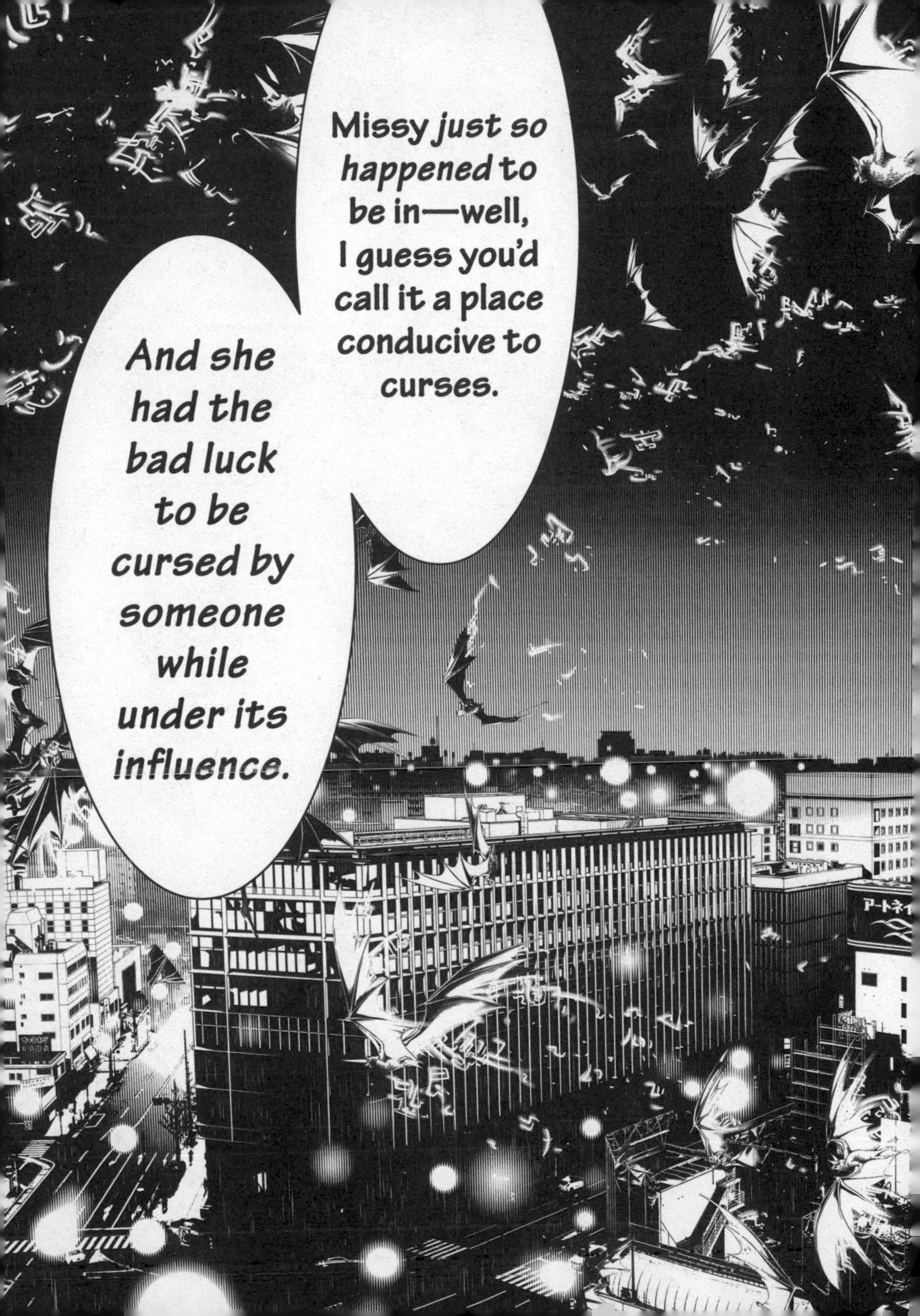
Missy just so happened to be in—well, I guess you'd call it a place conducive to curses.
And she had the bad luck to be cursed by someone while under its influence.
アートネイ

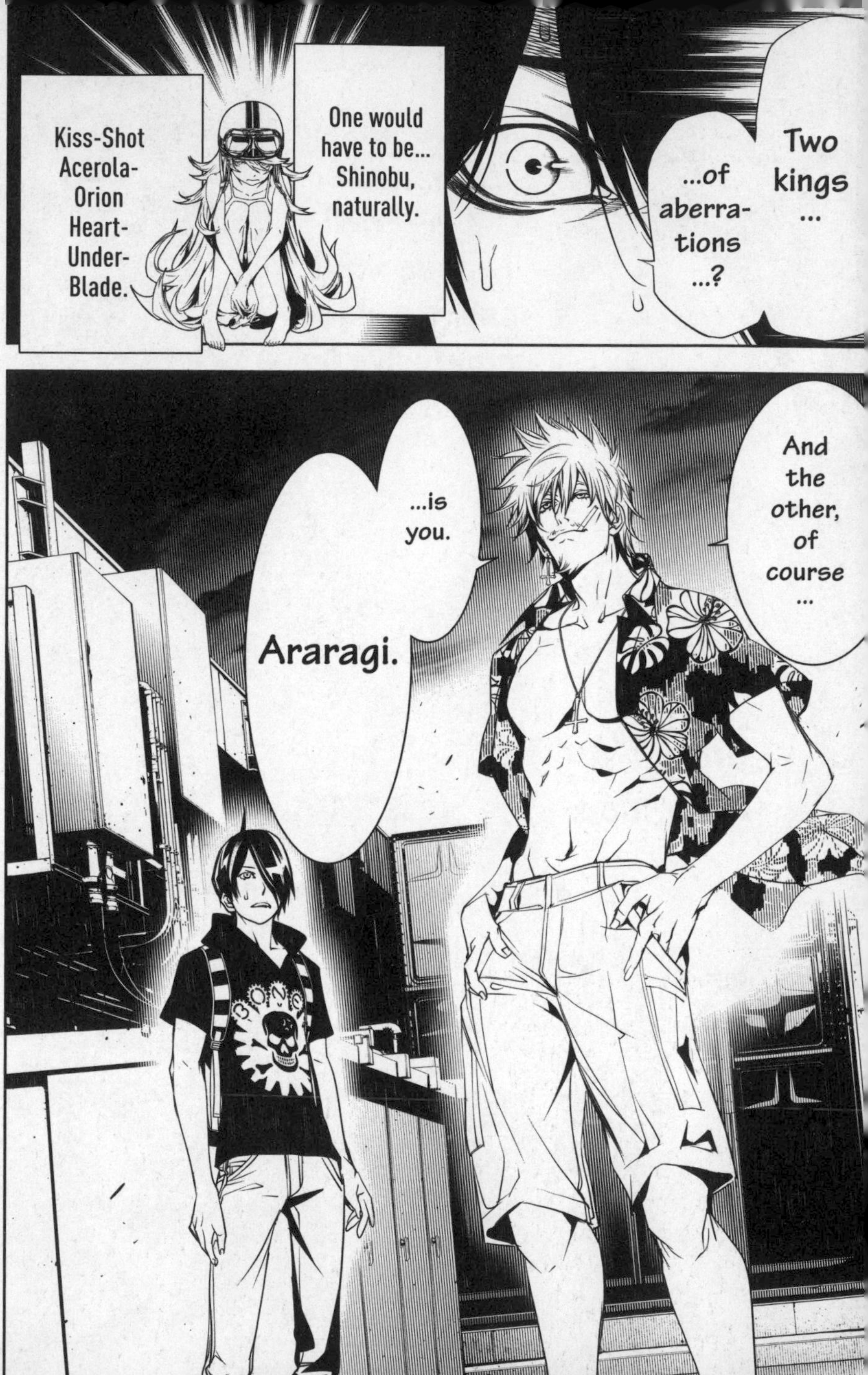
Two kings...
...of aberrations...?
One would have to be... Shinobu, naturally.
Kiss-Shot Acerola-Orion Heart-Under-Blade.
And the other, of course...
...is you.
Araragi.

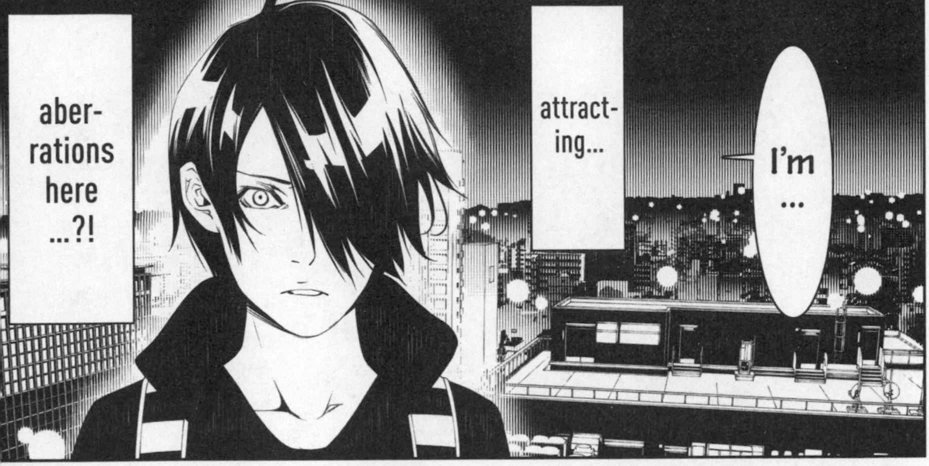
I'm ...
attract-
ing...
aber-
rations
here
...?!

The Two Kings of Aber-rations

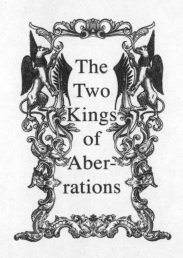

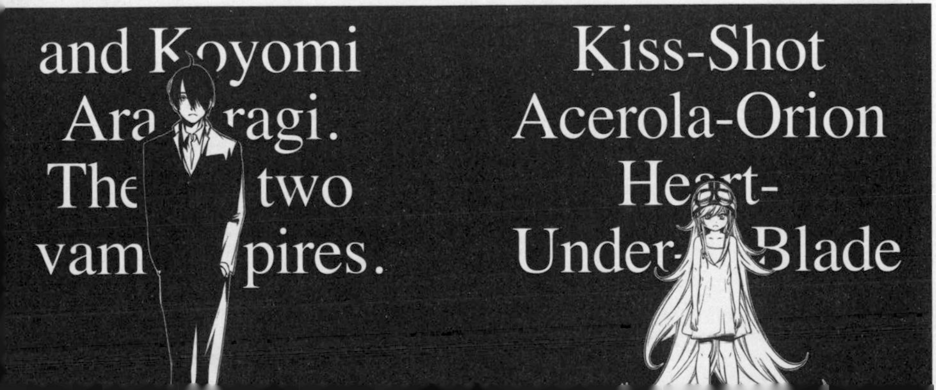
Kiss-Shot
Acerola-Orion
Heart-
Under-Blade
and Koyomi
Araragi.
The two
vampires.

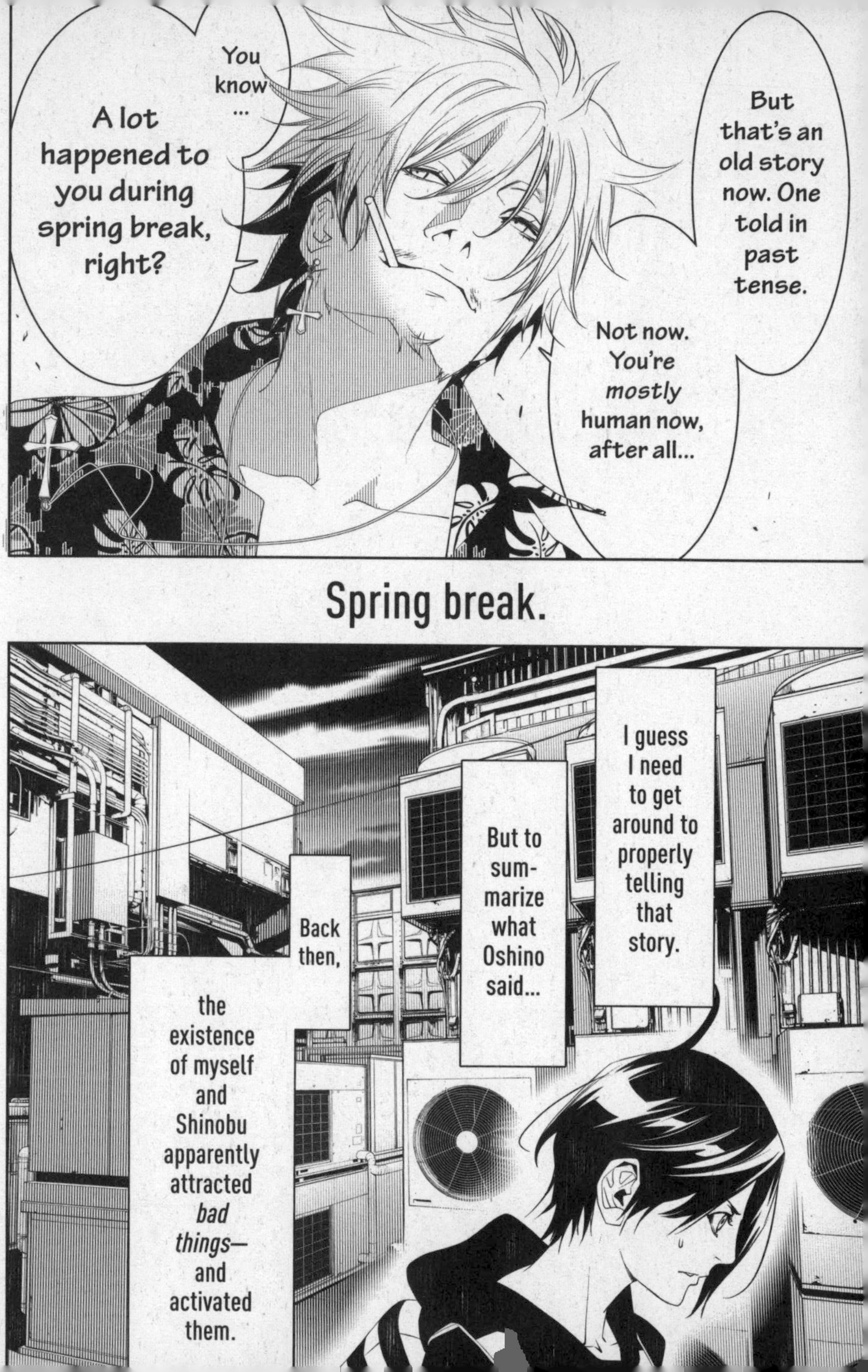
But that's an old story now. One told in past tense.
Not now. You're *mostly* human now, after all...
You know ...
A lot happened to you during spring break, right?
Spring break.
I guess I need to get around to properly telling that story.
But to sum-marize what Oshino said...
Back then,
the existence of myself and Shinobu apparently attracted *bad things*— and activated them.

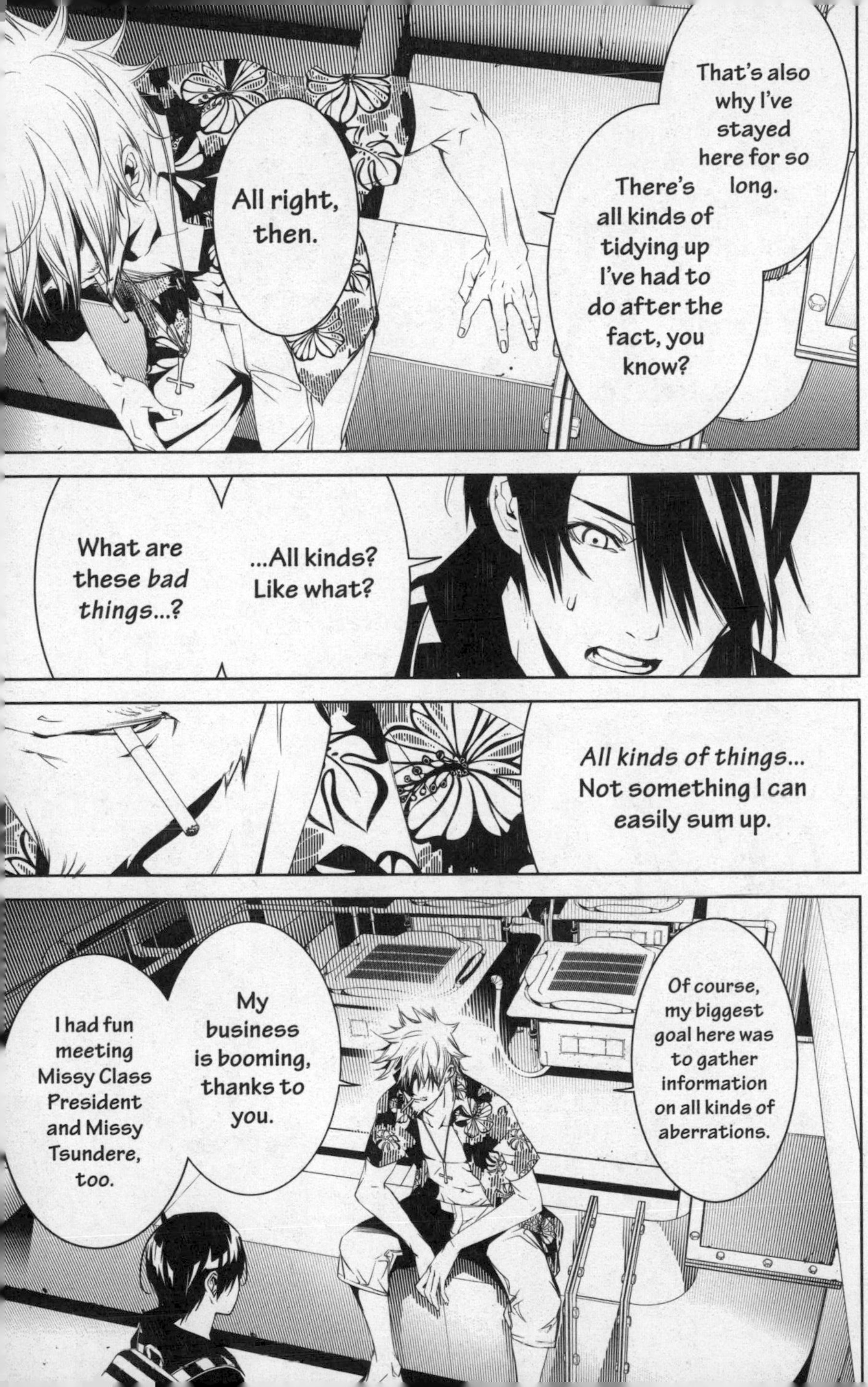
That's also why I've stayed here for so long.
There's all kinds of tidying up I've had to do after the fact, you know?
All right, then.
...All kinds? Like what?
What are these *bad* things...?
All kinds of things... Not something I can easily sum up.
Of course, my biggest goal here was to gather information on all kinds of aberrations.
My business is booming, thanks to you.
I had fun meeting Missy Class President and Missy Tsundere, too.

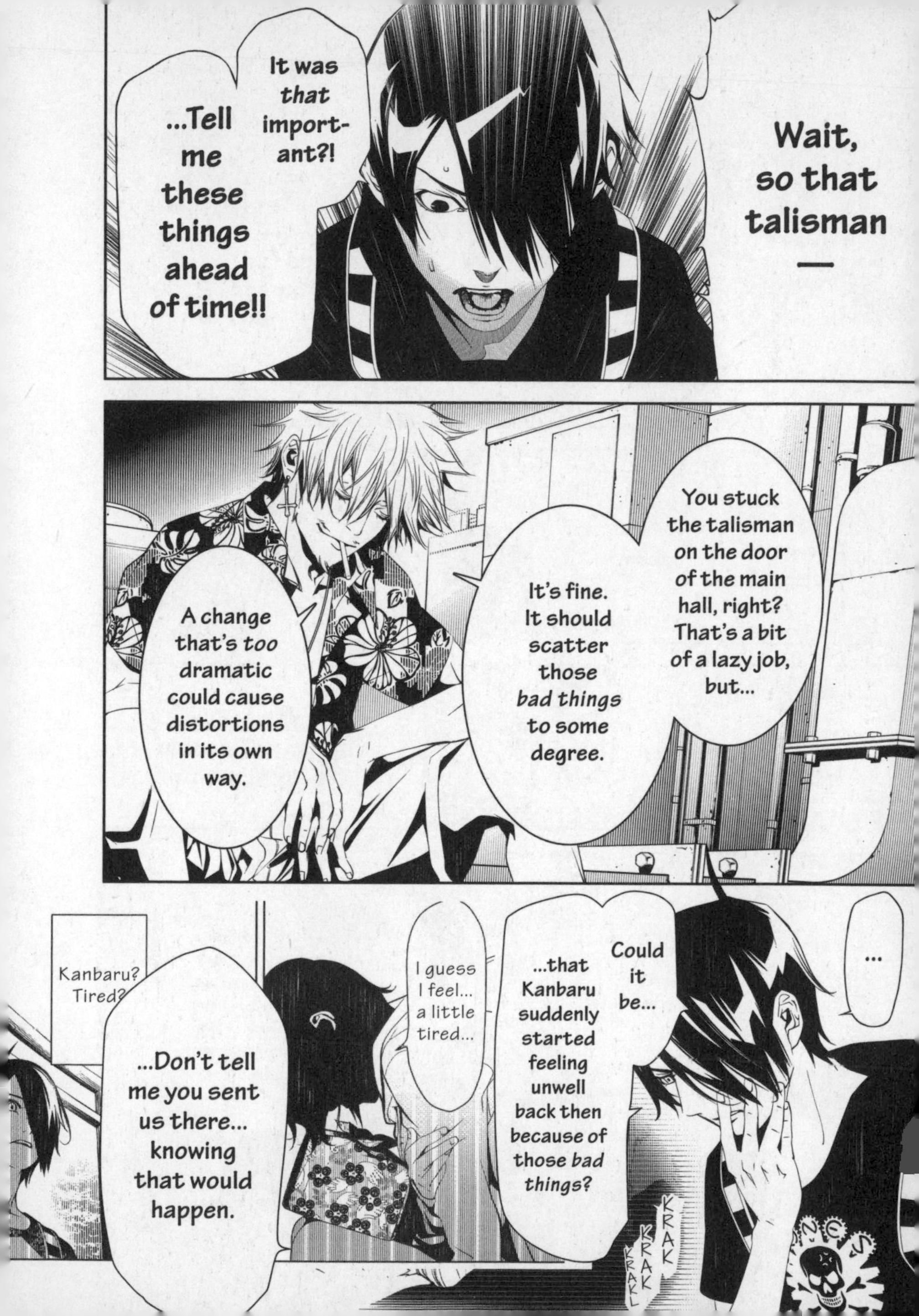
Wait, so that talisman —
It was *that* important?!
...Tell me these things ahead of time!!
You stuck the talisman on the door of the main hall, right? That's a bit of a lazy job, but...
It's fine. It should scatter those *bad things* to some degree.
A change that's *too* dramatic could cause distortions in its own way.
...
Could it be...
...that Kanbaru suddenly started feeling unwell back then because of those *bad things?*
I guess I feel... a little tired...
Kanbaru? Tired?
...Don't tell me you sent us there... knowing that would happen.
KRAK KRAK KRAK

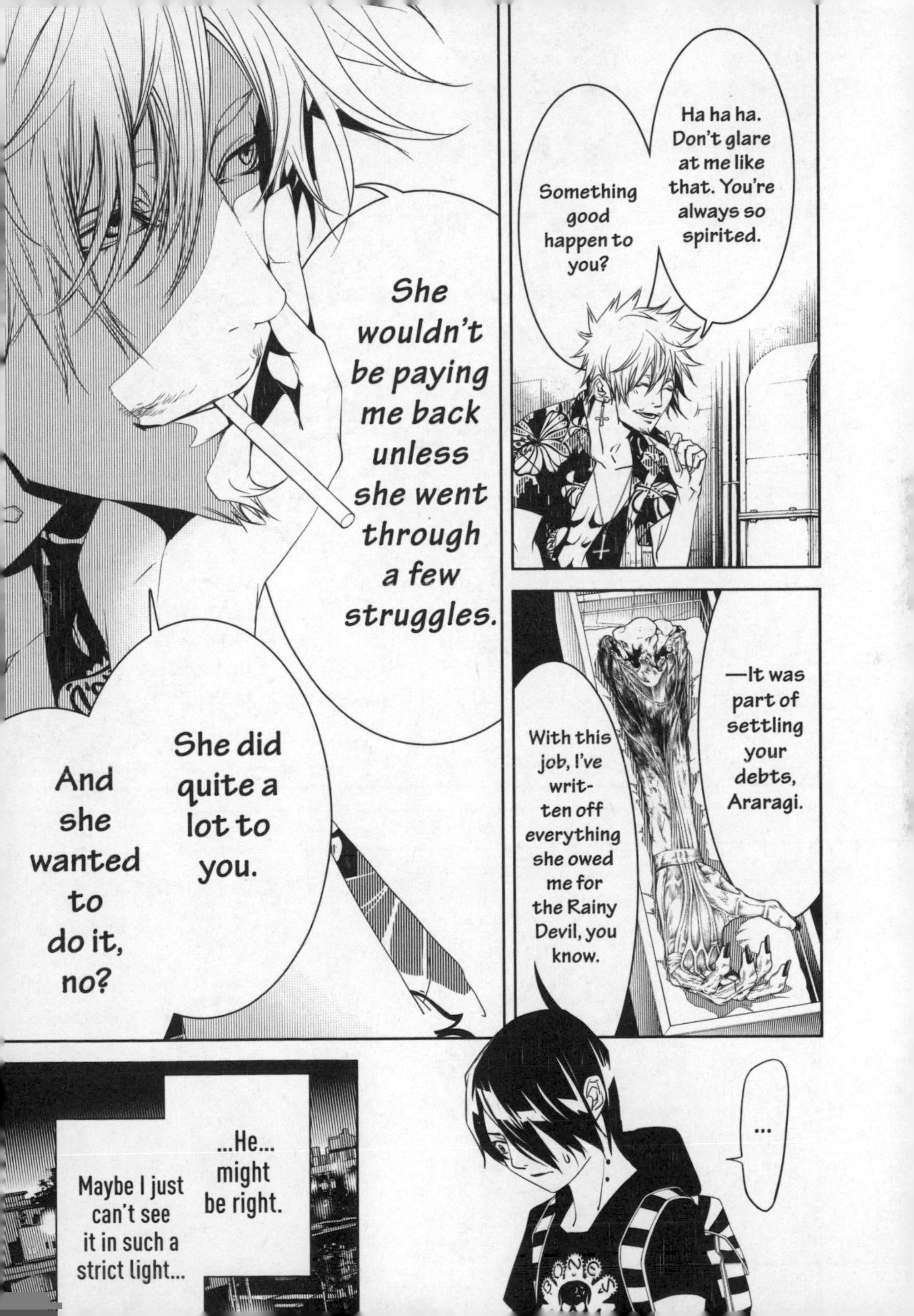
Ha ha ha. Don't glare at me like that. You're always so spirited.
Something good happen to you?
—It was part of settling your debts, Araragi.
With this job, I've writ-ten off everything she owed me for the Rainy Devil, you know.
She wouldn't be paying me back unless she went through a few struggles.
She did quite a lot to you.
And she wanted to do it, no?
...
...He... might be right.
Maybe I just can't see it in such a strict light...

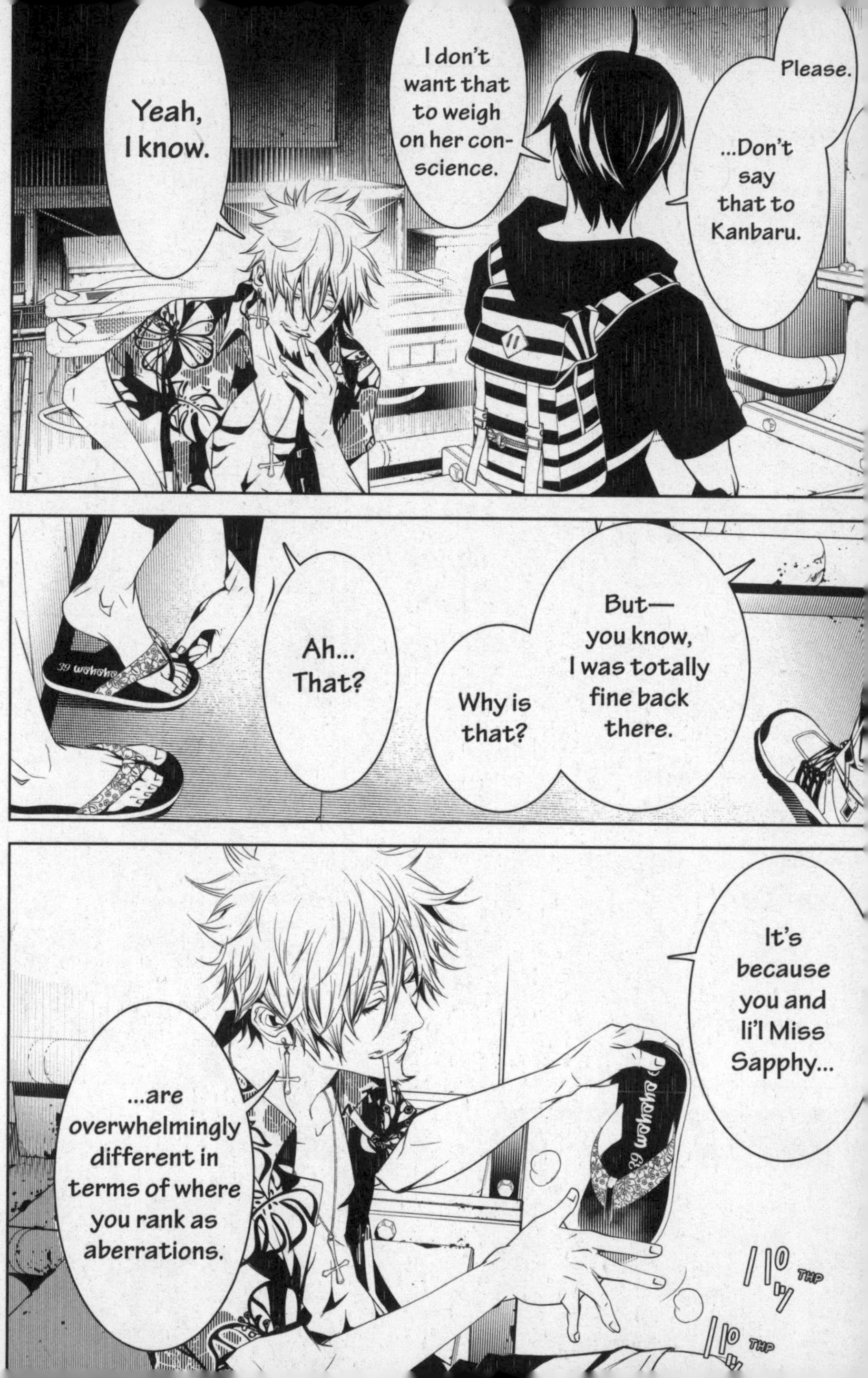
Please.
...Don't say that to Kanbaru.
I don't want that to weigh on her con-science.
Yeah, I know.
But— you know, I was totally fine back there.
Why is that?
Ah... That?
It's because you and li'l Miss Sapphy...
...are overwhelmingly different in terms of where you rank as aberrations.
THP
THP

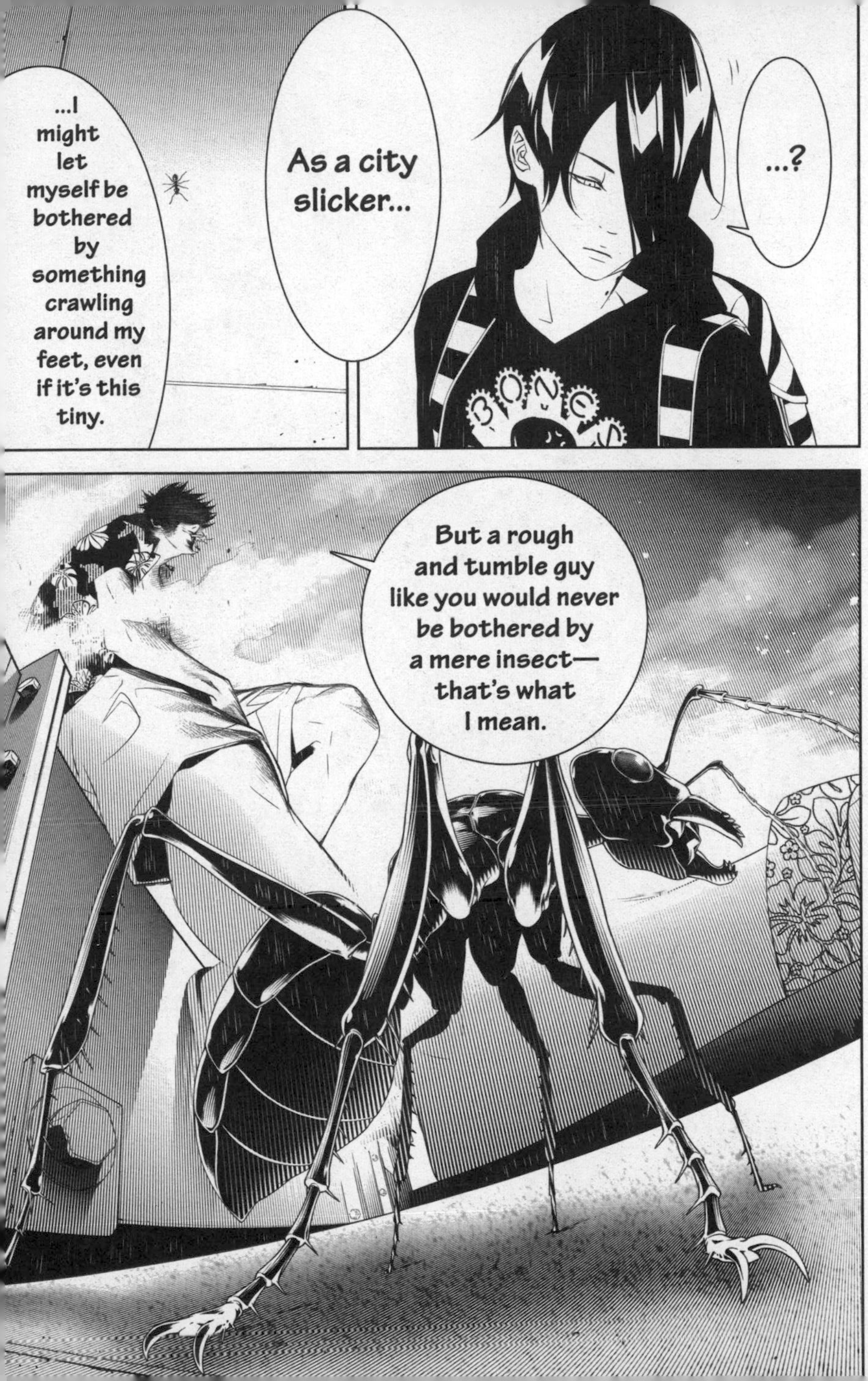
...?
As a city slicker...
...I might let myself be bothered by something crawling around my feet, even if it's this tiny.
But a rough and tumble guy like you would never be bothered by a mere insect— that's what I mean.

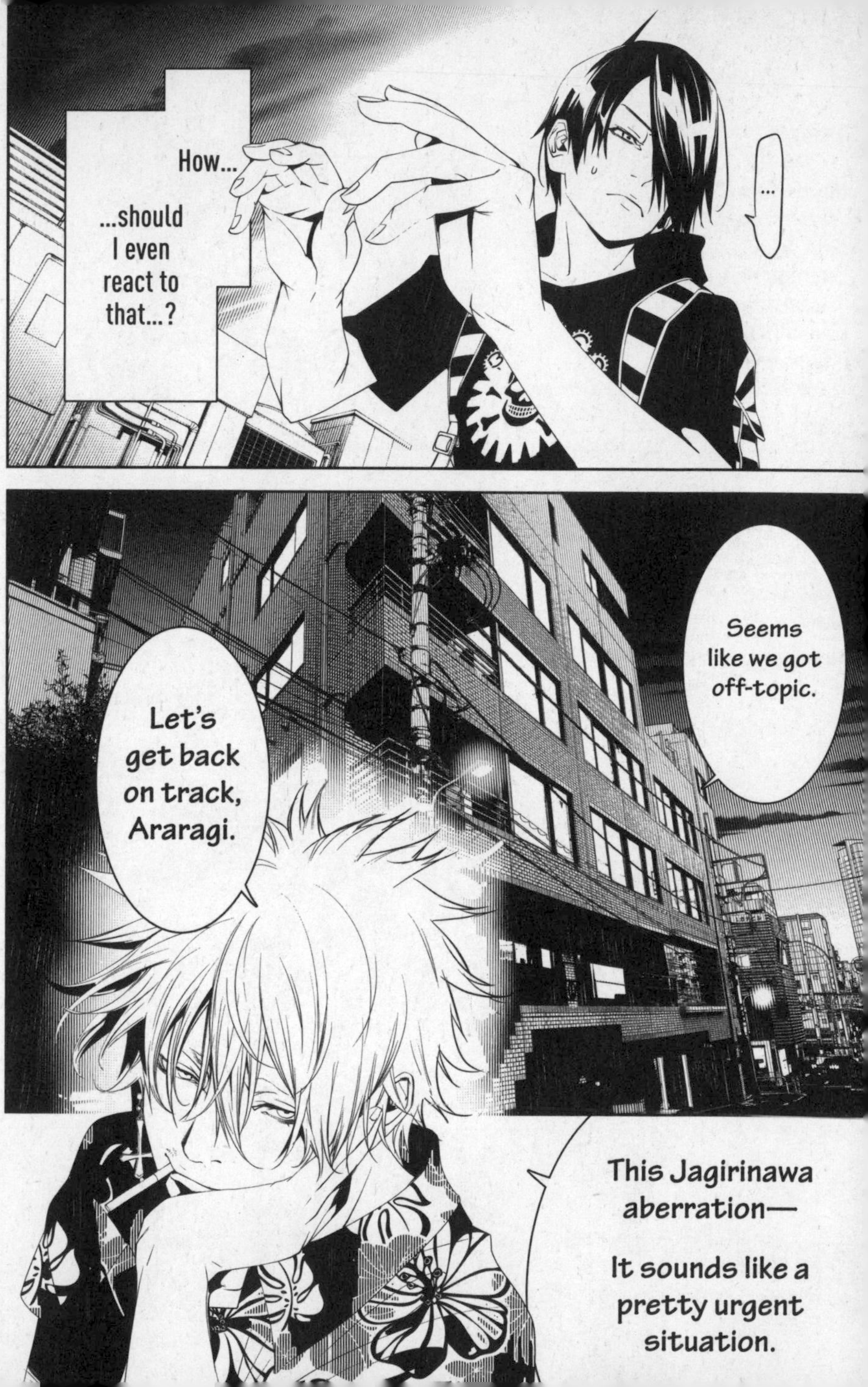
...
How...
...should I even react to that...?
Seems like we got off-topic.
Let's get back on track, Araragi.
This Jagirinawa aberration—
It sounds like a pretty urgent situation.

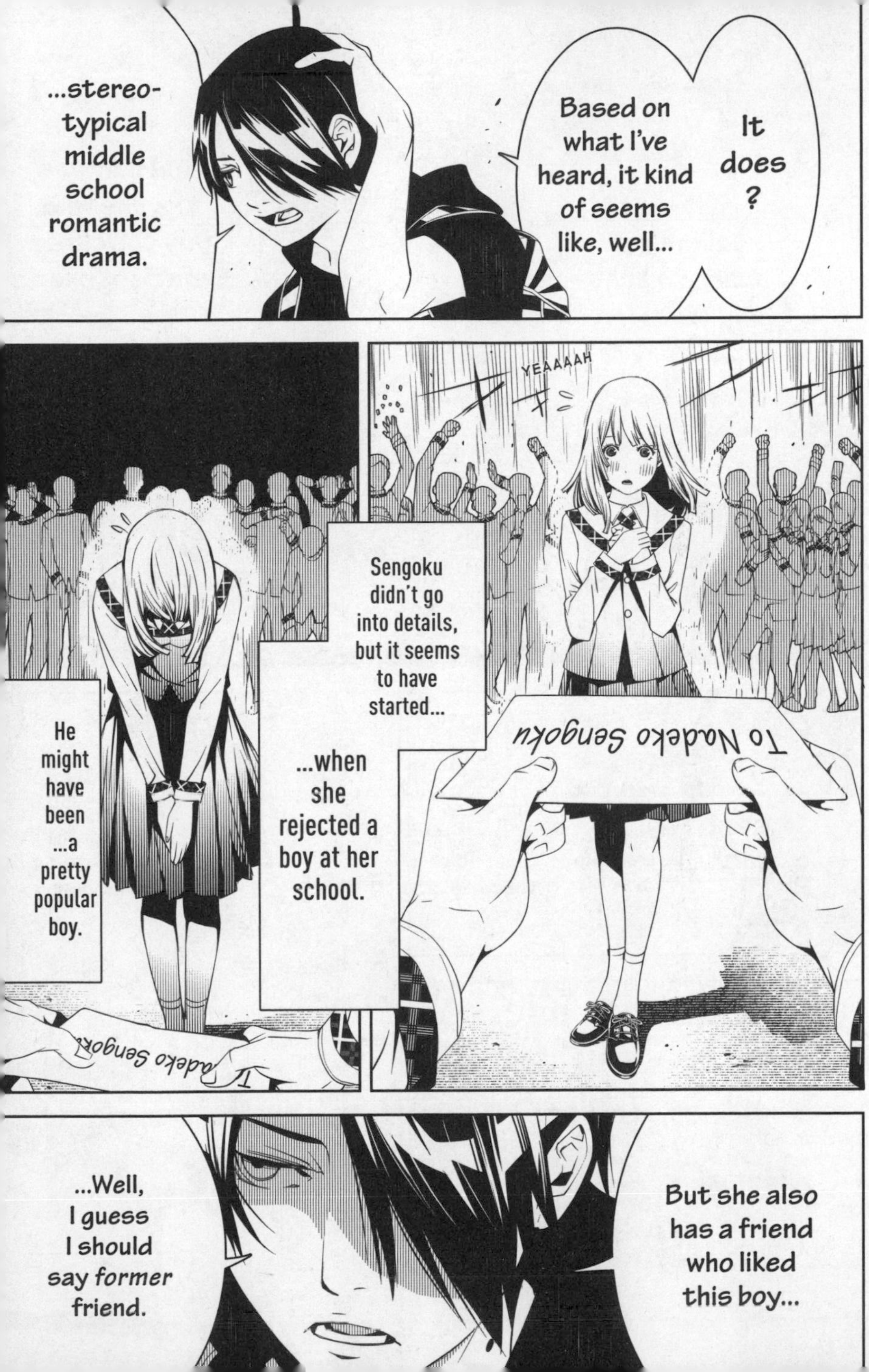

It does?
Based on what I've heard, it kind of seems like, well...
...stereotypical middle school romantic drama.
YEAAAAH
To Nadeko Sengoku
Sengoku didn't go into details, but it seems to have started...
...when she rejected a boy at her school.
He might have been ...a pretty popular boy.
adeko Sengok
But she also has a friend who liked this boy...
...Well, I guess I should say former friend.

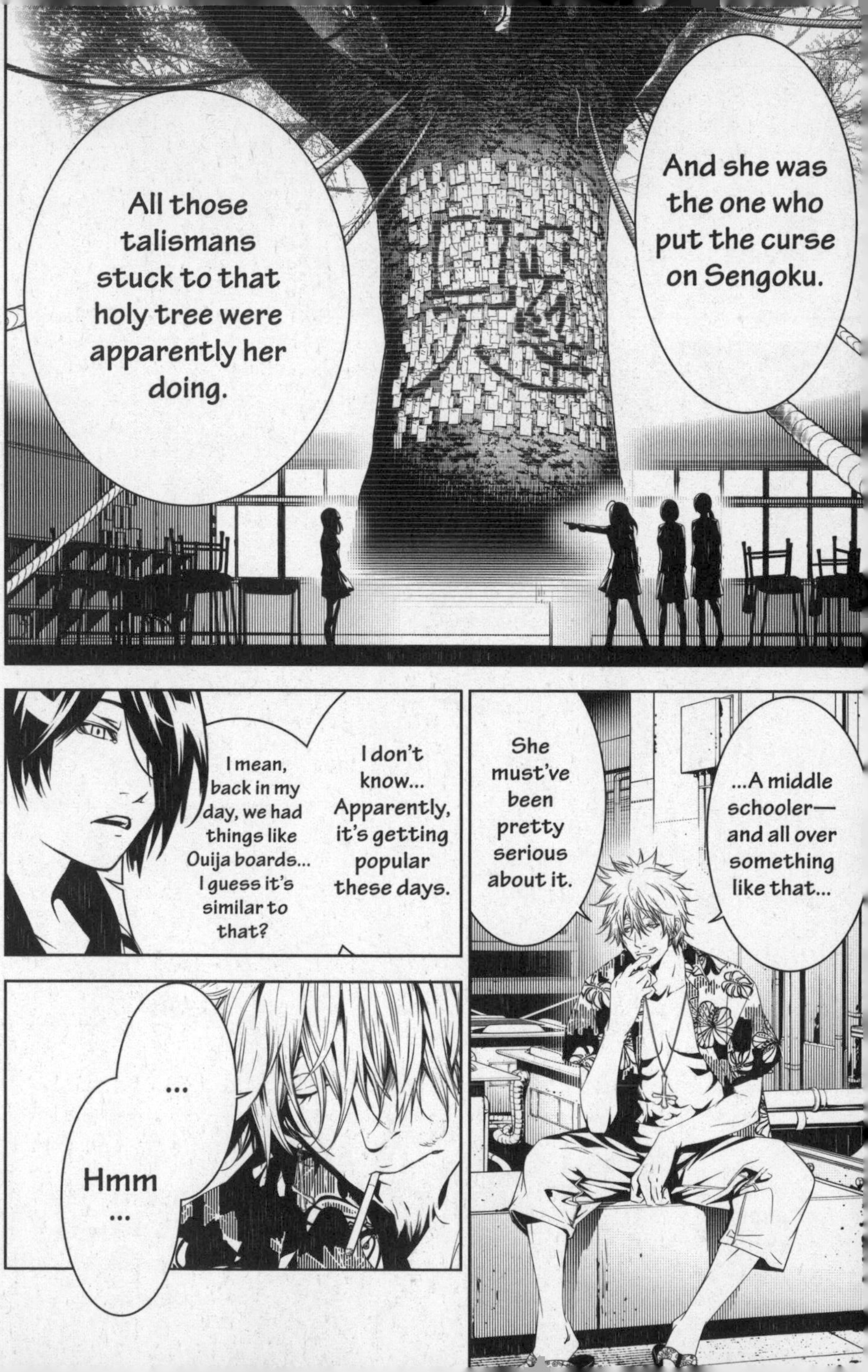
And she was the one who put the curse on Sengoku.
All those talismans stuck to that holy tree were apparently her doing.
...A middle schooler—and all over something like that...
She must've been pretty serious about it.
I don't know... Apparently, it's getting popular these days.
I mean, back in my day, we had things like Ouija boards... I guess it's similar to that?
...
Hmm
...

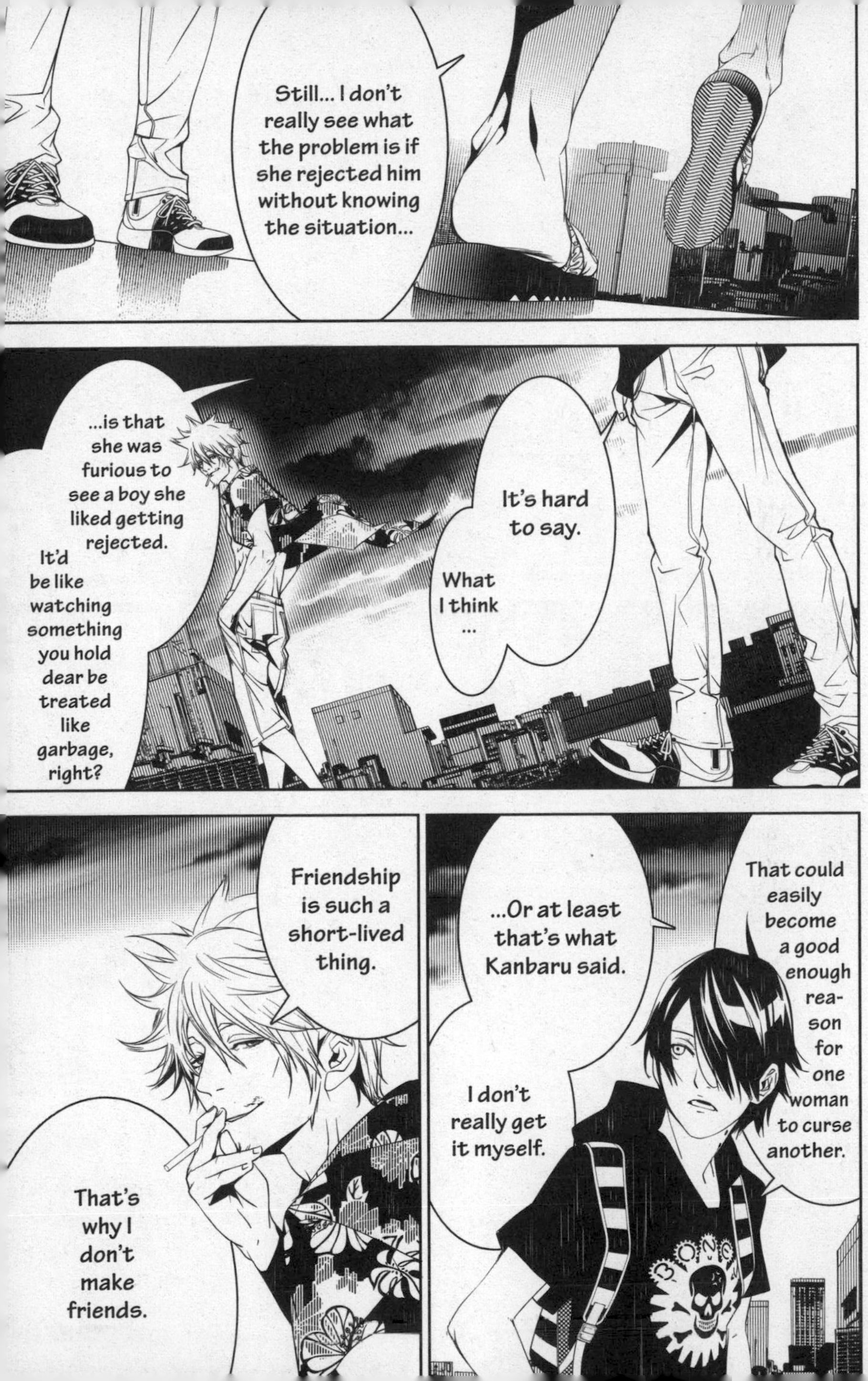
Still... I don't really see what the problem is if she rejected him without knowing the situation...
It's hard to say.
What I think ...
...is that she was furious to see a boy she liked getting rejected.
It'd be like watching something you hold dear be treated like garbage, right?
That could easily become a good enough rea-son for one woman to curse another.
...Or at least that's what Kanbaru said.
I don't really get it myself.
Friendship is such a short-lived thing.
That's why I don't make friends.

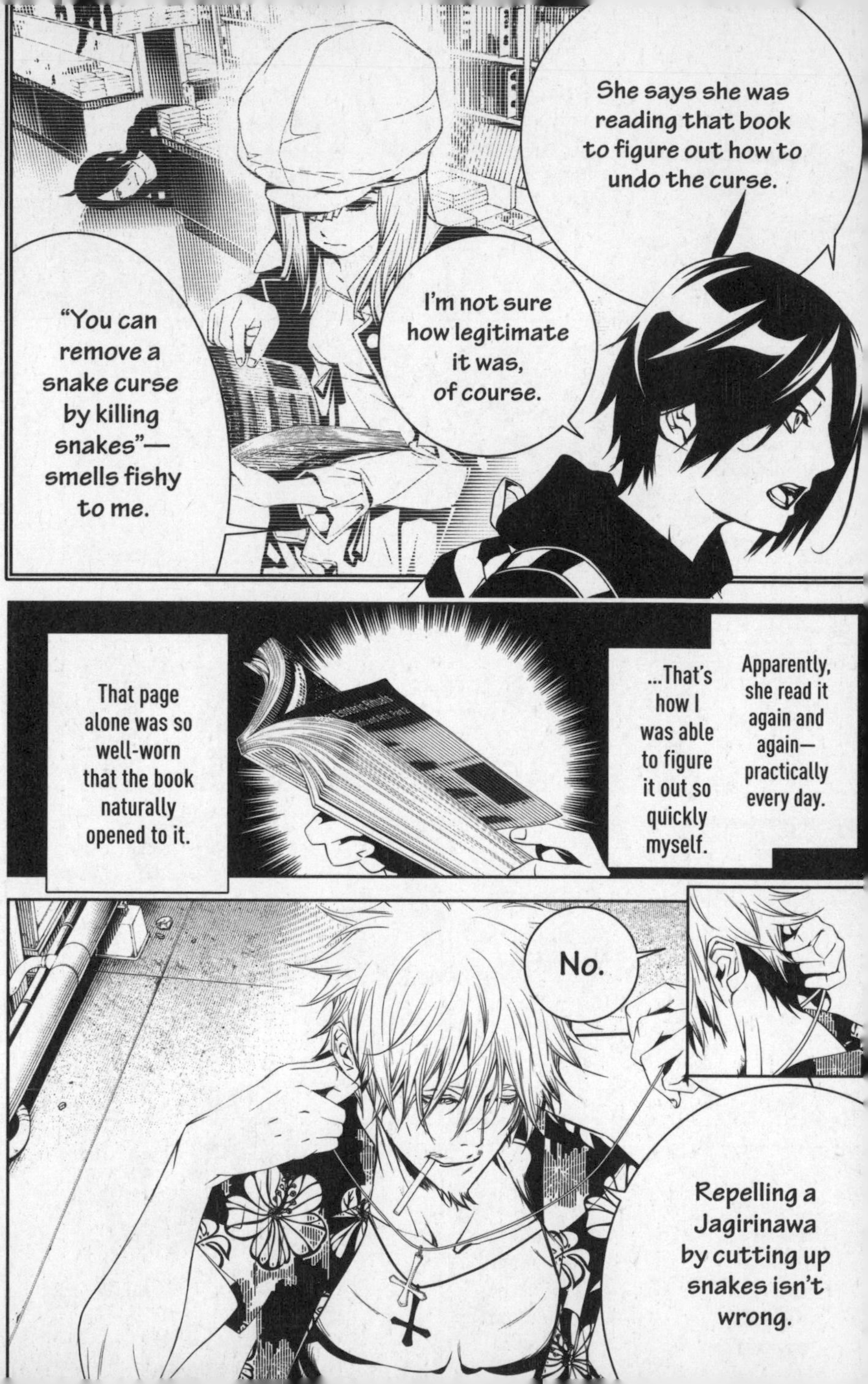
She says she was reading that book to figure out how to undo the curse.
I'm not sure how legitimate it was, of course.
"You can remove a snake curse by killing snakes"—smells fishy to me.
Apparently, she read it again and again—practically every day.
...That's how I was able to figure it out so quickly myself.
That page alone was so well-worn that the book naturally opened to it.
No.
Repelling a Jagirinawa by cutting up snakes isn't wrong.

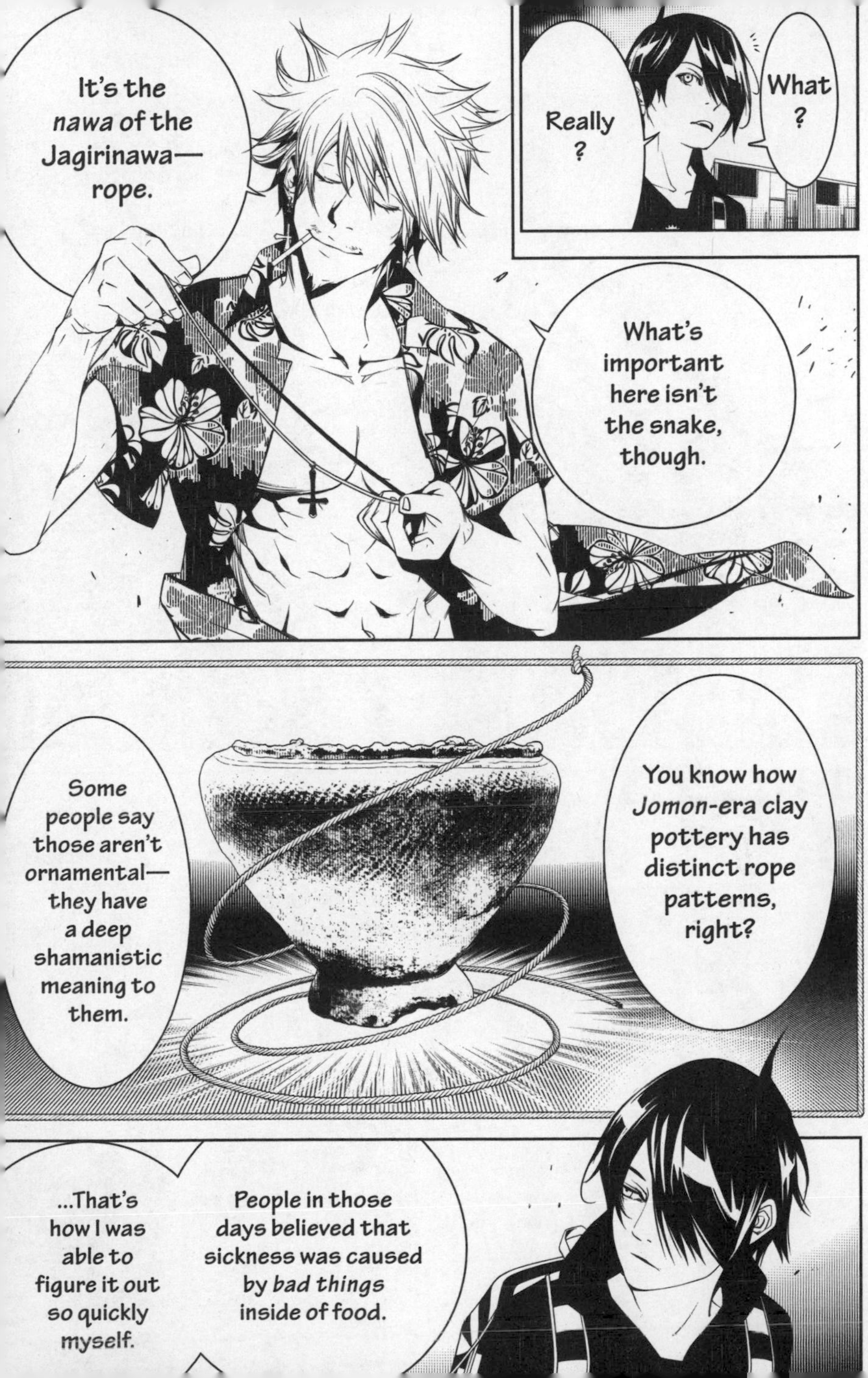

What?
Really?
It's the *nawa* of the Jagirinawa—rope.
What's important here isn't the snake, though.
You know how *Jomon*-era clay pottery has distinct rope patterns, right?
Some people say those aren't ornamental—they have a deep shamanistic meaning to them.
People in those days believed that sickness was caused by *bad things* inside of food.
...That's how I was able to figure it out so quickly myself.

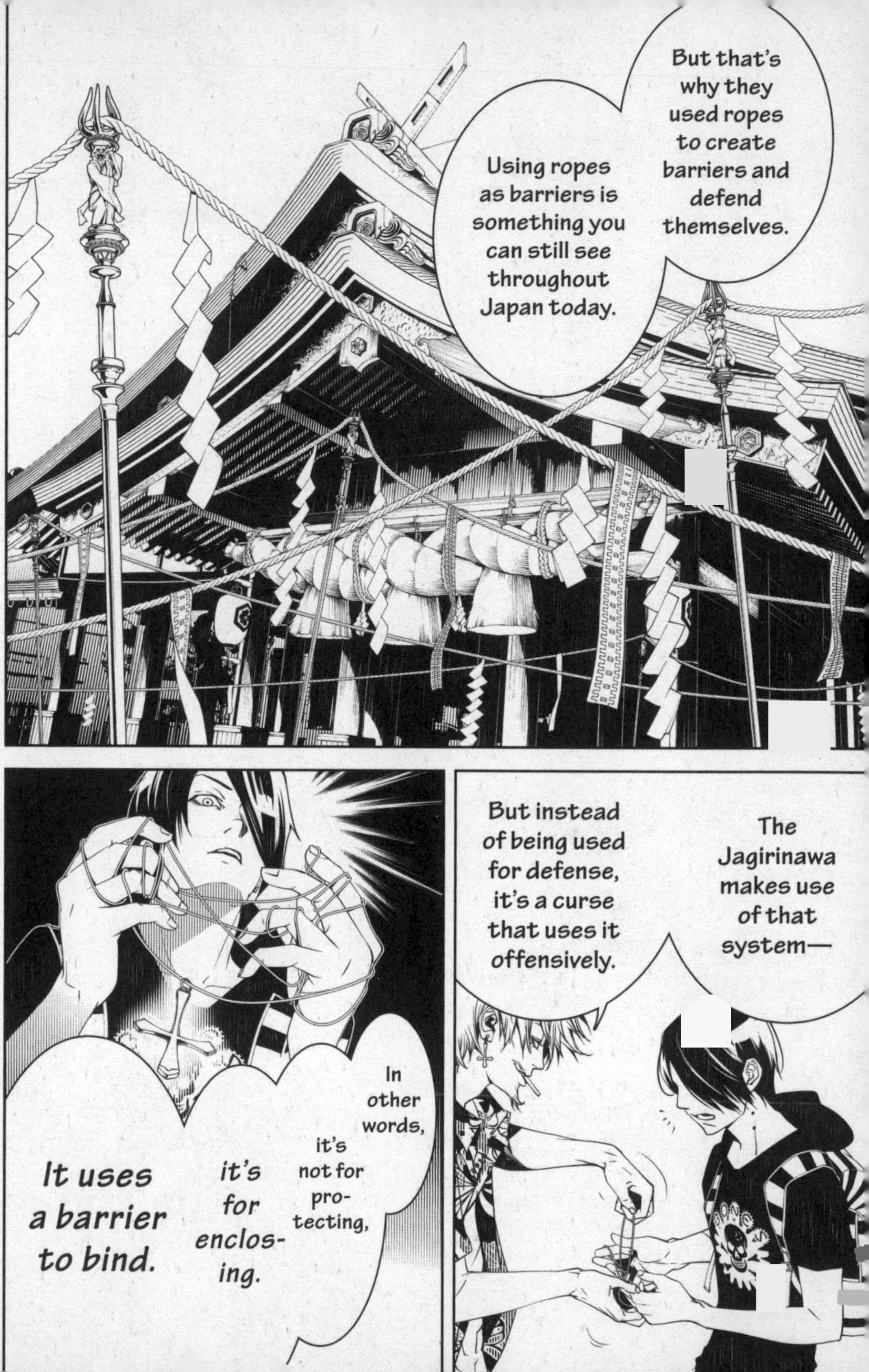
But that's why they used ropes to create barriers and defend themselves.
Using ropes as barriers is something you can still see throughout Japan today.
The Jagirinawa makes use of that system—
But instead of being used for defense, it's a curse that uses it offensively.
In other words,
it's not for pro-tecting,
it's for enclos-ing.
It uses a barrier to bind.

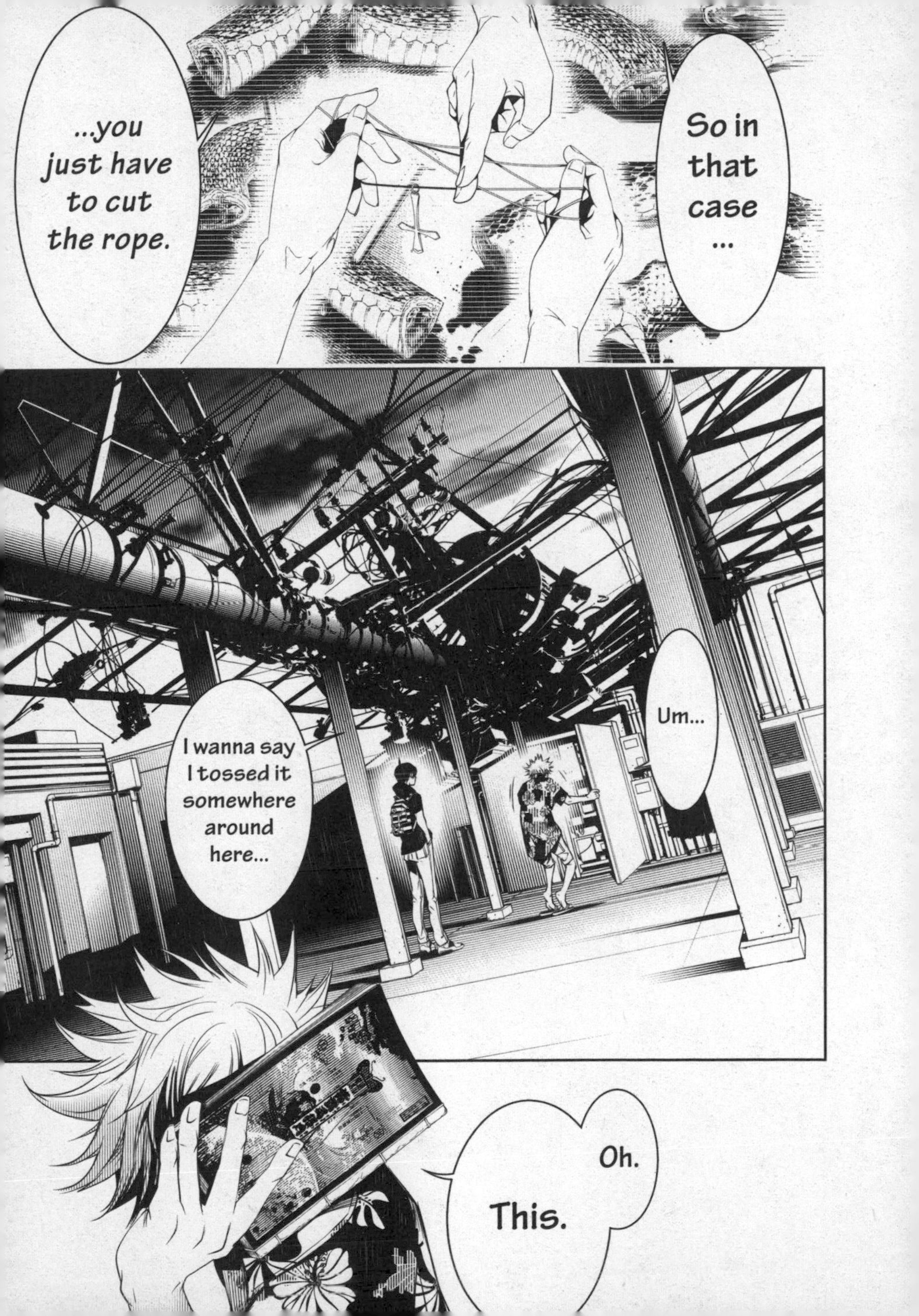
So in that case ...
...you just have to cut the rope.
Um...
I wanna say I tossed it somewhere around here...
Oh.
This.

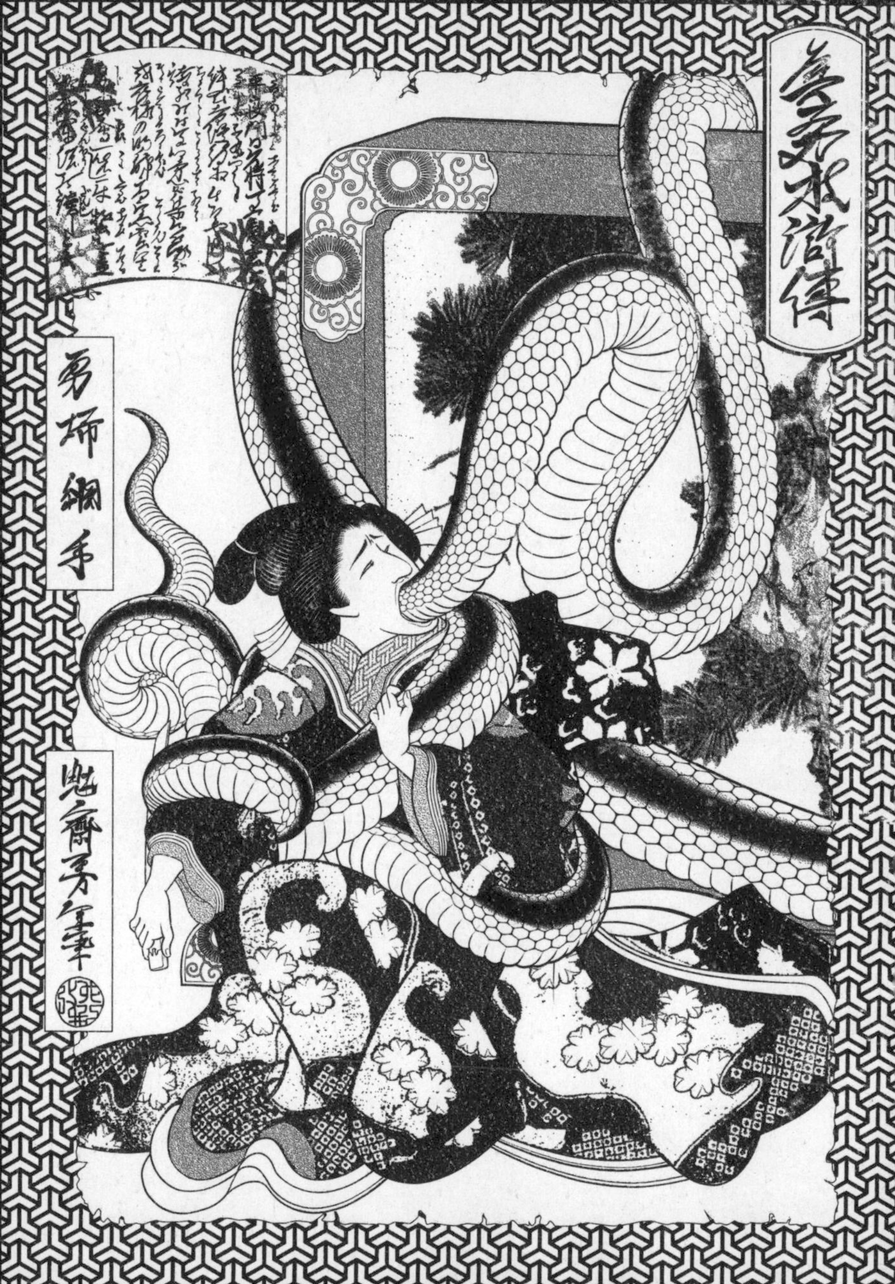
美勇水滸伝
勇婦綱手
魁齋芳年筆

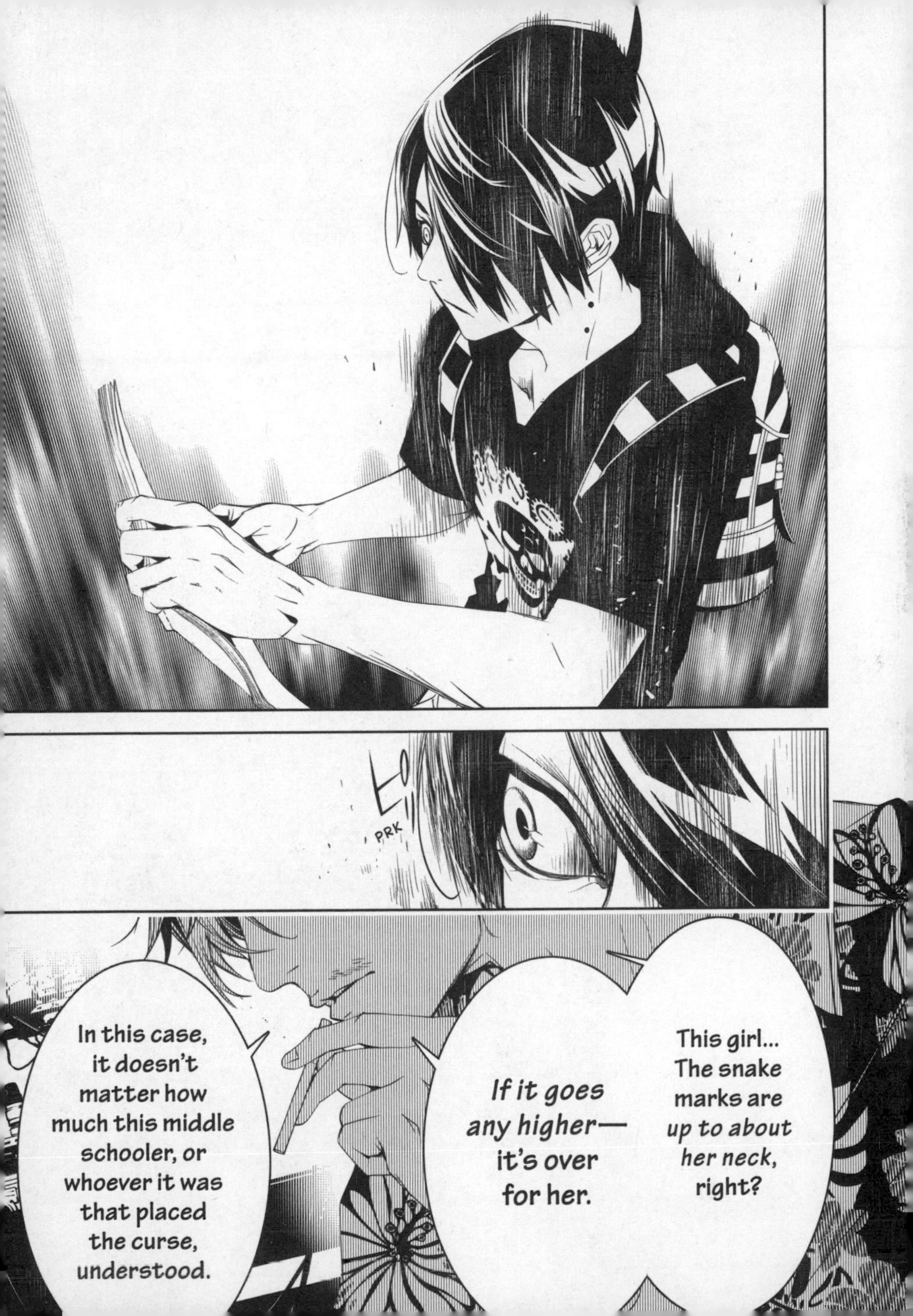
PRK
This girl... The snake marks are up to about her neck, right?
If it goes any higher— it's over for her.
In this case, it doesn't matter how much this middle schooler, or whoever it was that placed the curse, understood.

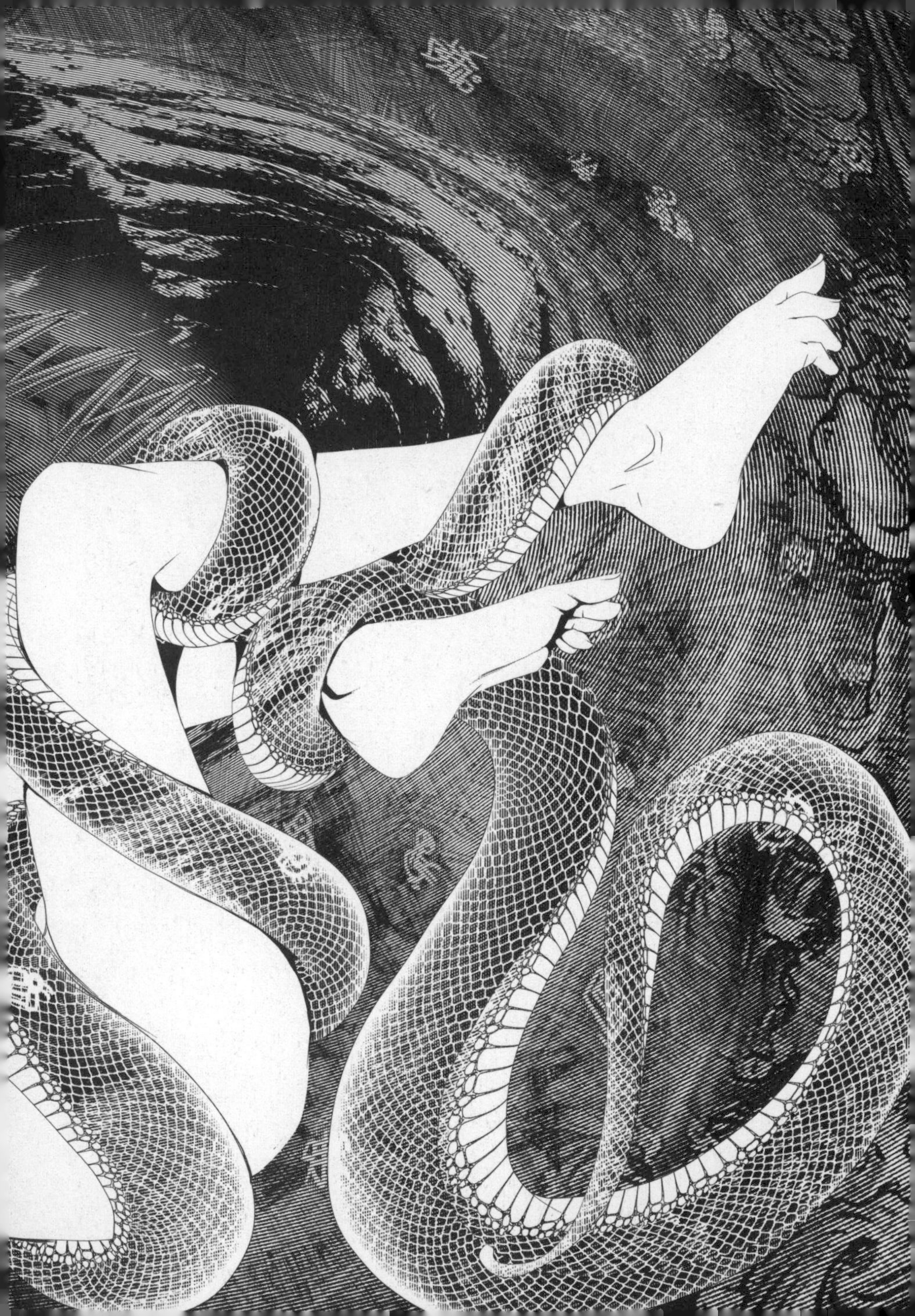

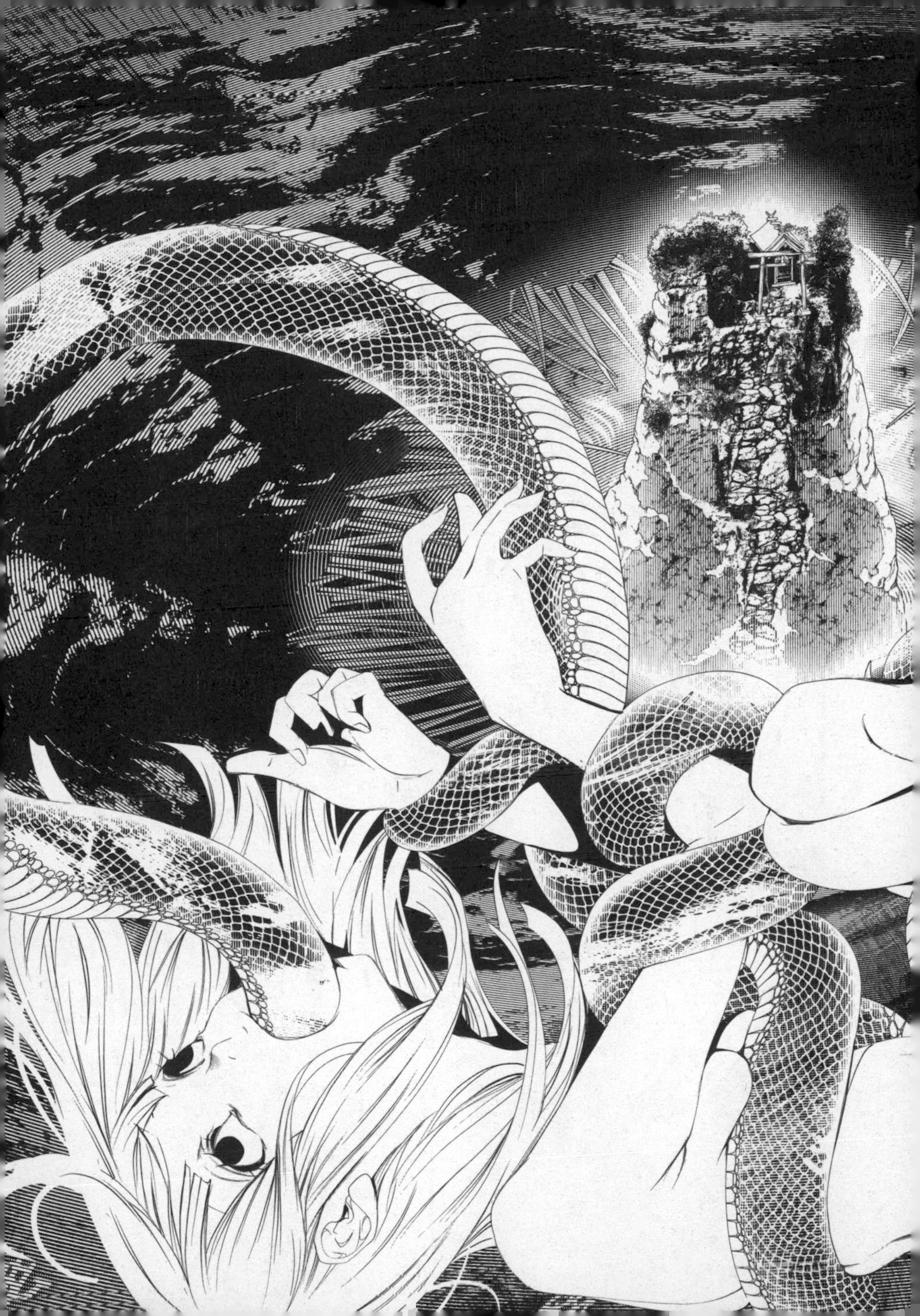

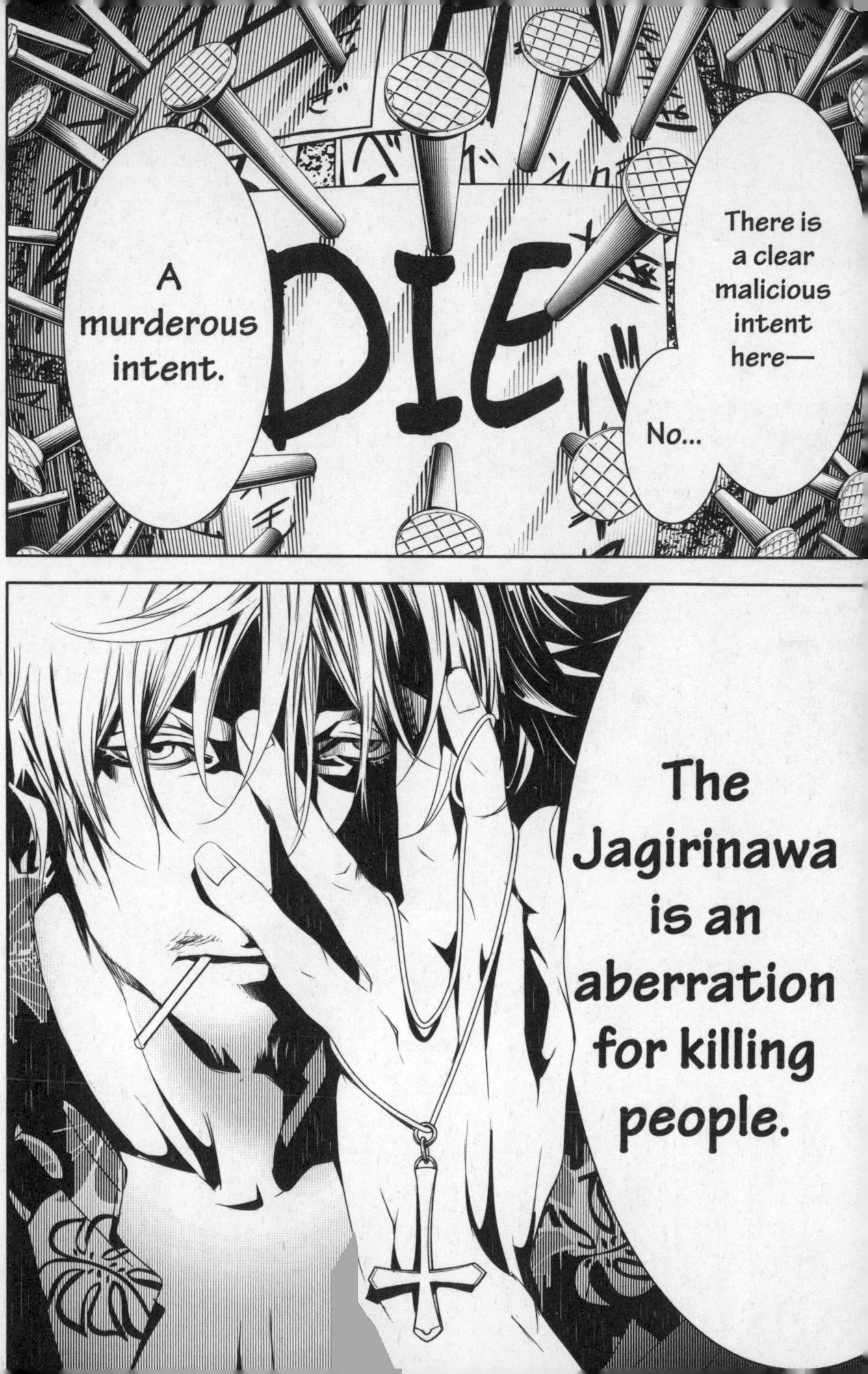
There is a clear malicious intent here—
No...
DIE
A murderous intent.
The Jagirinawa is an aberration for killing people.

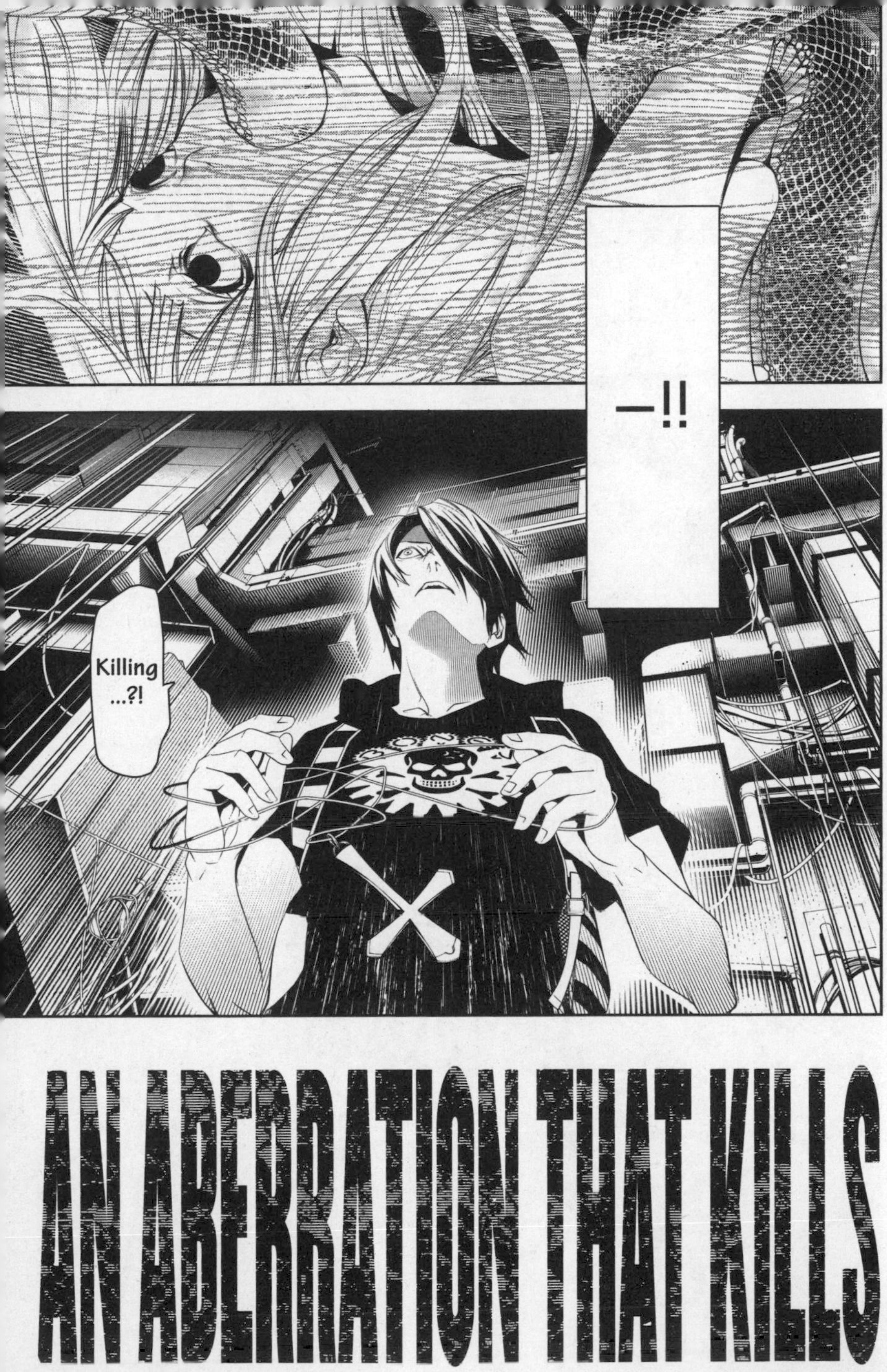
—!!
Killing ...?!

AN ABERRATION THAT KILLS

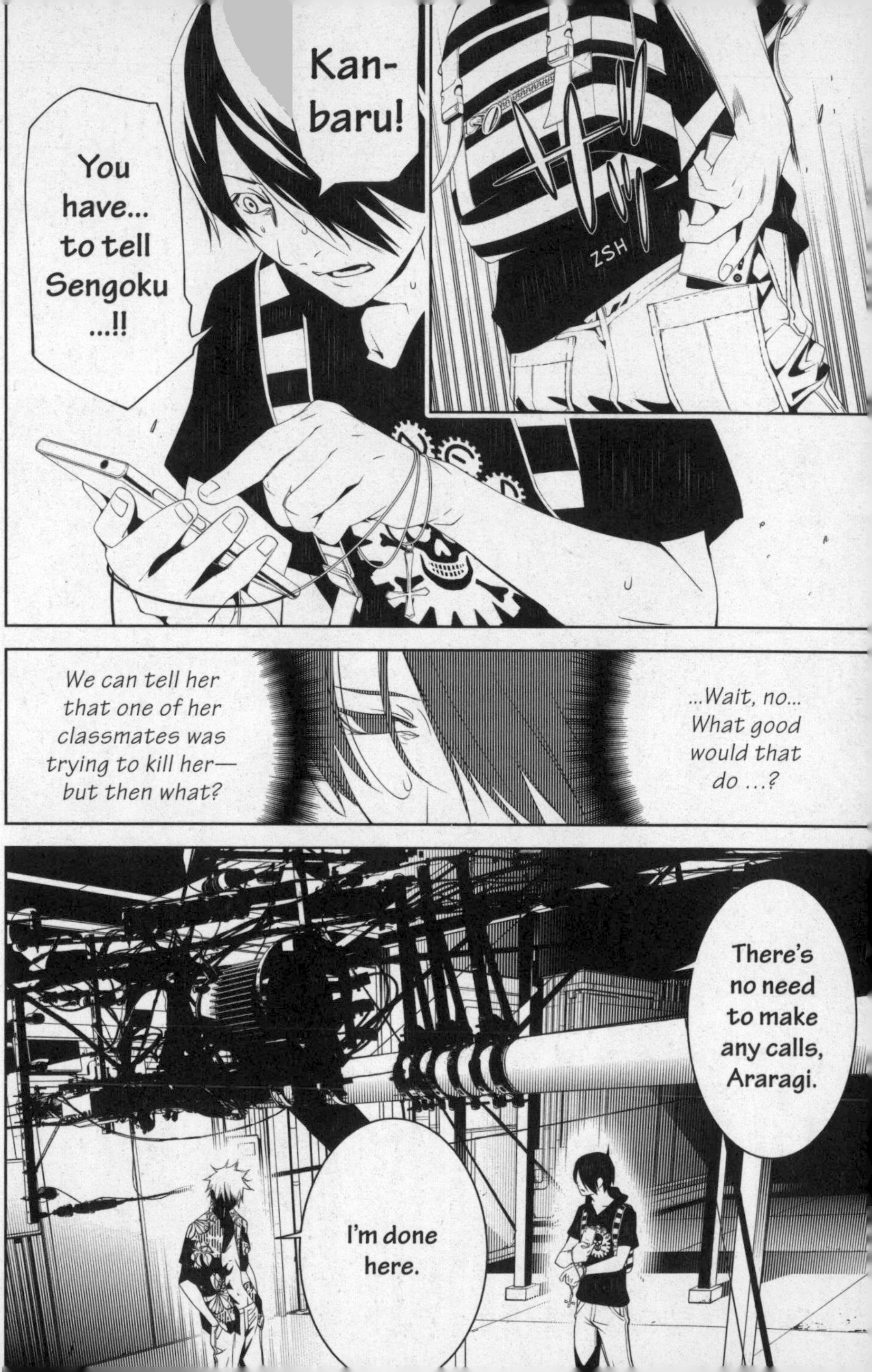
ZSH
Kan-baru!
You have... to tell Sengoku ...!!
...Wait, no... What good would that do ...?
We can tell her that one of her classmates was trying to kill her—but then what?
There's no need to make any calls, Araragi.
I'm done here.

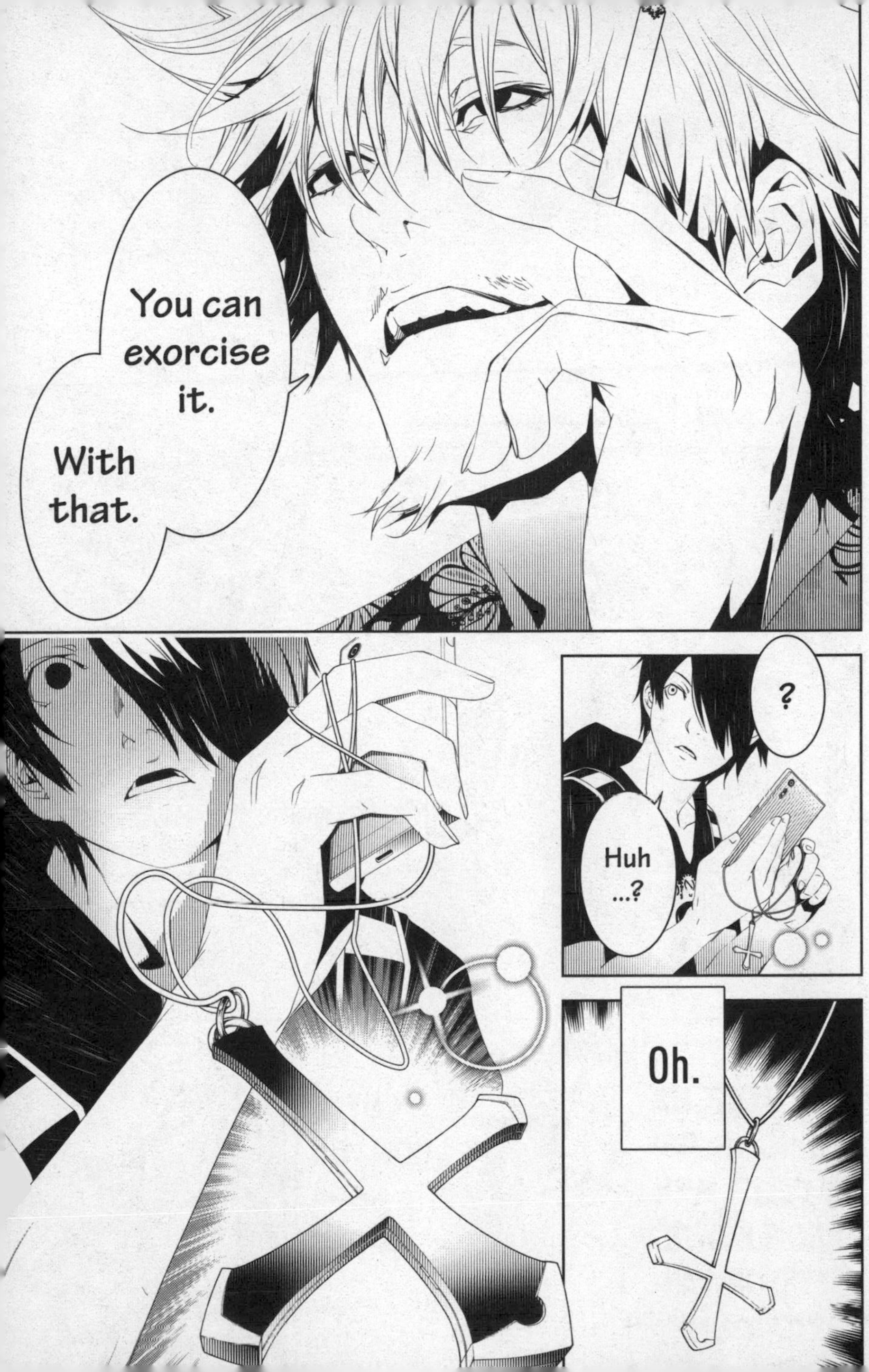

You can exorcise it.
With that.
?
Huh ...?
Oh.

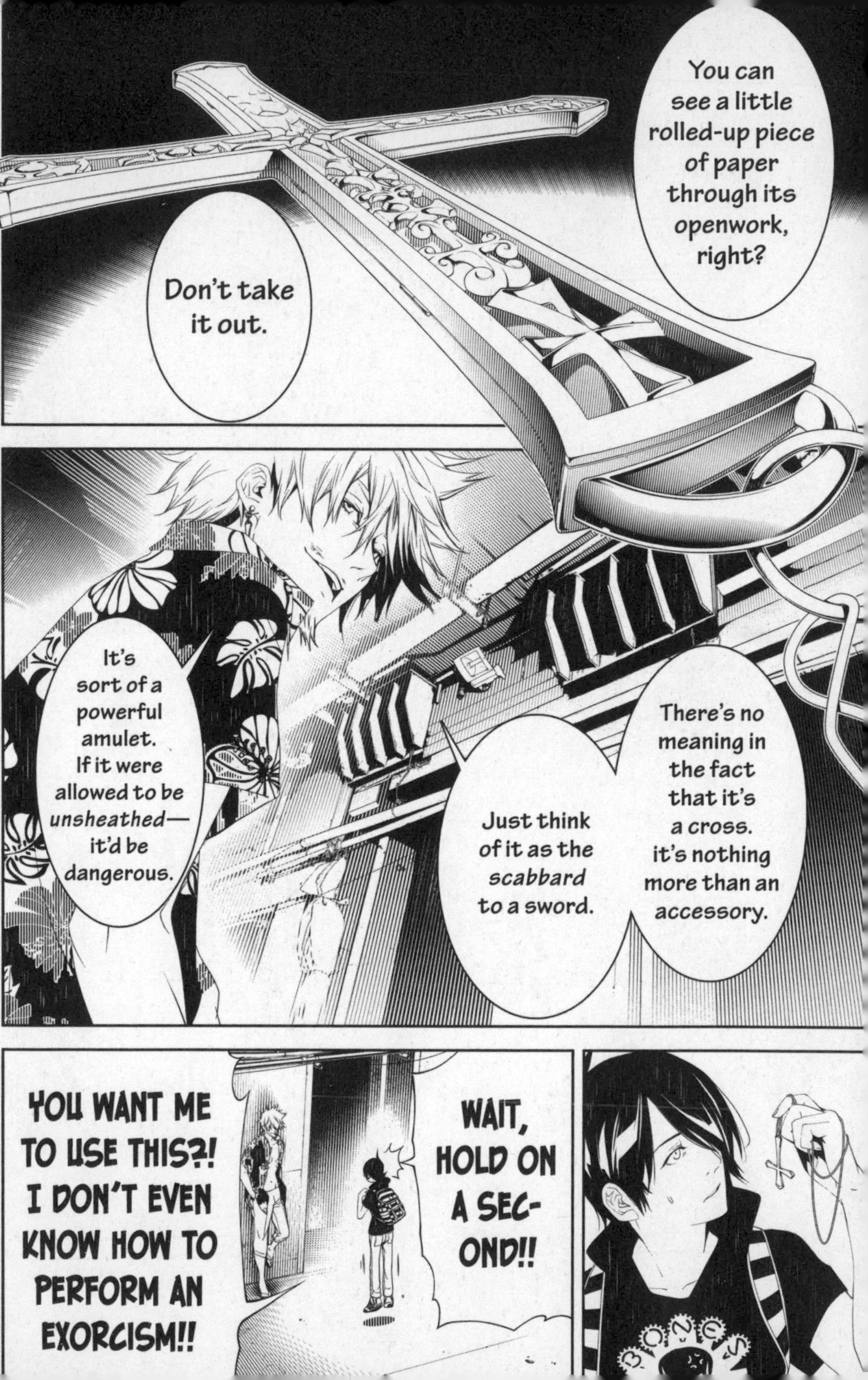
You can see a little rolled-up piece of paper through its openwork, right?
Don't take it out.
There's no meaning in the fact that it's a cross. it's nothing more than an accessory.
Just think of it as the *scabbard* to a sword.
It's sort of a powerful amulet. If it were allowed to be *unsheathed*—it'd be dangerous.
WAIT, HOLD ON A SEC-OND!!
YOU WANT ME TO USE THIS?! I DON'T EVEN KNOW HOW TO PERFORM AN EXORCISM!!

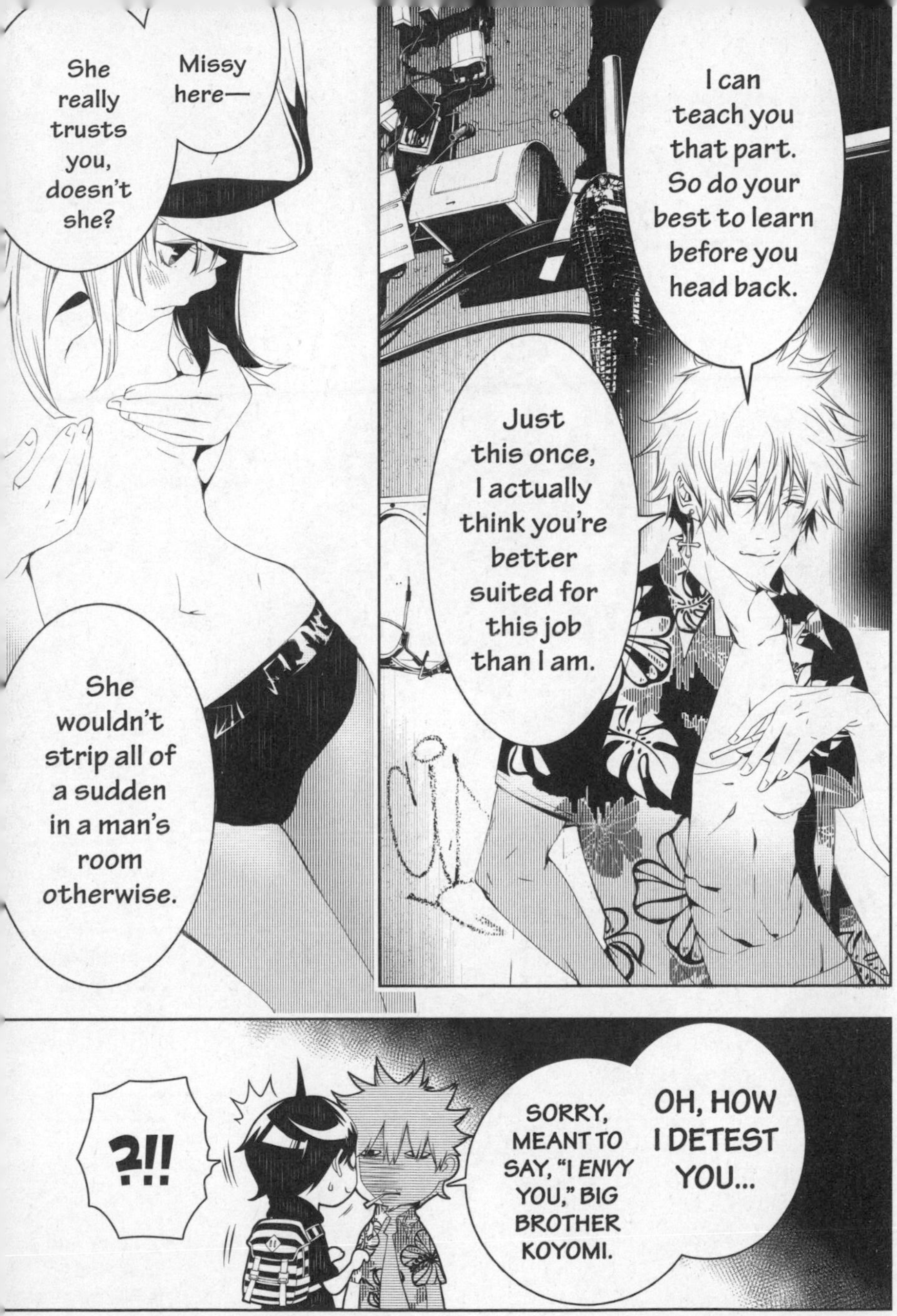
I can teach you that part. So do your best to learn before you head back.
Just this once, I actually think you're better suited for this job than I am.
Missy here— She really trusts you, doesn't she?
She wouldn't strip all of a sudden in a man's room otherwise.
OH, HOW I DETEST YOU...
SORRY, MEANT TO SAY, "I ENVY YOU," BIG BROTHER KOYOMI.
?!!

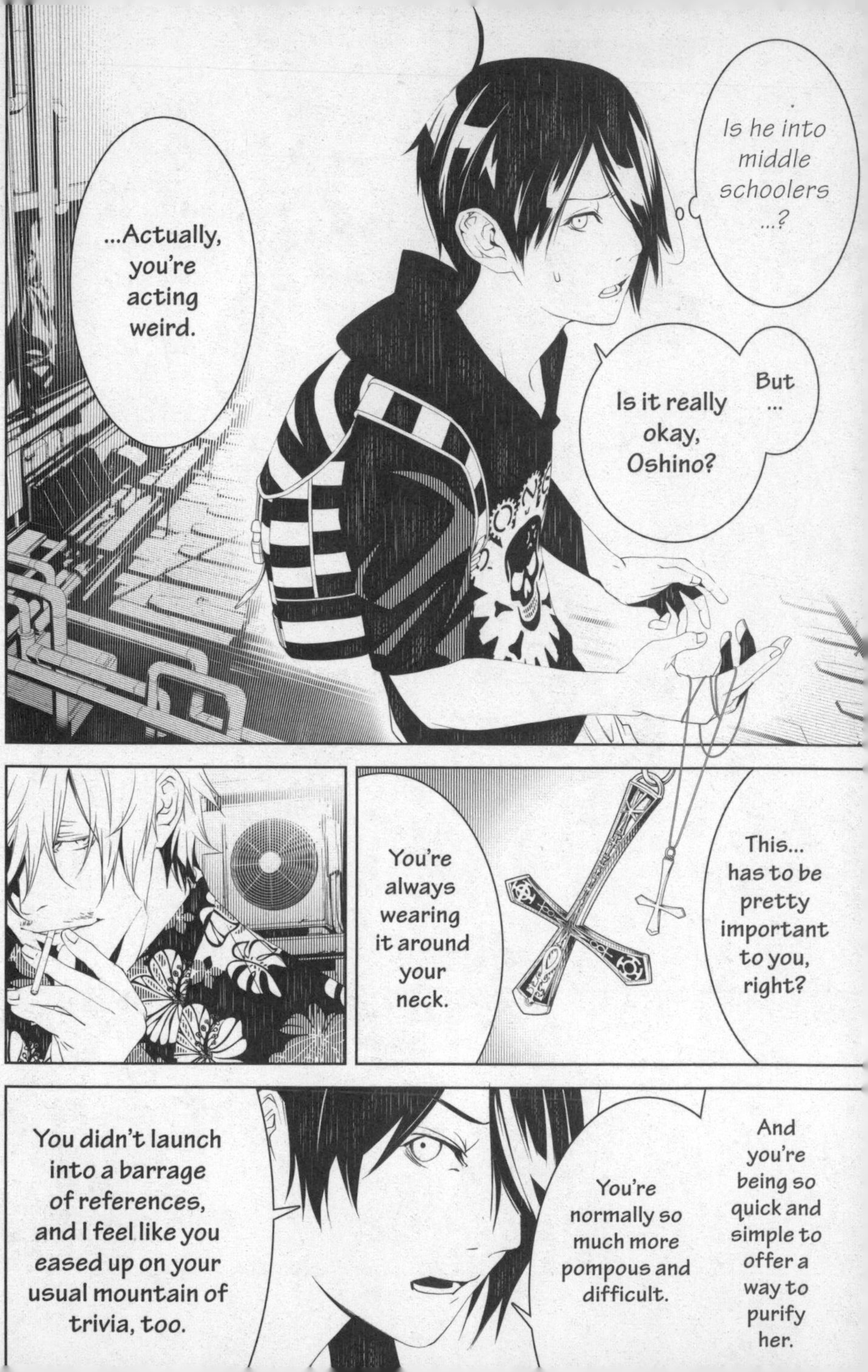
Is he into middle schoolers ...?
But ...
Is it really okay, Oshino?
...Actually, you're acting weird.
This... has to be pretty important to you, right?
You're always wearing it around your neck.
And you're being so quick and simple to offer a way to purify her.
You're normally so much more pompous and difficult.
You didn't launch into a barrage of references, and I feel like you eased up on your usual mountain of trivia, too.

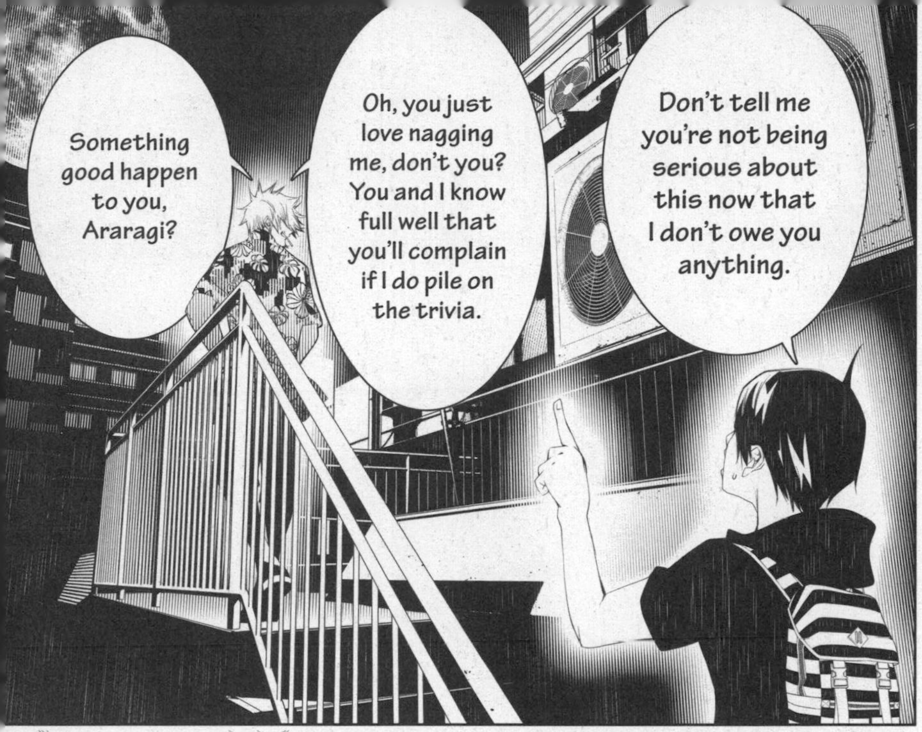
Don't tell me you're not being serious about this now that I don't owe you anything.
Oh, you just love nagging me, don't you? You and I know full well that you'll complain if I do pile on the trivia.
Something good happen to you, Araragi?

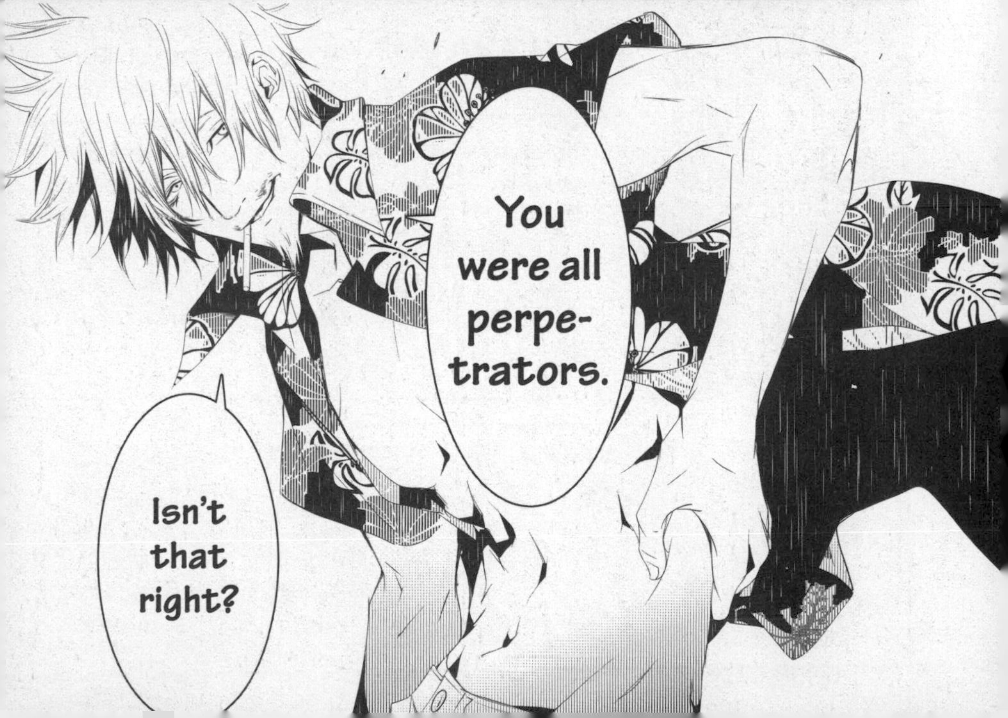
You were all perpe-trators.
Isn't that right?

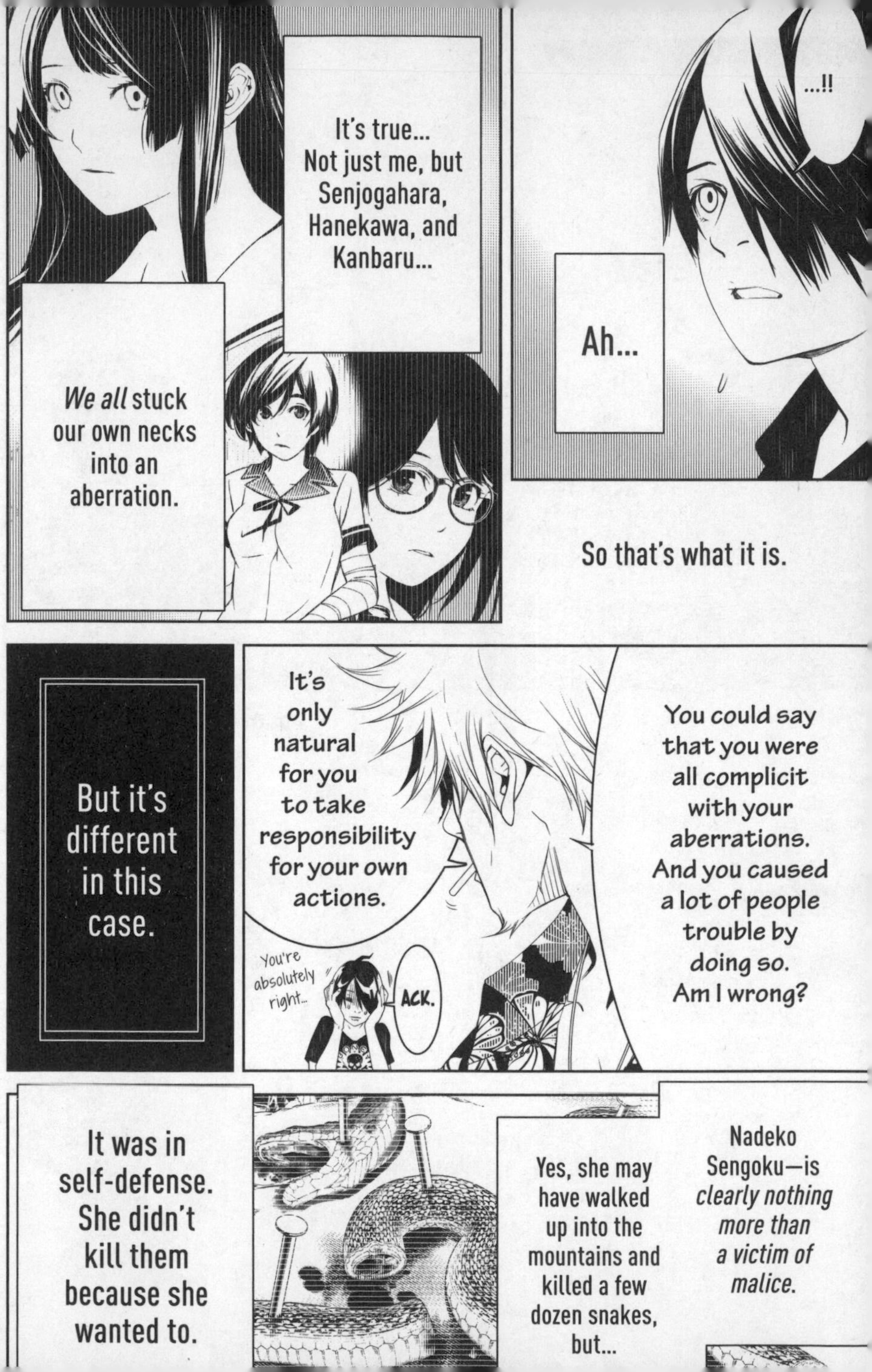
...!!
Ah...
So that's what it is.
It's true... Not just me, but Senjogahara, Hanekawa, and Kanbaru...
We all stuck our own necks into an aberration.
You could say that you were all complicit with your aberrations. And you caused a lot of people trouble by doing so. Am I wrong?
It's only natural for you to take responsibility for your own actions.
ACK.
You're absolutely right...
But it's different in this case.
Nadeko Sengoku—is *clearly nothing more than a victim of malice.*
Yes, she may have walked up into the mountains and killed a few dozen snakes, but...
It was in self-defense. She didn't kill them because she wanted to.

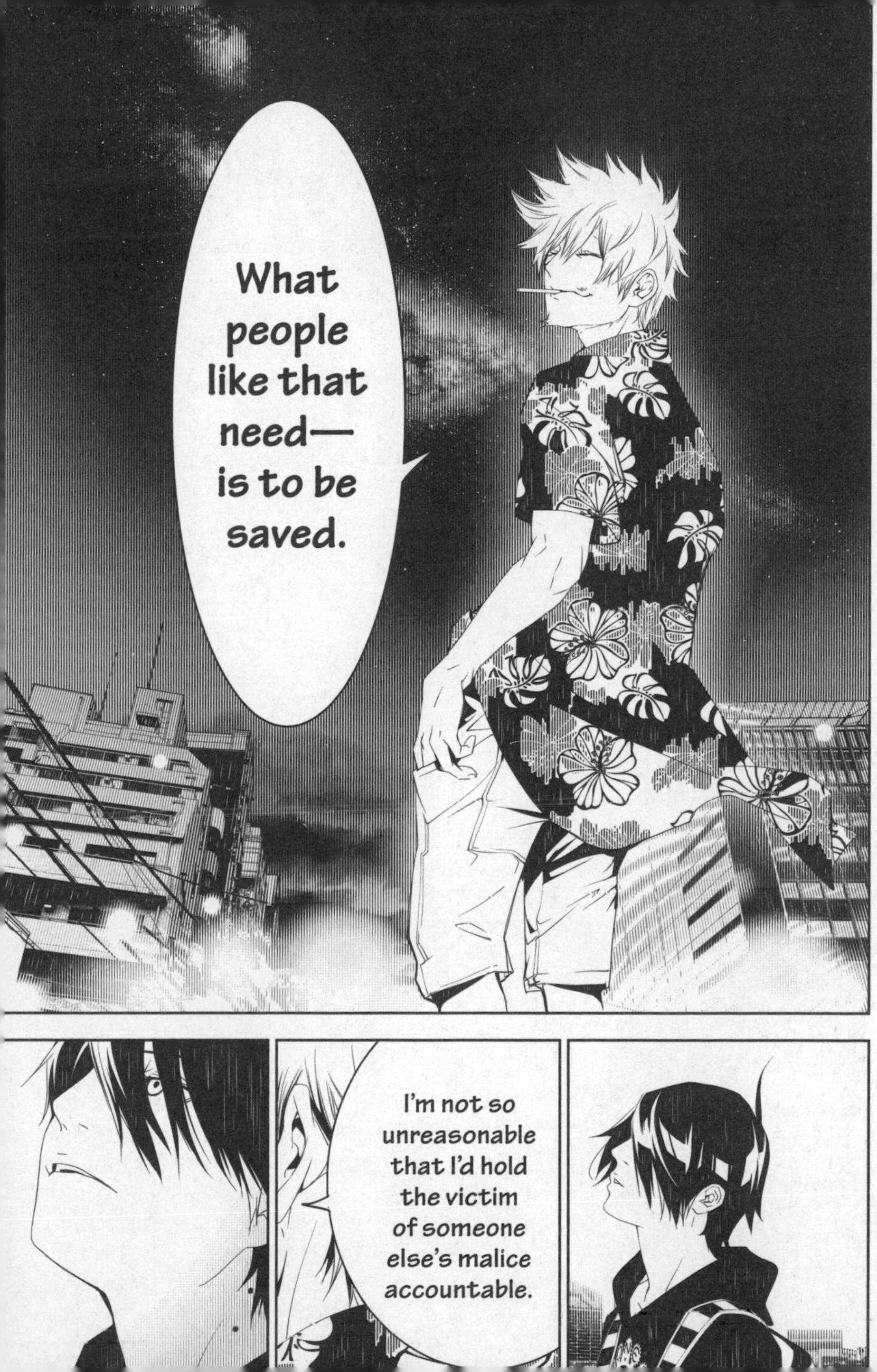
What people like that need— is to be saved.
I'm not so unreasonable that I'd hold the victim of someone else's malice accountable.

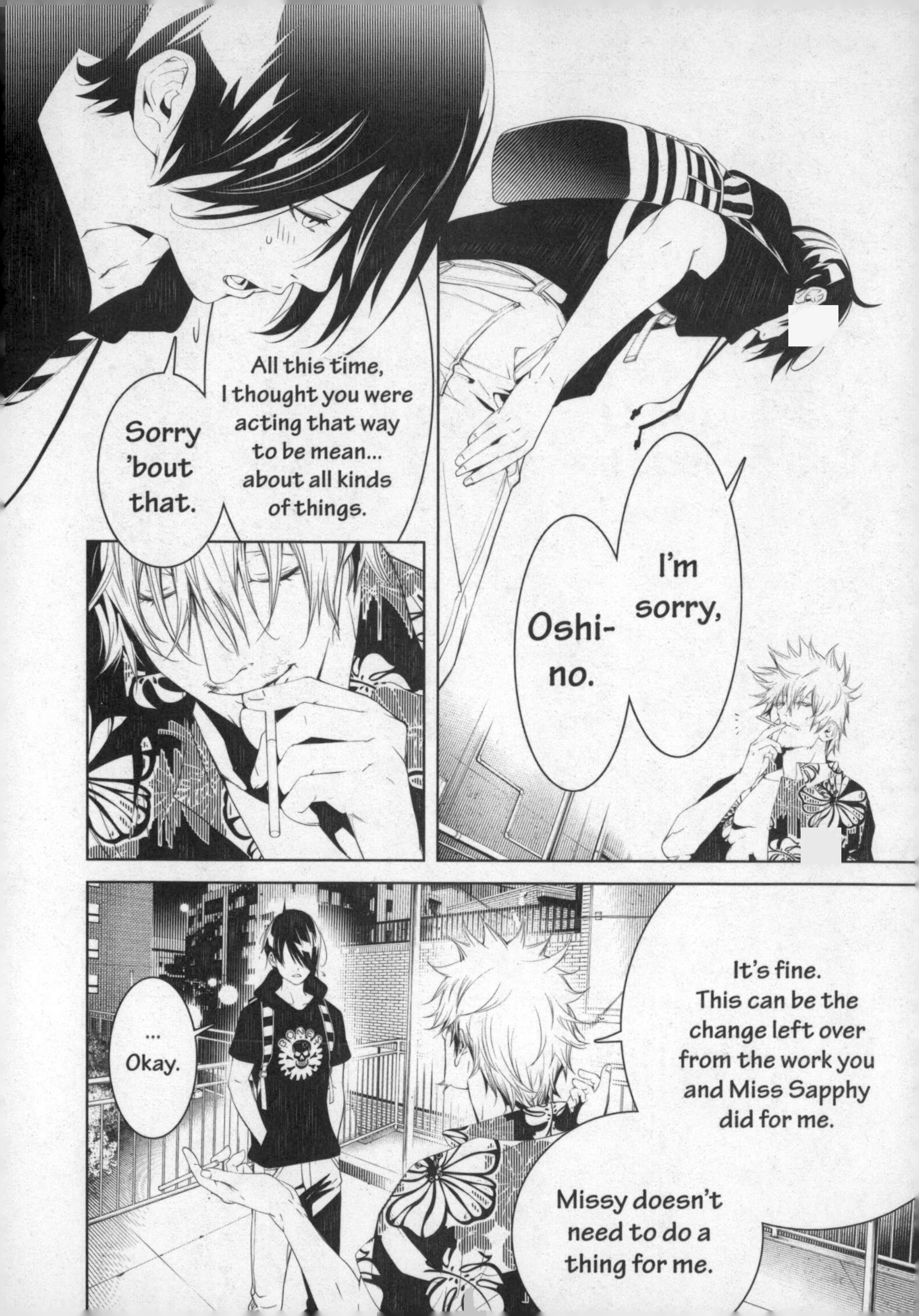
All this time, I thought you were acting that way to be mean... about all kinds of things.
Sorry 'bout that.
I'm sorry, Oshino.
It's fine. This can be the change left over from the work you and Miss Sapphy did for me.
Missy doesn't need to do a thing for me.
... Okay.

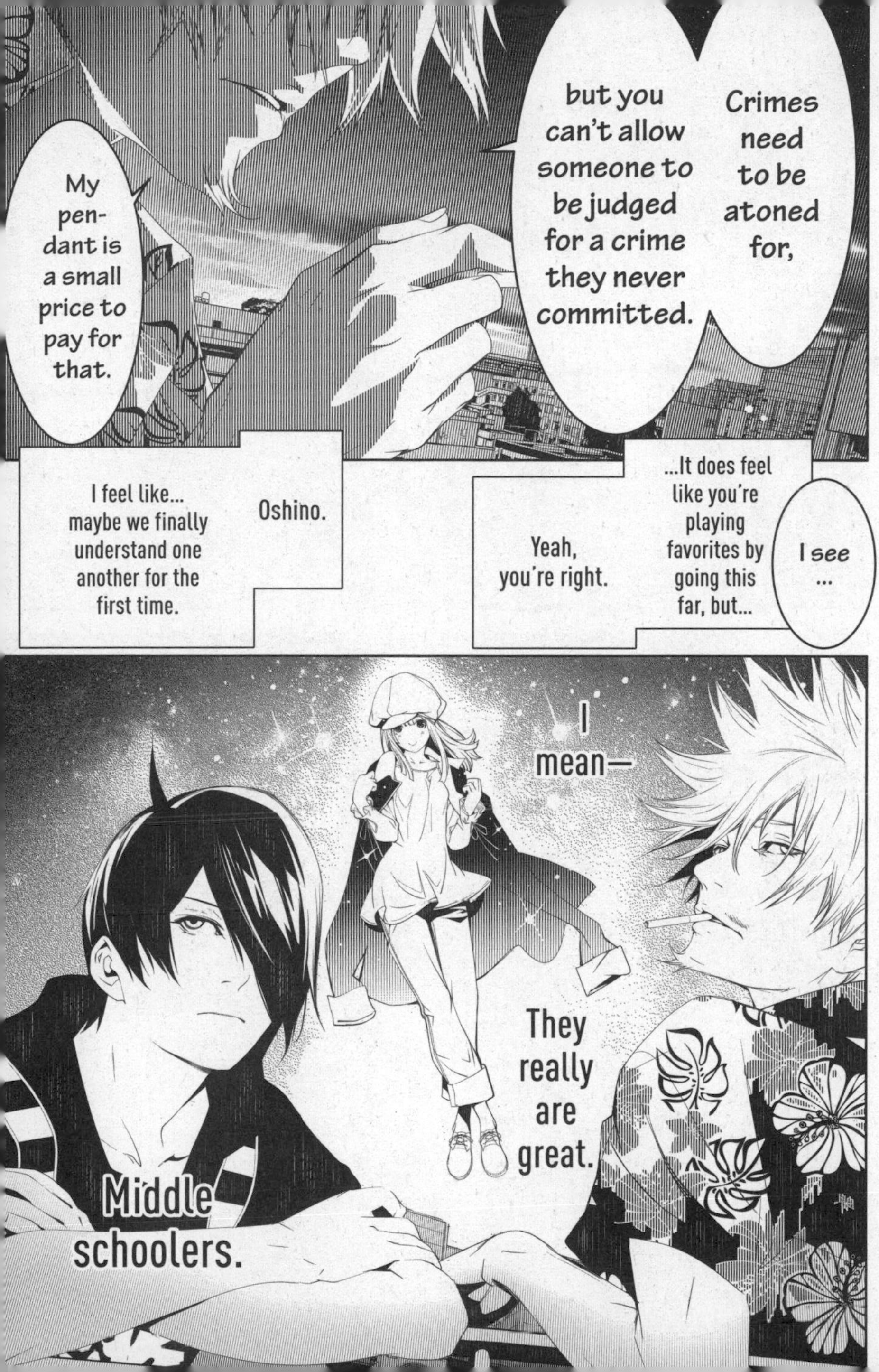
Crimes need to be atoned for,
but you can't allow someone to be judged for a crime they never committed.
My pen-dant is a small price to pay for that.
I see ...
...It does feel like you're playing favorites by going this far, but...
Yeah, you're right.
Oshino.
I feel like... maybe we finally understand one another for the first time.
I mean—
They really are great.
Middle schoolers.

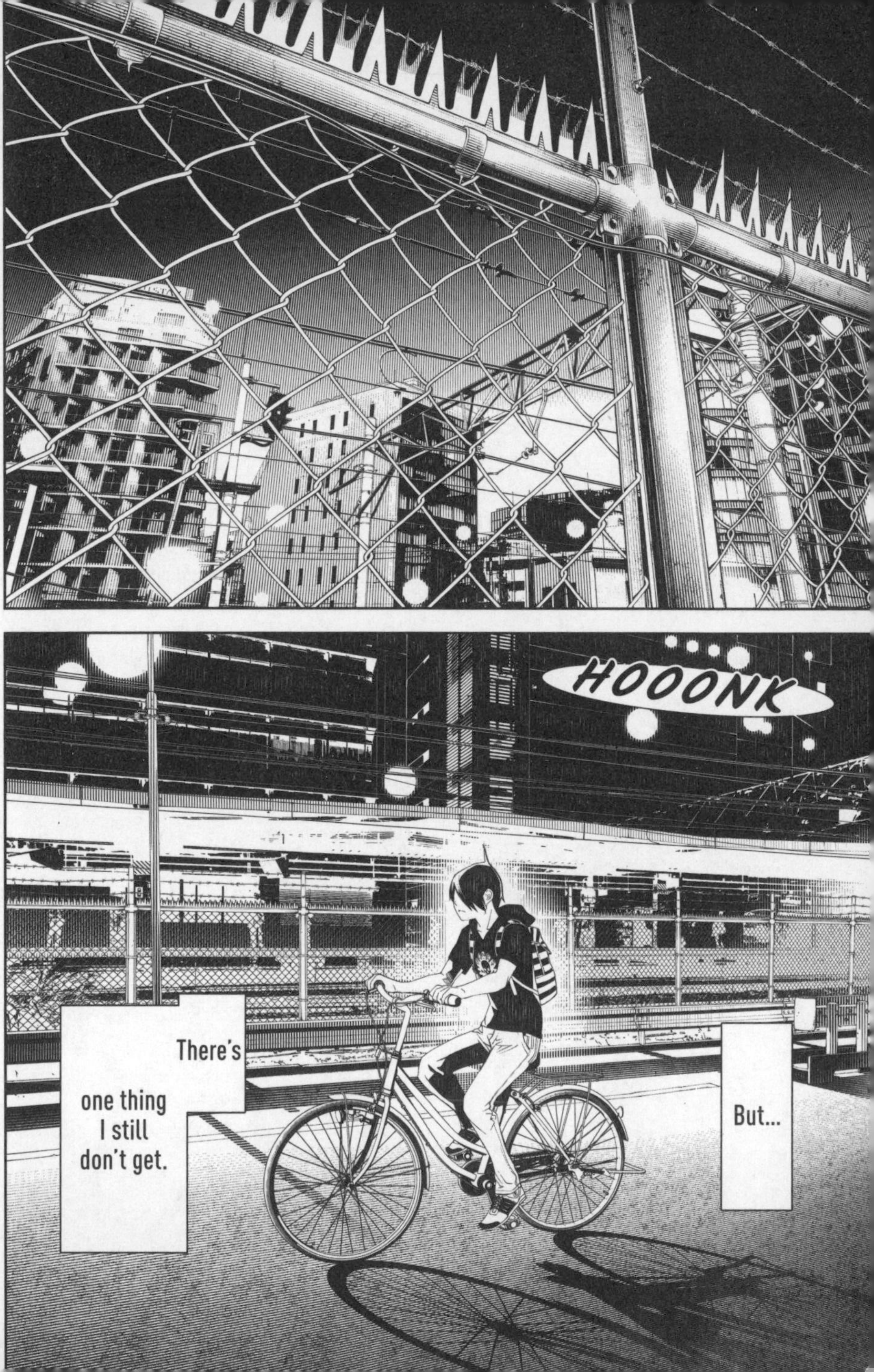
HOOONK
But...
There's one thing I still don't get.

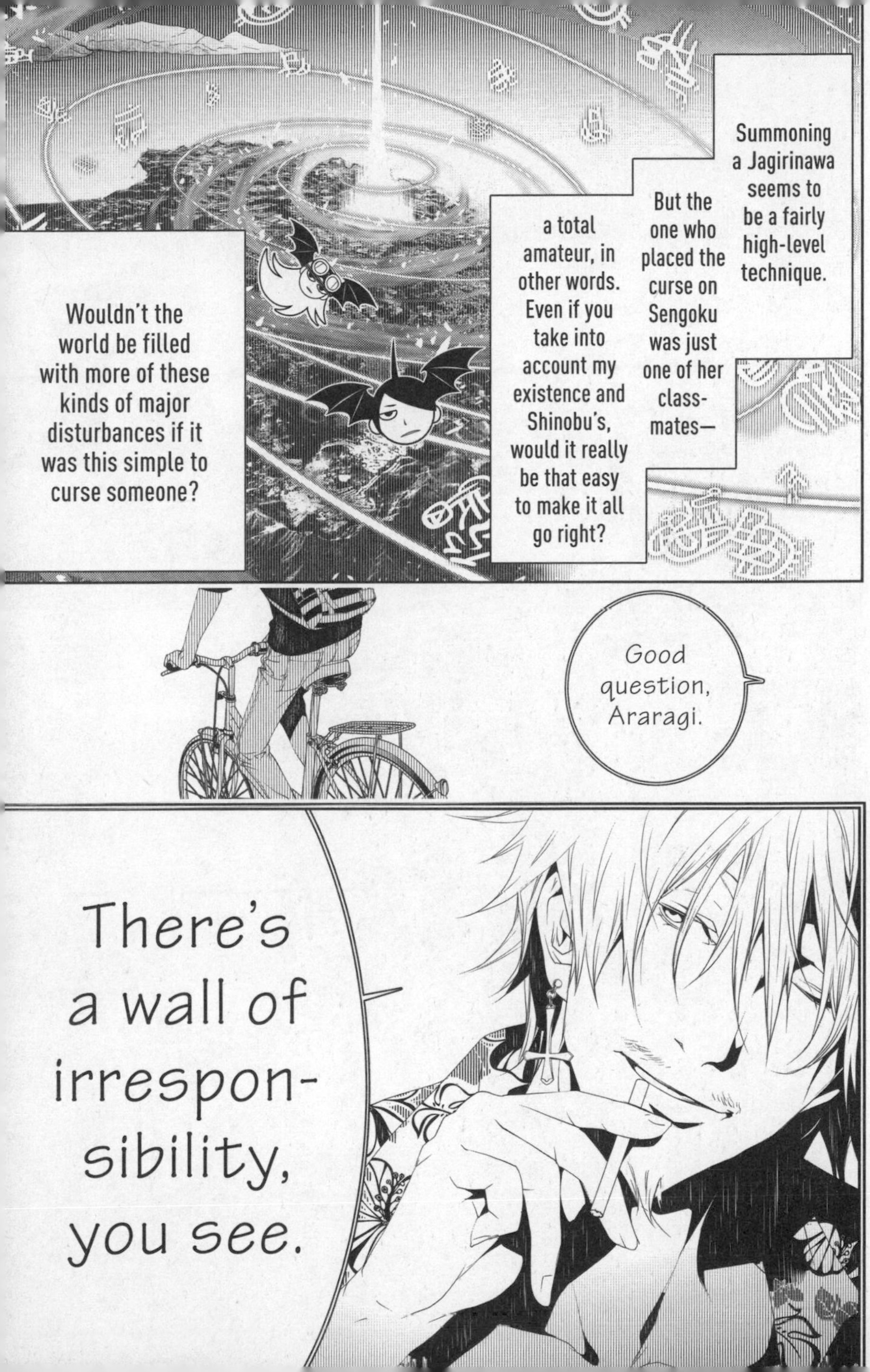
Summoning a Jagirinawa seems to be a fairly high-level technique.
But the one who placed the curse on Sengoku was just one of her classmates—
a total amateur, in other words. Even if you take into account my existence and Shinobu's, would it really be that easy to make it all go right?
Wouldn't the world be filled with more of these kinds of major disturbances if it was this simple to curse someone?
Good question, Araragi.
There's a wall of irrespon-sibility, you see.

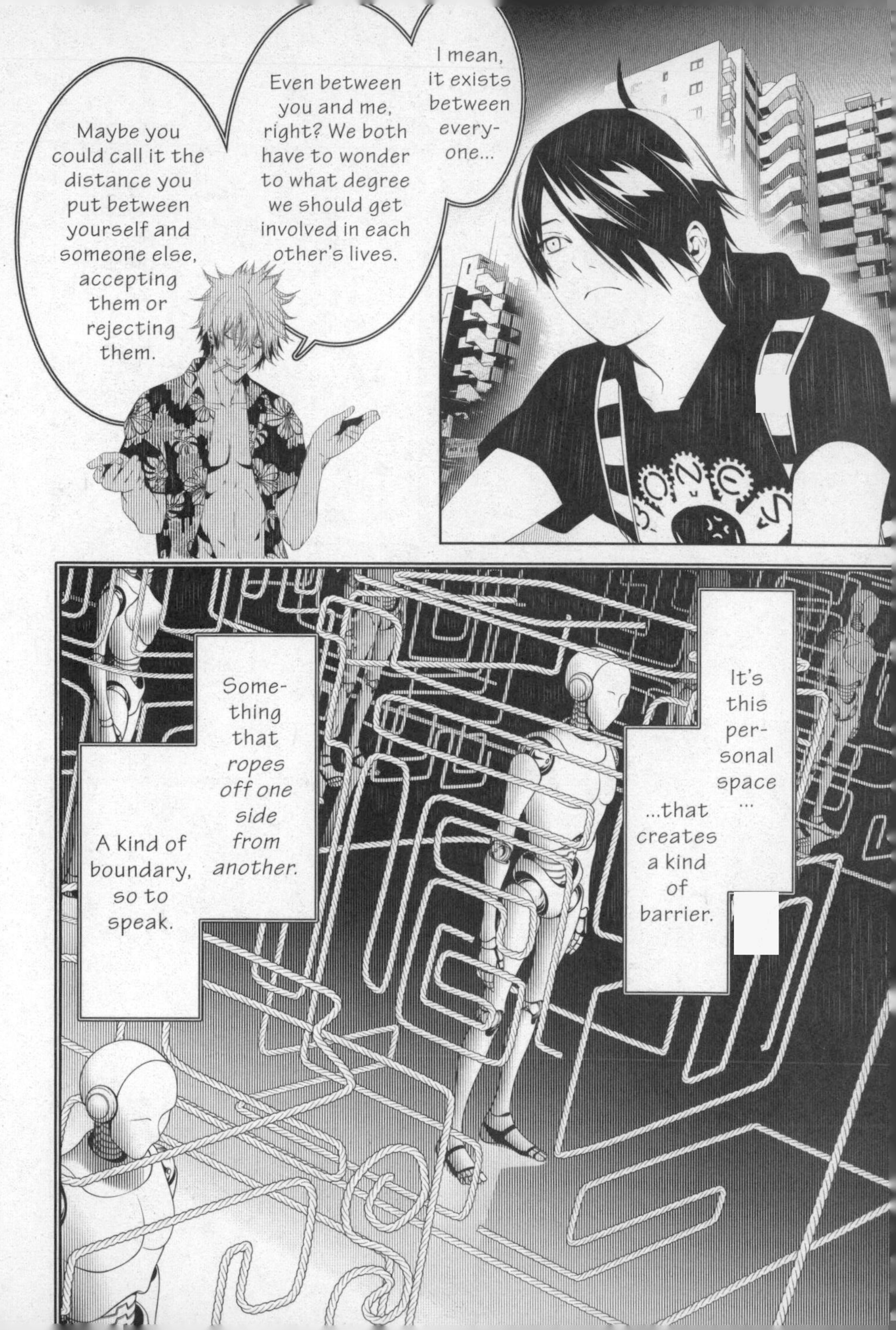
I mean, it exists between everyone...
Even between you and me, right? We both have to wonder to what degree we should get involved in each other's lives.
Maybe you could call it the distance you put between yourself and someone else, accepting them or rejecting them.
It's this personal space...
...that creates a kind of barrier.
Something that ropes off one side from another.
A kind of boundary, so to speak.

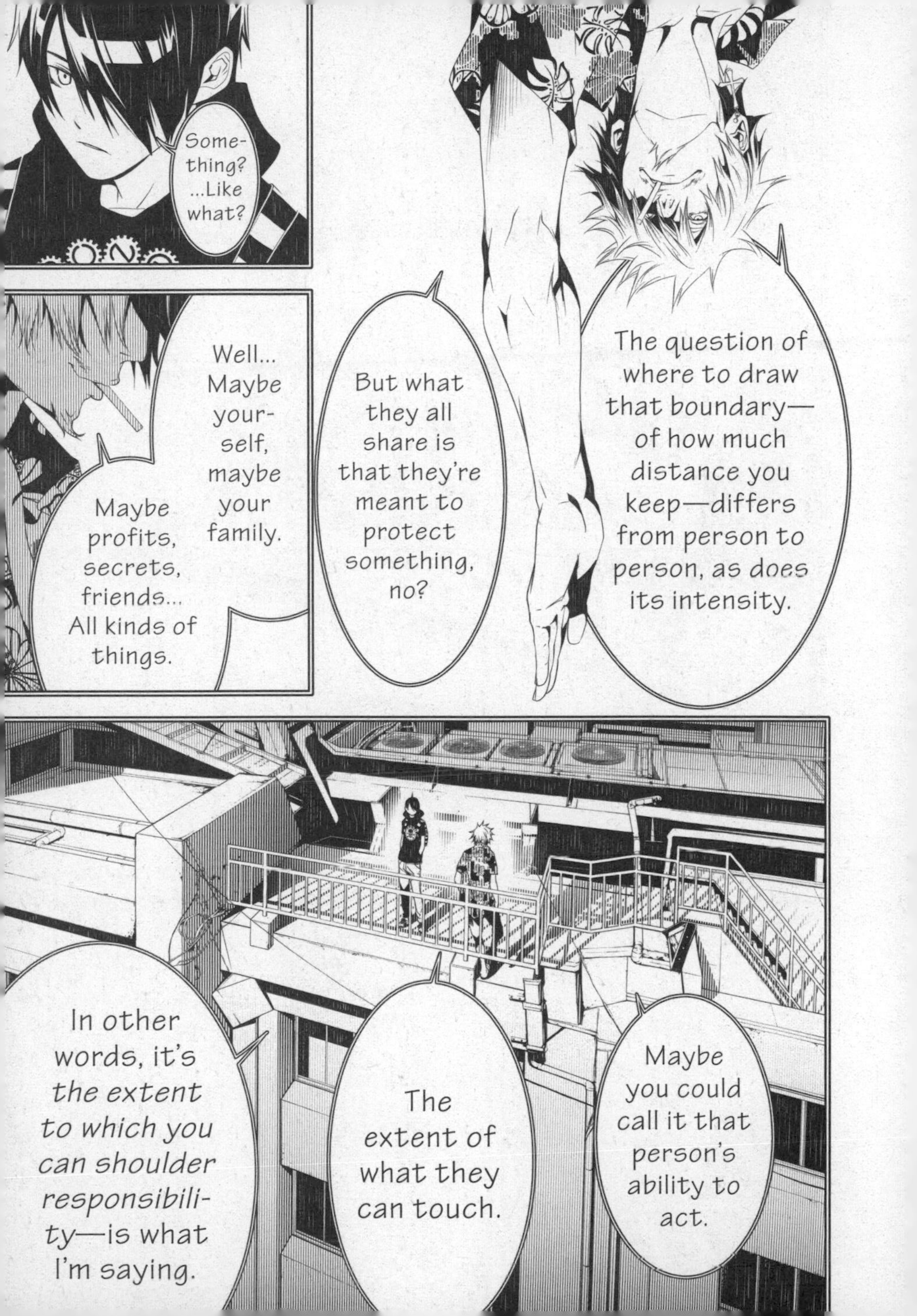
The question of where to draw that boundary—of how much distance you keep—differs from person to person, as does its intensity.
But what they all share is that they're meant to protect something, no?
Something? ...Like what?
Well... Maybe yourself, maybe your family.
Maybe profits, secrets, friends... All kinds of things.
Maybe you could call it that person's ability to act.
The extent of what they can touch.
In other words, it's *the extent to which you can shoulder responsibility*—is what I'm saying.

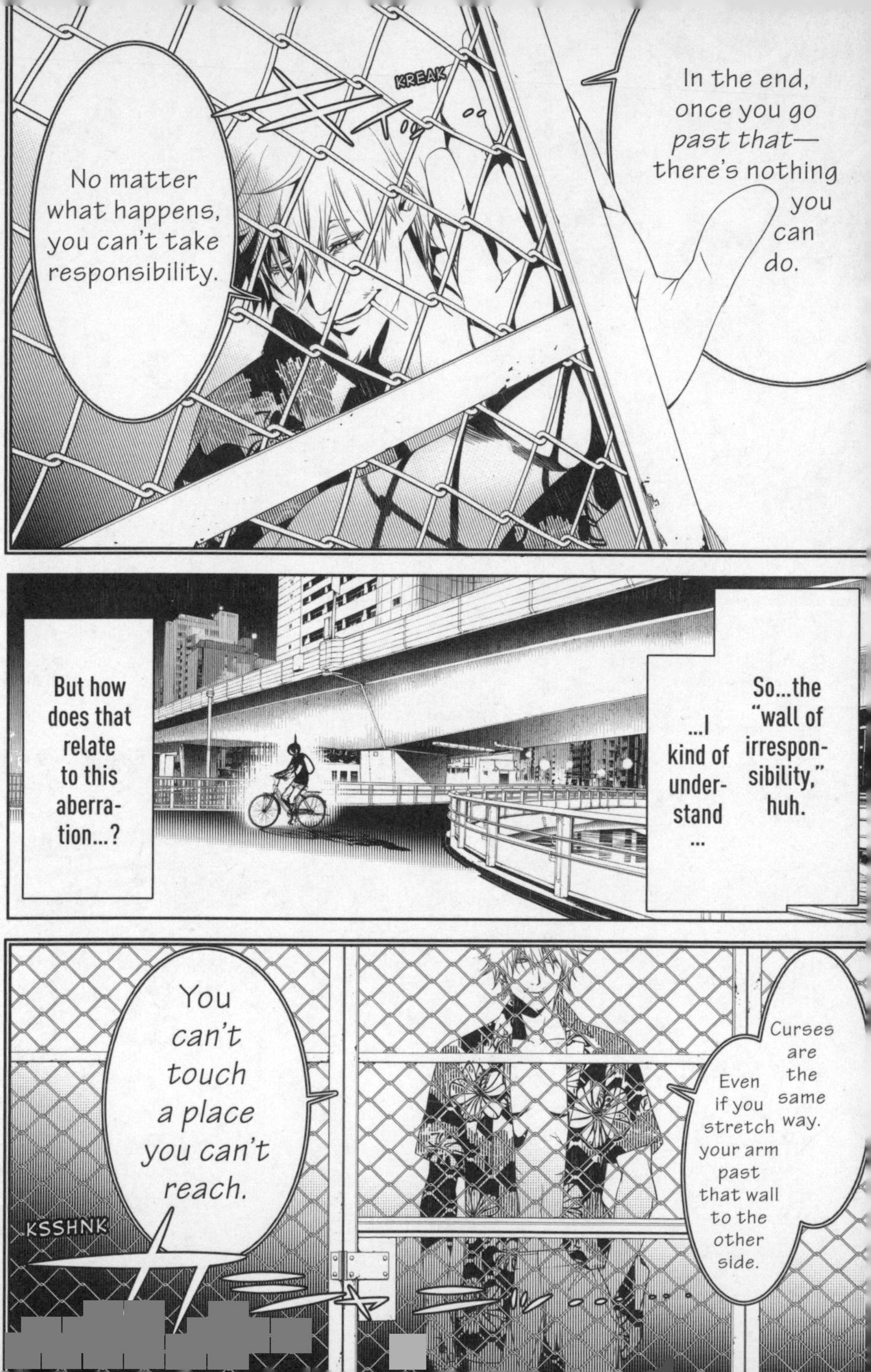
In the end, once you go past that— there's nothing you can do.
KREAK
No matter what happens, you can't take responsibility.
So...the "wall of irresponsibility," huh.
...I kind of understand...
But how does that relate to this aberration...?
Curses are the same way.
Even if you stretch your arm past that wall to the other side.
You can't touch a place you can't reach.
KSSHNK

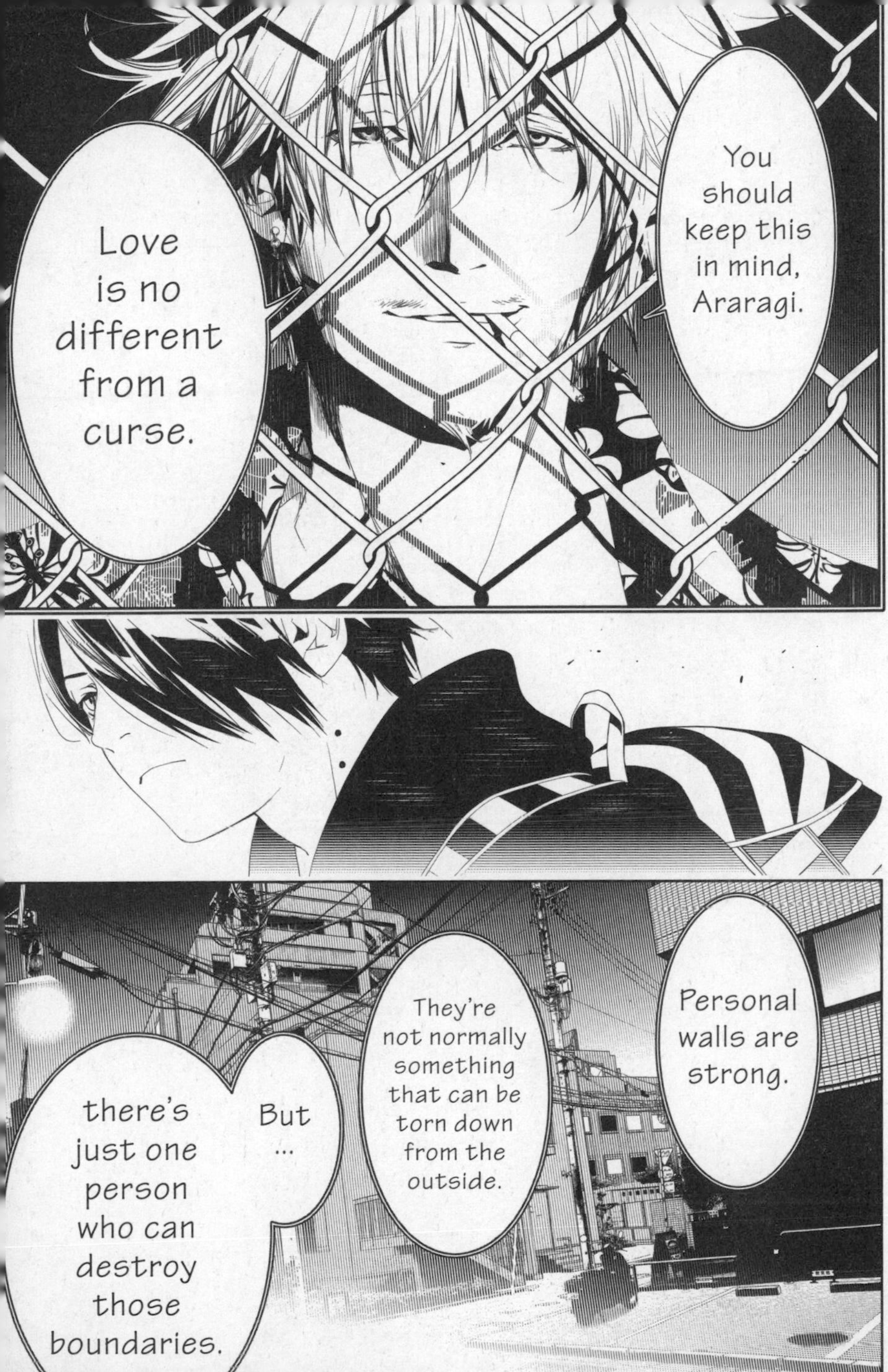
You should keep this in mind, Araragi.
Love is no different from a curse.
Personal walls are strong.
They're not normally something that can be torn down from the outside.
But ...
there's just one person who can destroy those boundaries.

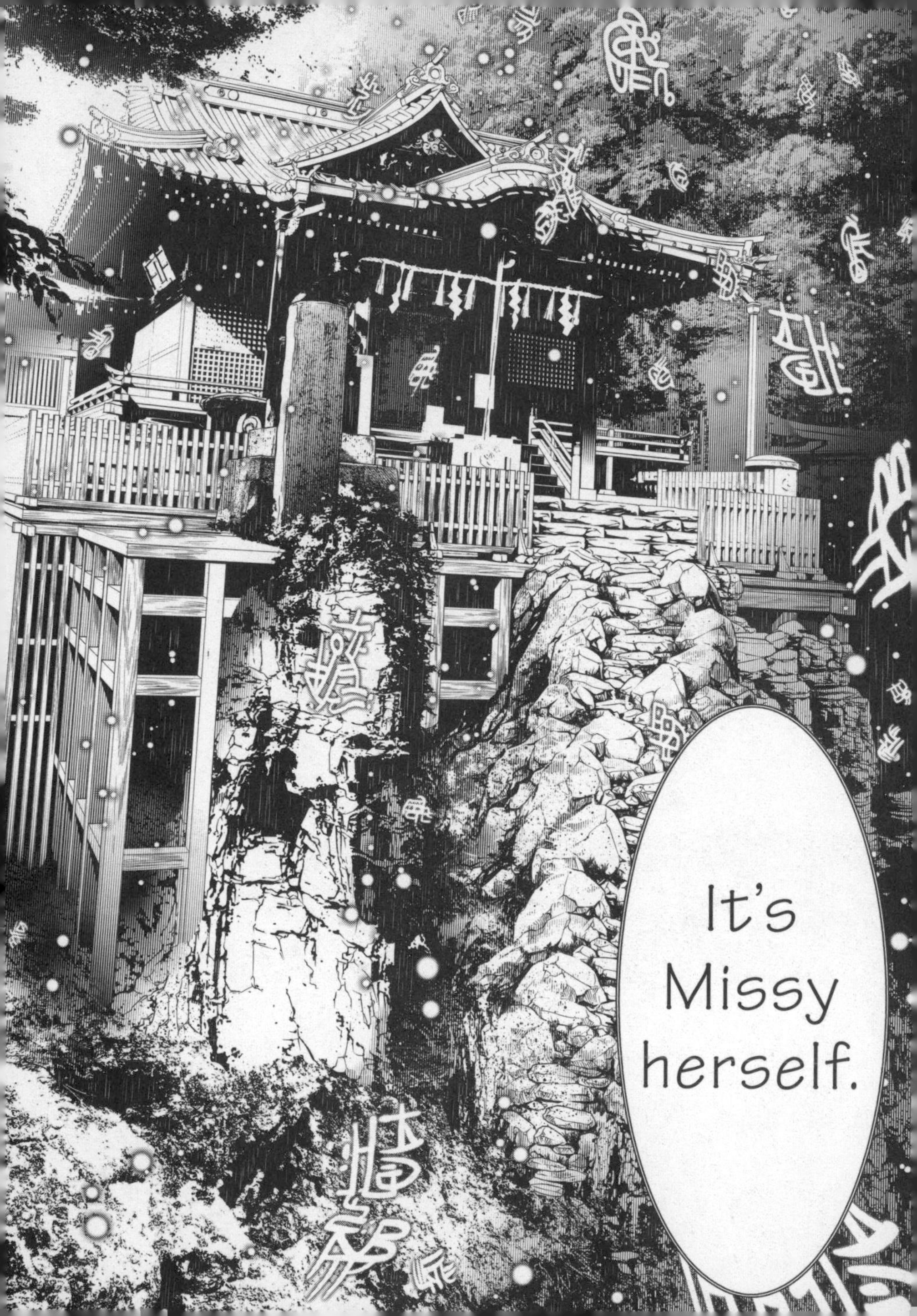
It's Missy herself.

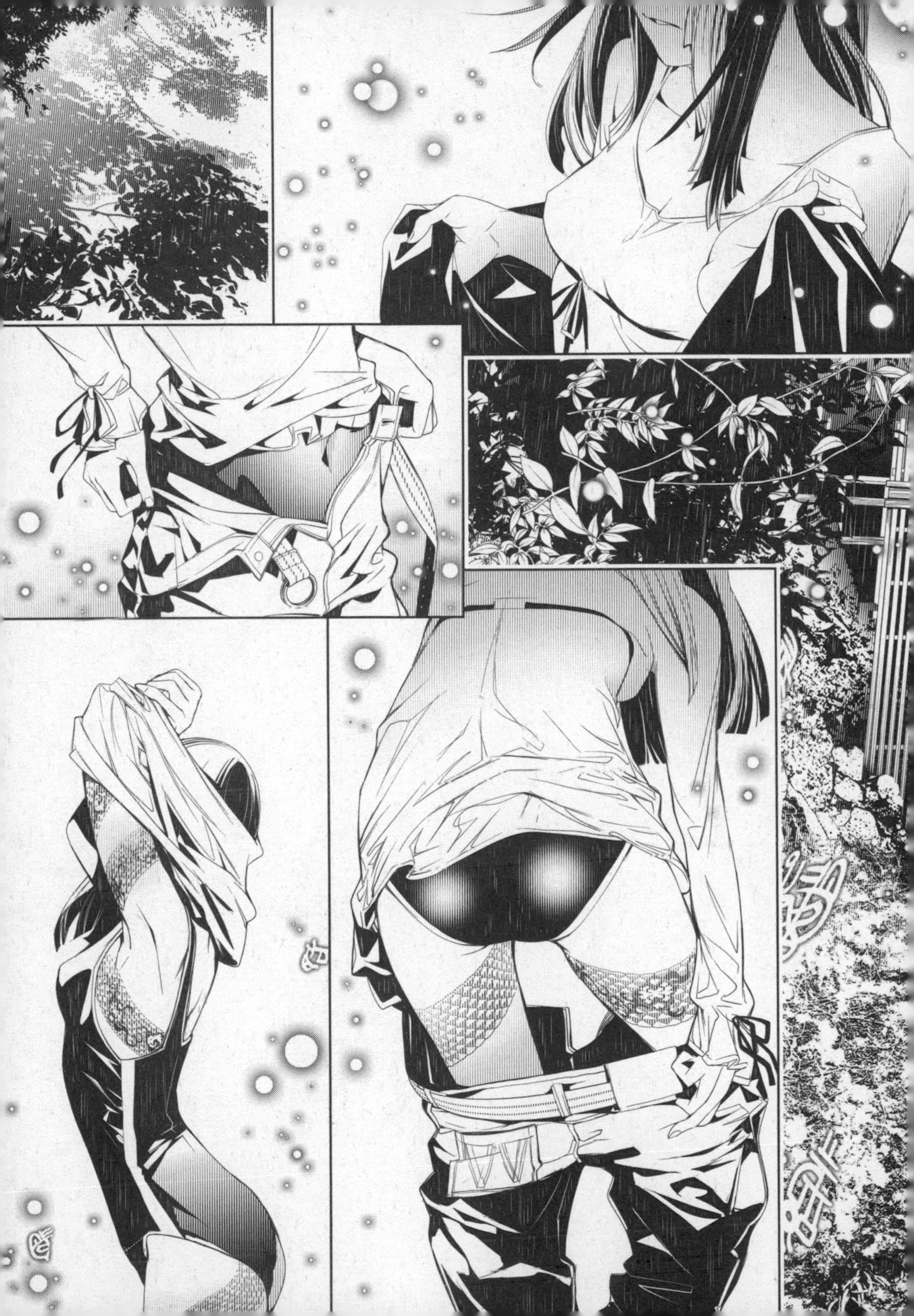

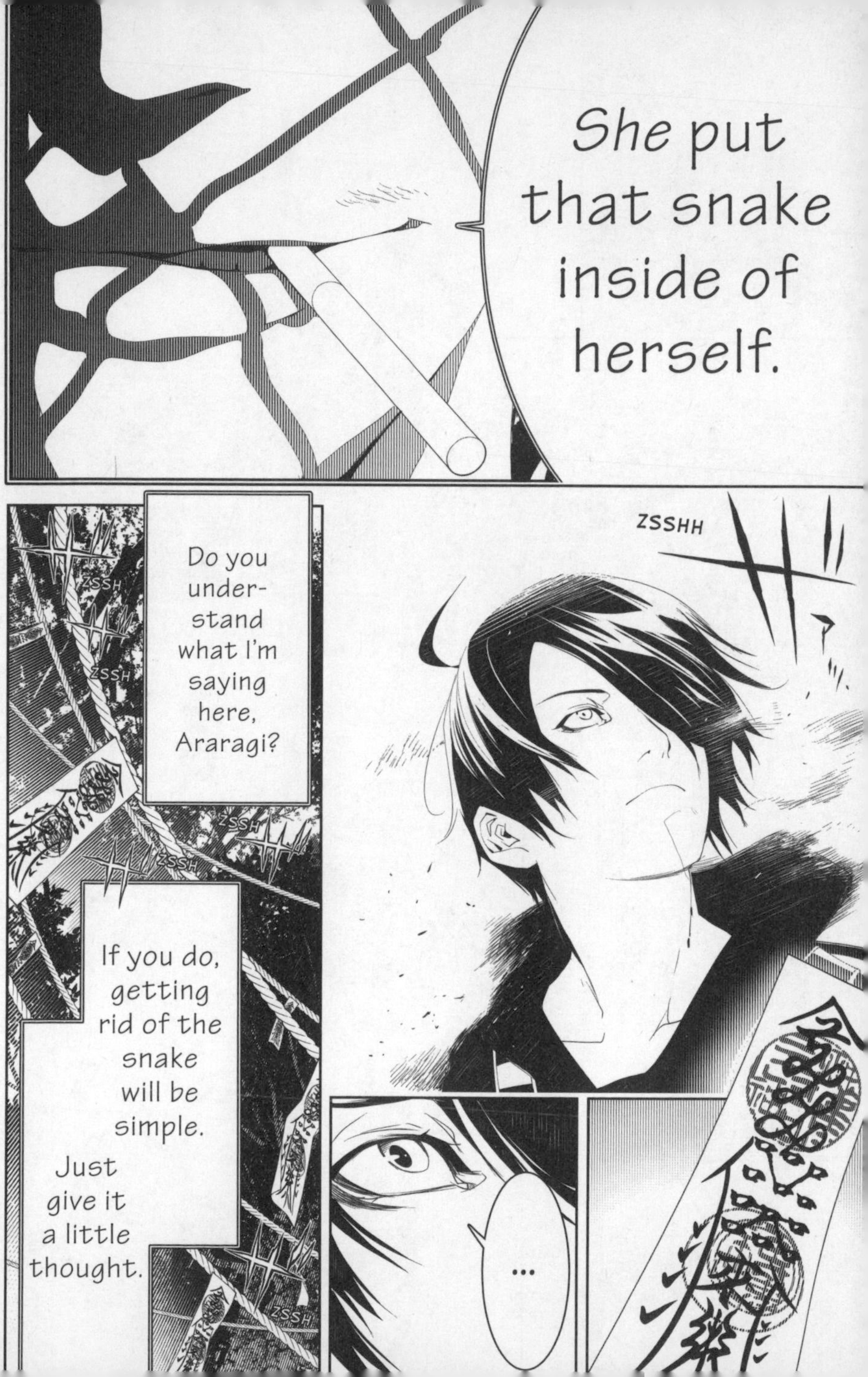
She put that snake inside of herself.
ZSSHH
...
Do you understand what I'm saying here, Araragi?
ZSSH
ZSSH
ZSSH
ZSSH
If you do, getting rid of the snake will be simple.
Just give it a little thought.
ZSSH

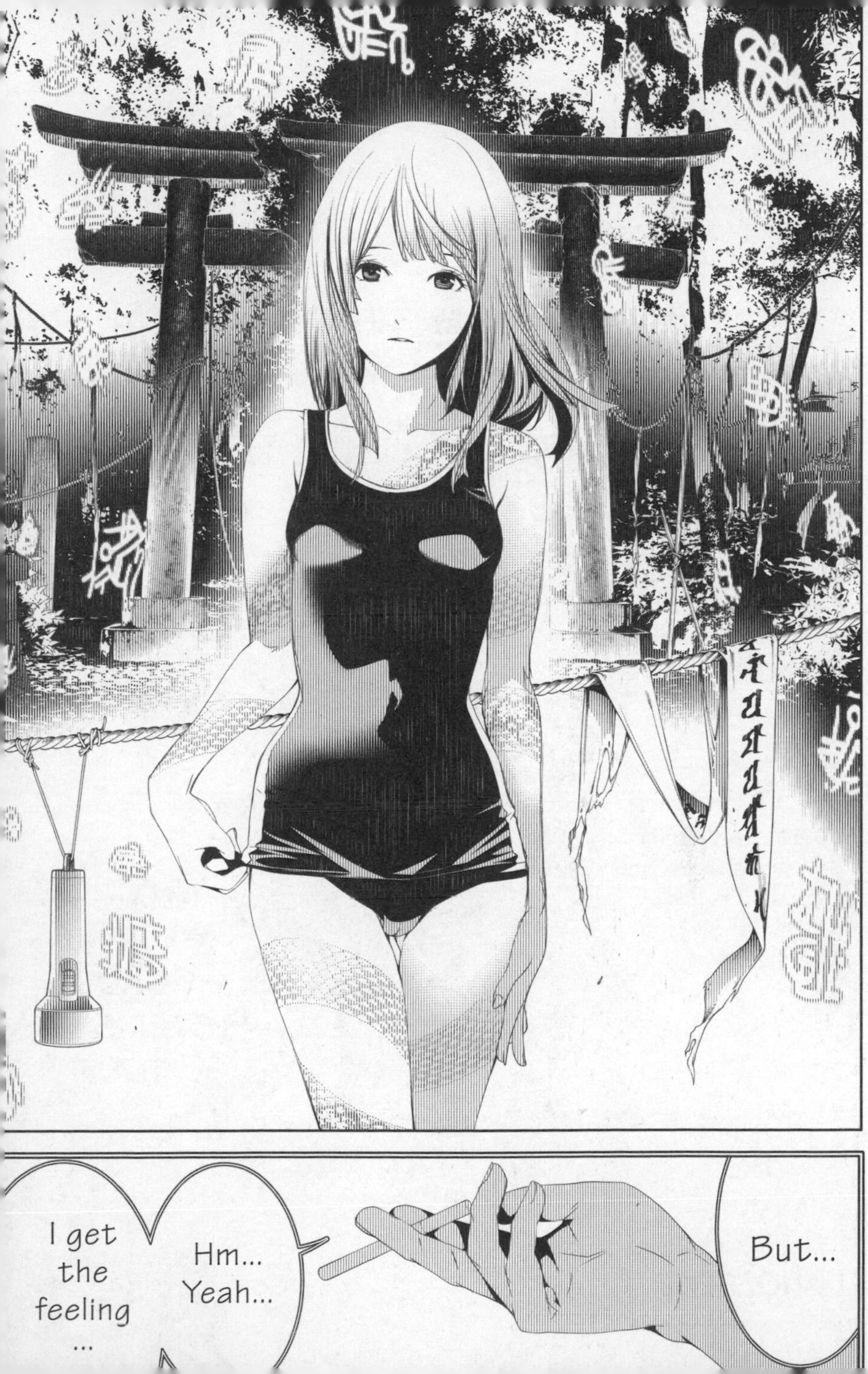

But...
Hm... Yeah...
I get the feeling ...

...that the reality of the situation...

...is going to be pretty tough on you.

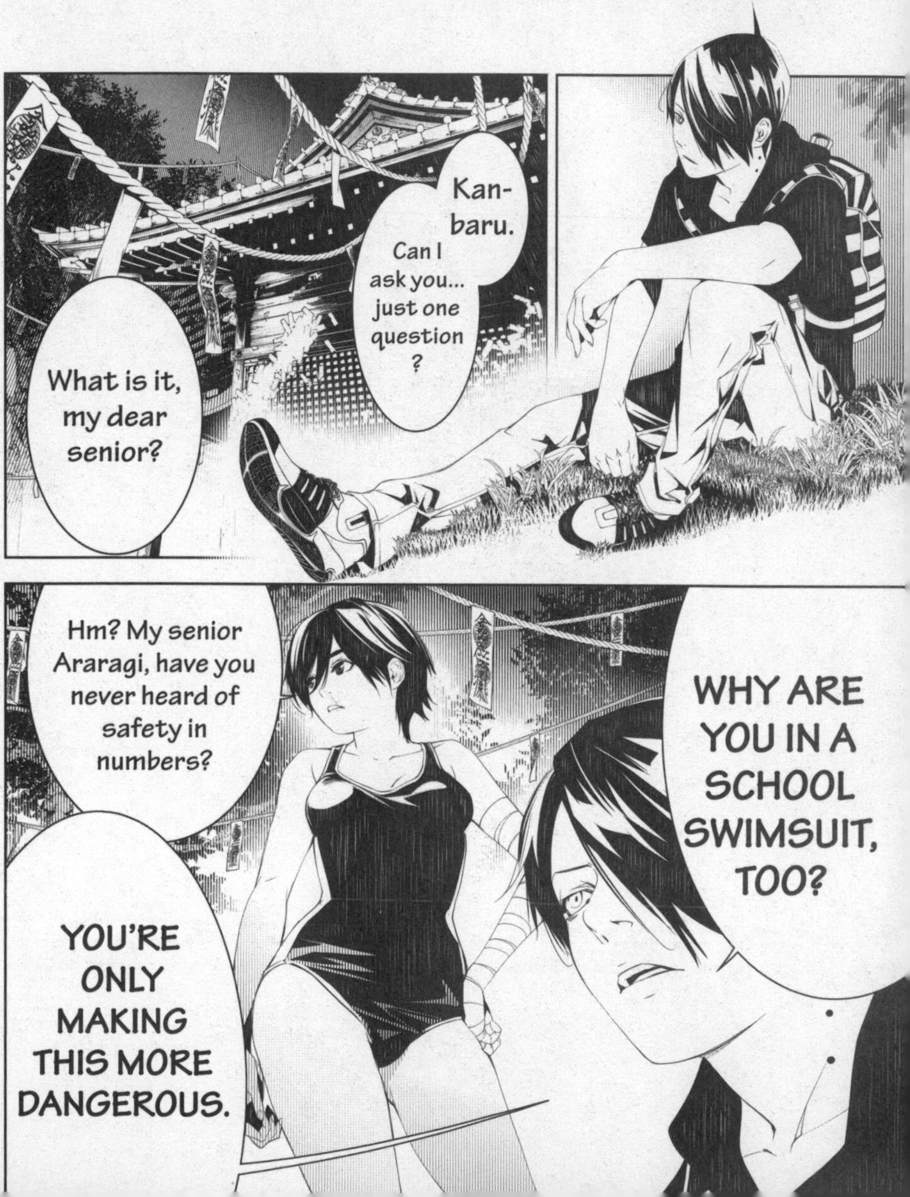

Kan-baru.
Can I ask you... just one question?
What is it, my dear senior?
WHY ARE YOU IN A SCHOOL SWIMSUIT, TOO?
Hm? My senior Araragi, have you never heard of safety in numbers?
YOU'RE ONLY MAKING THIS MORE DANGEROUS.

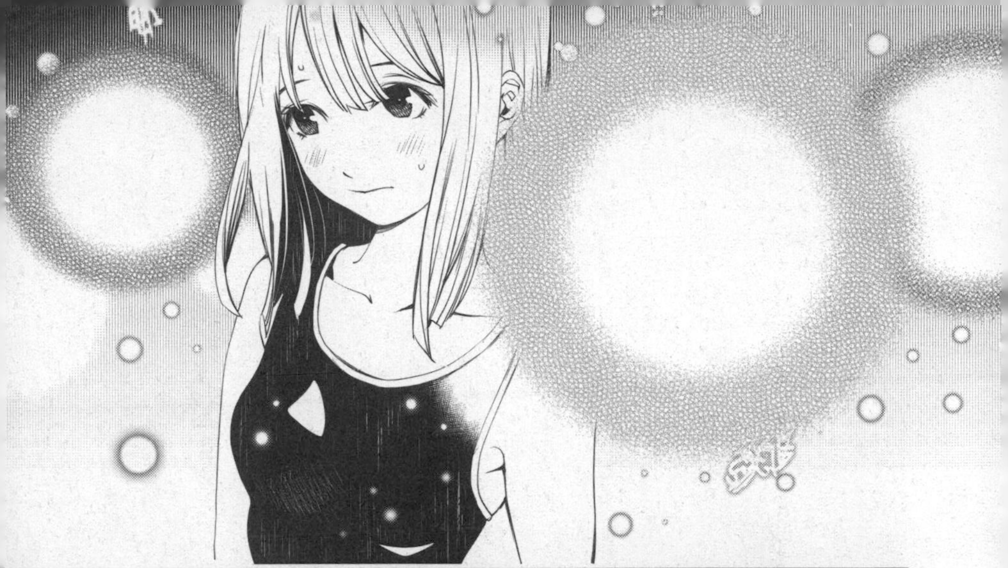

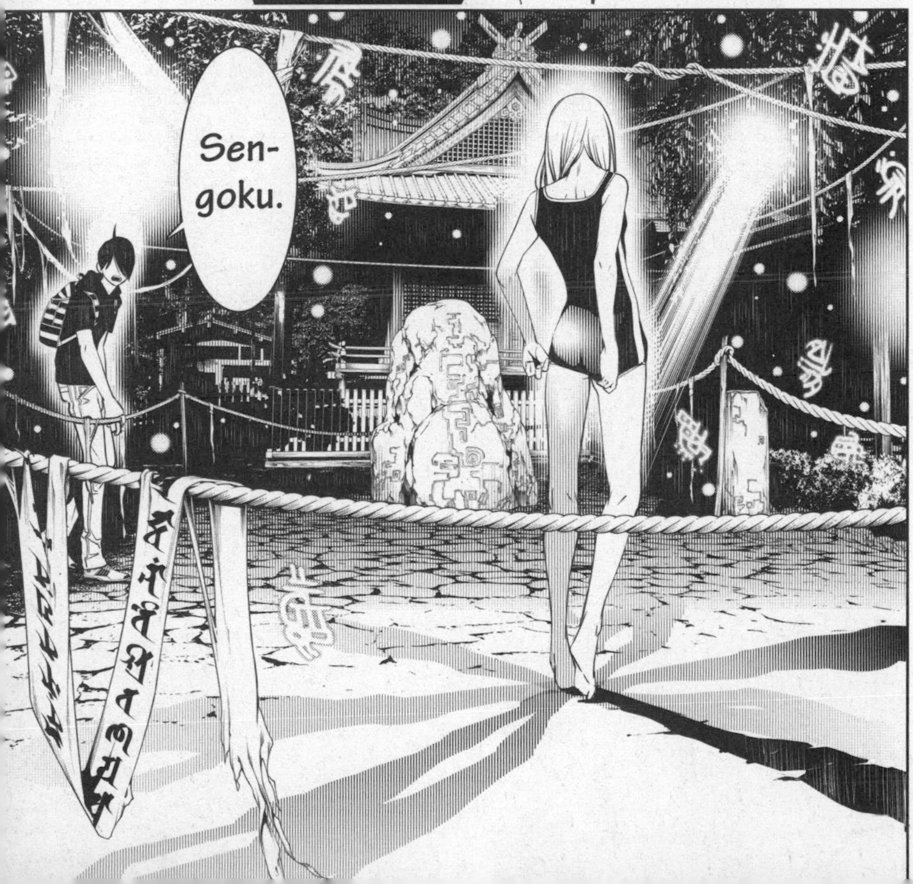
Sen-
goku.

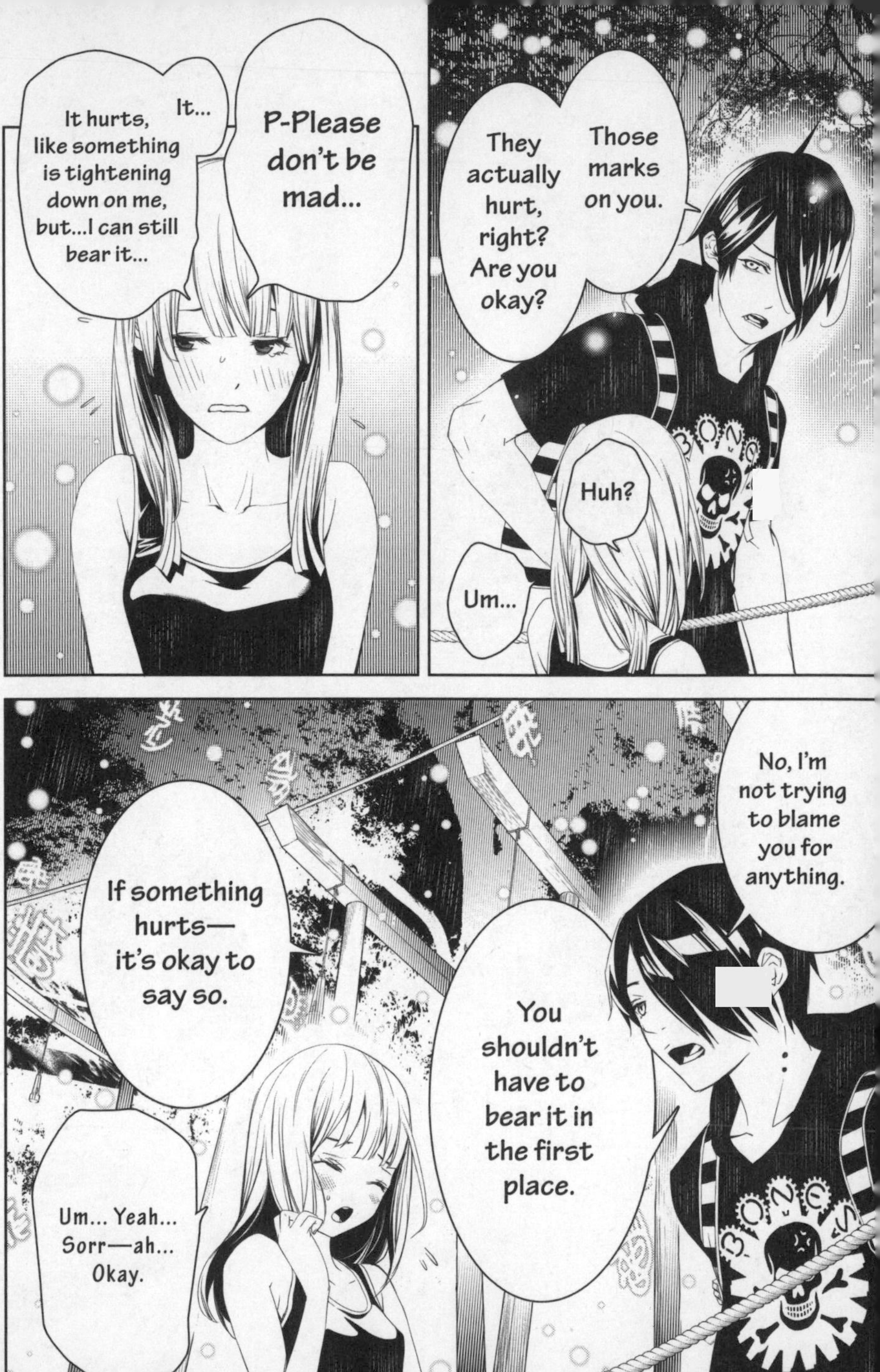
Those marks on you.
They actually hurt, right? Are you okay?
Huh?
Um...
P-Please don't be mad...
It...
It hurts, like something is tightening down on me, but...I can still bear it...
No, I'm not trying to blame you for anything.
You shouldn't have to bear it in the first place.
If something hurts— it's okay to say so.
Um... Yeah... Sorr—ah... Okay.

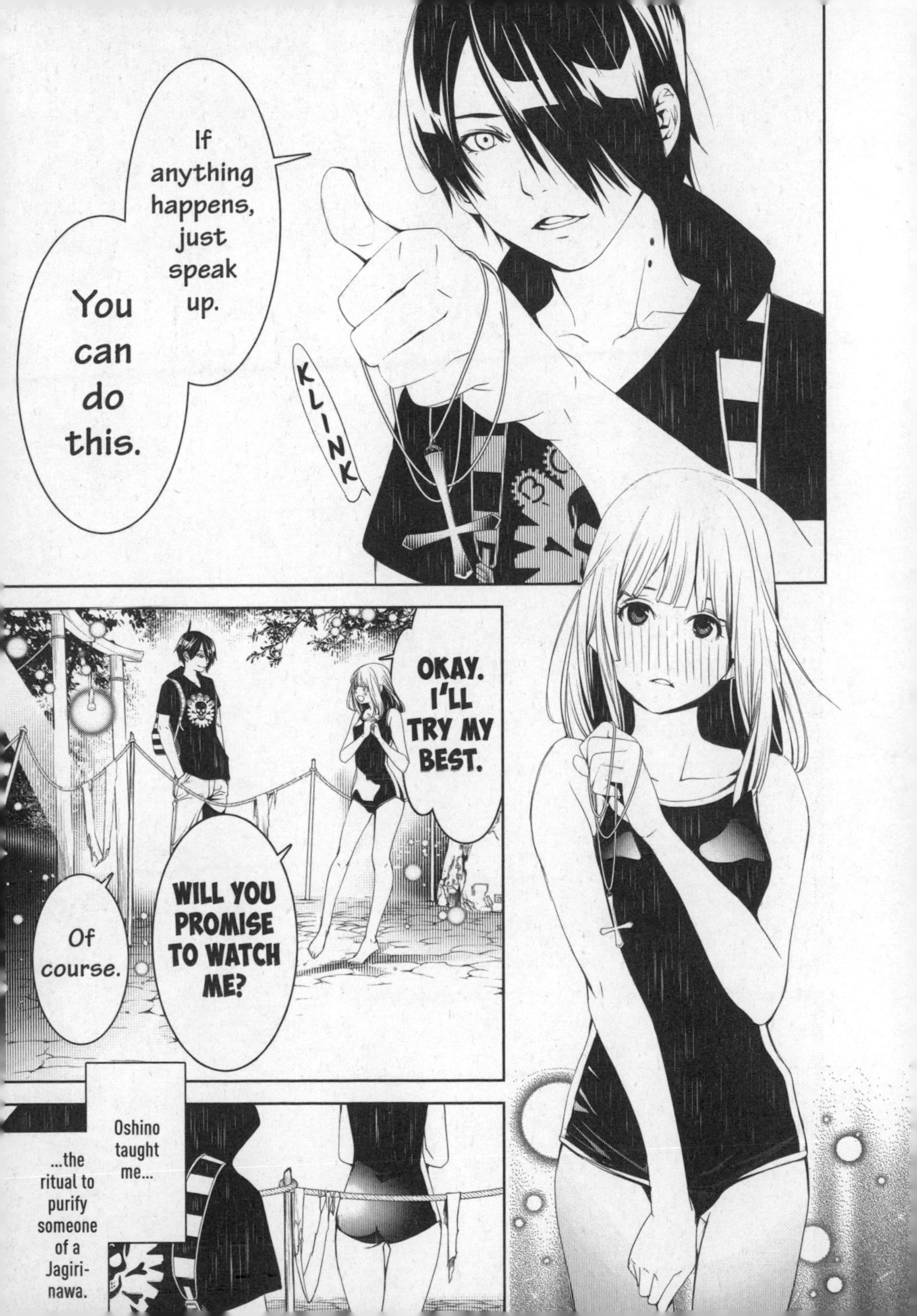

If anything happens, just speak up. You can do this.
KLINK
OKAY. I'LL TRY MY BEST.
WILL YOU PROMISE TO WATCH ME?
Of course.
Oshino taught me...
...the ritual to purify someone of a Jagiri-nawa.

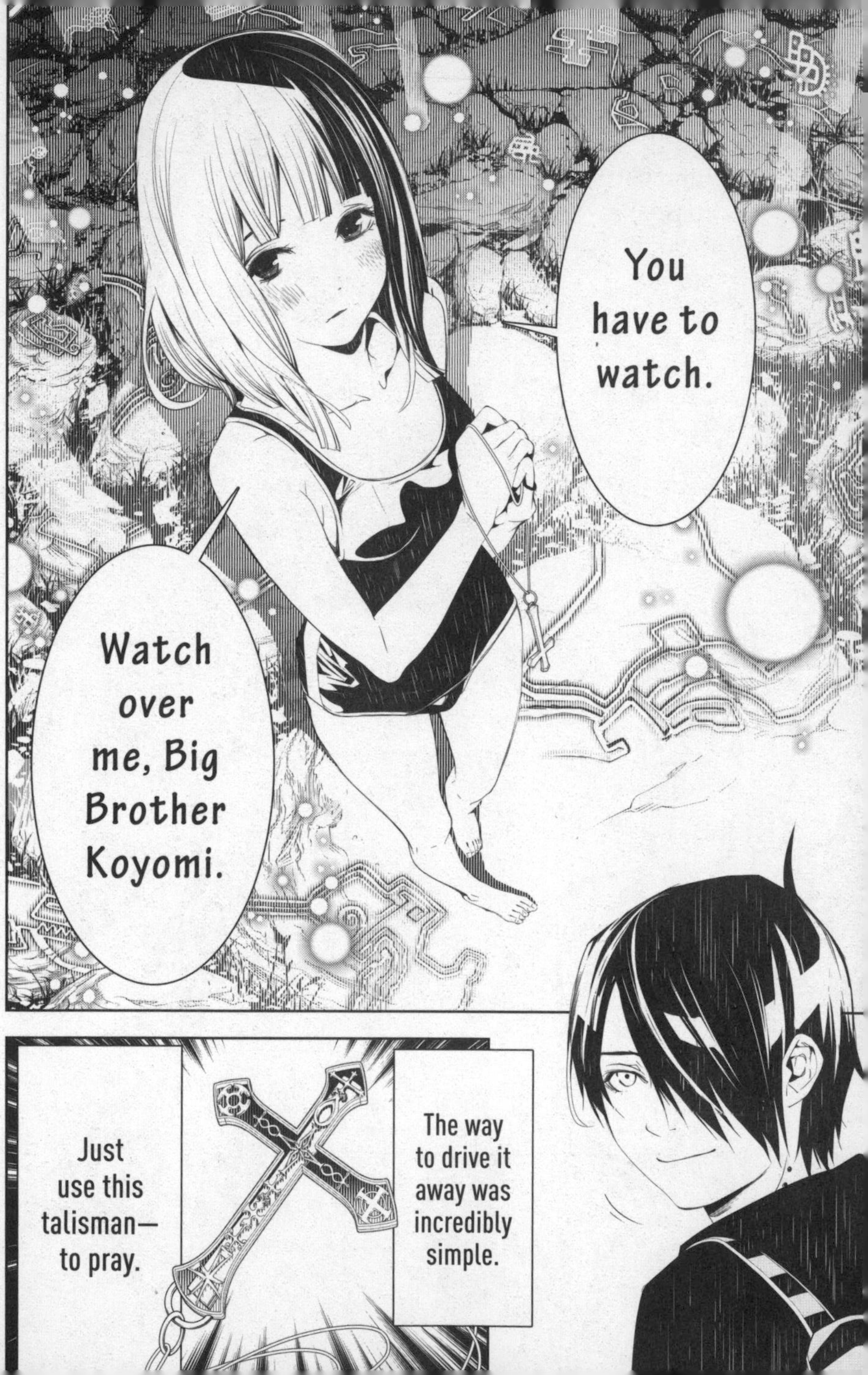
You have to watch.
Watch over me, Big Brother Koyomi.
The way to drive it away was incredibly simple.
Just use this talisman— to pray.

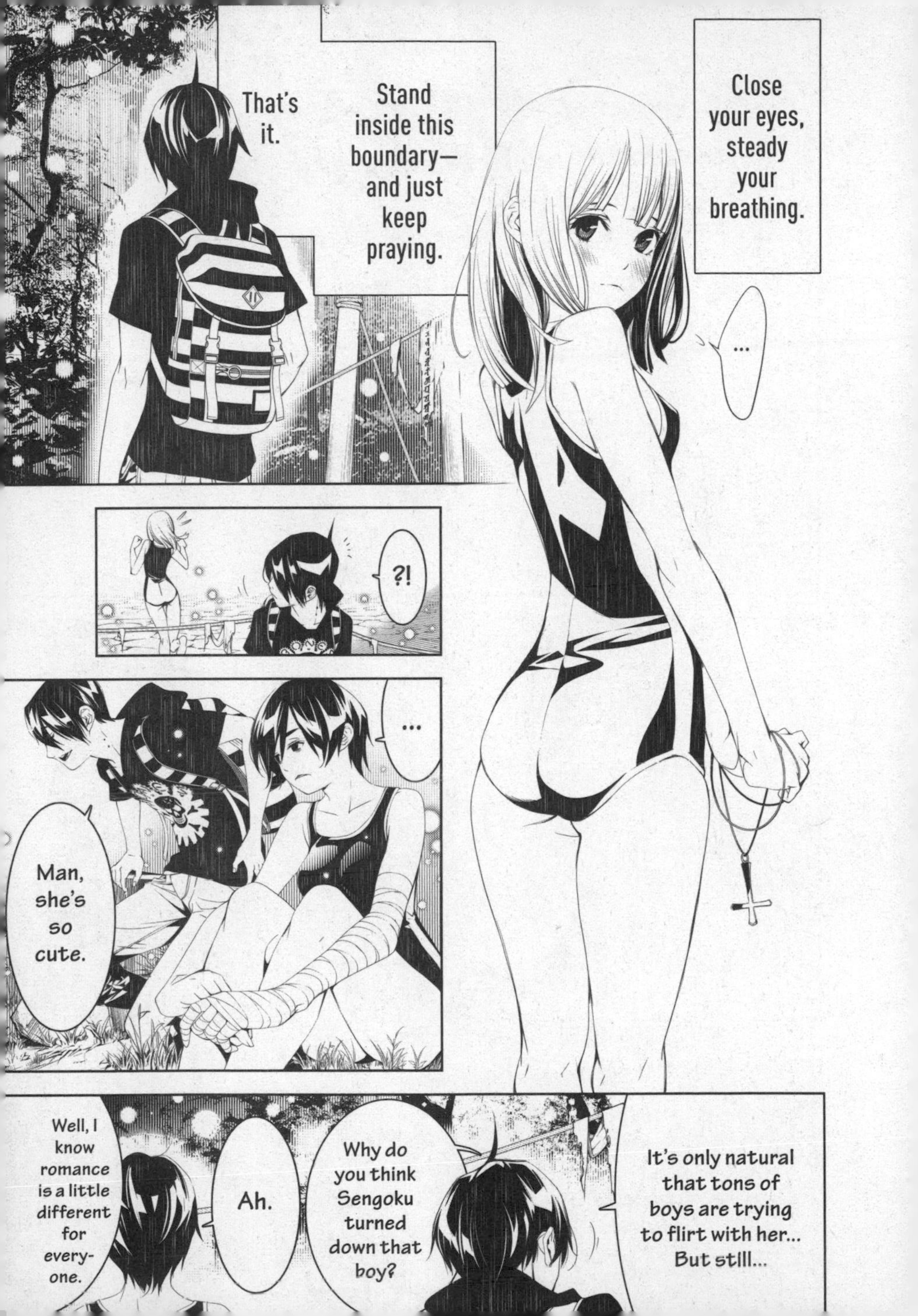
Close your eyes, steady your breathing.
...
Stand inside this boundary— and just keep praying.
That's it.
?!
...
Man, she's so cute.
It's only natural that tons of boys are trying to flirt with her... But still...
Why do you think Sengoku turned down that boy?
Ah.
Well, I know romance is a little different for everyone.

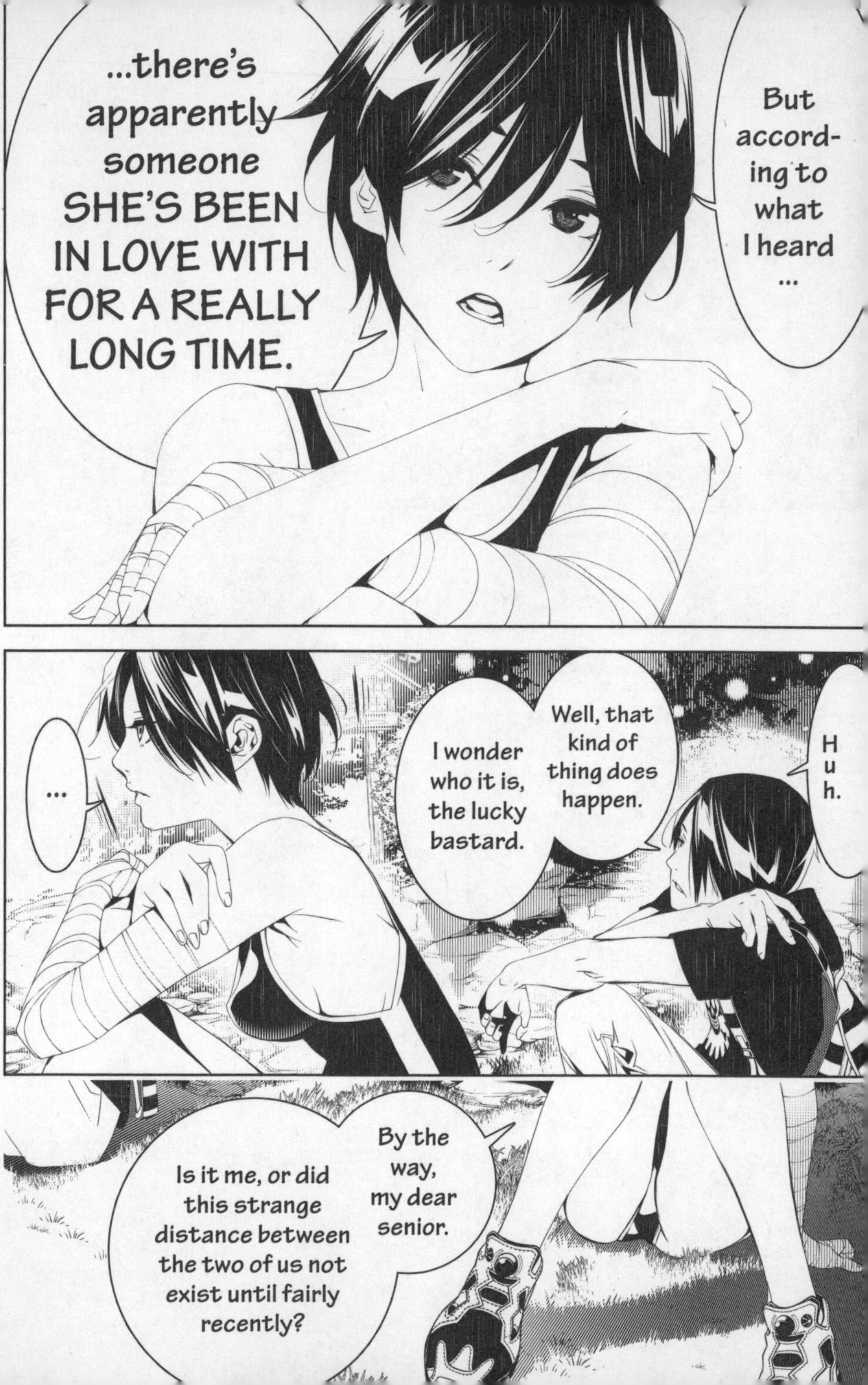
But according-ing to what I heard ...
...there's apparently someone SHE'S BEEN IN LOVE WITH FOR A REALLY LONG TIME.
Huh.
Well, that kind of thing does happen.
I wonder who it is, the lucky bastard.
...
By the way, my dear senior.
Is it me, or did this strange distance between the two of us not exist until fairly recently?

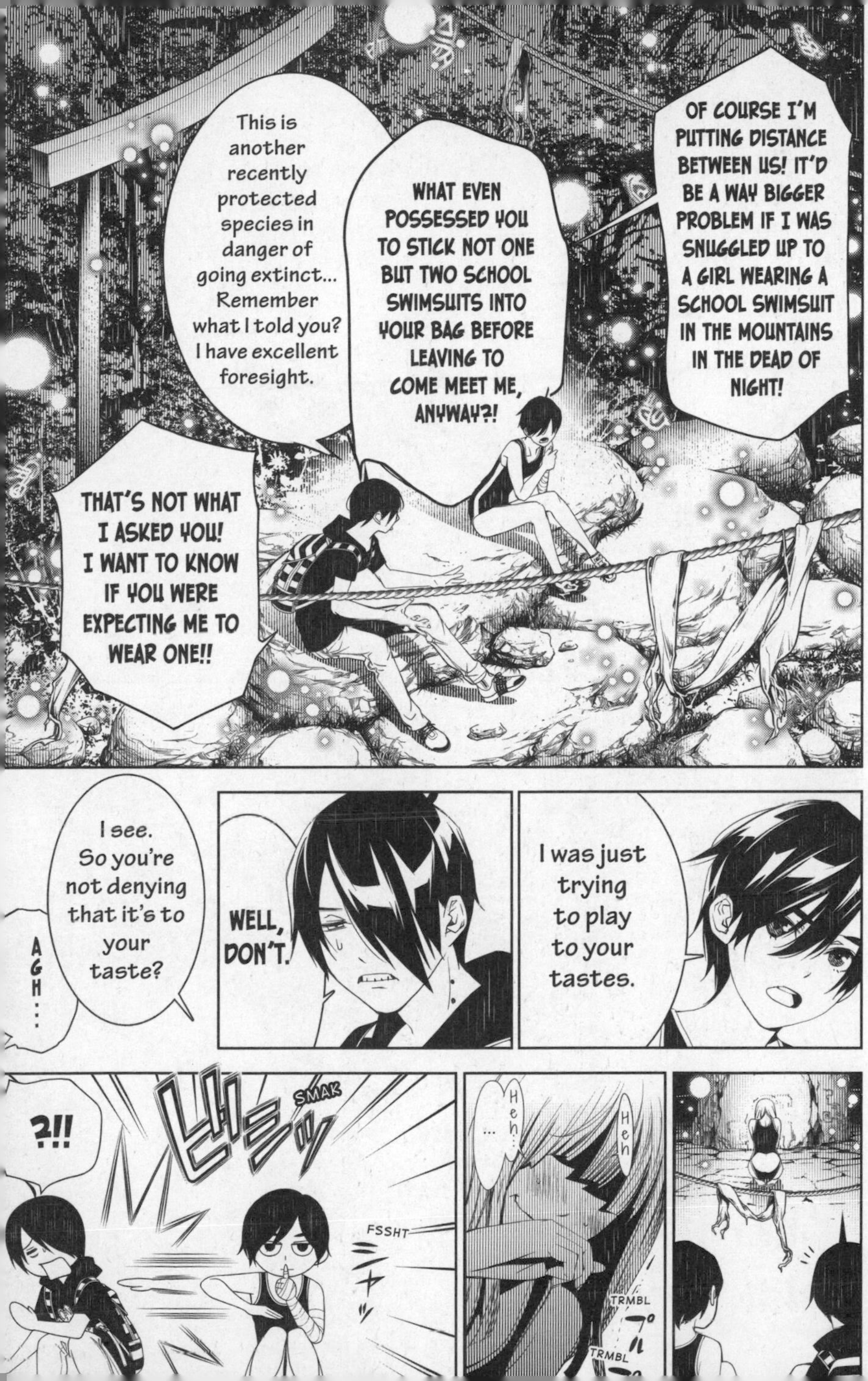
OF COURSE I'M PUTTING DISTANCE BETWEEN US! IT'D BE A WAY BIGGER PROBLEM IF I WAS SNUGGLED UP TO A GIRL WEARING A SCHOOL SWIMSUIT IN THE MOUNTAINS IN THE DEAD OF NIGHT!
WHAT EVEN POSSESSED YOU TO STICK NOT ONE BUT TWO SCHOOL SWIMSUITS INTO YOUR BAG BEFORE LEAVING TO COME MEET ME, ANYWAY?!
This is another recently protected species in danger of going extinct... Remember what I told you? I have excellent foresight.
THAT'S NOT WHAT I ASKED YOU! I WANT TO KNOW IF YOU WERE EXPECTING ME TO WEAR ONE!!
I was just trying to play to your tastes.
WELL, DON'T.
I see. So you're not denying that it's to your taste?
AGH...
Heh
Heh...
TRMBL
TRMBL
SMAK
?!!
FSSHT

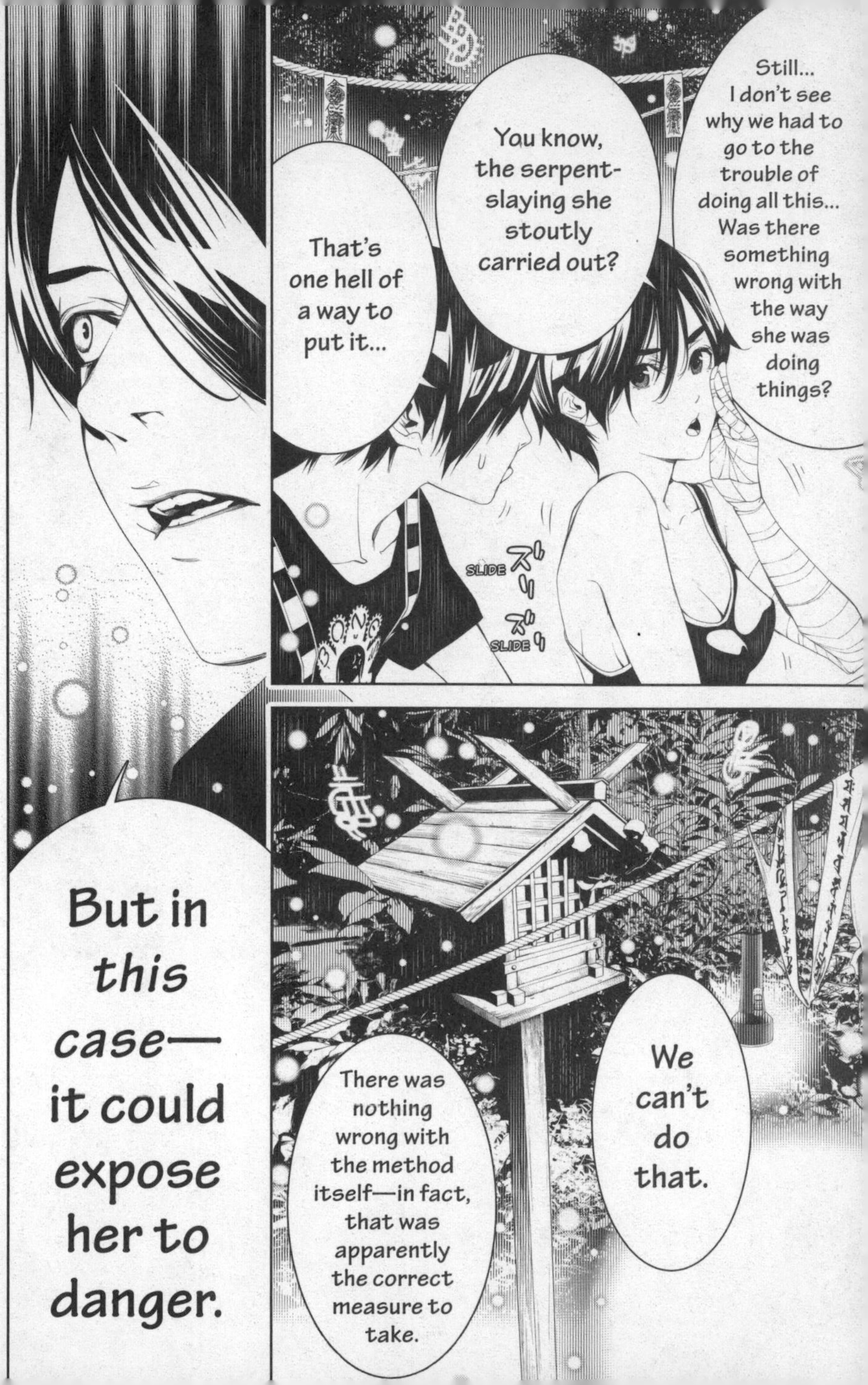
Still... I don't see why we had to go to the trouble of doing all this... Was there something wrong with the way she was doing things?
You know, the serpent-slaying she stoutly carried out?
That's one hell of a way to put it...
SLIDE
SLIDE
We can't do that.
There was nothing wrong with the method itself—in fact, that was apparently the correct measure to take.
But in this case— it could expose her to danger.

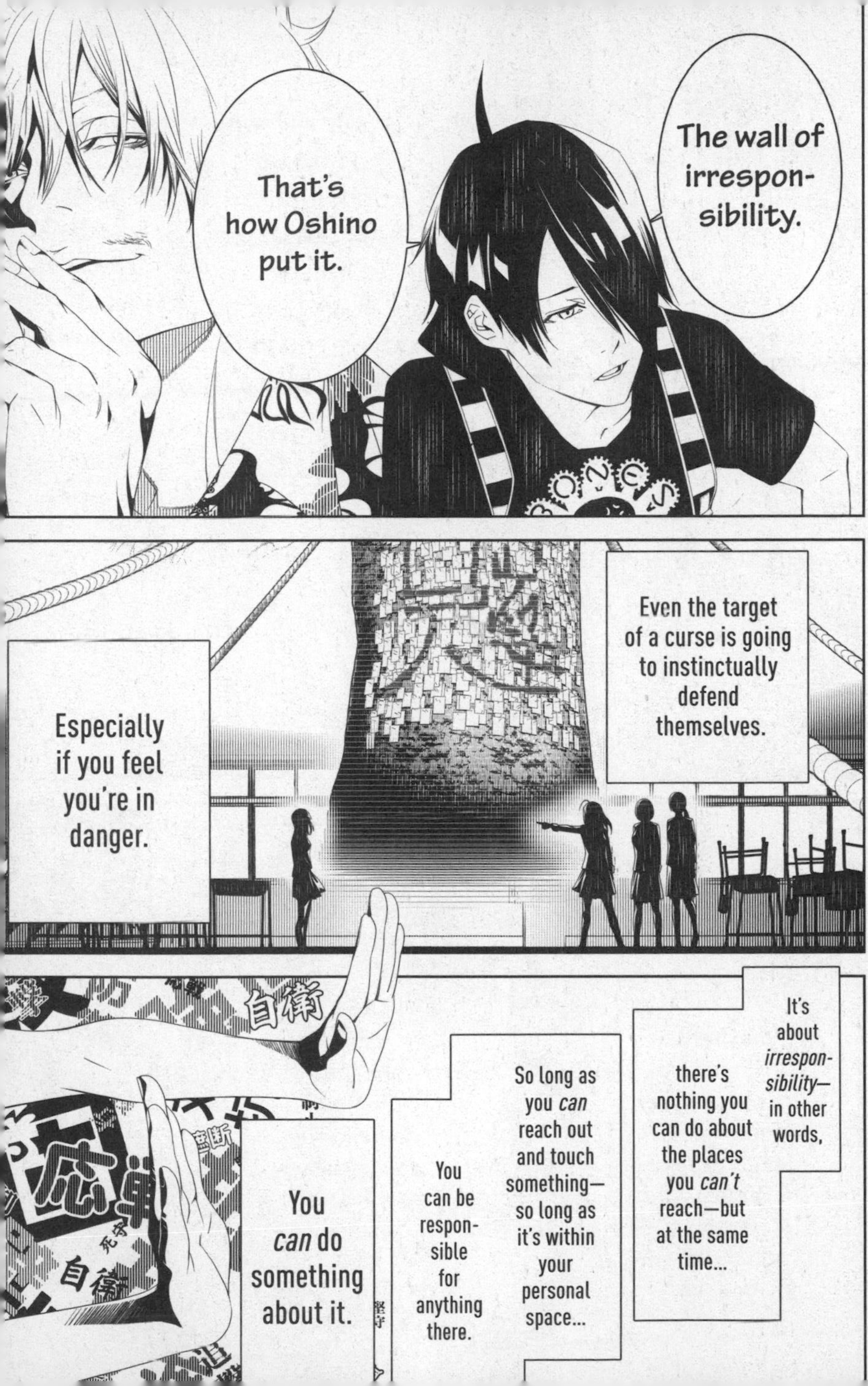

The wall of irresponsibility.
That's how Oshino put it.
Even the target of a curse is going to instinctually defend themselves.
Especially if you feel you're in danger.
It's about *irresponsibility*—in other words,
there's nothing you can do about the places you *can't* reach—but at the same time...
So long as you *can* reach out and touch something—so long as it's within your personal space...
You can be responsible for anything there.
You *can* do something about it.
自衛

Self-defense (自衛) / Shut out (遮断) / Interception (迎撃) / Wall (壁) / Resist (対抗) / Defense (防衛) /Defend to death (死守) /Firm (強固) / Strong defense (堅守) /Self-protection (護身) /Protection (防御)

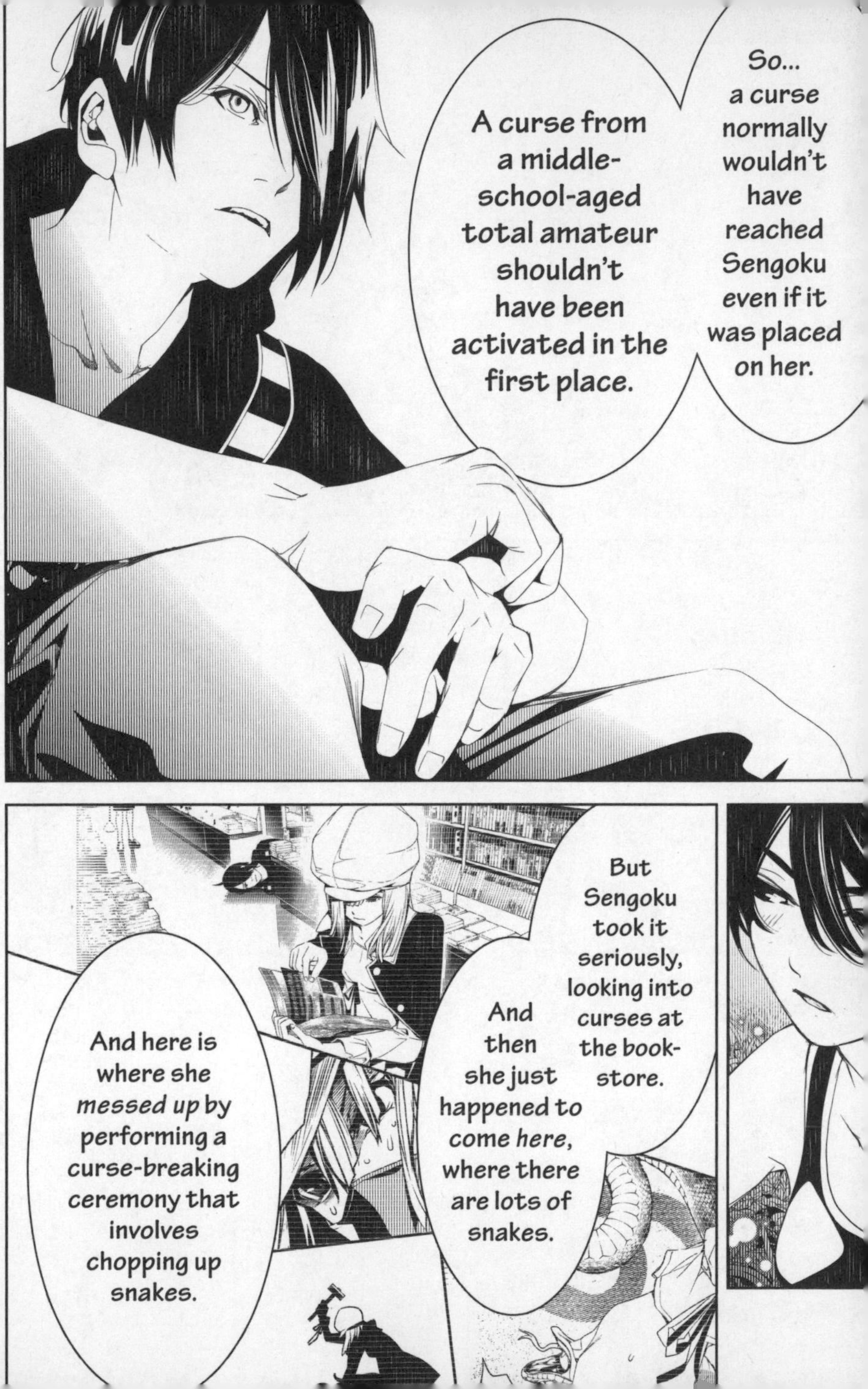

So... a curse normally wouldn't have reached Sengoku even if it was placed on her.
A curse from a middle-school-aged total amateur shouldn't have been activated in the first place.
But Sengoku took it seriously, looking into curses at the bookstore.
And then she just happened to come *here*, where there are lots of snakes.
And here is where she *messed up* by performing a curse-breaking ceremony that involves chopping up snakes.

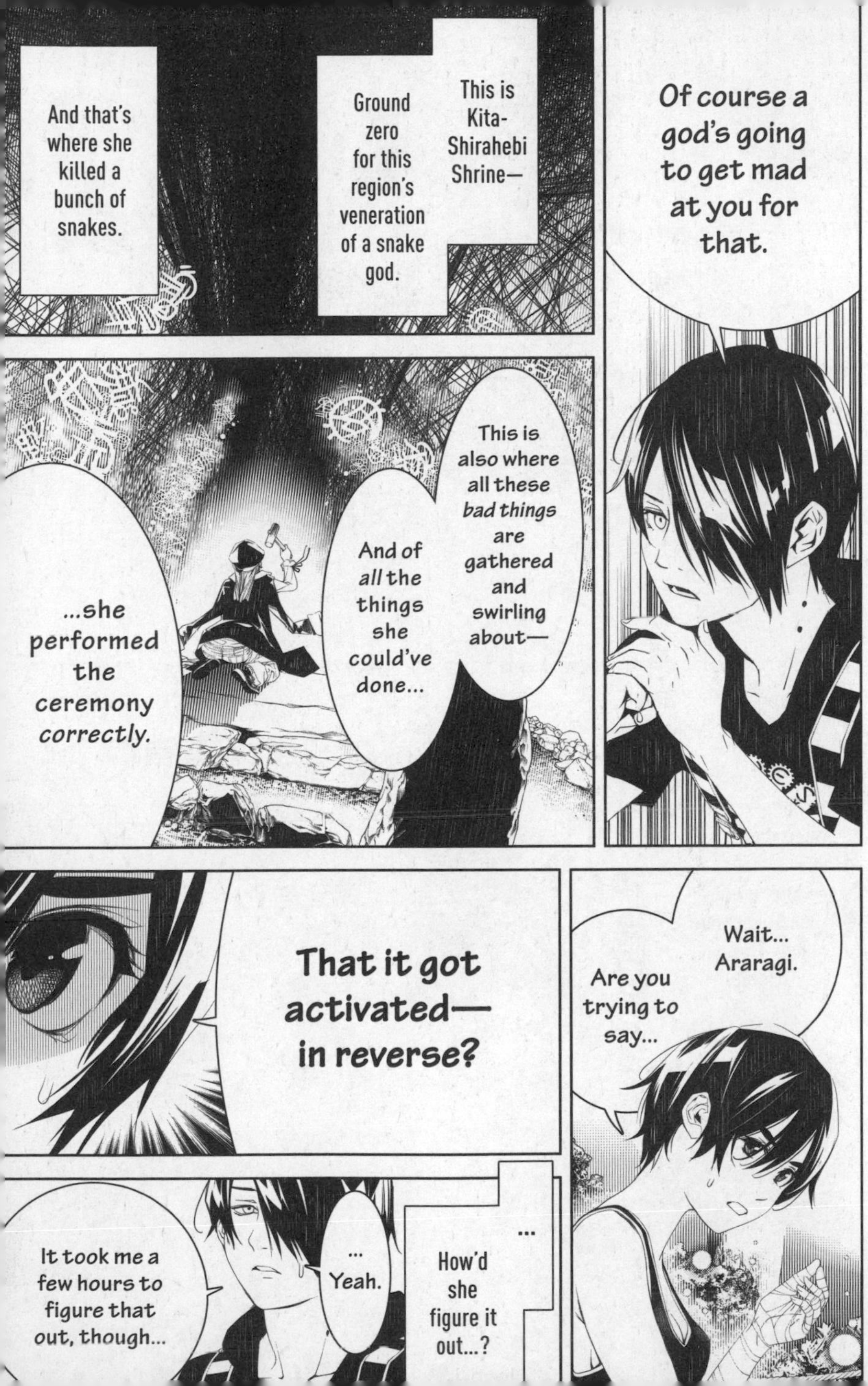
Of course a god's going to get mad at you for that.
This is Kita-Shirahebi Shrine—
Ground zero for this region's veneration of a snake god.
And that's where she killed a bunch of snakes.
This is also where all these *bad things* are gathered and swirling about—
And of *all* the things she could've done...
...she performed the ceremony *correctly.*
Wait... Araragi.
Are you trying to say...
That it got activated— in reverse?
...
How'd she figure it out...?
... Yeah.
It took me a few hours to figure that out, though...

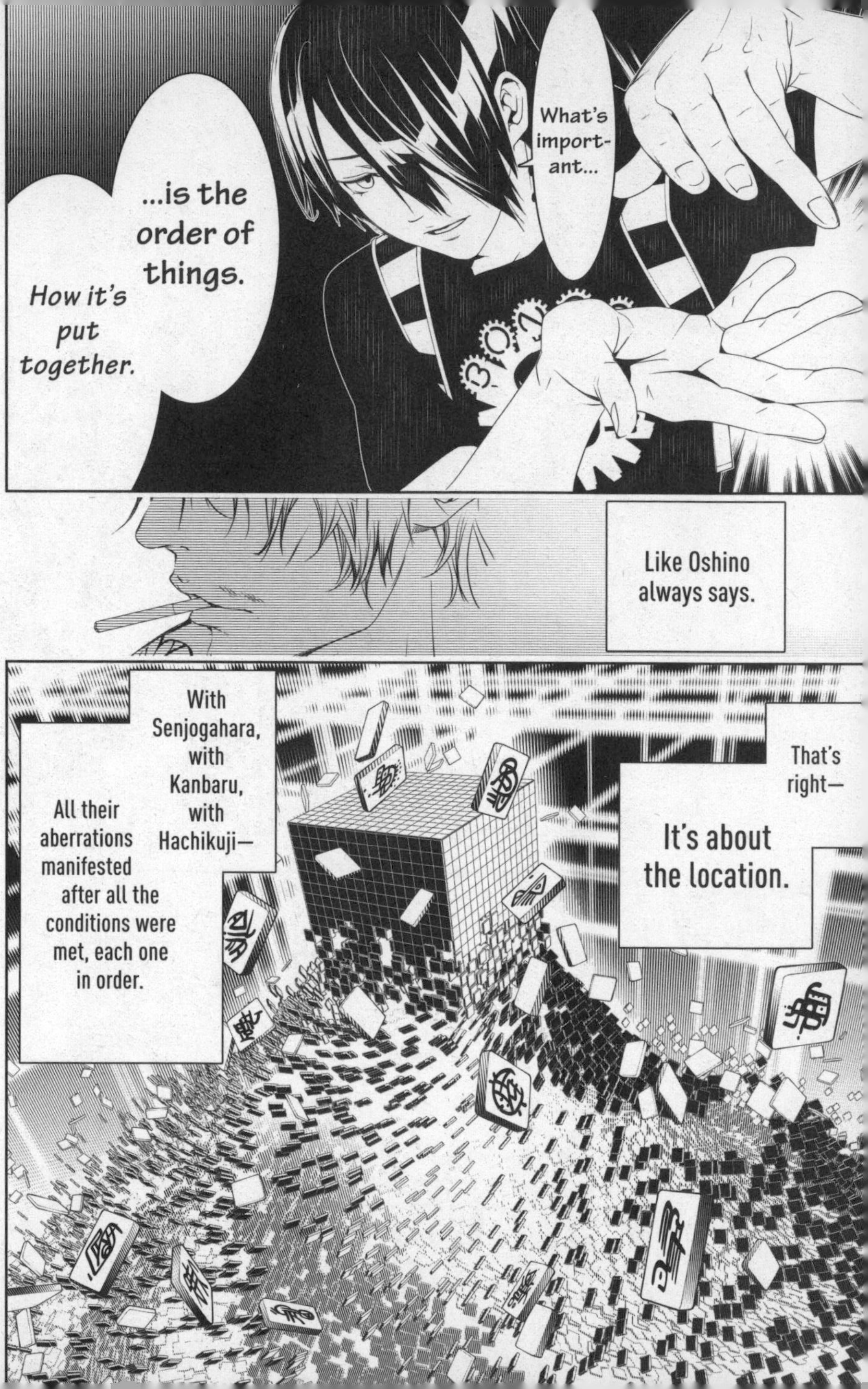
What's important...
...is the order of things.
How it's put together.
Like Oshino always says.
That's right—
It's about the location.
With Senjogahara, with Kanbaru, with Hachikuji—
All their aberrations manifested after all the conditions were met, each one in order.

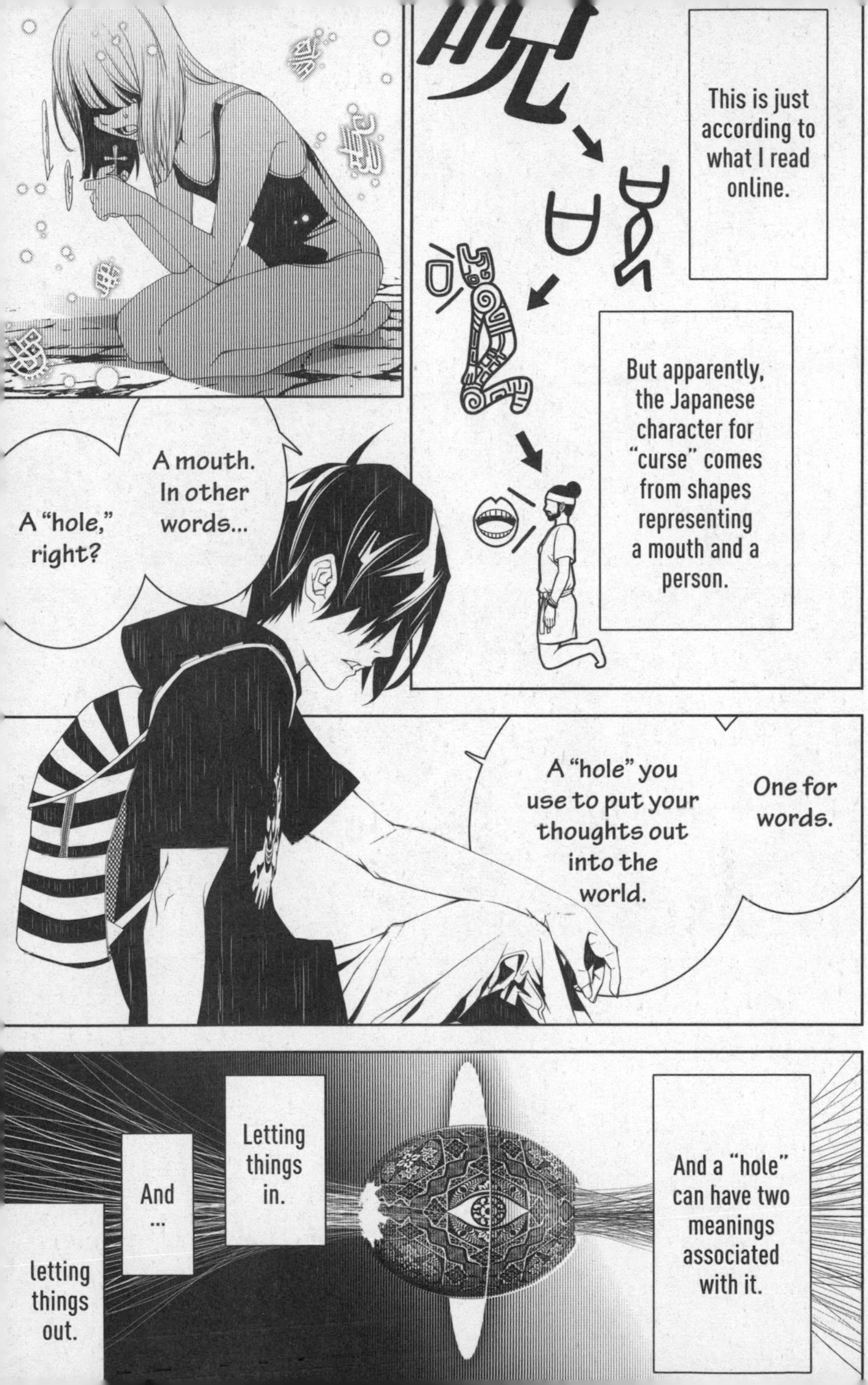
呪
This is just according to what I read online.
But apparently, the Japanese character for "curse" comes from shapes representing a mouth and a person.
A mouth. In other words...
A "hole," right?
One for words.
A "hole" you use to put your thoughts out into the world.
And a "hole" can have two meanings associated with it.
Letting things in.
And ...
letting things out.

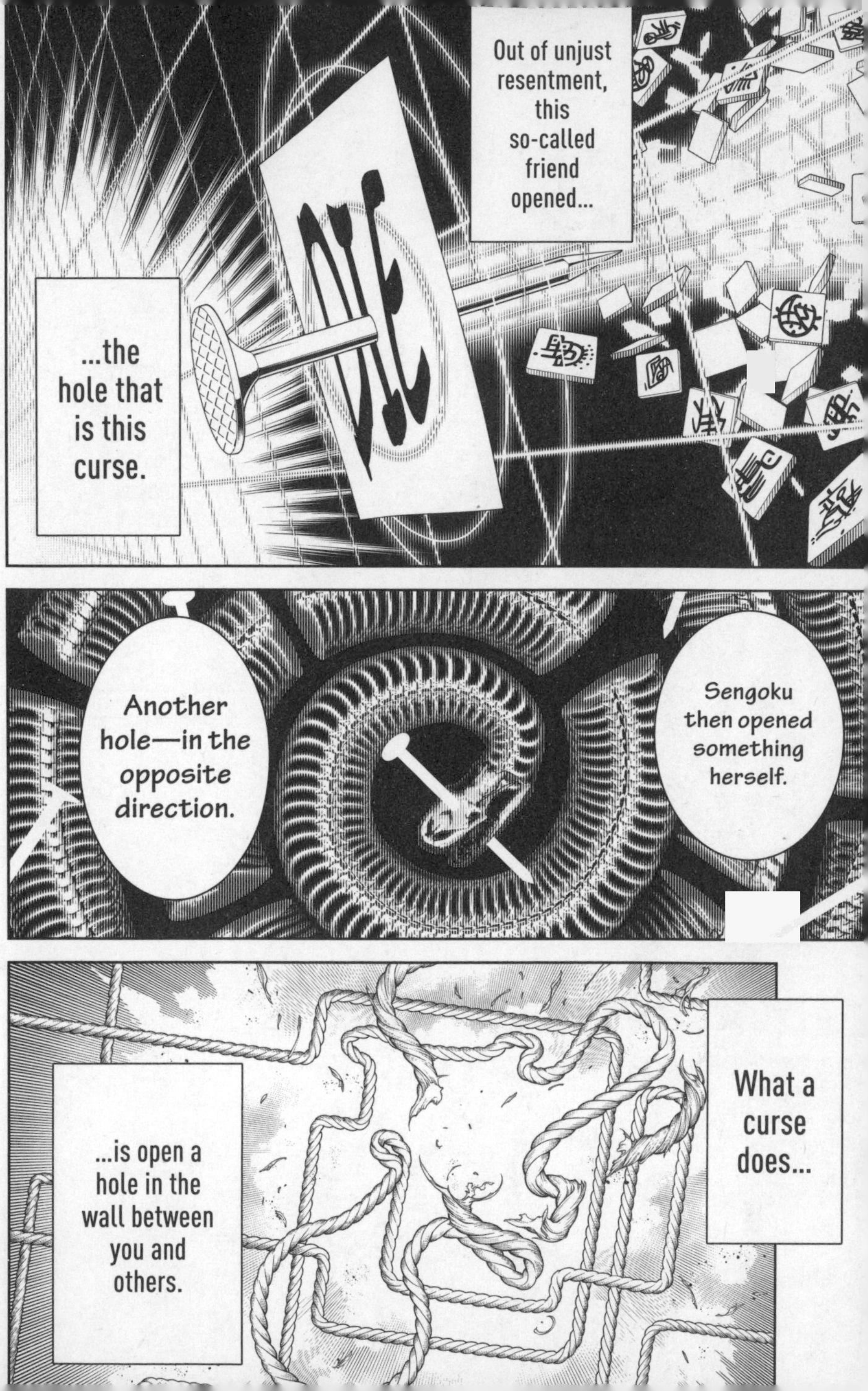
Out of unjust resentment, this so-called friend opened...
...the hole that is this curse.
Sengoku then opened something herself.
Another hole—in the opposite direction.
What a curse does...
...is open a hole in the wall between you and others.

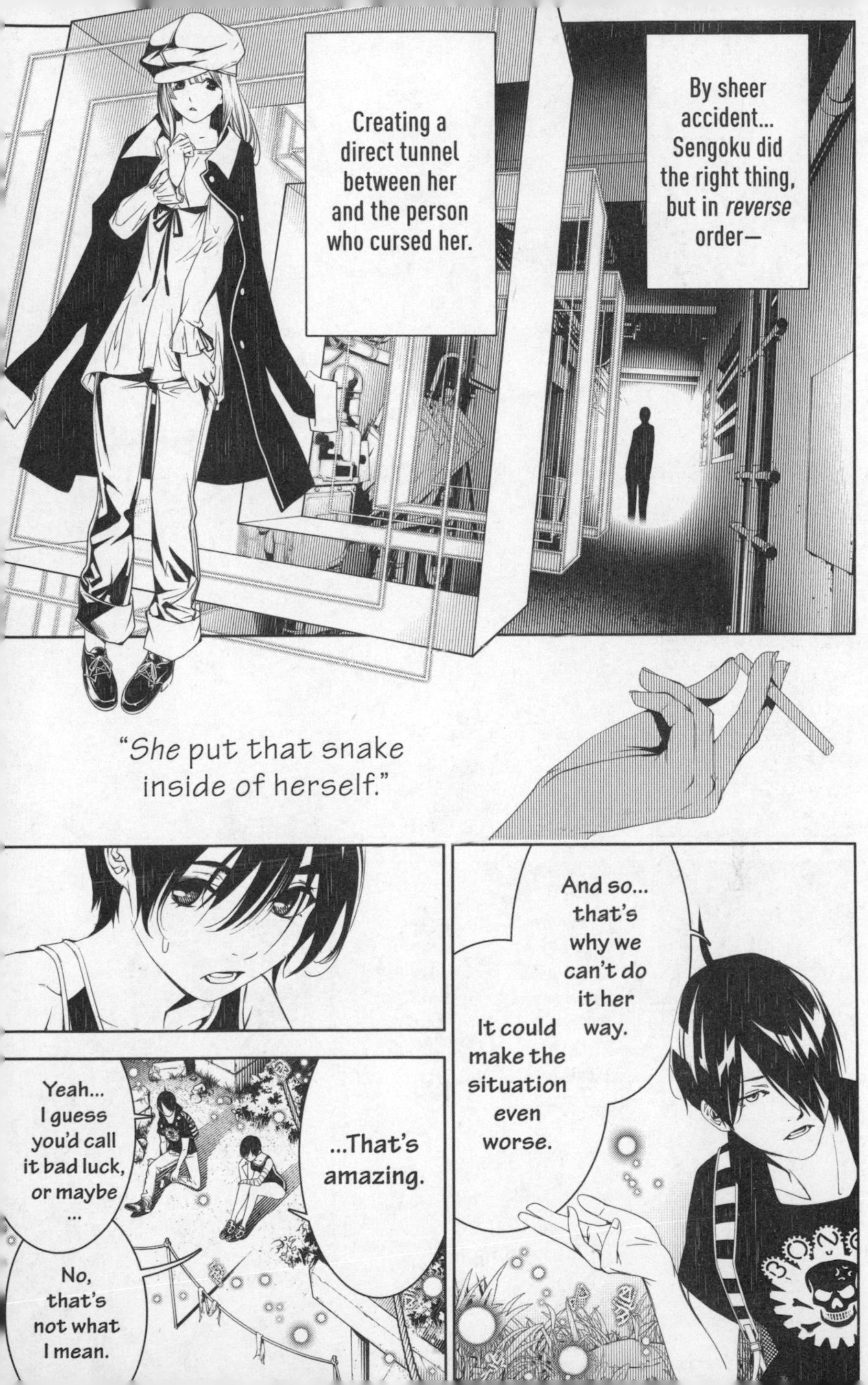
By sheer accident... Sengoku did the right thing, but in *reverse* order—
Creating a direct tunnel between her and the person who cursed her.
"*She* put that snake inside of herself."
And so... that's why we can't do it her way.
It could make the situation *even* worse.
...That's amazing.
Yeah... I guess you'd call it bad luck, or maybe ...
No, that's not what I mean.

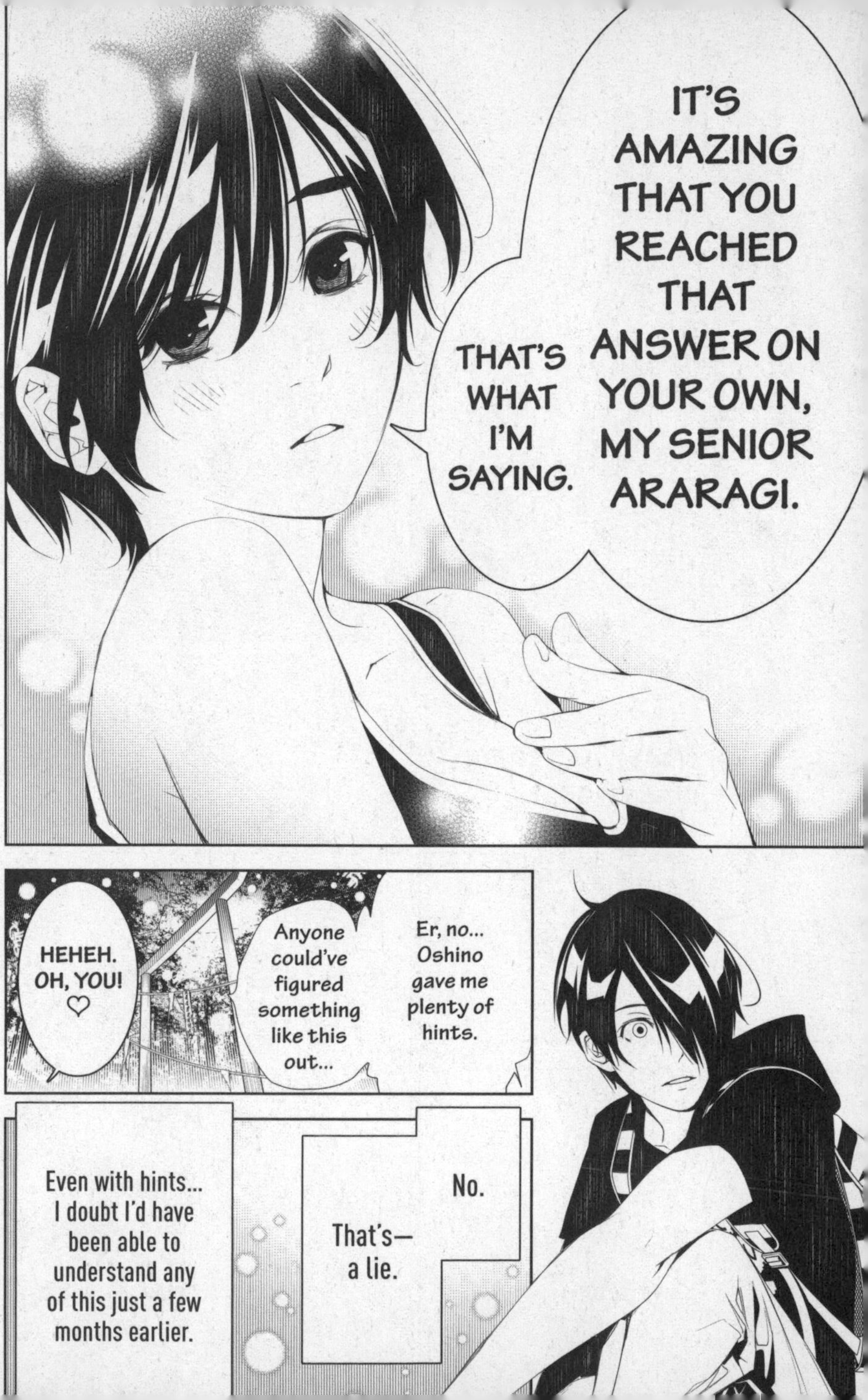
IT'S AMAZING THAT YOU REACHED THAT ANSWER ON YOUR OWN, MY SENIOR ARARAGI.
THAT'S WHAT I'M SAYING.
Er, no... Oshino gave me plenty of hints.
Anyone could've figured something like this out...
HEHEH. OH, YOU! ♡
No.
That's— a lie.
Even with hints... I doubt I'd have been able to understand any of this just a few months earlier.

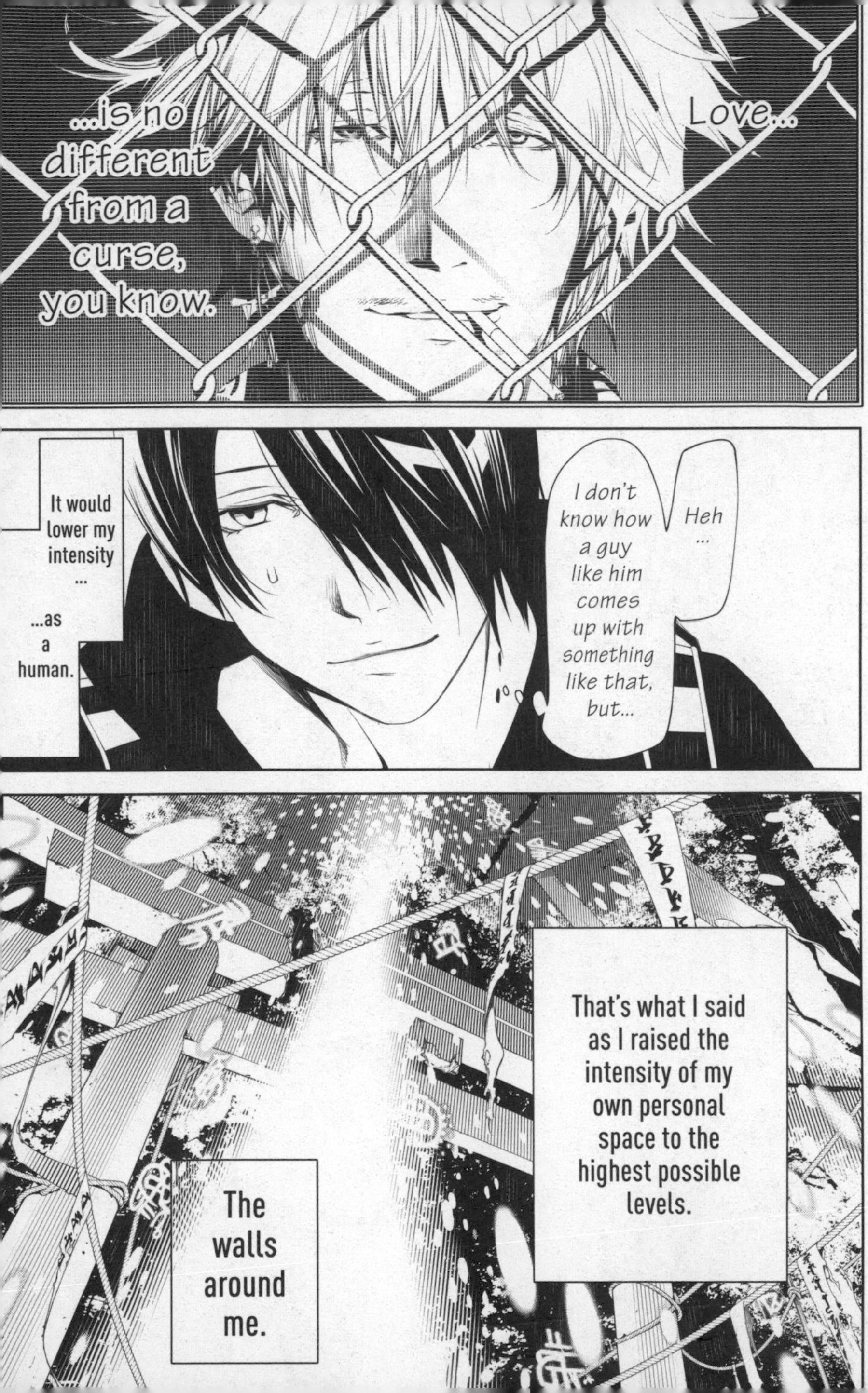
Love...
...is no different from a curse, you know.
Heh ...
I don't know how a guy like him comes up with something like that, but...
It would lower my intensity ...
...as a human.
That's what I said as I raised the intensity of my own personal space to the highest possible levels.
The walls around me.

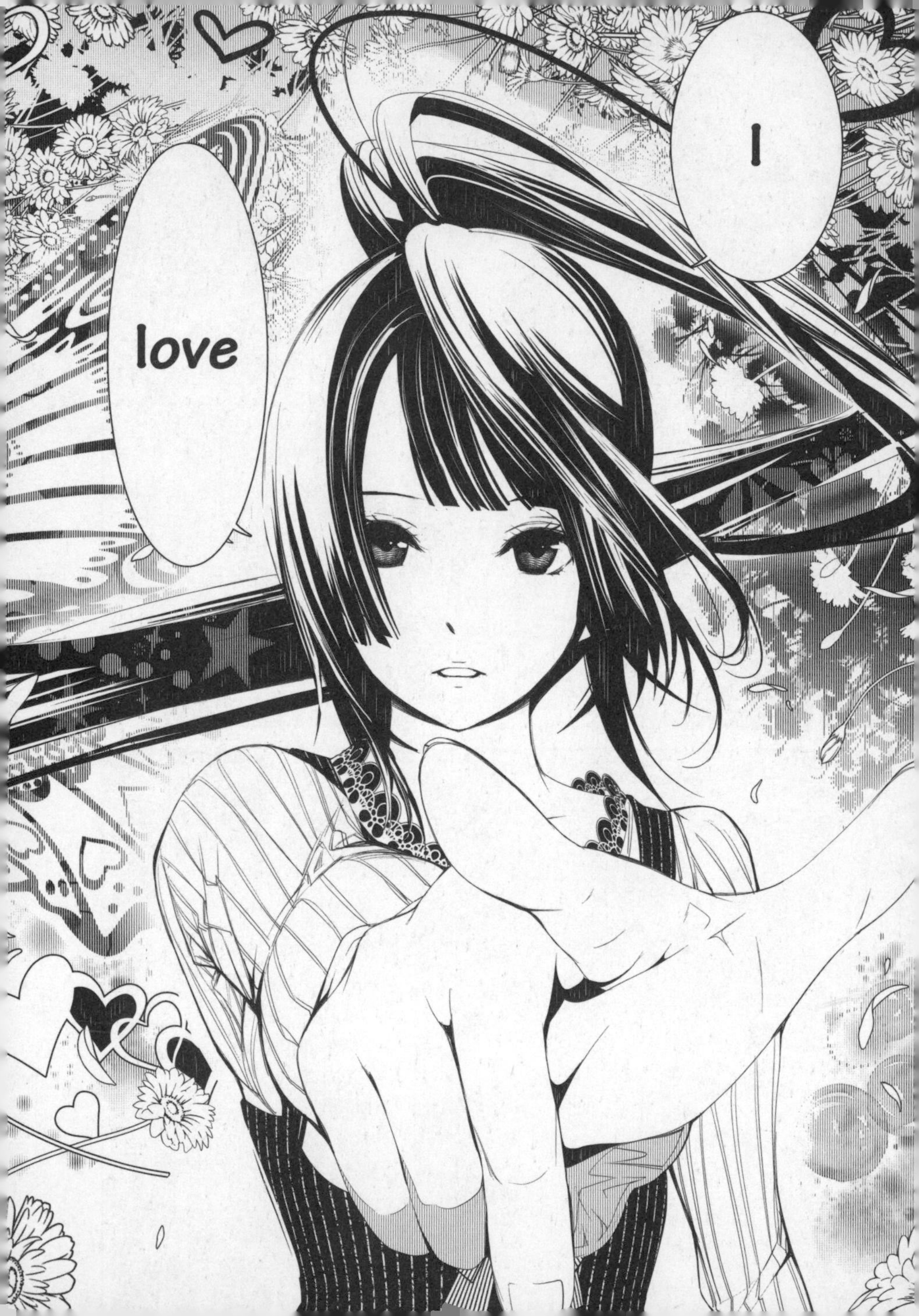
I
love

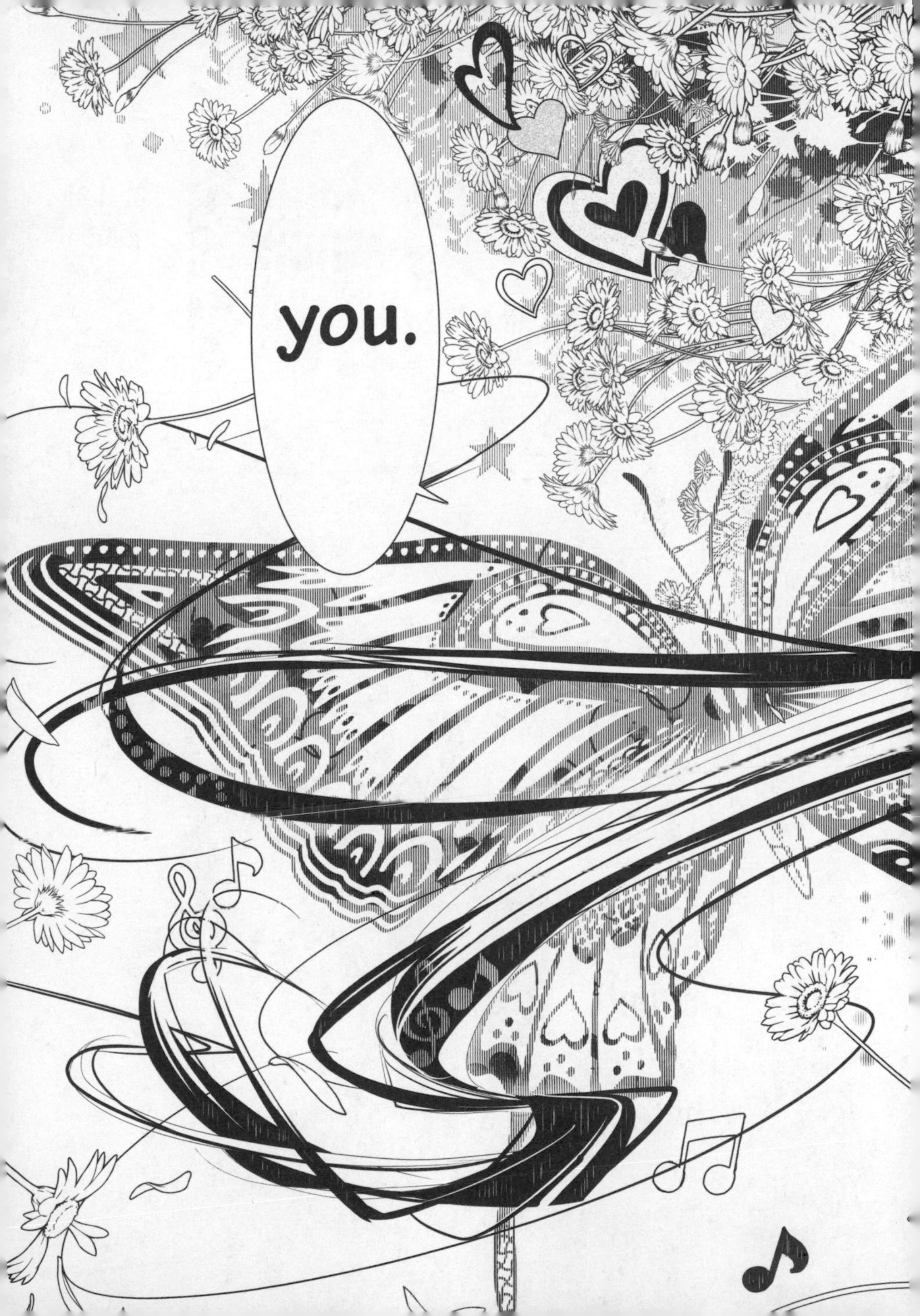
you.

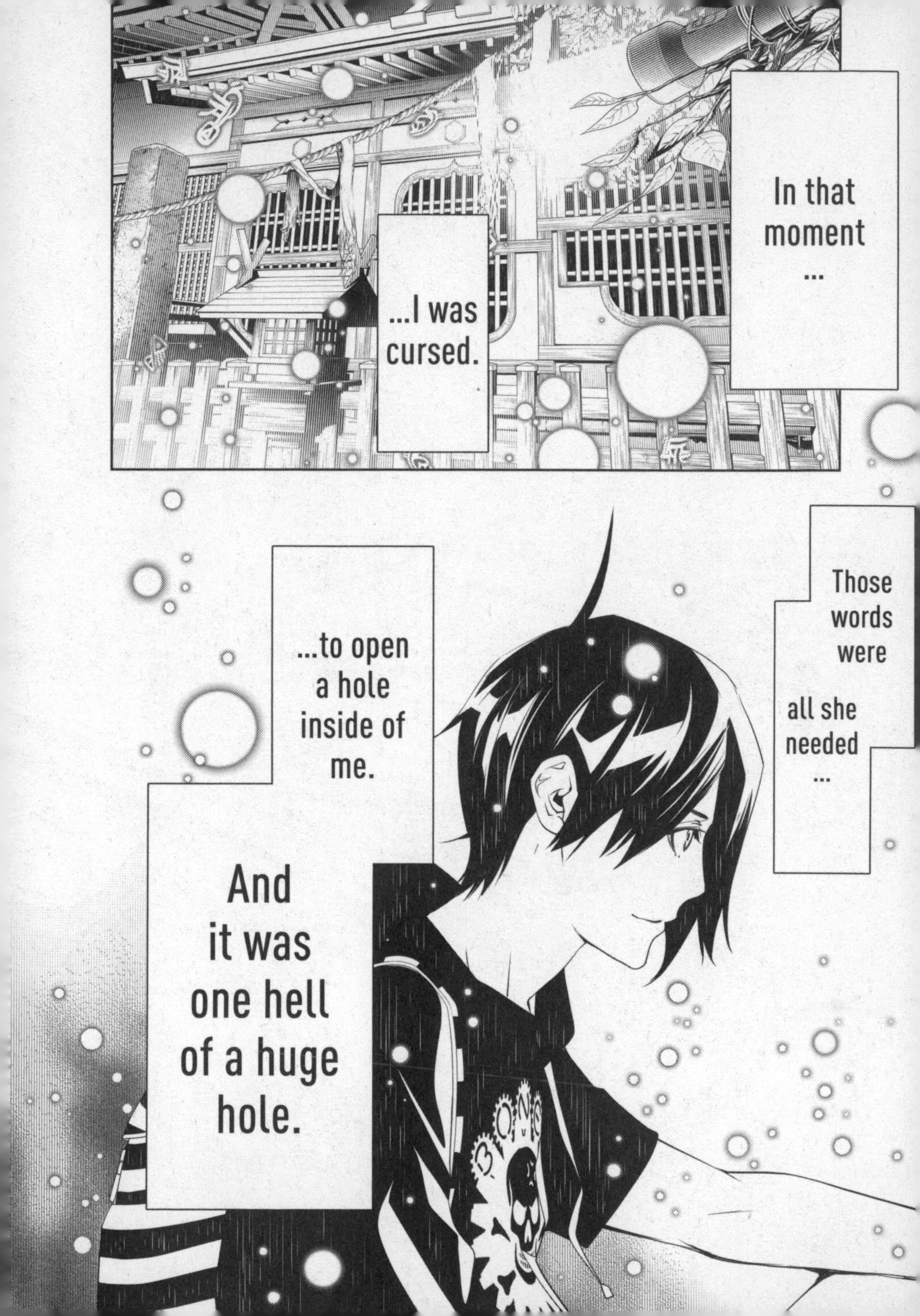
In that moment ...
...I was cursed.
Those words were all she needed ...
...to open a hole inside of me.
And it was one hell of a huge hole.

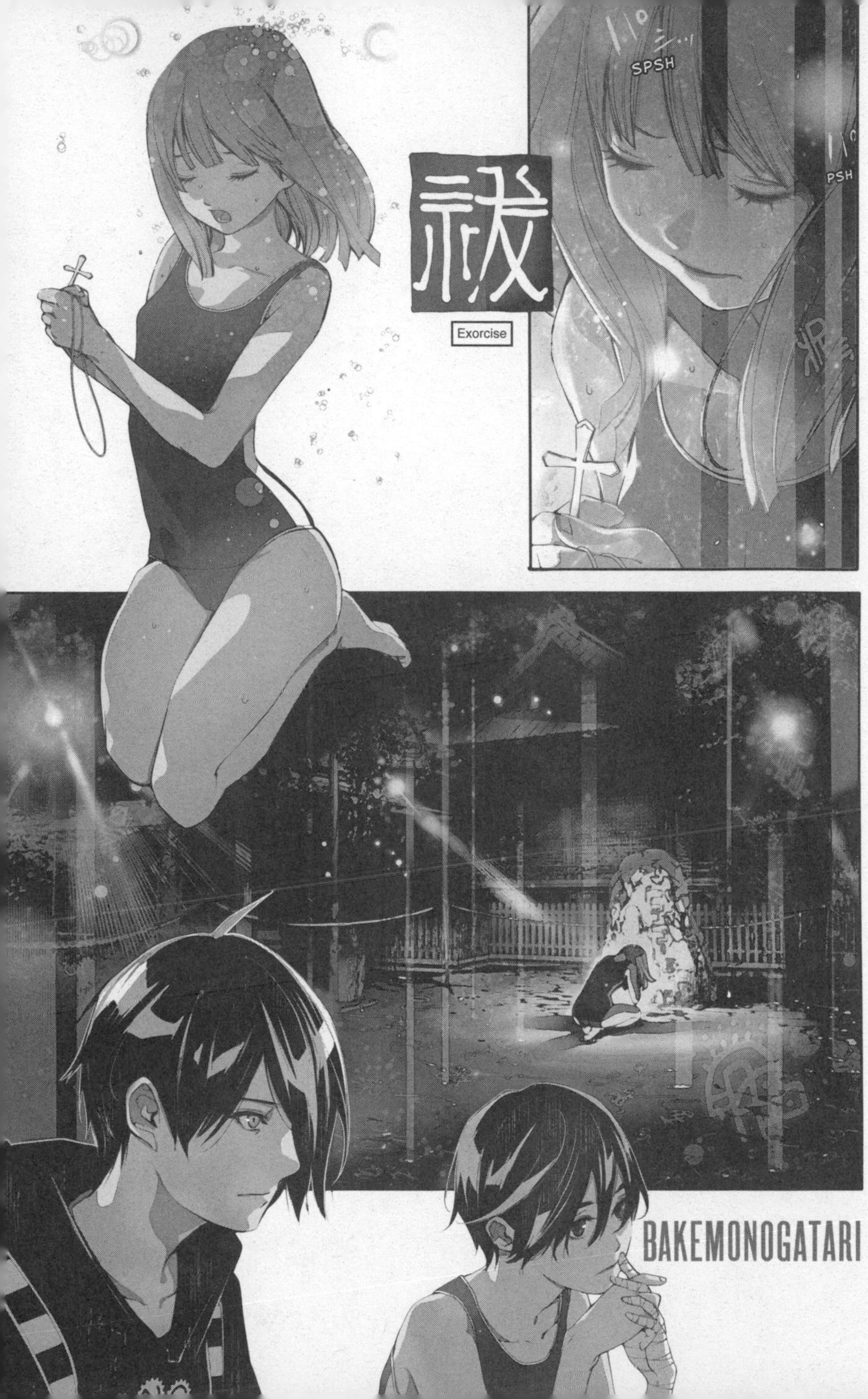
SPSH
PSH
祓
Exorcise
BAKEMONOGATARI

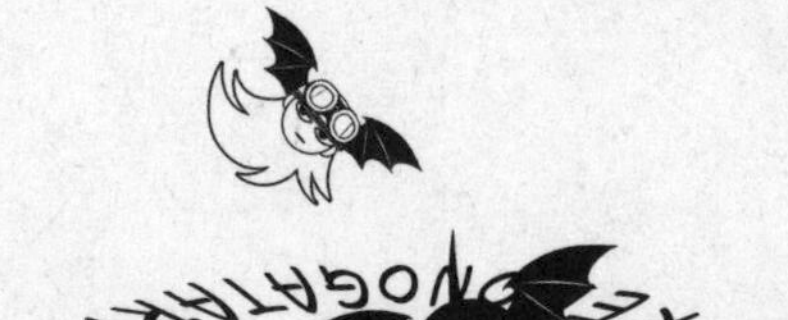
BAKEMONOGATARI
BAKEMONOGATARI

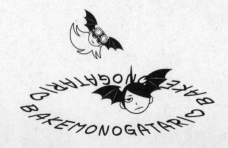

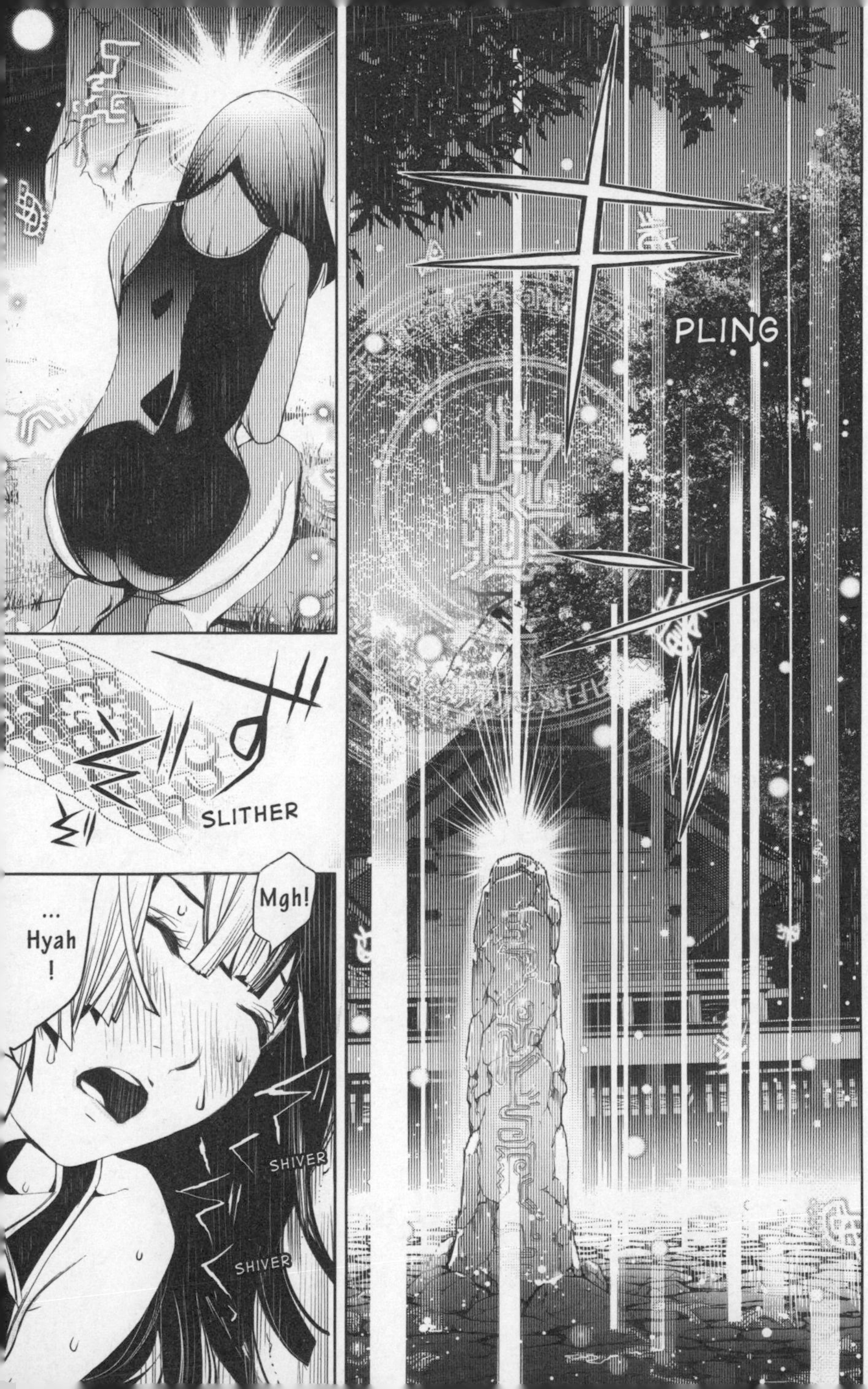
PLING
SLITHER
Mgh!
... Hyah!
SHIVER
SHIVER

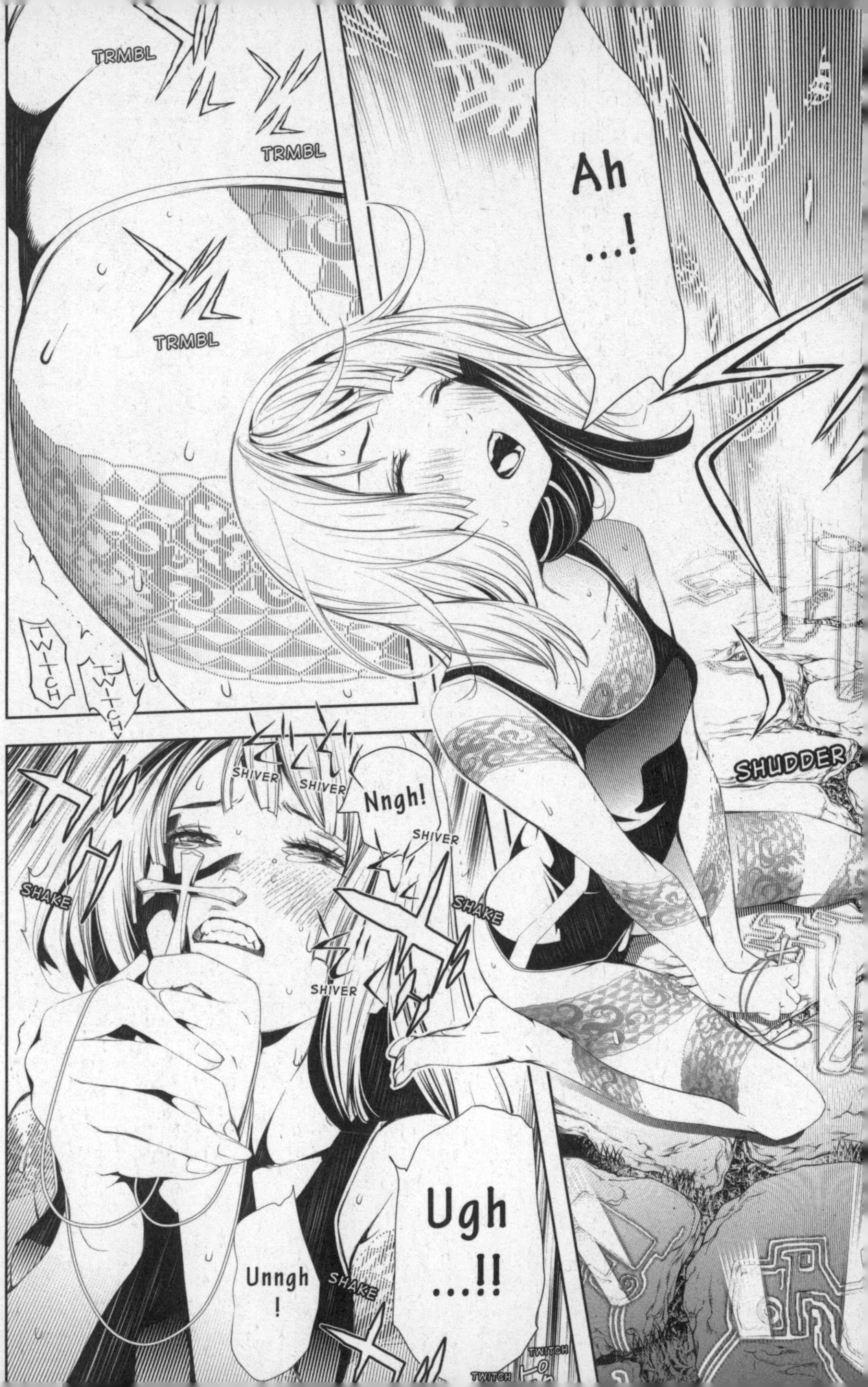
Ah ...!
SHUDDER
TRMBL
TRMBL
TRMBL
TWITCH
TWITCH
SHIVER
SHIVER
Nngh!
SHIVER
SHAKE
SHAKE
SHIVER
Ugh ...!!
SHAKE
Unngh !
TWITCH
TWITCH

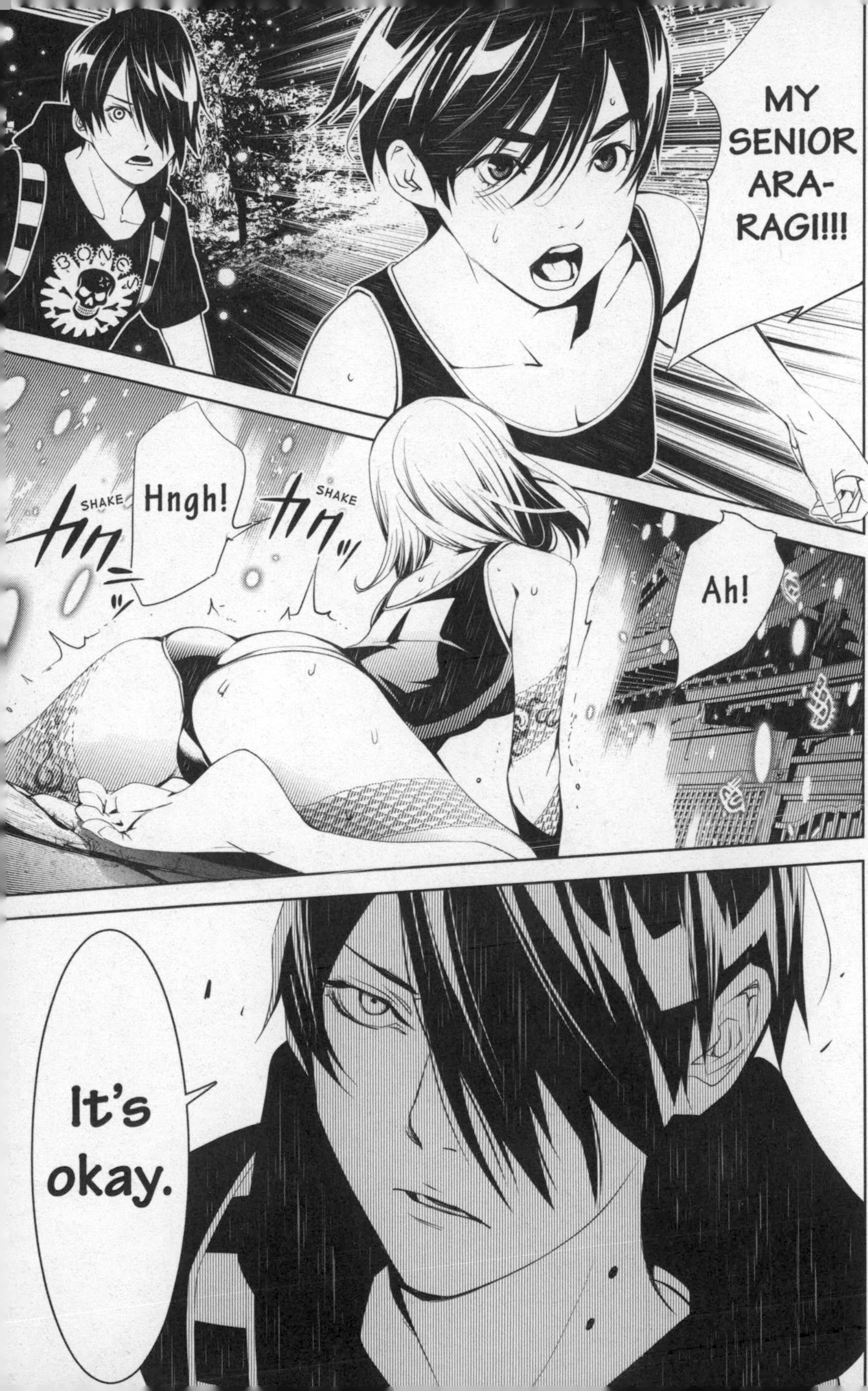
MY SENIOR ARA-RAGI!!!!
Ah!
SHAKE
カクッ
SHAKE
カク
Hngh!
It's okay.

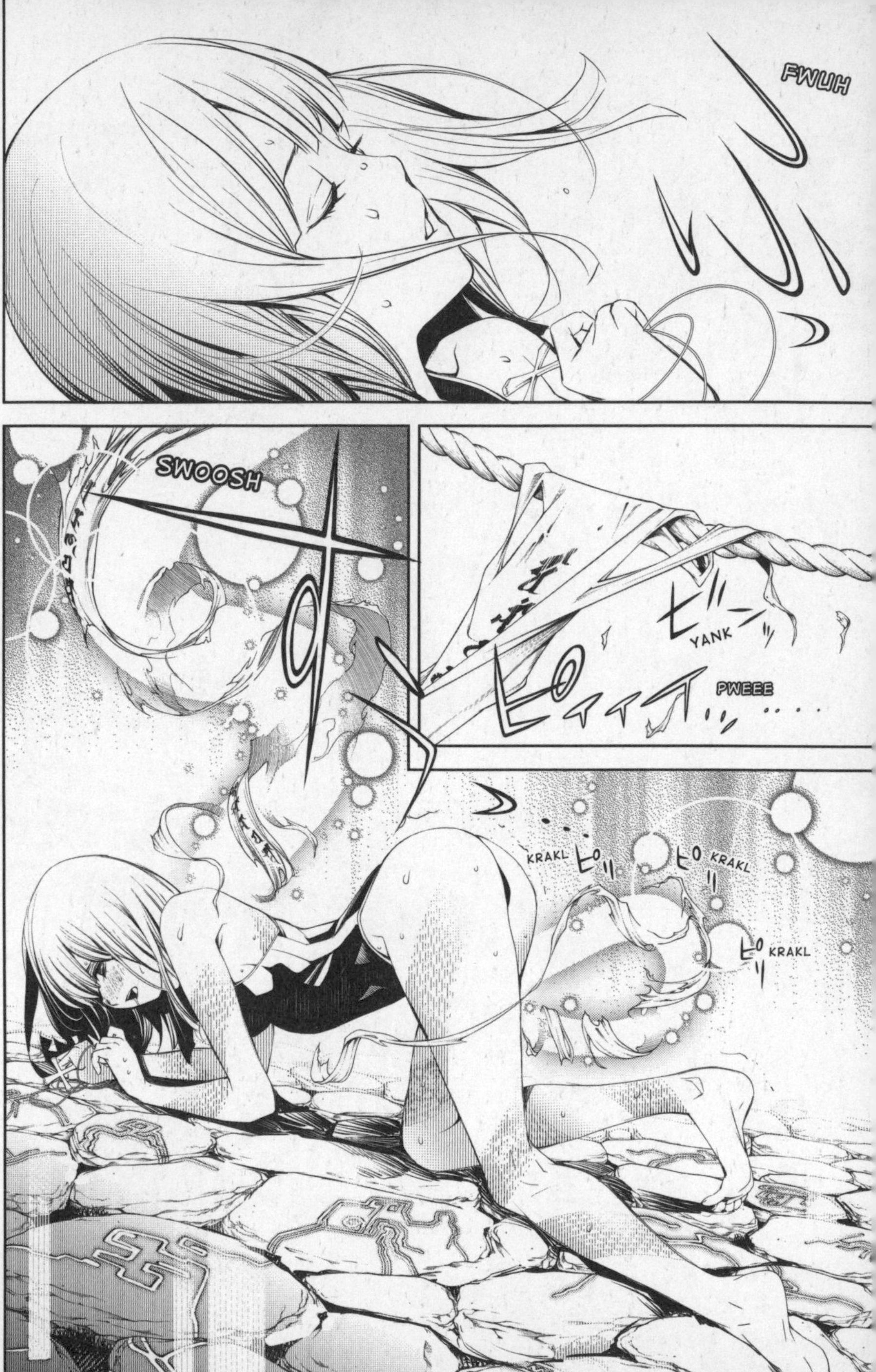
FWUH
YANK
PWEEE
SWOOSH
KRAKL
KRAKL
KRAKL

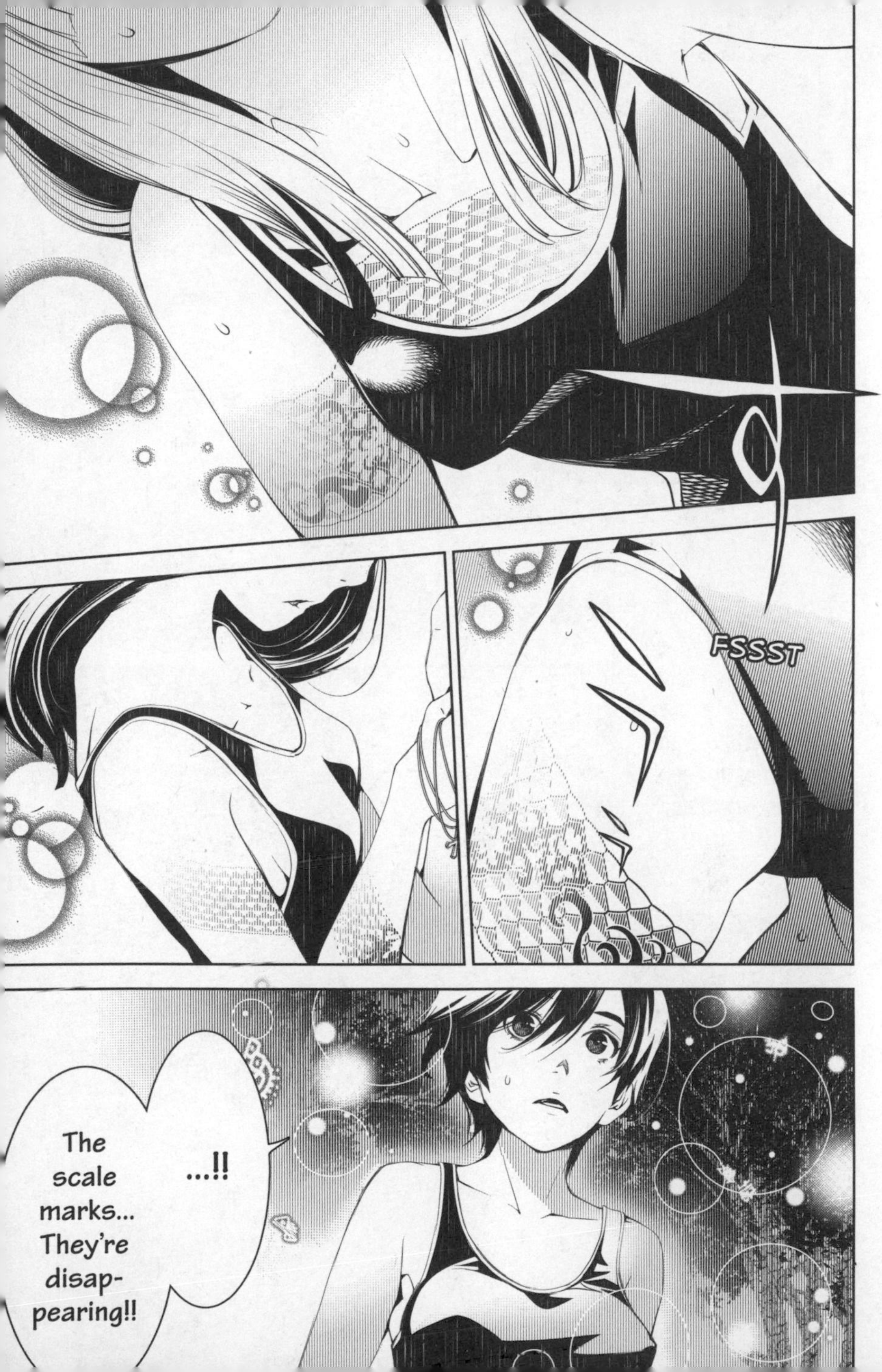
FSSST
...!!
The scale marks... They're disap-pearing!!

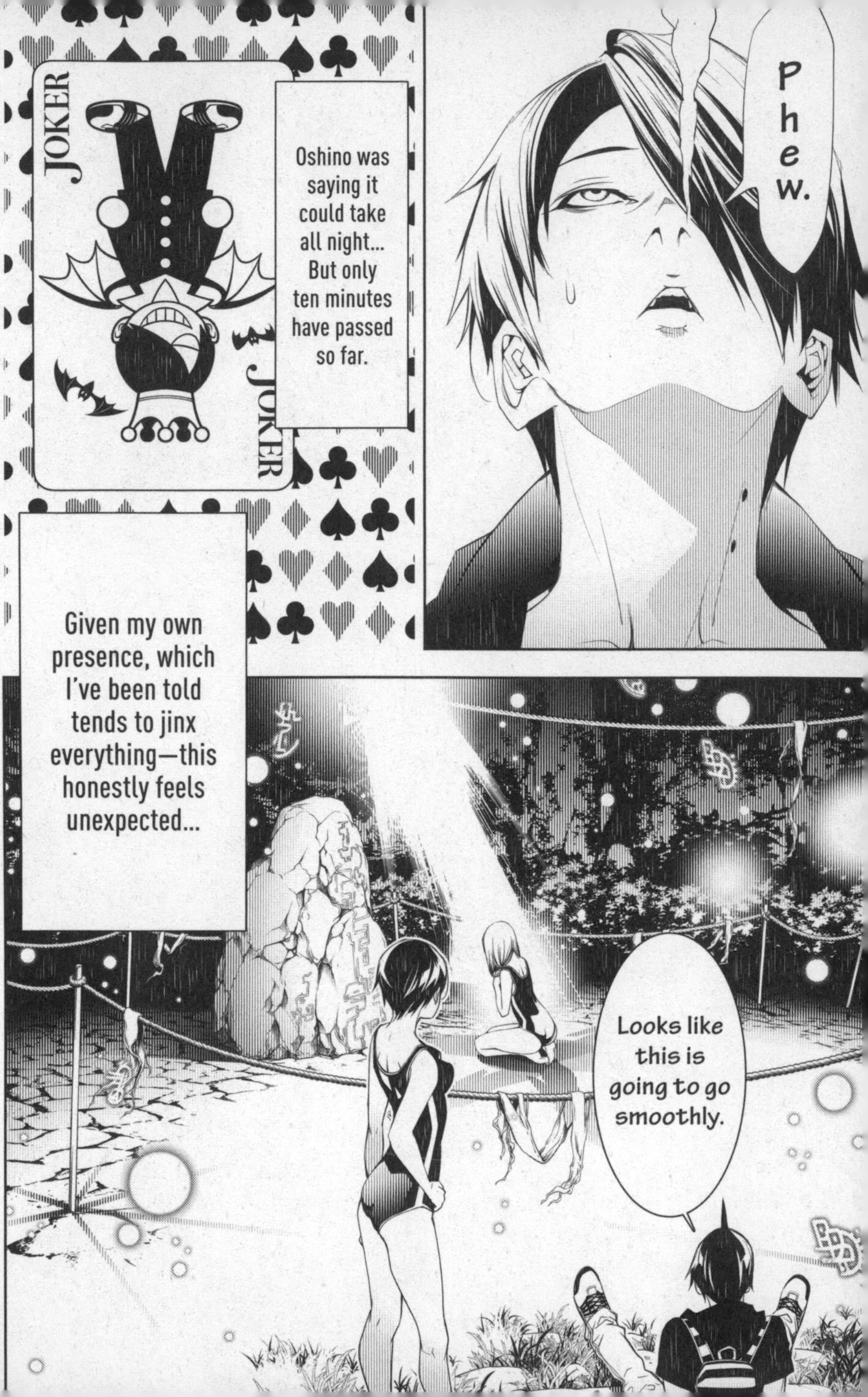
Phew.
Oshino was saying it could take all night... But only ten minutes have passed so far.
JOKER
JOKER
Given my own presence, which I've been told tends to jinx everything—this honestly feels unexpected...
Looks like this is going to go smoothly.

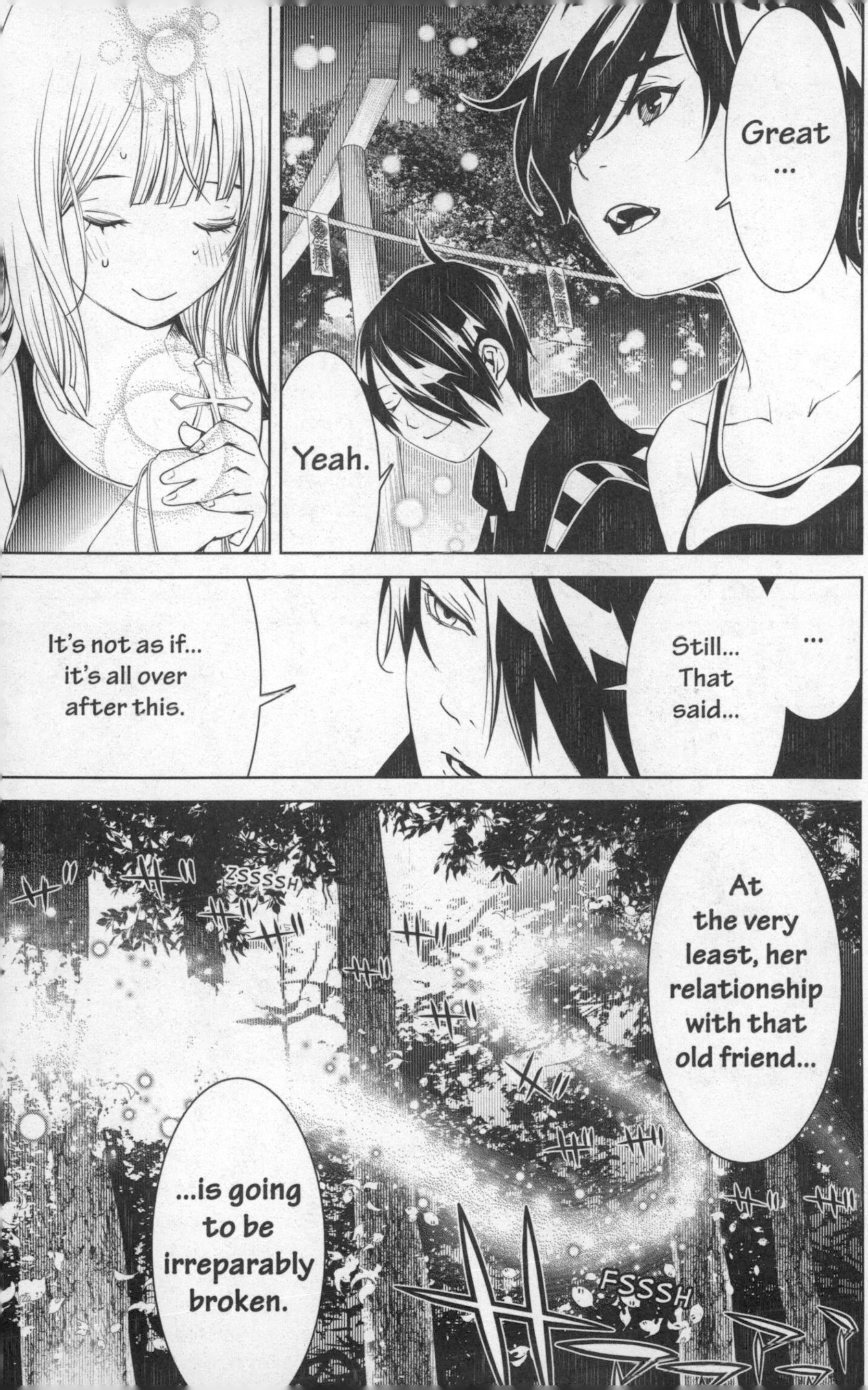
Great ...
Yeah.
...
Still... That said...
It's not as if... it's all over after this.
At the very least, her relationship with that old friend...
ZSSSSH
...is going to be irreparably broken.
FSSSH

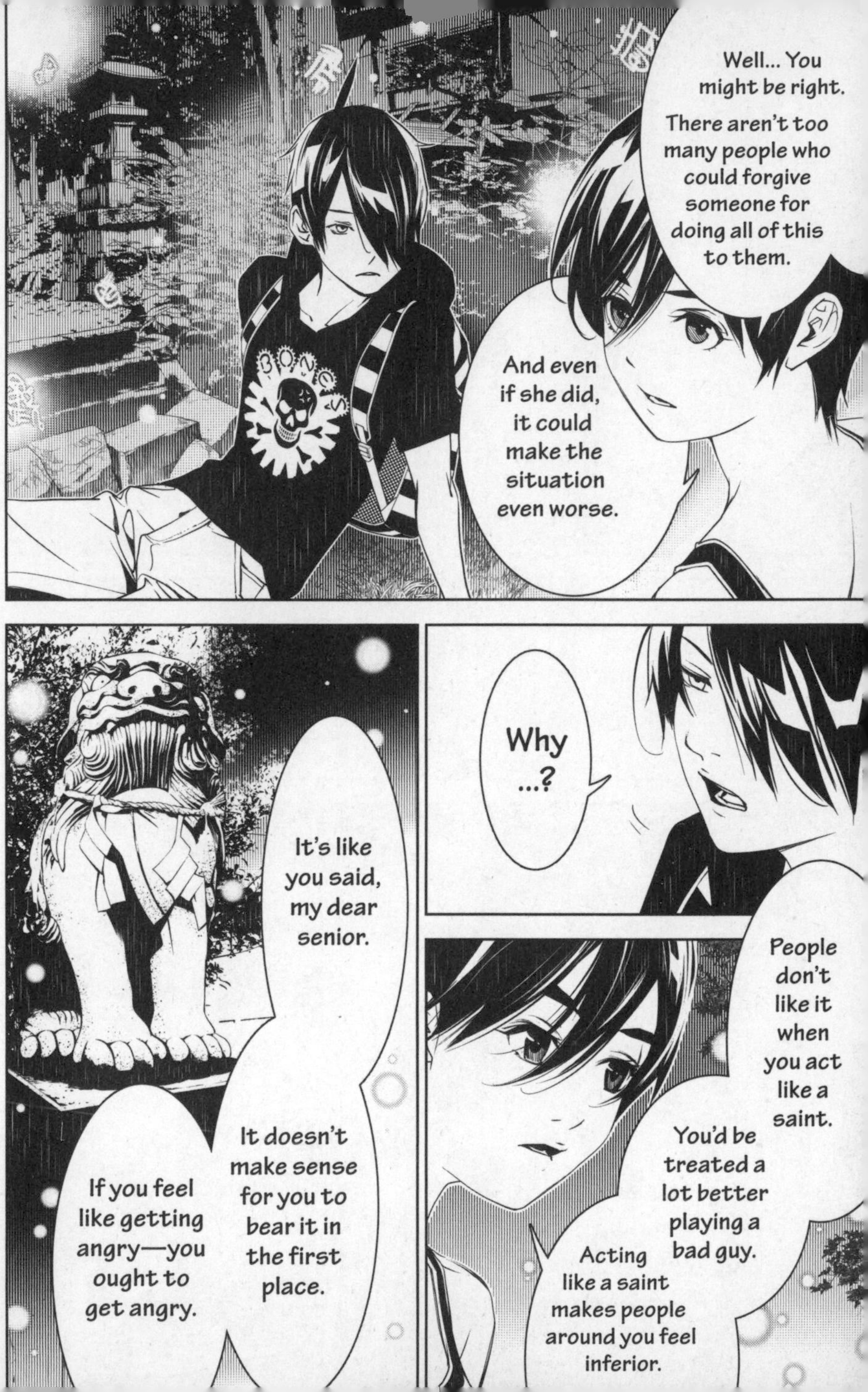
Well... You might be right.
There aren't too many people who could forgive someone for doing all of this to them.
And even if she did, it could make the situation even worse.
Why ...?
People don't like it when you act like a saint.
You'd be treated a lot better playing a bad guy.
Acting like a saint makes people around you feel inferior.
It's like you said, my dear senior.
It doesn't make sense for you to bear it in the first place.
If you feel like getting angry—you ought to get angry.

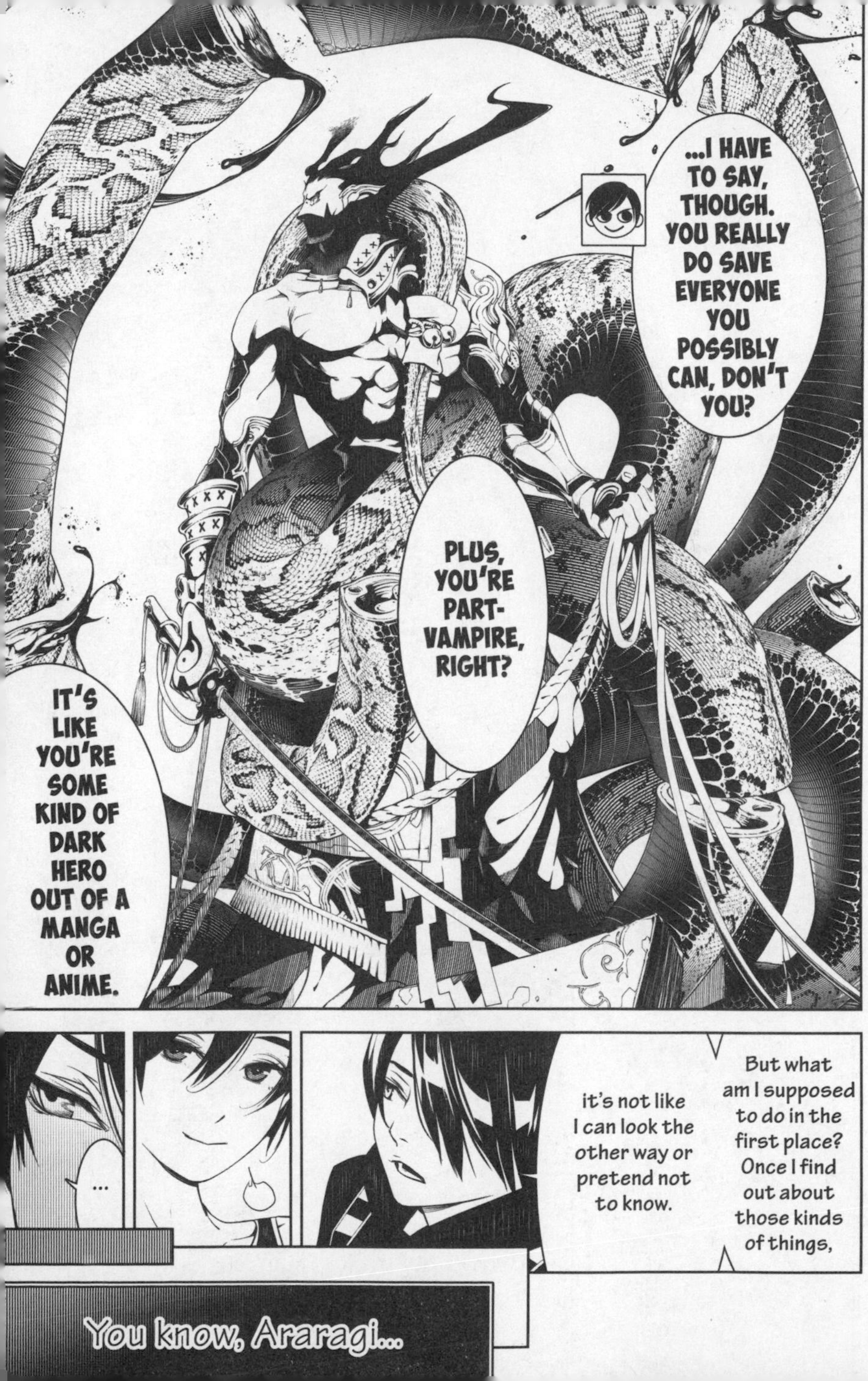
...I HAVE TO SAY, THOUGH. YOU REALLY DO SAVE EVERYONE YOU POSSIBLY CAN, DON'T YOU?
PLUS, YOU'RE PART-VAMPIRE, RIGHT?
IT'S LIKE YOU'RE SOME KIND OF DARK HERO OUT OF A MANGA OR ANIME.
But what am I supposed to do in the first place? Once I find out about those kinds of things,
it's not like I can look the other way or pretend not to know.
...
You know, Araragi...

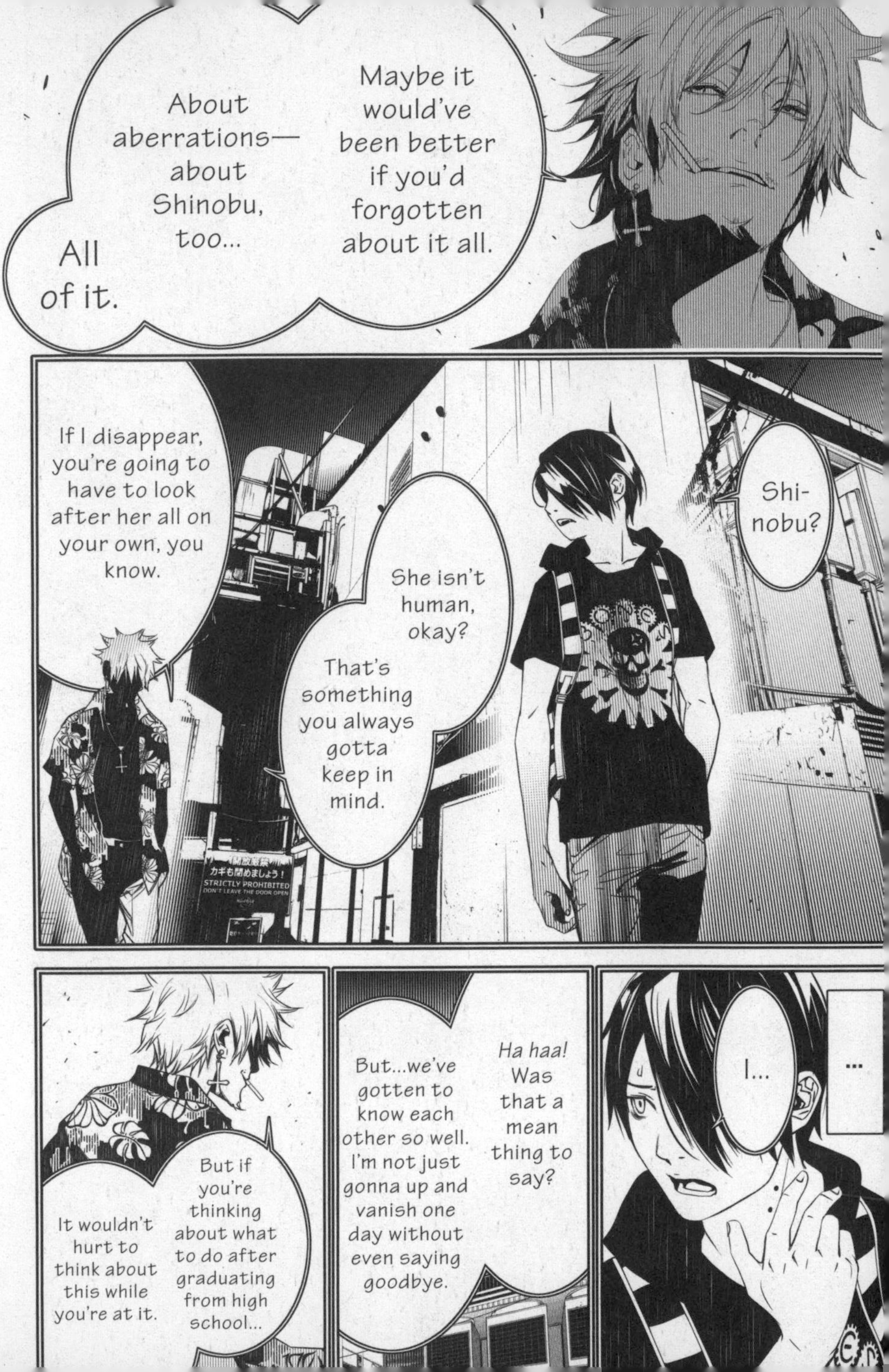
Maybe it would've been better if you'd forgotten about it all.
About aberrations—about Shinobu, too...
All of it.
Shi-nobu?
If I disappear, you're going to have to look after her all on your own, you know.
She isn't human, okay?
That's something you always gotta keep in mind.
開放厳禁
カギも閉めましょう！
STRICTLY PROHIBITED
DON'T LEAVE THE DOOR OPEN
...
I...
Ha haa! Was that a mean thing to say?
But...we've gotten to know each other so well. I'm not just gonna up and vanish one day without even saying goodbye.
But if you're thinking about what to do after graduating from high school...
It wouldn't hurt to think about this while you're at it.

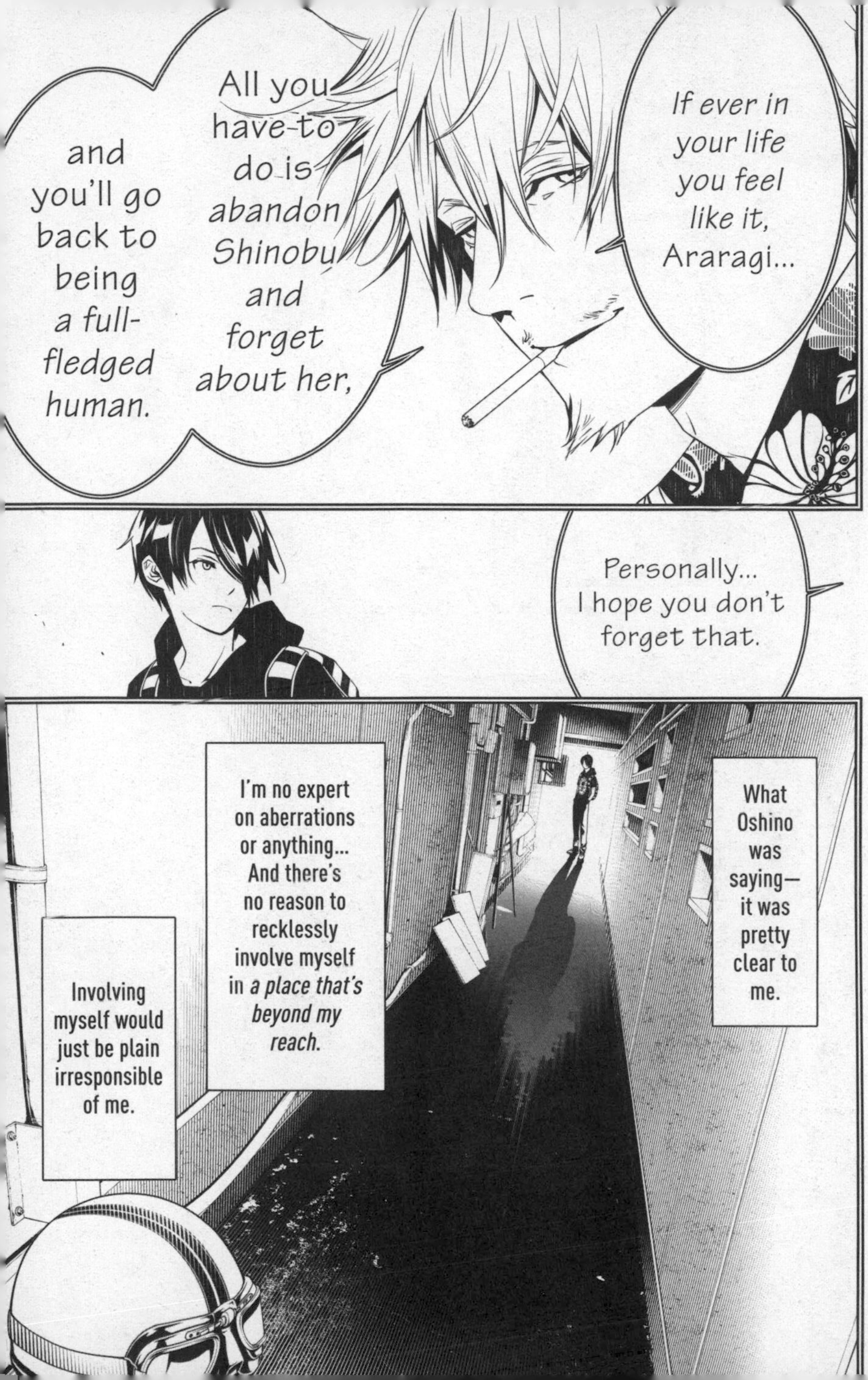
If ever in your life you feel like it, Araragi...
All you have to do is abandon Shinobu and forget about her,
and you'll go back to being a full-fledged human.
Personally... I hope you don't forget that.
What Oshino was saying—it was pretty clear to me.
I'm no expert on aberrations or anything... And there's no reason to recklessly involve myself in *a place that's beyond my reach.*
Involving myself would just be plain irresponsible of me.

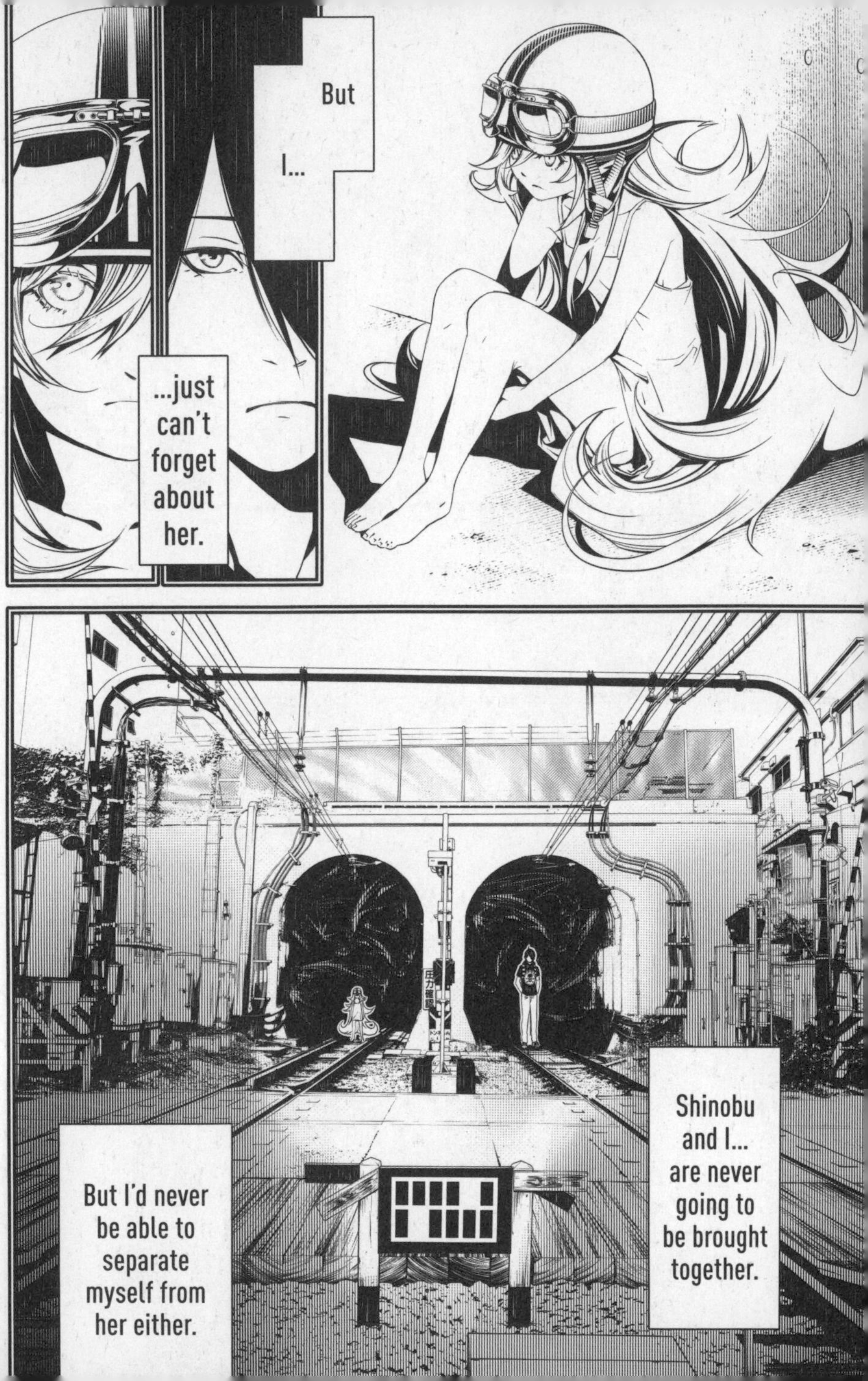
But I...
...just can't forget about her.
Shinobu and I... are never going to be brought together.
But I'd never be able to separate myself from her either.

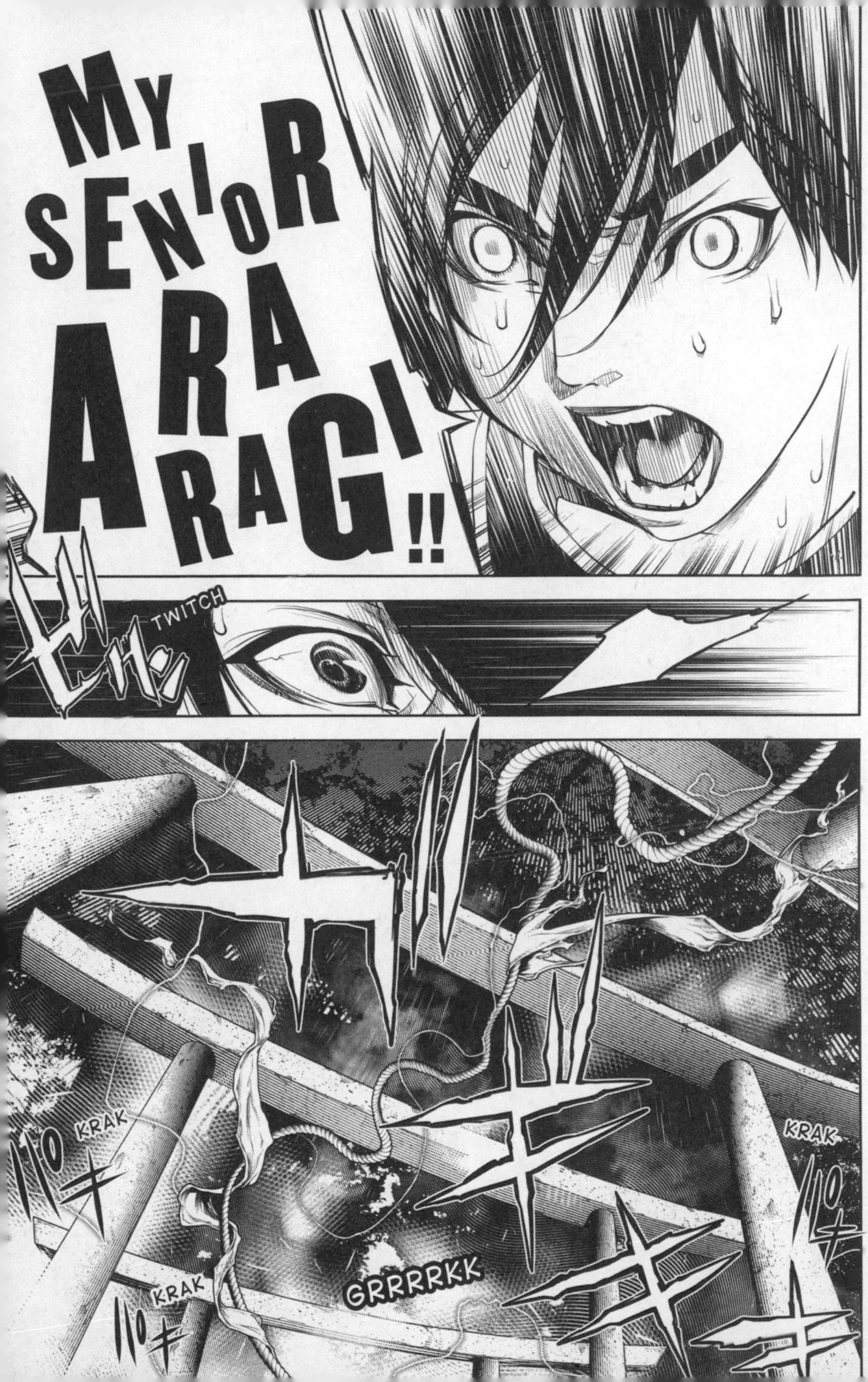
MY SENIOR ARARAGI!!
TWITCH
KRAK
KRAK
KRAK
GRRRRKK

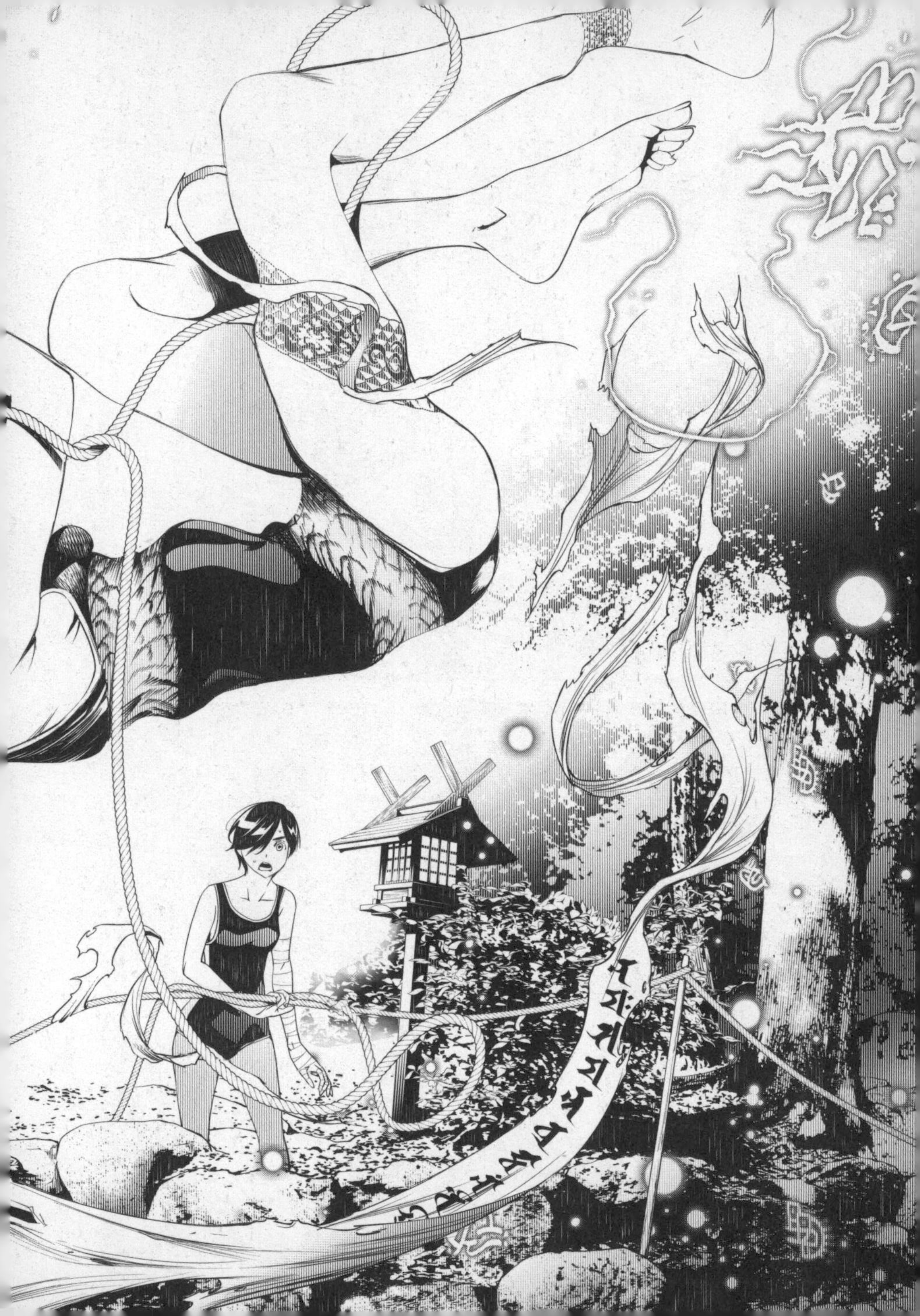

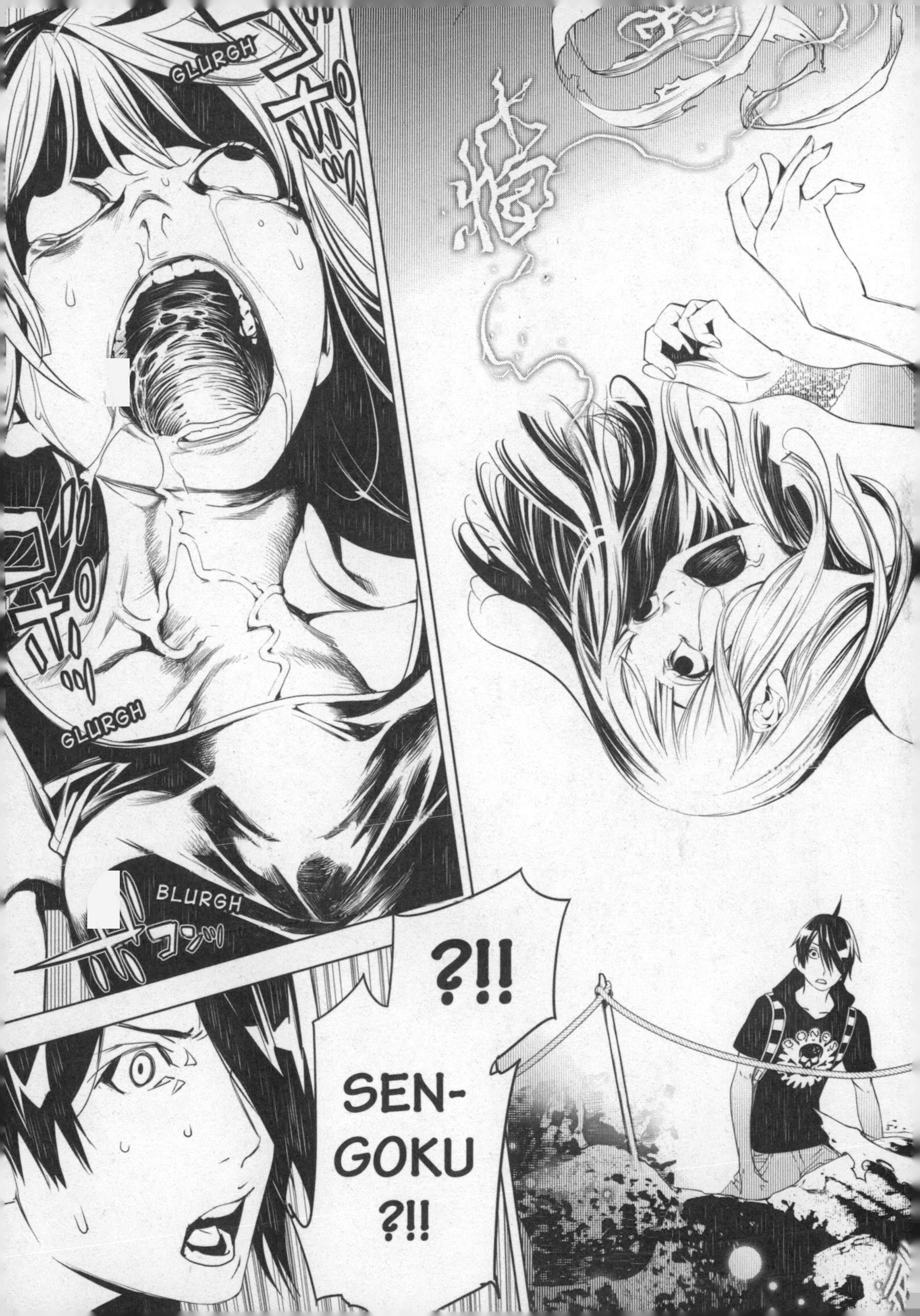
GLURGH
GLURGH
BLURGH
?!!
SEN-GOKU ?!!

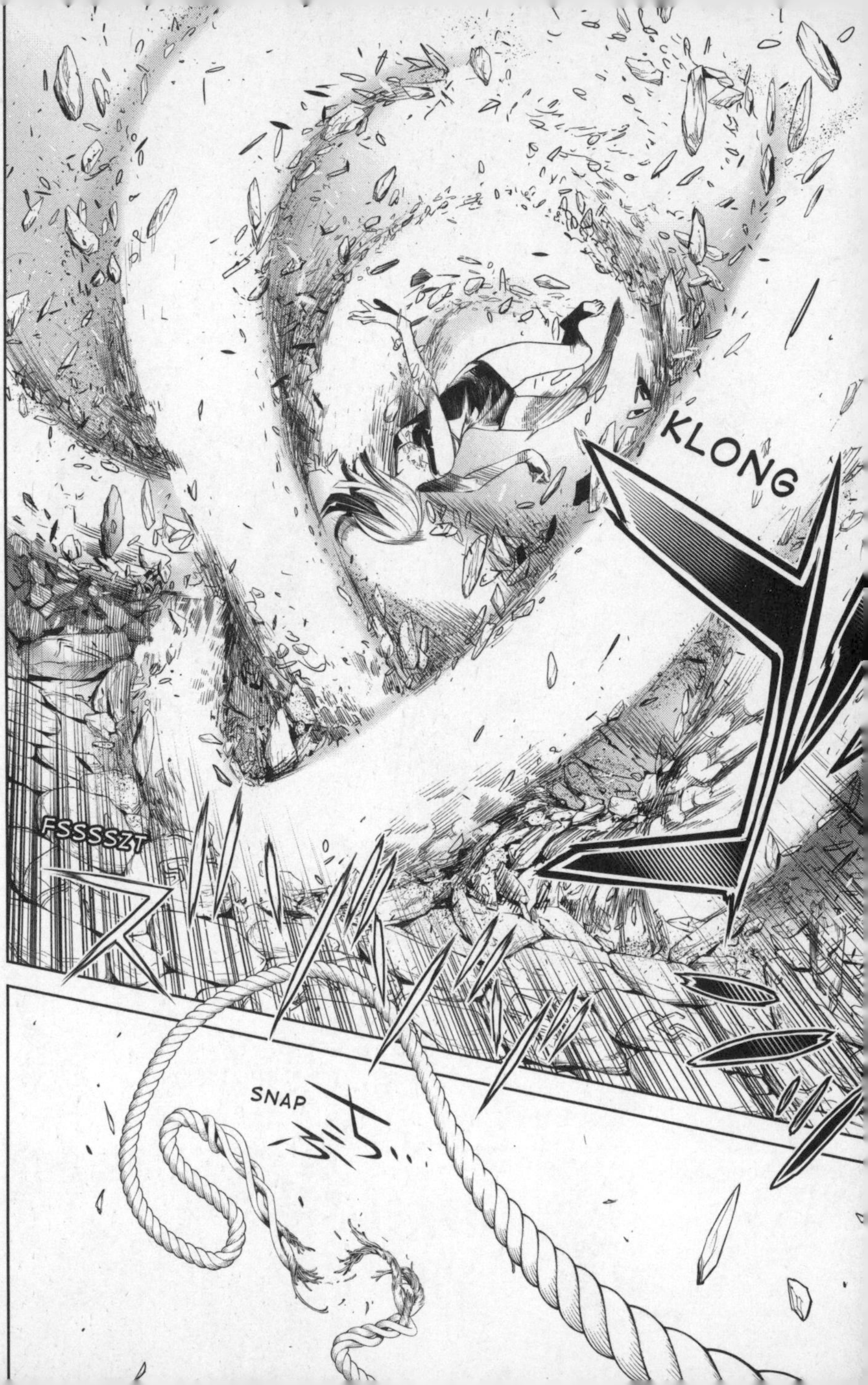
KLONG
FSSSSZT
SNAP

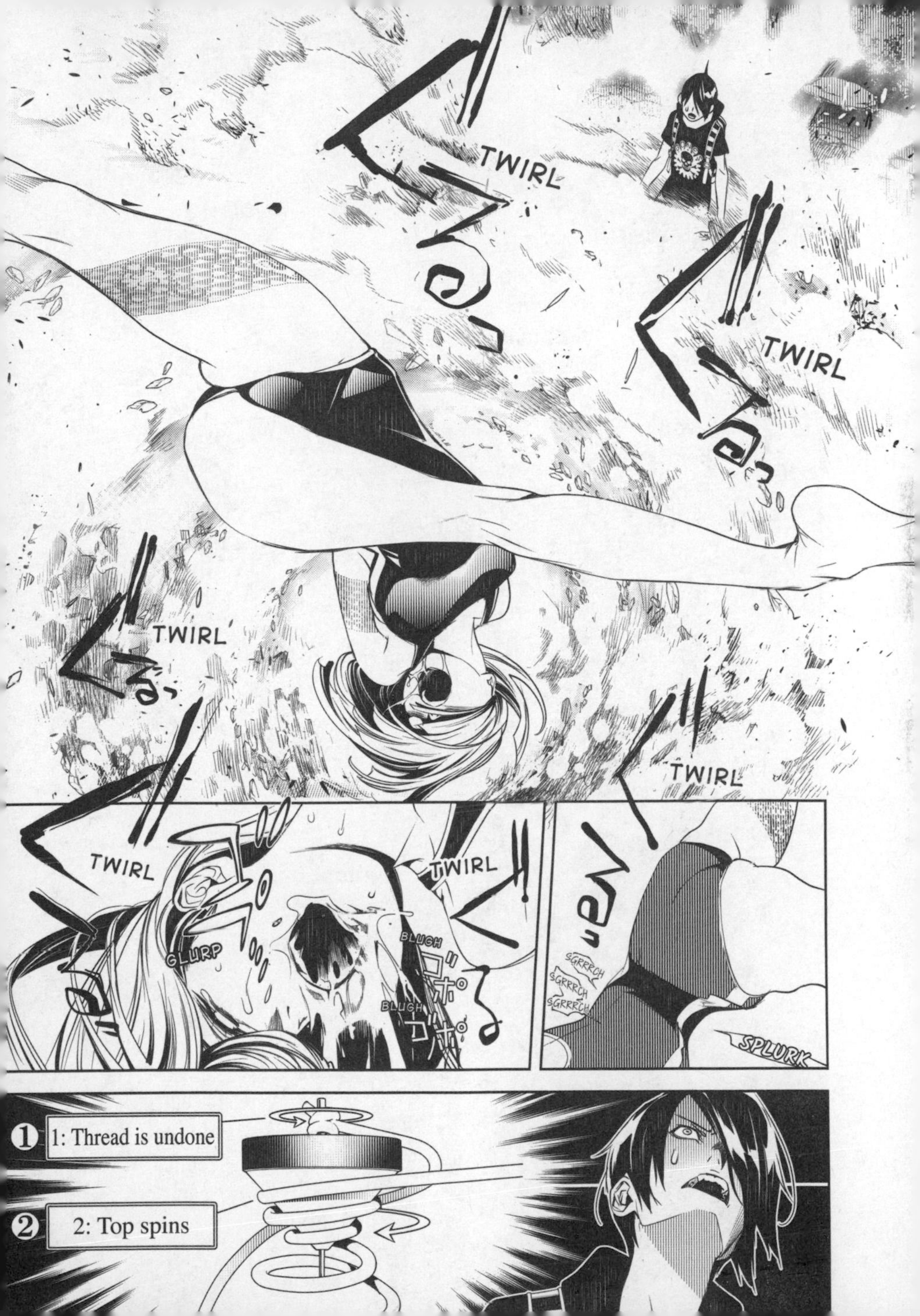
TWIRL
TWIRL
TWIRL
TWIRL
SGRRRCH
SGRRRCH
SGRRRCH
SPLURK
TWIRL
TWIRL
BLUGH
GLURP
BLUGH
① 1: Thread is undone
② 2: Top spins

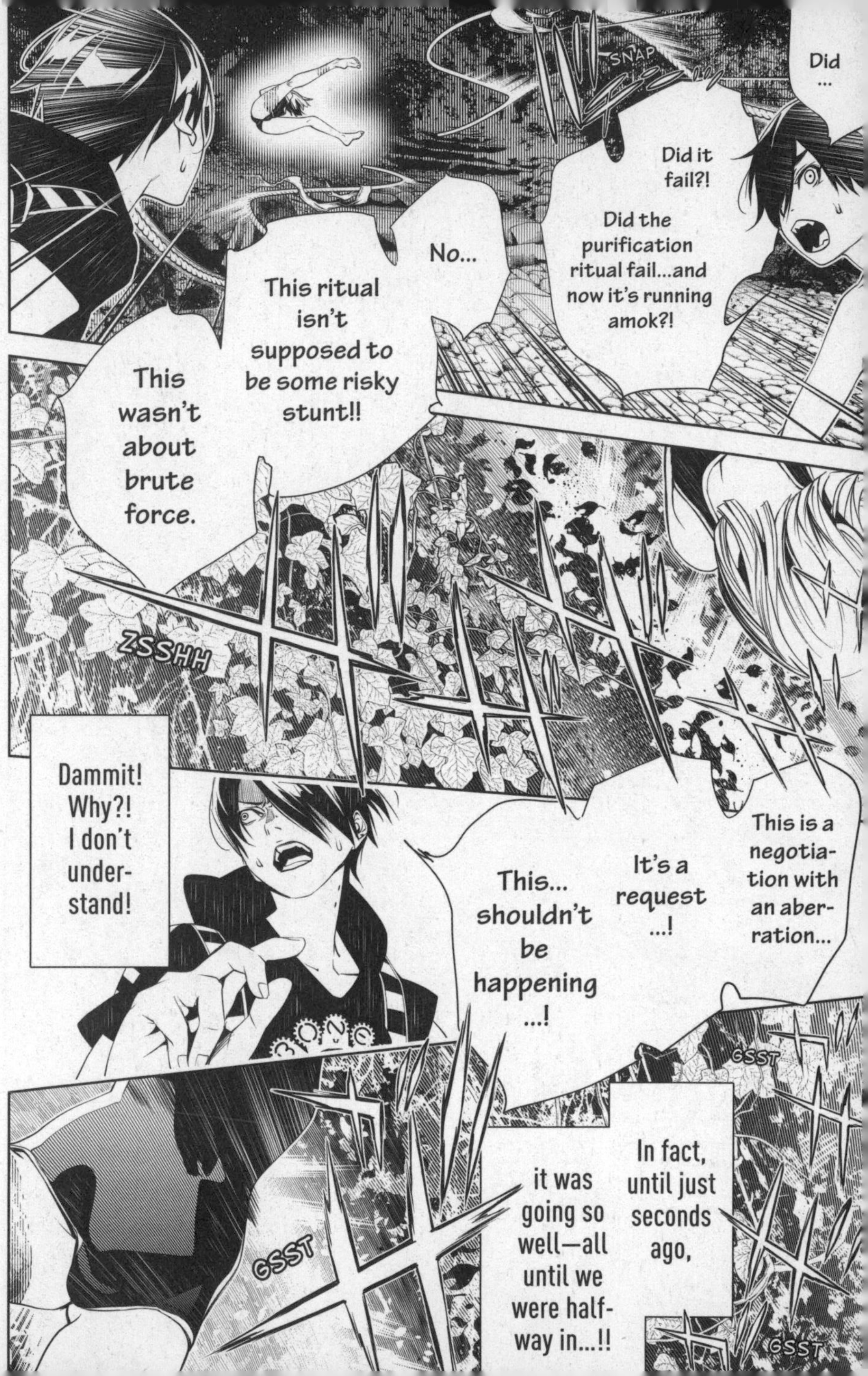
Did ...
SNAP
Did it fail?!
Did the purification ritual fail...and now it's running amok?!
No...
This ritual isn't supposed to be some risky stunt!!
This wasn't about brute force.
ZSSHH
This is a negotia-tion with an aber-ration...
It's a request ...!
This... shouldn't be happening ...!
Dammit! Why?! I don't under-stand!
GSST
In fact, until just seconds ago,
it was going so well—all until we were half-way in...!!
GSST
GSST

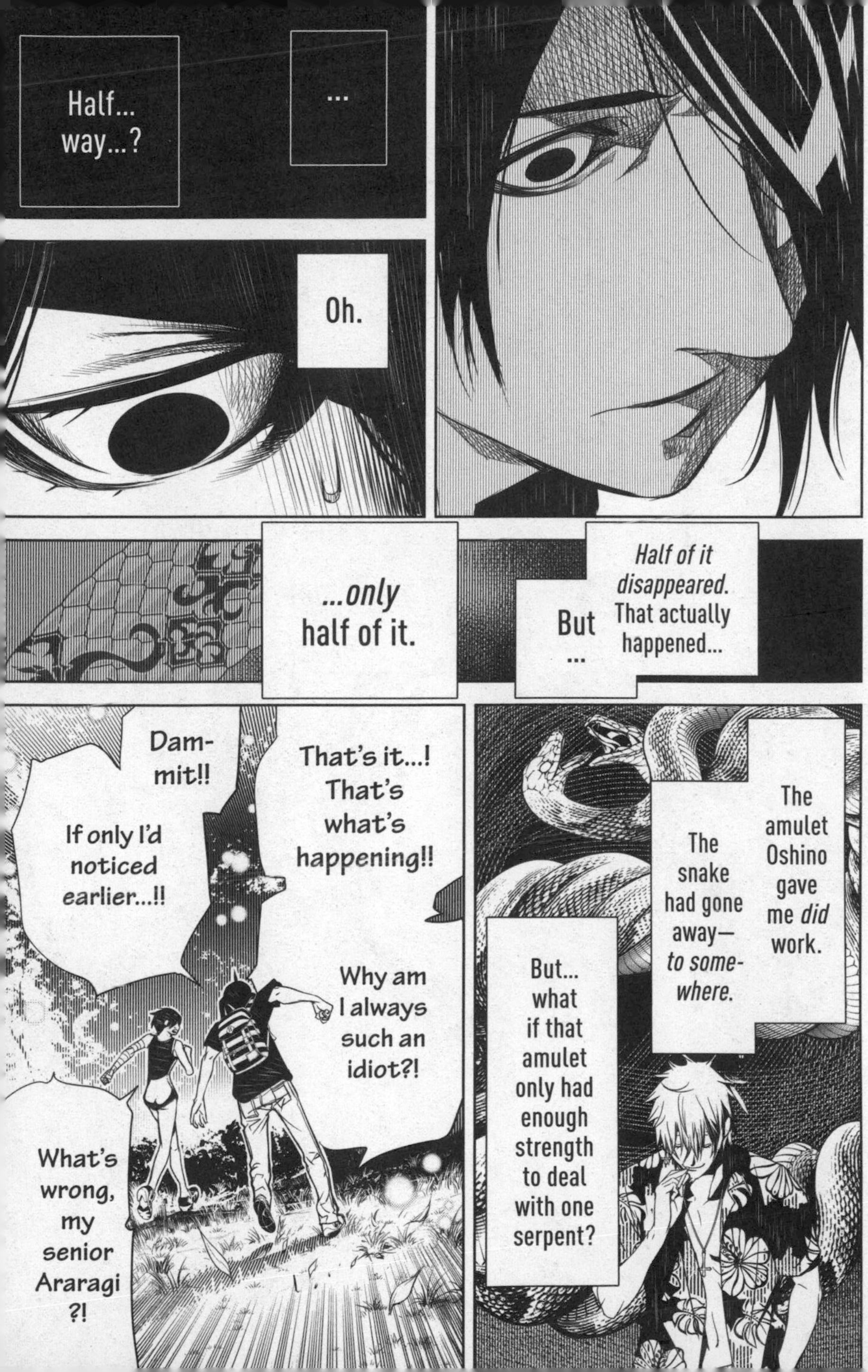
...
Half... way...?
Oh.
Half of it disappeared. That actually happened...
But ...
...only half of it.
The amulet Oshino gave me *did* work.
The snake had gone away— *to some-where.*
But... what if that amulet only had enough strength to deal with one serpent?
That's it...! That's what's happening!!
Dam-mit!!
If only I'd noticed earlier...!!
Why am I always such an idiot?!
What's wrong, my senior Araragi?!

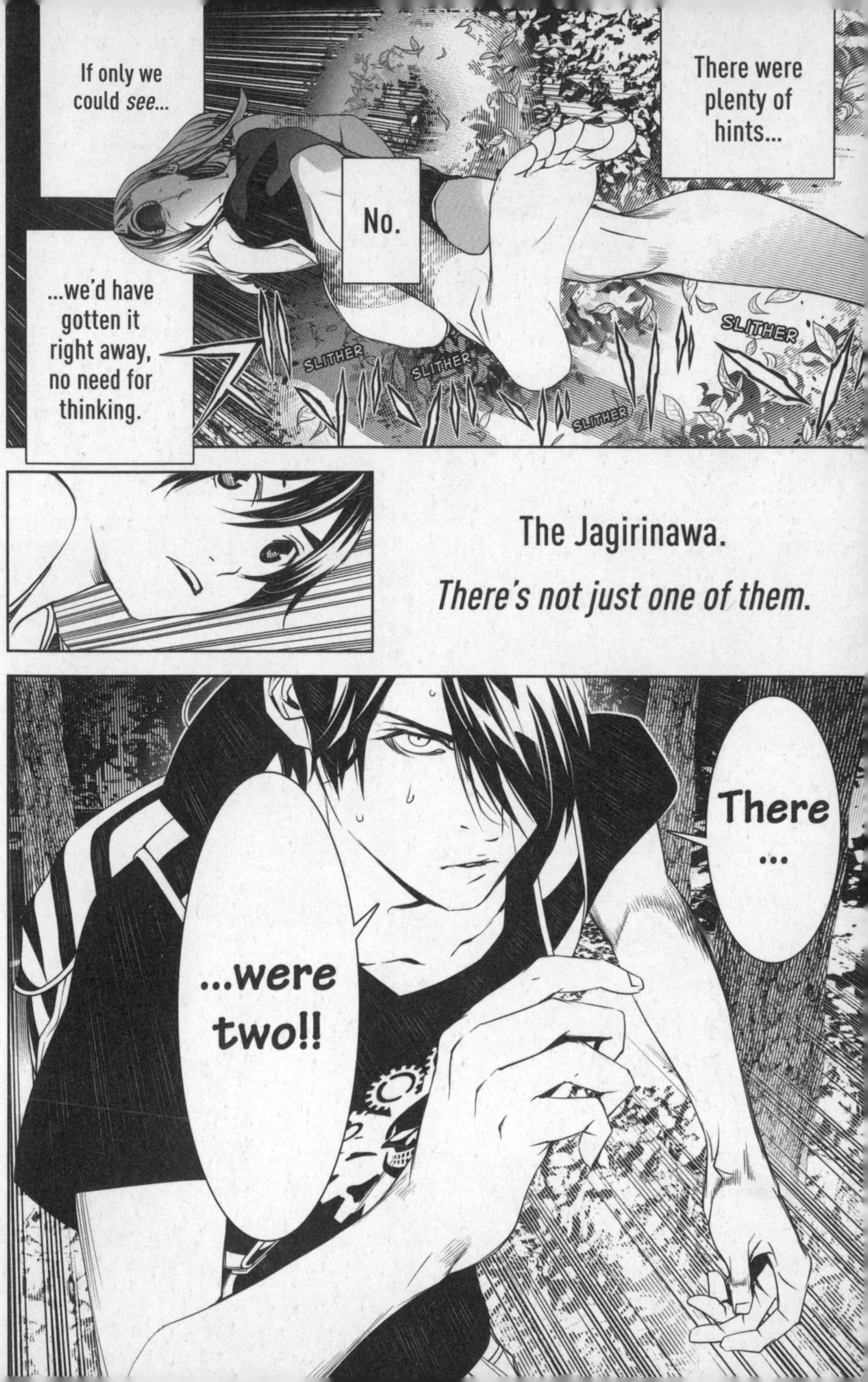
There were plenty of hints...
No.
If only we could *see*...
...we'd have gotten it right away, no need for thinking.
SLITHER
SLITHER
SLITHER
SLITHER
The Jagirinawa.
There's not just one of them.
There...
...were two!!

Continued in Volume 8

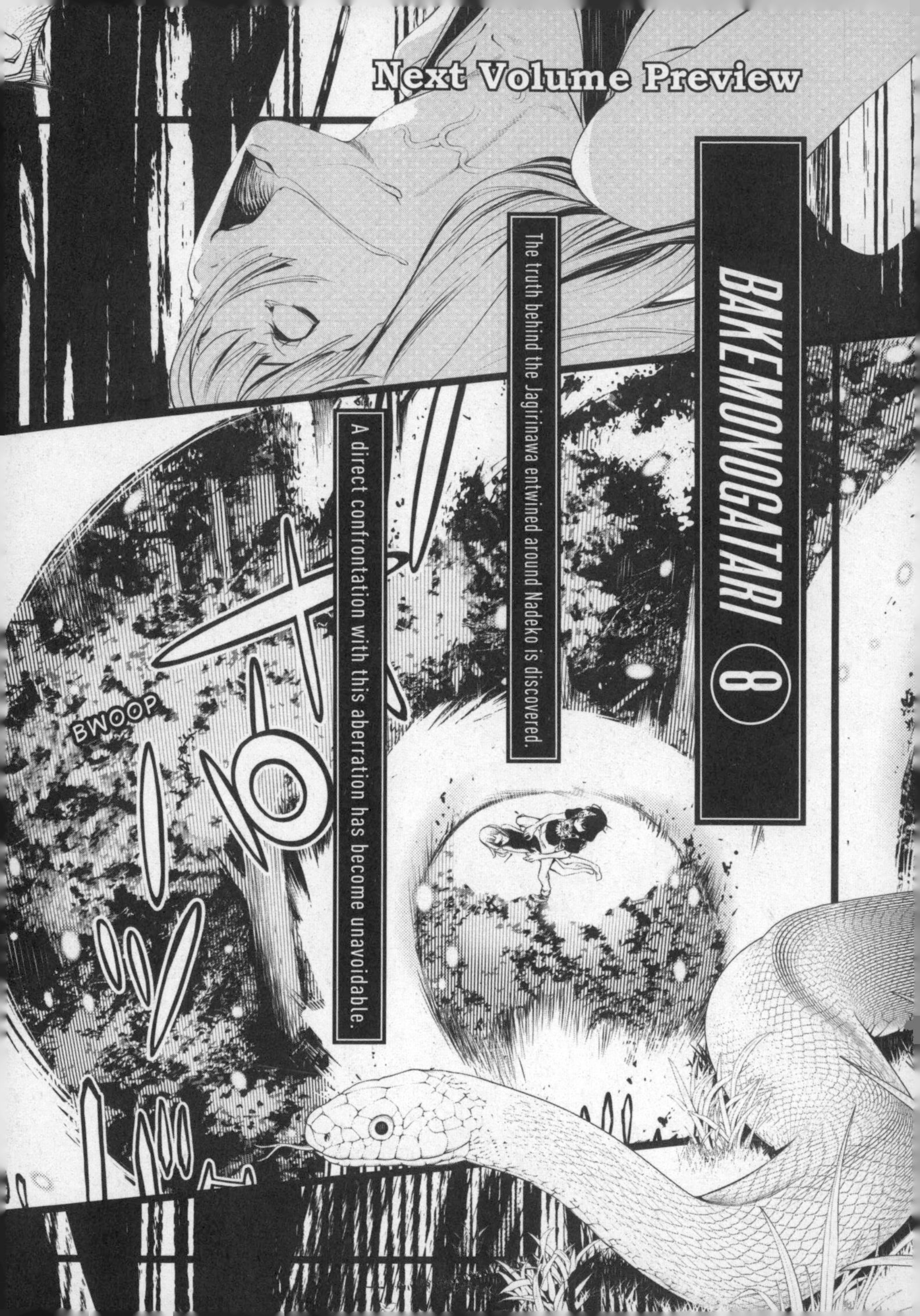
Next Volume Preview
BAKEMONOGATARI 8
The truth behind the Jagirinawa entwined around Nadeko is discovered.
A direct confrontation with this aberration has become unavoidable.
BWOOP

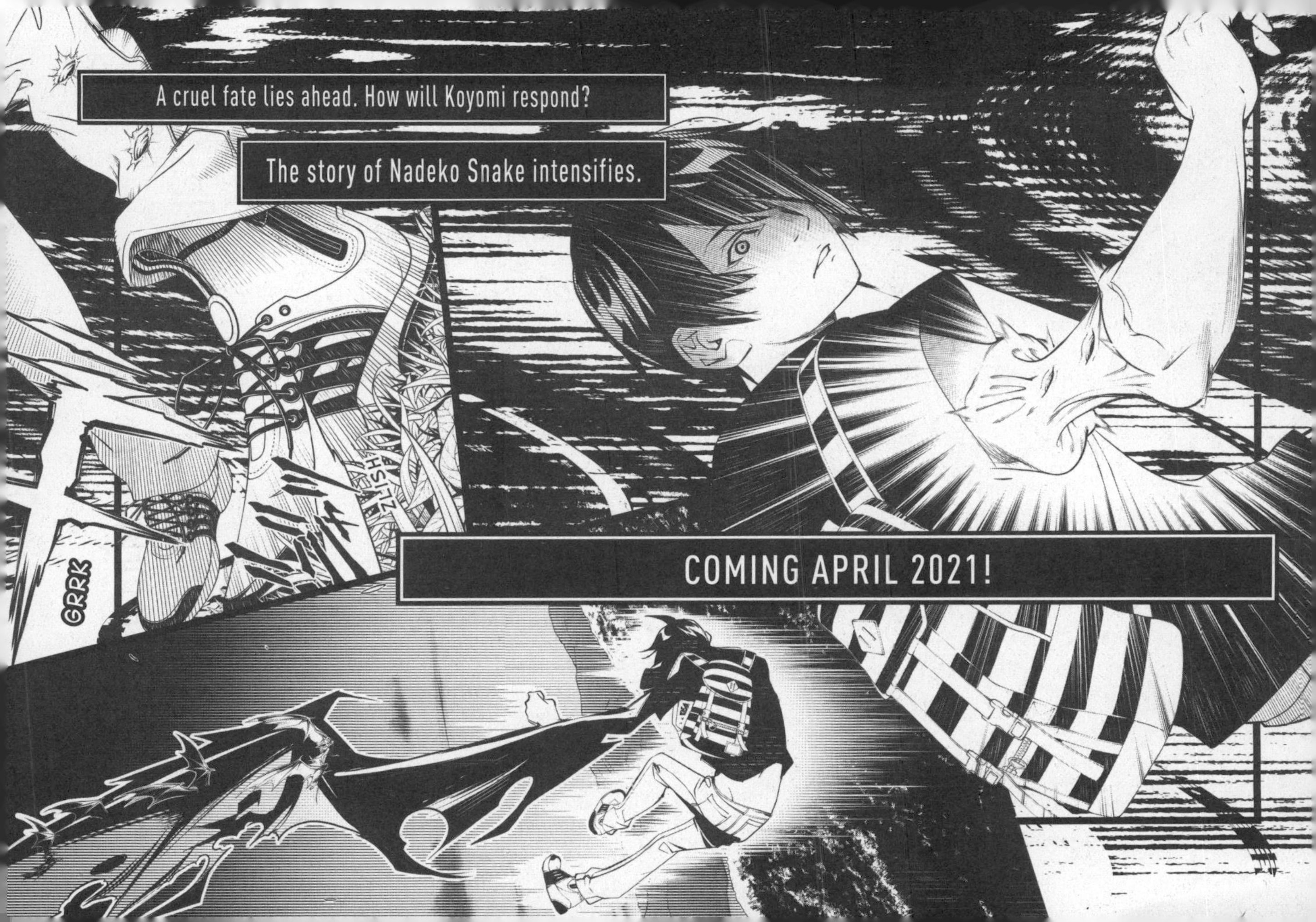
A cruel fate lies ahead. How will Koyomi respond?
The story of Nadeko Snake intensifies.
ZLISH
GRRK
COMING APRIL 2021!

BAKEMONOGATARI
volume 7

A Vertical Comics Edition

Editing: Ajani Oloye
Translation: Ko Ransom
Production: Grace Lu
           Hiroko Mizuno

First published in Japan in 2019 by Kodansha, Ltd., Tokyo
Publication for this English edition arranged through Kodansha, Ltd., Tokyo
English language version produced by Vertical Comics,
an imprint of Kodansha USA Publishing, LLC

Translation provided by Vertical Comics, 2021
Published by Kodansha USA Publishing, LLC, New York

Originally published in Japanese as *BAKEMONOGATARI 7* by Kodansha, Ltd.
BAKEMONOGATARI first serialized in *Weekly Shonen Magazine*,
Kodansha, Ltd., 2017-

This is a work of fiction.

ISBN: 978-1-949980-69-1

Manufactured in the United States of America

First Edition

Kodansha USA Publishing, LLC
451 Park Avenue South
7th Floor
New York, NY 10016
www.readvertical.com

Vertical books are distributed through Penguin-Random House Publisher Services.